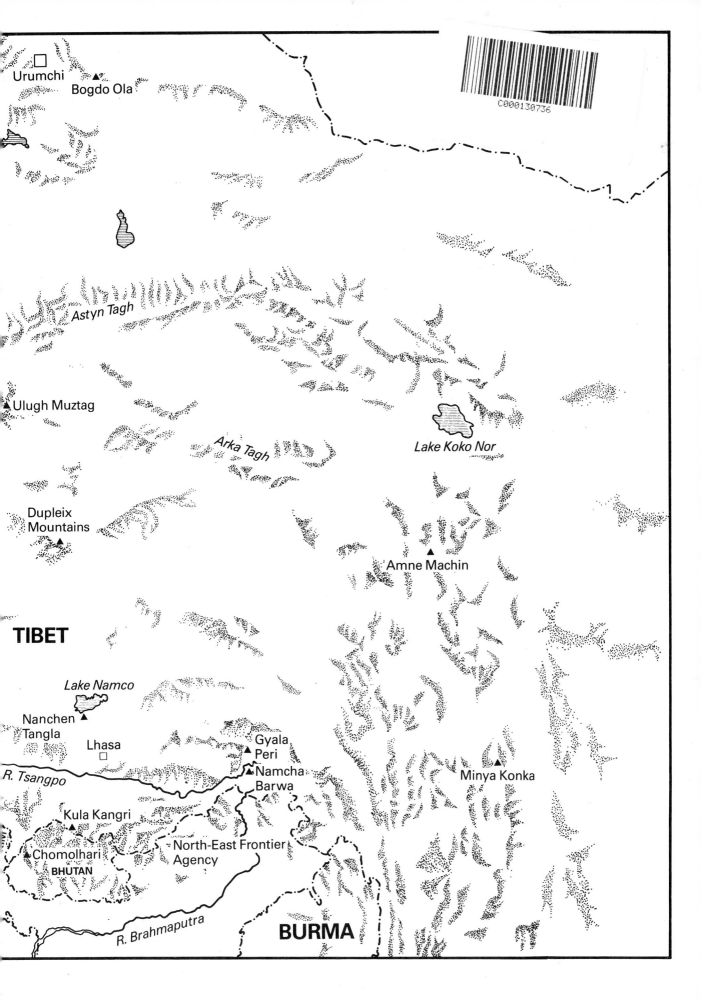

Urumchi □
▲ Bogdo Ola

C000130736

Astyn Tagh

▲ Ulugh Muztag

Arka Tagh

Lake Koko Nor

Dupleix
Mountains ▲

▲ Amne Machin

TIBET

Lake Namco

Nanchen ▲
Tangla

Lhasa □

Gyala
▲ Peri
▲ Namcha
Barwa

▲ Minya Konka

R. Tsangpo

Kula Kangri
▲

▲ Chomolhari
North-East Frontier
Agency

BHUTAN

R. Brahmaputra

BURMA

HIGH ASIA

HIGH ASIA

AN ILLUSTRATED HISTORY OF THE 7,000 METRE PEAKS

JILL NEATE

UNWIN
HYMAN
LONDON SYDNEY WELLINGTON

First published in Great Britain by the Trade Division
of Unwin Hyman Limited, 1989

UNWIN HYMAN LIMITED
15–17 Broadwick Street
London W1V 1FP

Allen & Unwin Australia Pty Ltd
8 Napier Street, North Sydney, NSW 2060, Australia

Allen & Unwin New Zealand Pty Ltd with the Port Nicholson Press
Compusales Building, 75 Ghuznee Street, Wellington, New Zealand

British Library Cataloguing in Publication Data

Neate, Jill
    High Asia : an illustrated history of the
    7000 metre peaks.
    1. Asia. Himalayas. Mountaineering
    I. Title
    796.5′22′0954

ISBN 0–04–440480–8

Designed by Julia Lilauwala
Disc Conversion by Columns Typesetters of Reading
Printed in Spain by Artes Gráficas Toledo, S.A.
D.L.TO:1714-1989

Contents

Acknowledgements   vii

Introduction   viii

World's Highest Peaks and First Ascents   1

Assam Himalaya   14

Bhutan Himalaya   16

Sikkim Himalaya   24
  Kangchenjunga Himal (Northern, Singalila)   25
  Janak Himal   32
  Dongkya Range   32

Eastern Nepal Himalaya (including peaks lying inside Tibet)   34
  Kangchenjunga Himal (Northern, Khumbhakarna)   34
  Mahalangur Himal (Barun, Makalu, Khumbu)   38
  Rolwaling Himal   48
  Pamari Himal   53
  Langtang Himal   53
  Jugal Himal   54

Central and Western Nepal Himalaya (including peaks lying inside Tibet)   56
  Ganesh Himal   56
  Serang (Sringi) Hiaml   60
  Mansiri (Manaslu) Himal   60
  Peri Himal   63
  Annapurna Himal   65
  Dhaulagiri Himal   71
  Nalakankar Himal   76
  Gurans Himal   78

Kumaun and Garhwal Himalaya 82
Kamet Group 83
Gangotri Group 86
Nanda Devi Group 87

Western Himalaya 96
Nun Kun Massif 96
Nanga Parbat (subsidiary peaks) 100

Greater Karakoram 102
Batura Muztagh 103
Hispar Muztagh 108
Panmah Muztagh 113
Baltoro Muztagh 116
Siachen Muztagh 124
Rimo Muztagh 127
Saser Muztagh 130

Lesser Karakoram 134
Rakaposhi Range 134
Haramosh 140
Masherbrum Range 142
Saltoro Range 148
Peaks Lying North of the Greater Karakoram 152

Hindu Kush 154
Northern Group 155
Saraghrar Group 156
Noshaq Group 159
Istor-O-Nal Group 160
Tirich Mir Group 163

Pamirs 168

Tien Shan 178

China and Tibet (excluding Himalayan peaks) 184
Transhimalaya 184
Kun Lun 186
Peaks in Central Tibet 194
Minya Konka Region, Szechuan 194

General Bibliography of Books and Reports 197

Peak Index 203

People Index 208

Acknowledgements

The initial stage in the preparation of this book was made very much easier by the earlier work done by Joydeep Sircar and published in his *Himalayan Handbook* (Calcutta, 1979), for which I am most grateful. Also I would like to thank Eugene Gippenreiter for checking and updating the sections on the Pamirs and Tien Shan; Xavier Eguskitza for checking much of the peak list; and Michael Ward for sight of his forthcoming article on the Kun Lun mountains and information about Tibet. My sincere thanks also to all the photographic contributors; and to Jim Scott for help with many of the older pictures. The attractive maps have been drawn by Ken Smith; and the whole thing was gently and skilfully drawn together by my editor Helen Wythers, who also helped a great deal with the collection of the illustrations.

▲ *Pumori South Face, see p. 32 (A. R. Allan)*

Introduction

The history of the exploration of the great peaks of the Himalaya and Central Asia is long and fascinating. When, in 1808, Lieutenant W. S. Webb took observations to some of the high peaks he was surprised by the heights he obtained. His calculation of the height of Dhaulagiri as 8,187 metres (only twenty metres greater than today's accepted figure) was derided by geographers outside India who held that the Andes were the highest mountains in the world, with Chimborazo the highest of all.

One of the early political factors affecting the course of exploration was the Nepalese War (1814–16). The settlement opened up the whole of the Kumaun and Garhwal Himalaya to British administration, but the drawback was the closure of Nepal to all foreigners, a state of affairs which persisted until 1949. With this very important exception, Britain thus had at least theoretical access to the whole of the vast southern approaches, from the Karakoram and Hindu Kush in the northwest as far as the autonomous kingdoms of Sikkim and Bhutan and the wild North-East Frontier Agency in Assam. To the north of these ranges lay Chinese Turkestan

(Sinkiang) and the secret land of Tibet, areas where Britain and Russia, both keen to gain influence, played the 'Great Game in Asia'.

The man responsible for the subsequent triumphs of the Survey of India was Sir George Everest. He created the linked system of triangulation which covers the whole region, based on his Great Arc of the Meridian, completed in 1841. This arc, measured through the centre of India to the Himalaya, provided the foundation for the mathematical spheroid from which the positions and heights of all Himalayan mountains are calculated. By means of this accurate base and the network of primary triangulations it was possible to make these calculations without actually visiting the peaks, unlike the topographical detail which could only be obtained on the spot.

By the middle of the nineteenth century the survey of India was well under way: Everest and K2 had been determined to be the highest mountains in the world. Notable among the early travellers was the eminent botanist Sir Joseph Hooker who, in 1848–49, made an almost complete circuit of the Kangchenjunga range in Sikkim on the eastern fringes of

Nepal. Reconnaissance surveys were made also of Karakoram glaciers. But travellers and surveyors alike were hungry for knowledge of what lay to the north of the great ranges, where they could not venture openly. Thus officers of the Great Trigonometrical Survey began to train Indian explorers (known as 'pundits') who could travel in disguise through Tibet, surreptitiously recording distances, bearings and high peaks, details which they concealed inside their prayer wheels.

The goal for many of these devoted servants of the Survey was Lhasa, the forbidden city, as it was for later Western travellers who observed the high peaks of the Kun Lun range. Also, in 1865 the surveyor W. H. Johnson made an illicit visit to the Kun Lun and claimed an ascent of Peak E61, measured in 1862 at 7,281 metres. But many years later it was demonstrated conclusively that his plane table had been set up wrongly, as a consequence of which he was on a different peak. He was not to be the last to fall into this trap.

In 1883 William Woodman Graham went out from England with the main object of climbing mountains 'more for sport and adventures than for the advancement of scientific knowledge'. Accompanied by Swiss guides, he visited Sikkim first, then travelled to the Garhwal Himalaya where, among other things, he made a brief attempt to penetrate the Rishiganga gorge to the Nanda Devi basin. Returning to Sikkim he ascended a high peak which he believed to be Kabru (7,338 metres), a claim which is no longer taken seriously. In all he reached heights of about 6,100–6,300 metres on four different peaks. Later he is said to have lost his money and emigrated to the USA where he became a cowboy.

Outside Nepal the greatest peaks lie in the Karakoram, and it was in this range that two of the most important expeditions in mountaineering history took place in 1892 and 1909. The first was led by Sir Martin Conway. In the course of much exploration Conway attempted Baltoro Kangri ('Golden Throne'), reaching a height of over 6,550 metres. The very successful 1909 expedition was led by the Duke of the Abruzzi; although he failed to climb K2 the Duke and his guides did reach a height of about 7,500 metres on Chogolisa, bad weather alone preventing a certain ascent. However, the first ascent of a 7,000–metre peak had been made already in 1907 when T. G. Longstaff climbed Trisul (7,120 metres) in the Garhwal Himalaya. Around this time, the Americans Dr and Mrs Workman made a series of expeditions in the Karakoram and Nun Kun massif, where Fanny Bullock Workman reached just under 7,000 metres – a women's

height record which she vigorously and successfully defended against the claims of her compatriot Annie Peck who had climbed the north peak of Huascarán in Peru.

In the 1920s and 1930s major expeditions from Britain and other countries concentrated on the greatest prizes then available to them – Everest, K2, Kangchenjunga and Nanga Parbat. Smaller than these giants but more attractive to informal private groups, the 7,000–metre peaks drew considerable attention with attempts on and ascents of peaks such as Masherbrum and Saltoro Kangri in the Karakoram, and Kamet and Nanda Devi in the Garhwal Himalaya. The biggest prize was the ascent of Nanda Devi in 1936, which was made possible by the fine exploration done by Eric Shipton and Bill Tilman two years previously. Another remarkable success was the ascent of Minya Konka (7,590 metres) in China's Szechuan province by four young Americans. At this time, too, Russia's Pamir mountains were being opened up, with ascents of Pik Lenin (7,134 metres) and Pik Kommunizma (7,495 metres) in 1928 and 1933 respectively. Finally, one of the best known of climbing stories, the ascent in 1937 of Chomolhari (7,315 metres) in Bhutan, was the work of F. Spencer Chapman, who had been with Gino Watkins in the Arctic.

All this was as nothing compared with the explosion in mountaineering activity which began after the Second World War when Nepal opened its frontiers for the

first time. As expeditions scrambled to make first ascents of the fourteen peaks in the world over 8,000 metres more and more nationalities poured into the new playgrounds, including the Japanese, now possibly the most numerous and enthusiastic climbers in the world. First ascents of 7,000–metre peaks became commonplace. Standards of technique, clothing and equipment advanced in leaps and bounds; swift alpine-style ascents began to take the place of the cumbersome siege tactics hitherto employed. After many first ascents had been made, climbers turned to harder routes on known peaks, always a sign of a new era. Despite all this some 7,000–metre peaks held out for a considerable time and provided a fresh epoch of mountaineering history; some are still unclimbed.

And still, throughout all these dramatic developments, the peaks of China and Tibet remained a mystery to all but a handful of Westerners. Their heights, even their locations, were not accurately known in many cases. Not only these peaks but also the whole of the northern approaches to the Himalaya and Karakoram remained closed to foreigners, except for one or two special cases. Until 1980 that is, when the Chinese announced that certain high peaks were being made available immediately. This relaxation continues and, as the author of an article in the 1985 *Alpine Journal* noted, in China 'One hundred years of first ascents remain'.

Note on Chinese Pinyin spelling

The new Chinese Pinyin system of spelling the Western equivalents of Chinese and Tibetan place-names is gradually being adopted in mountaineering literature. The older forms have been given precedence in this historical record, with the new forms shown where appropriate.

Journals

The following abbreviations have been used for journals cited:

AJ   *Alpine Journal* (Alpine Club, London)

AAJ   *American Alpine Journal* (American Alpine Club, New York)

HJ   *Himalayan Journal* (Himalayan Club, Bombay)

MW   *Mountain World* (Allen & Unwin)

Author's Note

The Harvard system of bibliography has been substitued by the publishers, against my wishes, in order to conform with their house style.

The World's Highest Peaks and First Ascents

Headings:
Name (of peak or subsidiary peak)
Group (i.e. physical location)
Height (in metres)
Year (of first ascent)
Summiters (first on summit)
Nationality (of expedition)

This list has been compiled principally from the following sources:
Bolinder, A. and Dyrenfurth G.O. (1968/69), 'Table of all known peaks in the world over 7,300 metres', *MW*, pp. 179–84.
Boothman, F. (1982), 'Mountains of Tibet and the Tibet/China border', *AJ*, 87, pp. 83–99.
Carter, H. A. (1985), 'Classification of the Himalaya', *AAJ*, 27 pp. 109–41.
Dyrenfurth, G.O. (1972), 'Sommets de huit mille et sept mille metres', *Les Alpes*, pp. 228–33 (list of unclimbed summits).
Kohli, M. S. (1985), 'Mountaineering in Bhutan', *AJ*, 90, pp. 18–20.
Kowalewski, Z. and Kurzab, J. *Na szczytach Himalajów*, pp. 406–17.
Mountaineering maps of the world.

★ No Ascent Traced

Not all heights are certain; in particular, most of the heights of peaks in Bhutan Himal should be regarded as doubtful.

NAME	GROUP	HEIGHT	YEAR	SUMMITERS	NATIONALITY
Everest	Khumbu	8848	1953	E. Hillary, Tenzing	British
-South summit		8760	1953	T. Bourdillon, C. Evans	British
K2(Chogori)	Baltoro	8611	1954	A. Compagnoni, L. Lacedelli	Italian
Kangchenjunga	Kangchen.Nth	8586	1955	G. Band, J. Brown	British
-Yalung Kang		8505	1973	Y. Ageta, T. Matsuda	Japanese
-Central Peak		8482	1978	W. Branski, Z. Heinrich, K. Olech	Polish
-South		8476	1978	W. Wroz, E. Chrobak	Polish
-P.7741(Z'Hütl)		7741	1931	H. Hartmann, K. Wien	German
-Zemu Peak		7780	★		
Lhotse	Khumbu	8516	1956	E. Reiss, F. Luchsinger	Swiss
-Middle		8430	★		
-Lhotse Shar		8400	1970	S. Mayerl, R. Walter	Austrian
Makalu	Makalu	8463	1955	J. Couzy, L. Terray	French
-Southeast		8010	1970	M. Asami, Y. Ichikawa	Japanese
Cho Oyu	Khumbu	8201	1954	H. Tichy, J. Jöchler, Pasang Dawa Lama	Austrian

NAME	GROUP	HEIGHT	YEAR	SUMMITERS	NATIONALITY
Dhaulagiri	Dhaulagiri	8167	1960	K. Diemberger, P. Diener, E. Forrer, A. Schelbert Nyima Dorji, Nawang Dorji	Swiss
Manaslu	Mansiri	8163	1956	T. Imanishi, Gyalzen Norbu	Japanese
-East Pinnacle		7992	★		
Nanga Parbat	Nanga Parbat	8125	1953	H. Buhl	German
-South Peak		8042	1982	V. Bühler	German
-Forepeak		7910	1971	J. Psotka, A. Puskac, I. Urbanovic	Czech
-North Peak(1)		7817	1978	M. Zatko, J. Zatko, J. Just A. Belica	Czech
-North Peak(2)		7785	★		
-Silberzacken		7597	★		
-Northeast		7530	1971	J. Psotka, A. Puskac, I. Urbanovic	Czech
-Rakhiot Peak		7070	1932	P. Aschenbrenner, H. Kunigk	German
Annapurna	Annapurna	8091	1950	M. Herzog, L. Lachenal	French
-Central Peak		8051	1980	U. Böning, L. Greissl H. Oberrauch	German
-East Peak		8010	1974	J. Anglada, E. Civis, J. Pons	Spanish
Gasherbrum I	Baltoro	8068	1958	P. Schoening, A. Kauffman	U.S.A.
-South		7069	1980	M. Barrard, G. Narbaud	French
Gasherbrum II	Baltoro	8035	1956	J. Larch, F. Moravec, H. Willenpart	Austrian
-East		7772	1983	W. Kurtyka, J. Kukucka	Polish
Broad Peak	Baltoro	8047	1957	M. Schmuck, F. Wintersteller	Austrian
-Central		8016	1975	K. Glazek, M. Kesicki, J. Kulis, B. Nowaczyk, A. Sikorski	Polish
-South		7721	★		
-North		7550	1983	R. Casarotto	Italian
Shisha Pangma	Jugal	8046	1964	Hsu Ching, Chang Chun-yen Wang Fu-chou, Chen-san, Cheng Tien-Liang, Wu Tsung-yueh, Sodnam Dorji, Minar Trashi, Dorji, Tontan	Chinese
Gasherbrum IV	Baltoro	7980	1958	W. Bonatti, C. Mauri	Italian
Gyachung Kang	Khumbu	7952	1964	Y. Kato, K. Sakaizawa, Pasang Phutar	Japanese
-Southeast		7850	★		
Gasherbrum III	Baltoro	7952	1975	J. Onyskiewicz, A. Chadwick, W. Rutkeiwicz, K. Zdzito-wiecki	Polish
Annapurna II	Annapurna	7937	1960	C. Bonington, R. Grant, Ang Nyima	British
Ngojumba Kg.I	Khumbu	7916	1982	Kim Yong-Han, Ang Tsering, Dorje	S. Korea-Nepal
Kangbachen	Kangchen.Nth	7903	1974	K. Olech, W. Branski, W. Klaput, M. Malatynski, A. Rubinowski	Polish
Himalchuli	Mansiri	7893	1960	M. Harada, H. Tanabe	Japanese
Disteghil Sar	Hispar	7885	1960	G. Starker, D. Marchart	Austrian
-Central		7760	★		
Ngadi Chuli	Mansiri	7871	1970	H. Watanabe, Tsering	Japanese
-South Shoulder		7514	★		

NAME	GROUP	HEIGHT	YEAR	SUMMITERS	NATIONALITY
Nuptse	Khumbu	7855	1961	D. Davis, Tashi	British
-Central		7845	★		
-Northwest		7745	1977	O. Kunji, Zambu	Japanese
-East		7703	★		
-West		7784	1988	Chun Bong-Gon, Bae Hyun-Jong, Kim Hwa-Gon, Oh Se-Cheul, Lhakpa Norbu, Pasang Dawa	Sth Korean
Khunyang Chhish	Hispar	7852	1971	A. Zawada, Z. Heinrich, J. Stryczynski, R. Szafirski	Polish
-South		7620	★		
-East		7320	★		
-West		7350	★		
-North		7108	1979	K. Echizenya, O. Hanai, S. Irikawa, A. Ishimura, A. Koizumi, H. Shiga, E.Shimozawa, J. Takahashi	Japanese
Masherbrum	Masherbrum	7821	1960	G. Bell, W. Unsoeld	U.S.A.
-Southwest		7806	1981	Z. Heinrich, M. Maltynski, P. Nowacki	Polish
-P.7200(Far West)	7200	1988			Italian
-P.7200		7200	★		
-P.7000		7000	★		
Nanda Devi	Nanda Devi	7816	1936	N. Odell, H. Tilman	Brit-U.S.A.
Chomolönzo	Makalu	7790	1954	J. Couzy, L. Terray	French
-Northwest		7540	★		
-P.7150		7150	★		
Rakaposhi	Rakaposhi	7788	1958	M. Banks, T. Patey	British
-P.7290		7290	★		
-East Peak		7010	1985	G. Fellner, G. Haberl, E. Koblmüller, F. Pressl	Austrian
Batura I(East)	Batura	7795	1976	H. Bleicher, H. Oberhofer	German
-West		7794	★		
Namcha Barwa	Assam	7782	★		
Batura II	Batura	7762	★		
Kanjut Sar	Hispar	7760	1959	C. Péllissier	Italian
Kamet	Kamet	7756	1931	R. Holdsworth, F. Smythe, E. Shipton, Lewa	British
Dhaulagiri II	Dhaulagiri	7751	1971	A. Huber, Jangbu	Austrian
-North		7239	★		
Ngojumba Kg.II	Khumbu	7743	1965	N. Uemura, Pemba Tenzing	Japanese
Saltoro Kang.I	Saltoro	7742	1962	Y. Takamura, A. Saito, Capt.Bashir	Jap-Pakistani
P.7739	Annapurna	7739	★		
Batura III	Batura	7729	★		
Gurla Mandhata	Nalakankar	7728	1985	Cirenuoji, Jiabu, Jin Junxi, K. Matsubayashi, Song Zhiyu, K. & Y. Suita, T. Wada	Jap-Chinese
Trivor	Hispar	7728	1960	W. Noyce, J. Sadler	Brit-U.S.A.
-Southwest		7000	★		
Kongur	Kun Lun	7719	1981	P. Boardman, C. Bonington, A. Rouse, J. Tasker	British
Dhaulagiri III	Dhaulagiri	7715	1973	G. Haberl, H. Saler, K. Schreckenbach	German
Jannu	Kumbhakarna	7710	1962	P. Keller, R. Paragot	French

NAME	GROUP	HEIGHT	YEAR	SUMMITERS	NATIONALITY
-East Peak		7468	★		
Tirich Mir	Hindu Kush	7706	1950	P. Kvernberg	Norwegian
-South		7100	1950?		
Saltoro Kg.II	Siachen	7705	★		
P.7700	Annapurna	7700	★		
Disteghil East	Hispar	7696	1980	A. Bielun, J. Gronczewski, R. Kowalewski, T. Piotrowski, J. Tillak	Polish
Tirich Mir East	Hindu Kush	7692	1964	R. Höibakk, A. Opdal	Norwegian
Ngojumba Kg.III	Khumbu	7681	★		
Kangchungtse	Makalu	7678	1954	J. Franco, L. Terray, Gyalzen Norbu, Pa Norbu	French
Saser Kangri I	Saser	7672	1973	Dawa Norbu, Da Tenzing, Nima Tenzing, Thondup	Indian
-West Forepeak		7620	1987	M. Bissa & 4 others	Indo-British
Chogolisa	Masherbrum	7665	1975	G. Ammerer, A. Pressl	Austrian
-Northeast		7654	1958	M. Fujihira, K. Hirai	Japanese
Phola Gangchen	Jugal	7661	1981	B. Farmer, R. Price	New Zealand
Dhaulagiri IV	Dhaulagiri	7661	1975	S. Kawazu, E. Yusuda	Japanese
Varah Shikar	Annapurna	7647	1980	S. Mayerl, H. Neumair, Ang Chappal	Austrian
P.7640	Batura	7640	★		
Dhaulagiri V	Dhaulagiri	7618	1975	M. Morioka, Pemba Tsering	Japanese
Shispare	Batura	7611	1974	H. Bleicher, L. Cichy, M. Grochowski, J. Holnicki-Szulc, A. Mlynarczyk, H. Oberhofer, J. Poreba	Polish-German
-Northwest		7100	★		
P.7600(between Gash.III/IV)	Baltoro	7600	★		
Kongur Tobe	Kun Lun	7595	1956	J. Ivanov, K. Kuzmin, V. Potapov, V. Rachimov, B. Rukodelnikov, V. Sibarakov, Cheng Chung-chang, Pchen Chung-mu	Sino-Soviet
Batura IV	Batura	7594	1978	Y. Ishikawa, M. Itoh, M. Ohkubo	Japanese
Sheratse Chuli	Khumbu	7591	★		
Minya Konka	Szechuan	7590	1932	T. Moore, R. Burdsall	U.S.A.
Changtse	Khumbu	7580	1982	U. Zehetleitner	German
Yazghil Dome S	Hispar	7559	1980	A. Bielún, J. Gronczewski, R. Kowalewski, T. Piotrowski, J. Tillak	Polish
Annapurna III	Annapurna	7555	1961	M. Kohli, Sonam Gyatso, Sonam Girmi	Indian
Kula Kangri	Bhutan	7554	1986	C. Itani, E. Ohtani, H. Ozaki, A. Sakamoto	Japanese
Mustagata	Kun Lun	7546	1956	19 Russians, 12 Chinese. (See note at end of list)	Sino-Soviet
Skyang Kangri	Baltoro	7544	1976	Y. Fujiohji, H. Nagata	Japanese
-Southwest		7500	★		
Gangkar Puenzum	Bhutan	7541	★		
-P.7532		7532	★		
-P.7516		7516	★		
Himalchuli Wst	Mansiri	7540	1978	Y. Ogata, K. Sugeno	Japanese
P.7532(Yalung)	Kangchen.Nth	7532	★		

NAME	GROUP	HEIGHT	YEAR	SUMMITERS	NATIONALITY
-Southwest		7385	★		
Batura V	Batura	7531	1983	A. Heinrich, V. Stallbohm	Polish
Yukshin Gar.Sar	Hispar	7530	1984	W. Bauer, W. Bergmayr, W. Brandecker, R. Streif	Austrian
-South		7100	★		
Annapurna IV	Annapurna	7525	1955	H. Biller, H. Steinmetz, J. Wellenkamp	German
Saser Kang.II	Saser	7518	★		
-West		7518	1985	Phu Dorje, Sherup Choldon, Sonam Wangdu, Tsering Smanla	Indo-Japan
Mamostong Kang.	Rimo	7516	1984	N. Yamada, K. Yoshida, R. Sharma, P. Das, H. Chauhan	Ind-Japanese
Saser Kg.III	Saser	7495	1986	Dawa Tsering, Magan Singh, Rubgias, Sharap Shalden, Suddi Man, Tsering Sherpa	Indian
Pumari Chhish	Hispar	7492	1979	S. Chiba, K. Minami M. Ohashi, H. Yokoyama	Japanese
Noshaq	Hindu Kush	7492	1960	G. Iwatsabo, T. Sakai	Japanese
Tir,Mir West I	Hindu Kush	7487	1967	J. Cervinka, I.Galfy, V. Smida, I.Urbanovic	Czech
Khangsar Kang	Annapurna	7485	1969	R. Obster, P.Schubert, K. Winkler	German
Jongsong Peak	Janak	7483	1930	E. Hoerlin, E. Schneider,	International
Kommuniszma	Pamirs	7482	1933	E. Abalakov	U.S.S.R.
Noshaq East	Hindu Kush	7480	1963	G. Gruber, R. Pischinger	Austrian
Pasu Sar	Batura	7476	★		
Teram Kangri	Siachen	7462	1975	K. Kodaka, Y. Kobayashi	Japanese
Shartse	Khumbu	7459	1974	K. Diemberger, H. Warth	Austro-German
Malubiting W	Rakaposhi	7458	1971	K. Pirker, H. Schell, H. Schindlbacher, H. Sturm	Austrian
-Northwest		7300	★		
Gangapurna	Annapurna	7455	1965	G. Hauser, L. Greissl, H. Kollensperger, E. Reis-müller, Ang Temba, Phu Dorje	German
Muchu Chhish	Batura	7453	★		
-East		7280	★		
P.7451	Janak	7451	★		
Tir.Mir West II	Hindu Kush	7450	1974	G. Machetto, B.Re	Italian
Pungpa Ri	Jugal	7446	1982	D. Scott, R. Baxter-Jones, A. MacIntyre	British
Dome Kang	Janak	7442	1930	G. Dyrenfurth	International
Pik Pobeda	Tien Shan	7439	1956	V. Abalakov, J. Arkin, P. Budanov, L. Filimonov, N. Gusak, V. Kiziel, K. Klecko, J. Leonov, S. Musajev, J. Tur, V. Usienov	U.S.S.R.
Nanda Devi East	Nanda Devi	7434	1939	J. Bujak, J. Klarner	Polish
Ganesh I	Ganesh	7429	1955	E. Gavechat, C. Kogan, R. Lambert	French
-East		7400	1960	P. Wallace, Gyalzen, Pa Norbu	British
K12	Saltoro	7428	1974	S. Takagi, T. Ito	Japanese

NAME	GROUP	HEIGHT	YEAR	SUMMITERS	NATIONALITY
–P.7200		7200	★		
–P.7100		7100	★		
–P.7100		7100	★		
Muztagh Ata Nth	Kun Lun	7427	1981	K. Matsui, T. Sakahara	Japanese
Sia Kangri	Siachen	7422	1934	H. Ertl, A. Höcht	International
Saser Kg.IV	Saser	7416	1987	M. Bazire, D. Howie	Indo-British
Haramosh	Haramosh	7409	1958	H. Roiss, F. Mandl, S. Pauer	Austrian
Istor-o-Nal	Hindu Kush	7403	1969	J. Anglada, J. Cerda, E. Civis, J. Pons	Spanish
Teram Kang.II	Siachen	7402	1975	Y. Kobayashi, K. Kodaka	Japanese
Batura VI	Batura	7400	★		
Ghaint I	Saltoro	7400	1961	W. Axt	Austrian
Noshaq Central	Hindu Kush	7400	1963	G. Gruber, R. Pischinger, & 5 others	Austrian
Tir.Mir W. III	Hindu Kush	7400	1974	J. Kelle, J. Lemoine, G. Lucazeau, M. Pompei, S. Strathou	French
Kabru IV	Singalila	7395	★		
–P.7245		7245	★		
–P.7129		7129	★		
–P.7149		7149	★		
–P.7278		7278	★		
Ultar Sar (Boj. Duanasir II)	Batura	7388	★		
–West		7350	★		
Rimo I	Rimo	7385	1988	Y. Ogata, N. Sherpa, Sumanla, Yoshida	Indo-Jap
Teram Kang.III	Siachen	7382	1979	M. Kudo, J. Kurotaki, M. Oka	Japanese
–West		7300	★		
Sherpi Kangri	Saltoro	7380	1976	S. Ogata, T.Inoue	Japanese
–South		7370	★		
Rimo II	Rimo	7373	★		
Ist-o-Nal Nth	Hindu Kush	7373	1967	K. Lapuch, M. Oberegger	Austrian
–North II		7350	1967	K. Lapuch, M.Oberegger	Austrian
–North III		7300	★		
Churen West	Dhaulagiri	7371	1970	K. Hasegawa, A. Norbu	Japanese
–Central		7320	1970	M. Fukui, K. Hasegawa	Japanese
Churen East	Dhaulagiri	7371	1970	Kim Hosup, R. Angyal	South Korean
Himalchuli Nth	Mansiri	7371	1985	Lee Jae-Hong, Lhakpa Norbu, Pasang Dawa, Ang Pasang, Zangbu	South Korean
Chongtar	Baltoro	7370	★		
Labuche Kang	Pamari Himal	7367	1987	A. Deuchi, H. Furukawa, K. Sudo, Diaqiog, Gyala, Lhaji, Wanjia	Tibet-Japan
Kirat Chuli	Kangchen. Nth	7365	1939	E. Grob, H. Paidar, L. Schmaderer	Swiss-German
Istor-o-Nal SE	Hindu Kush	7365	1969	J. Anglada, J. Cerda, E. Civis, J. Pons	Spanish
Skil Brum	Baltoro	7360	1957	M. Schmuck, F. Wintersteller	Austrian
Abi Gamin	Kamet	7355	1950	G. Chevalley, R. Dittert, A. Tissières, Dawa Tondup	Swiss
Kabru III	Singalila	7353	★		

NAME	GROUP	HEIGHT	YEAR	SUMMITERS	NATIONALITY
P.7353	Tibet(inter'l)	7353	★		
Jasamba	Khumbu	7351	★		
Gimmigela I	Kangchen. Nth	7350	★		
Cho Aui	Khumbu	7350	1986	K. Emura, Y.Endo, K. Matsuki, Y. Shikoda	Japanese
Karun Kuh	Less.K'-koram	7350	1984	H. Grün, W. Krampf, H. Zimmermann	Austrian
Pumarikish SE	Hispar	7350	★		
Chongtar Nth.	Baltoro	7350	★		
-Northeast		7300	★		
Talung	Singalila	7349	1964	F. Lindner, Tenzing Ninda	German
-South		7181	1964	F. Lindner, Tenzing Ninda	German
Saraghrar	Hindu Kush	7349	1959	F. Alleto, P. Consiglio	Italian
-Central		7330	★		
Momhil Sar	Hispar	7343	1964	H. Schell, R. Wiederhofer, L. Schlömmer, H. Schindl-bacher, R. Pischinger	Austrian
Ghaint II	Saltoro	7343	1977	W. Axt, G. Brenner, H. Holat, B. Klausbruckner, F. Pucher	Austrian
-East		7000	★		
Kabru North	Singalila	7338	1935	C. Cooke	British
-P.7290(North)		7290	★		
-P.7279(West)		7279	★		
Tir.Mir W. IV	Hindu Kush	7338	1967	K. Diemberger, D. Proske	Austrian
Yutmaru Sar	Hispar	7330	1980	M. Motegi, T. Sugimoto, M. Watanabe	Japanese
Chongtar South	Baltoro	7330	★		
-South II		7180	★		
Boj.Duanasir	Batura	7329	1984	E. Kisa, M. Nagoshi, R. Okamoto	Japanese
-South		7250	1984	E. Kisa M. Nagoshi, R. Okamato	Japanese
Sia Kangri II	Siachen	7325	1934	H. Ertl, A. Hocht	International
-Central		7273	1934	H. Ertl, A. Hocht	International
Yazghil Dome N	Hispar	7324	1983	C. Casolari	Italian
Gasherbrum V	Baltoro	7321	★		
-East		7300	1978	K. Mukaide, M. Sakaguchi, T. Sato	Japanese
Chamlang	Barun	7319	1962	S. Anma, Pasang Phutar	Japanese
-South		7316	★		
-Central		7180	1984	J. Afanassieff, Ang Phurba D. Scott, M. Scott	International
Kabru South	Singalila	7317	★		
-P.7080		7080	★		
-P.7060		7060	★		
P.7316	Dhaulagiri	7316	★		
Chomolhari	Bhutan	7315	1937	F. Chapman, Pasang Dawa	British
Sia Kangri III	Siachen	7315	1934	G. Dyrenfurth, H. Dyren-furth, & others	International
P.7308	Khumbu	7308	★		
Istor-o-Nal S	Hindu Kush	7308	1969	J. Anglada, J. Cerda, E. Civis, J. Pons	Spanish
Saraghrar S.	Hindu Kush	7307	1967	H. Hara, Y. Sato	Japanese

NAME	GROUP	HEIGHT	YEAR	SUMMITERS	NATIONALITY
Sherpi Kang.E	Saltoro	7303	★		
Jeje Kangphu	Bhutan	7300	★		
Urdok I	Baltoro	7300	1975	K. Hub, R.Schauer, H. Schell L. Schell, H. Zefferer	Austrian
P.7300(between Gash.III/IV)	Baltoro	7300	★		
Saraghrar NW	Hindu Kush	7300	★		
-Northwest II		7200	1982	N. Bohigas, J. Díaz, E. Lucas	Spanish
Istor-o-Nal W.	Hindu Kush	7300	1955	J. Murphy, T. Mutch	U.S.A.
-West II		7280	★		
-Rock Pinnacle		7200	1969	M. Meres, J. Psotka	Czech
P.7291	Batura	7291	★		
Malubit.Cent	Rakaposhi	7291	1975	H. Atsumi, K. Moro, M. Onodera, T. Takahashi	Japanese
Shingeik Zom	Hindu Kush	7291	1966	K. Holch, I. Trübswetter	German
-II		7170	1969	A.& A. Aichhorn	Austrian
-III		7150	1969	A.& A. Aichhorn	Austrian
Baintha Brakk	Biafo	7285	1977	C. Bonington, D. Scott	British
Porong Ri	Jugal	7284	1982	Y. Eto, M. Wada	Japanese
Pasu Diar	Batura	7284	1978	C. Ando, M. Inove, K. Wakui, S. Yamada, Sher Khan, E. Anwar, I. Wali	Japanese
Baltistan Pk	Masherbrum	7281	1970	von der Hecken, G. Haberl, E. Koblmüller, G. Pressl	Austrian
Baltoro Kg.III	Baltoro	7280	1963	S. Kono, T. Shibata	Japanese
Istor-o-Nal NE	Hindu Kush	7276	★		
Mustagh Tower	Baltoro	7273	1956	J. Hartog, T. Patey	British
-West		7270	1956	J. Brown, I. McNaught-Davis	British
Mana	Kamet	7272	1937	F. Smythe	British
Dhaulagiri VI	Dhaulagiri	7268	1970	S. Kawazu, S. Kimura, H. Nakamura, S. Yamamura	Japanese
Crown	Less.K'koram	7265	★		
Summa-ri	Baltoro	7263	★		
Baltoro Kg.V	Masherbrum	7260	1934	J. Belaieff, P. Ghiglione, A. Roch	International
Diran	Rakaposhi	7257	1968	R. Göschl, R. Pischinger, H. Schell	Austrian
Baltoro Kg.IV	Masherbrum	7250	[Possibly Japanese in 1963 or 1976]		
Noshaq West		7250	1963	S. Jungmaier, G. Gruber, E. Werner, M. Hofpointner, H. Pilz, R. Pischinger, M. Schober	Austrian
Saraghrar SW		7250	1971	T. Nagano	Japanese
-Southwest II		7200	1971	M. Furukawa, Y. Katsumi, T. Nagano, M. Nakachi,	Japanese
P.7249	Dhaulagiri	7249	★		
Putha Hiunchuli	Dhaulagiri	7246	1954	J. Roberts, Ang Nyima	British
Apsarasas I	Siachen	7245	1976	Y. Inagaki, T. Miyamoto, K. Yabuta	Japanese
-South		7117	1976	(Members of same exped.)	
Mukut Parbat	Kamet	7242	1951	H. Riddiford, E. Cotter, Pasang Dawa	New Zealand
-East		7130	★		
Baltoro Kg.I	Masherbrum	7240	1976	G. Sueki, Y. Toyama	Japanese

NAME	GROUP	HEIGHT	YEAR	SUMMITERS	NATIONALITY
P.7239	Bhutan	7239	★		
P.7239	Bhutan	7239	★		
Apsarasas II	Siachen	7239	★		
Chamlang East	Barun	7235	1984	D. Scott, J. Afannassief, M. Scott, Ang Phurba	International
-East II		7290	★		
Langtang Lirung	Langtang	7234	1978	S. Wada, Pemba Tsering	Japan-Nepal
Rimo III	Rimo	7233	1985	J. Fotheringham, D. Wilkinson	British
Apsarasas III	Siachen	7230	★		
Khartaphu	Khumbu	7227	1935	E. Kempson, E. Shipton, C. Warren	British
Ningchin Kang.	Tibet(int'l)	7223	1986	(12 climbers)	Tibetan
Karjiang	Bhutan	7221	★		
-Central		7216	1986	H. Iwasaki, N.Shingo, K. Tomoda	Japanese
Apsarasas IV	Siachen	7221	★		
Baltoro Kg.II	Masherbrum	7220	1976	G. Sueki, Y. Toyama	Japanese
Annapurna Dakshin	Annapurna	7219	1964	S. Uyeo, Mingma Tsering	Japanese
-Central		7071	1964	Y. Ageta, M. Kimura, H. Yoshino	
-North		7010	★		
Darban Zom	Hindu Kush	7219	1965	U. Kossler, M. Schmuck	Austrian
Gang Benchen	Langtang	7211	1982	G. Hitomi, H. Kondo, S. Koshima, K. Matsubayashi, R. Morimoto, T. Morito, K. Nakagawa, K. Ushida	Japanese
Saraghrar SE		7208	★		
-Southeast II		7184	1971	T. Nagano	Japanese
Langtang Ri	Langtang	7205	1981	N,Yamaha, M. Wakao, S. Nasu, A. Rinji	Japanese
Singhi Kangri	Siachen	7202	1976	M. Katayama, S. Takahashi, J. Imai	Japanese
Kangphu Gang	Bhutan	7200	★		
Gang Chhen	Bhutan	7200	★		
Matsa Gang	Bhutan	7200	1985	G. Hitami, S. Nakayama, T. Tsukihara, S. Yokoyama	Japanese
Gieu Gang	Bhutan	7200	★		
Bularung Sar	Hispar	7200	★		
Lupghar Sar	Hispar	7200	1979	T. Nazuka, H. Shimizu, Y. Watanabe	Japanese
-West		7199	1979	H.& S. Gloggner	German
-West II		7010	★		
-East		7200	★		
P.7199	Makalu	7199	★		
Gurja Himal	Dhaulagiri	7193	1969	T. Saeki, Lhakpa Tenzing	Japanese
Tarke Kang	Annapurna	7193	1964	M. Nishimura, Sherpa Dorje	Japanese
Tsogaka	Langtang	7193	★		
Chamar	Serang	7187	1953	M. Bishop, Namgyl	New Zealand
-South		7183	★		
Apsarasas V	Siachen	7187	★		
P.7186(East of Cho Aui)	Khumbu	7186	★		
Apsarasas VI	Siachen	7184	★		

NAME	GROUP	HEIGHT	YEAR	SUMMITERS	NATIONALITY
-East		7000	★		
Menlungtse	Rolwaling	7181	★		
-West		7023	1988	A. Fanshawe, A. Hinkes	British
Rimo IV	Rimo	7168	1984	G. Sharma, M. Yadev	Indian
P.7167	Kun Lun	7167	1986	T. Baba, S.Kobayashi, S. Nakashima, Y. Numano, M. Sato	Japanese
Hachinder Chhish	Batura	7163	1982	K. Hayami, Y. Higashi, K. Kimura, T. Saito, K. Sakai, T. Takinami, K. Yoshida	Japanese
Yermanendi Kg.	Masherbrum	7163	★		
Nyenchen Tang.	Tibet(int'l)	7162	1986	Y. Maruyama, H. Naganuma, M. Wada	Japanese
Pumori	Khumbu	7161	1962	G. Lenser, U. Hürlimann, E. Forrer	German-Swiss
Manaslu North	Mansiri	7157	1964	F. Driessen, J. De Lint, H. Schriebl, Nima Tenzing, Ila Tsering	Dutch
-North II		7157?	1979	J. Cervinka, O. Srovonal	Czech
Savoia I	Baltoro	7156	★		
Hardeol	Nanda Devi	7151	1978	N. Dorje, N. Tensing, Kanhaya Prahlad, D. Rinzing, P. Tharkey, Thondup	Indian
Latok II	Panmah	7151	1977	E. Alimonta, T. Mase, R. Valentini	Italian
-South		7080	★		
Gyala Peri	Assam	7150	1986	Y. Hashimoto, H. Imamura, Y. Ogata	Japanese
Gama Peak	Dhaulagiri	7150	1970	K. Nakajima, G. Nabeyama	Japanese
P.7150(Ch'lisa)	Masherbrum	7150	★		
Depak	Saltoro	7150	1960	M. Anderl, E. Senn	German
Latok 1	Panmah	7145	1979	S. Matsumi, T. Shigehiro, Y. Watanabe	Japanese
Kampire Dior	Batura	7143	1975	Y. Hayashi, K. Takami, S. Mori, Y. Teranishi	Japanese
P.7139	Peri	7139	★		
Chaukamba I	Gangotri	7138	1952	L. George, V. Russenberger	French
Nun	Kashmir	7135	1953	C. Kogan, P. Vittoz	French
Gaurishankar	Rolwaling	7134	1979	J. Roskelley, M. Dorje	U.S.A.
-South		7010	1979	P. Boardman, T. Leach, G. Naifhardt, Pemba Lama	British-Nep
Tilitso	Annapurna	7134	1978	E. Schmutz	French
Pik Lenin	Pamirs	7134	1928	E. Allwein, E. Schneider, K. Wien	Russo-German
Api	Gurans	7132	1960	K. Hirabayashi, Gyaltsen Norbu	Japanese
-West		7100	★		
Baruntse	Barun	7129	1954	G. Harrow, C. Todd	New Zealand
-Central		7066	★		
-North		7059	★		
Pauhunri	Dongkya	7128	1910	A. Kellas, Sonam, Ang Tharke	British
Himlung	Peri	7126	1983	M. Minami, W.Saito, K. Takahashi, Kirkin Lama	Japanese
Pathibara	Kangchen. Nth	7123	★		
-Northeast		7100	1949	R. Dittert, J.Pargätzi, A.	Swiss

NAME	GROUP	HEIGHT	YEAR	SUMMITERS	NATIONALITY
				Sutter, Arjeeba, Dawa Thondup, Gyalgen	
Trisul	Nanda Devi	7120	1907	T. Longstaff, A.& H. Brocherel, Karbir	British
P.7120	Kun Lun	7120	[May be the same as P.7167]		
Ganesh II	Ganesh	7111	1979	H. Ogura, Dawa Norbu, Pemba Tsering	Jap-Nepalese
Nang.Gosum III	Khumbu	7110	★		
Ganesh III	Ganesh	7110	1981	H. Warth, Ang Chappal, Nga Temba, Nima Tenzing, N. Kuwahara, J.Nakamura, N. Hase, Tendi Sherpa, Kirke Sherpa	Nep-German & Japanese
Savoia II	Baltoro	7110	★		
P.7108	Dhaulagiri	7108	1972	T. Fujika, T. Sato, 2 Sherpas	Japanese
Udren Zom	Hindu Kush	7108	1964	G. Gruber, R. Pischinger	Austrian
Pik E. Korzhen-evskoi	Pamirs	7105	1953	B. Dimitriev, A. Goziev, A. Kovyrkov, L. Krasavin, E. Ryspajev, R. Sielidzanov, P. Skorobogatov, A. Ugarov	U.S.S.R.
Savoia III	Baltoro	7103	★		
Tsenda	Bhutan	7100	★		
Mazeno	Nanga Parbat	7100	★		
P.7100(between Gash.IV/V)	Baltoro	7100	★		
Baltistan NW	Masherbrum	7100	★		
-Cima Abruzzi		7040	1969	D. Alessandri, C.Leone (possibly)	Italian
Istor-o-Nal E	Hindu Kush	7100	★		
P.7098	Peri	7098	★		
Loinbo Kangri	Transhi-malaya	7093	★		
Mana Northwest	Kamet	7092	★		
Changtok I	Panmah	7091	★		
Kangtö	Assam	7090	★		
Ghenta Peak	Batura	7090	1974	J. Kurczab	Polish-German
Kun	Kashmir	7086	1913	L. Borelli, M.Piacenza, G. Gaspard, Carrel, Ali Ramin	Italian
Shakaur	Hindu Kush	7084	1964	G. Gruber, R. Pischinger	Austrian
Udren Z. Cent.	Hindu Kush	7080	1977	T. Ishii, M. Kubota, K. Morita, T. Niwa, N. Sakurai	Japanese
Urdok II	Baltoro	7079	★		
Satopanth	Gangotri	7075	1947	R. Dittert, A. Graven, A. Roch, A. Sutter	Swiss
-West		7045	1983	H. Hisamatsu, M.Omiya, A. Suzuki	Japanese
Tirsuli	Nanda Devi	7074	1966	N. Mallik, S. Chakravorty Tashi, Dorji	Indian
Nyanang Ri	Jugal	7071	★		
Kellas Rock Pk	Khumbu	7071	1935	E. Shipton, H. Tilman, E. Wigram	British
Langar Zom	Hindu Kush	7070	1964	O. Huber	German
-Southeast		7061	1967	K. Umezu, S. Yokoyama	Japanese

NAME	GROUP	HEIGHT	YEAR	SUMMITERS	NATIONALITY
Nobaisum Zom	Hindu Kush	7070	1967	K. Diemberger, K. Lapuch	Austrian
P.7069	Annapurna	7069	★		
Chong Kumdang I	Rimo	7069	★		
Chaukamba II	Gangotri	7068	★		
Dunagiri	Nanda Devi	7066	1939	A. Roch, F. Steuri, D. Zogg	Swiss
Nilgiri North	Annapurna	7061	1962	L. Terray, H. Campagne, P.& P. Campagne, Wongohj	French-Dutch
Summa-ri North	Baltoro	7060	★		
Kharta Changri	Khumbu	7056	1935	E. Kempson, C. Warren	British
Ganesh IV	Ganesh	7052	1978	K. Aogagi, M.& Y. Hashimoto, Y. Okuma, T. Shimoji, T. Suzuki, T. Tomita, I. Yasuda, H. Yoshio, Y. B. Thpa, M. Tenzing, O. Sonam, K. Bhandari, E. Okutani & 2 others	Japan-Nepal
Risum	Jugal	7050	★		
P.7050	Jugal	7050	★		
Udren Zom Sth	Hindu Kush	7050	1967	H. Hara, K. Kurachi, H. Sato, Y. Sato	Japanese
Nyegyi Kangsang	Assam	7047	★		
Changtok II	Panmah	7045	★		
P.7044	Janak	7044	★		
Naipeng	Assam	7043	1984	(7 climbers)	Chinese
Link Sar	Masherbrum	7041	★		
Saraghrar Nth	Hindu Kush	7040	1959	F. Alleto, P. Consiglio	Italian
Vostochnaya	Tien Shan	7039	1958	(44 climbers)	U.S.S.R.
P.7038	Peri	7038	★		
Koh-i-Urgend	Hindu Kush	7038	1963	S. Burkhardt, M. Eiselin, H. Ryf, A. Strickler	Swiss
Hungchi	Khumbu	7036	★		
P.7036	Mansiri	7036	★		
Janak	Janak	7035	★		
Ratna Chuli	Annapurna	7035	★		
Tirsuli West	Nanda Devi	7035	★		
Pauhunri South	Dongkya	7032	★		
Shudu Tsenpa	Dongkya	7032	★		
Saipal	Gurans	7031	1963	K. Hirabayashi, Pasang Phutar III	Japanese
Spantik	Rakaposhi	7027	1955	R. Diepen, E. Reinhardt, J. Tietze	German
Malangutti Sar	Hispar	7025	1985	Y. Muranaka, K. Nakahara, T. Sugimoto, Ang Nima	Japanese
Mt.Hardinge	Siachen	7024	★		
P.7023	Khumbu	7023	★		
Akher Chioh	Hindu Kush	7020	1966	R. Göschl, H. Schell	Austrian
P.7018	Khumbu	7018	1935	E. Shipton, H. Tilman, E. Wigram	British
Mamostong K. II	Rimo	7017	★		
P.7016	Batura	7016	1986	D. Alessandri, A. Capassi D. Mancinelli, A. Tansella	Italian
P.7013	Khumbu	7013	★		
Palung Ri	Khumbu	7013	★		

NAME	GROUP	HEIGHT	YEAR	SUMMITERS	NATIONALITY
P.7013	Jugal	7013	★		
P.7011	Khumbu	7011	1935	H. Tilman, E. Wigram	British
Mayër Kangri	Tibet(int'l)	7011	★		
P.7010	Annapurna	7010	★		
Gimmigela II	Kangchen. Nth	7005	★		
Chong Kum.II	Rimo	7005	★		
Gasherbrum VI	Baltoro	7003	1985	M. Ercalani (claimed)	Italian
Chura Gang	Bhutan	7000	★		
Melunghi Kang	Bhutan	7000	★		
Chumari Gang	Bhutan	7000	★		
Table Mountain	Bhutan	7000	★		
Gangchen Tag	Bhutan	7000	★		
Teri Kang	Bhutan	7000	★		
Chomolhari Gang	Bhutan	7000	★		
Prupoo Burahka	Masherbrum	7000	1977	S. Anji, S. Kobayashi, T. Nakamura, M. Yajima	Japanese
Saraghrar West	Hindu Kush	7000	★		

The names of the nineteen Russian and twelve Chinese climbers who made the first ascent of Muztagata are as follows: E. Beletskij, I. Bogatjev, B. Dimitrijev, A. Gozhev, I. Grek, E. Ivanov, V. Kovaljev, A. Kovyrkov, K. Kuzmin, V. Potapov, R. Potaptjuk, V. Rachimov, B. Rukodelnikov, A. Sebastianov, G. Senatjev, I. Shumichin, A. Sidorenko, P. Skorobogatov, J. Tjernovlivin, Shih Chan-chun, Chen Rongchan, Hsu Chin, Lyu Dayi, Liu Lien-man, Ben Shu-li, Chen De-yu, Pchen Chung-mu, Go De-cung, Bon Gin-zhan, Si Syu, Khu Beymin.

N.B. (1) Some of the above unclimbed peaks have been attempted without success.

(2) Other peaks of doubtful and/or reduced height are dealt with in the main text.

Assam Himalaya

East of the Kuru Chu (in eastern Bhutan) lies the least known part of the entire Himalayan chain. The highest peaks lie on the ill-defined border between China (Tibet) and the Indian state of Arunchal Pradesh (Assam), culminating in the fine peak Namcha Barwa which lies on the Great Bend of the Tsangpo. The country has never been accurately surveyed except in a few places and the unadministered frontier tracts of Assam are populated by unfriendly tribes.

Starting from the west, in the area between the Kuru Chu and the Chayul Chu-Subansiri rivers lie several peaks in the Kangtö Range – Gori Chen, Kangtö and Nyegyi Kangsang. In the spring of 1939 H. W. Tilman travelled north from Tezpur, east of the Mönyul corridor, to the Gorjo Chu valley in the vicinity of Gori Chen (6,858 metres) and briefly glimpsed a high peak he thought might be Kangtö. His trip was cut short by illness in the party. From the Chayul Chu east to the Siyon is a tract of country where the frontier peaks, known here as the Pachakshiri Range, apparently do not reach the height of 7,000 metres. The Namcha Barwa Range lies between the Siyon and the Tsangpo.

Namcha Barwa is generally recognized as marking the eastern end of the Himalaya. However, east of the Great Bend of the Tsangpo, in northern Assam and Burma, there are more ranges with the possibility of another high peak (Chompo, 7,000 metres?) to the west of the Ata Kang La. This pass was visited by Ronald Kaulback and crossed by Frank Kingdon Ward.

KANGTÖ
Location: east of Rodung col (in NEFA) – a massif barbed with ice ridges which forms a southern spur of the main range
Height: 7,090 metres
Lat./Long.: 27°48' 92°24'

NYEGYI KANGSANG
Height: 7,047 metres
Lat./Long.: approx. 28° 93°

NAMCHA BARWA (Namjag Barwa Feng)
Height: 7,782 metres
Lat./Long.: 29°37'51" 95°03'31"

Although there were several recorded sightings of this peak in the nineteenth century, from 1879 onwards, its true position was only fixed in 1912, by the observations of Captains Oakes and Field of the Abor Expedition, and by Captain Henry Morshead from the Mishmi hills. The following year F. M. Bailey and Morshead saw it from close quarters during their survey of the Dihang and the Tsangpo gorge, and discovered the neighbouring peak Gyala Peri. No further reconnaissances of the two peaks are recorded until the Chinese activity of recent years. In the early 1980s the Chinese reserved the first ascent of Namcha Barwa for themselves and began making determined efforts to effect its ascent. Studies of the region and reconnaissances of the climbing possibilities were carried out by various parties between August 1982 and April 1984. Among other things the weather in the region was found to be generally unsettled with much fog and cloud. As part of their programme in 1984 they ascended the neighbouring peak Nai Peng from the southwest, placing seven climbers on the summit. From there they could see six possible routes on Namcha Barwa, all of them complicated and with mixed snow, ice and rock. Unsuccessful attempts were made to climb Namcha Barwa in April 1983 and 1984.

NAI PENG
Height: 7,043 metres
First ascent: 1983 via Southwest
Flank

Chinese climbers ascended the stee and avalanche prone southwest flank between 18–21 April.

GYALA PERI (Jialabiali Feng)
Location: north of Namcha Barwa
Height: 7,150 metres
First ascent: 1986 via South Ridge

In 1985 the Himalayan Association of Japan sent a two-man party to reconnoitre this peak. The following year a climbing party returned, led by Kazuo Tobita. After an approach rendered difficult by constant rain and dangerous river crossings, camp was established below the west face by mid-September. The climbers gained the south ridge at 6,000 metres and placed their fourth camp at 6,750 metres on 21 October. The summit was reached on 31 October after two unsuccessful attempts.

Bibliography

Tilman, H. (1940) 'Assam Himalaya unvisited', *AJ* 52, pp. 53–62.

Tilman, H. (1946) *When Men and Mountains Meet.* pp. 1–47 (Cambridge: Cambridge University Press).

(Alpine Club Collection)

Henry Treise Morshead (1882–1931)

Lieutenant Colonel Morshead was the son of a Devon squire and nephew of the climber Frederick Morshead. He was commissioned in the Royal Engineers in December 1901 and joined the Survey of India five years later. In the winter of 1911–12 he was with a survey party in the Assam hills, and again a year later when he triangulated the Dibang valley. In the spring of 1913 he and F. M. ('Eric') Bailey, the political officer, carried out their adventurous exploration of the great bend of the Tsangpo river between Namcha Barwa and Gyala Peri. Returning to India after the war he served in Waziristan in 1920, later accompanying A. M. Kellas on an attempt to climb Kamet, which they might have succeeded in doing but for the refusal of their porters to place a camp on Meade's Col. Morshead then took part in the 1921 and 1922 Everest expeditions, the second time as a member of the climbing team and reached an altitude of 26,985 ft (8,225 metres). Although badly frostbitten on the hands and feet, with great strength and fortitude he suffered the agonising evacuation cheerfully. While on leave in 1927 he joined the Cambridge University expedition to Spitsbergen, and on his return to India was appointed Director of the Survey in Burma where he was murdered on Sunday 17 May 1931 while out riding. Although not first and foremost a climber, Morshead had a well deserved reputation as a great mountain man, and was looked upon as the leading authority of his day on the eastern Himalaya.

Bhutan Himalaya

This small Himalayan kingdom has remained closed to all but a handful of foreigners until this decade, and even now the authorities continue to exercise great restraint by putting a high price on the small amount of tourism and mountaineering permitted. Bhutan is still not accurately surveyed, except in a few places and along certain routes. Thus the heights and topography of all but one or two of the high peaks are, to some extent, matters for conjecture.

In the seventeenth century a few Jesuit priests travelled briefly in Bhutan, and in the eighteenth century there were a few small trade missions. But these visitors added very little to our geographical knowledge, the first person to do so being the pundit explorer R.N. (Rinzin Namgyal) in 1885–6. Later, J. Claude White, the first Political Officer appointed to Sikkim, was on official missions to Bhutan in 1905 and 1907. He also explored the eastern parts of the country in 1906, crossing the difficult Mon La Kar Chung La (5,316 metres) into Tibet, thus viewing the Kula Kangri group at close quarters. He was handicapped in his travels by the lack of local guides.

Apart from Spencer Chapman's ascent of Chomolhari in 1937 other visits by Westerners this century have been confined, until recently, to officials and men of science. In 1933 G. Sherriff and F. Ludlow carried out botanical exploration, in the course of which they ascended to the difficult glacier pass Mon

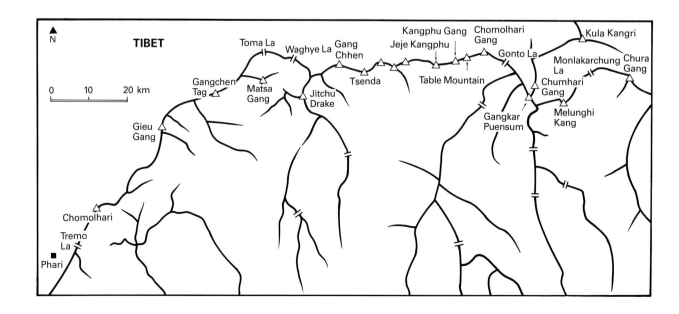

La Kar Chung La which gives a magnificent view of the Kula Kangri massif. They then travelled eastwards and crossed into Tibet, following in part Claude White's route. There appears to have been no further activity until the visits of doctors Michael Ward and Peter Steele, geologist August Gansser, and historian Dr Blanche Olschak in the 1960s. Peter Steele and his family journeyed across Bhutan, and he paid a visit to the Mon La Ka Chung La. Michael Ward and his companions visited the Laya region. They went up the valley of the Mo-Chu, had a distant view of the Lunana peaks from the Kangla Ka Chu La, then followed the southern flanks of the frontier range westwards to Chomolhari, crossing a number of passes. While doing medical research in 1965 Michael Ward obtained a good deal of topographical information about the little known area of Lunana. The Swiss geologist August Gansser climbed a subsidiary summit on the southern flank of Chomolhari and approached the Melunghi Kang massif in 1963. In 1967 he was able to carry out his own researches in the Lunana region, taking a number of spectacular photographs of the principal massifs.

The first foreign mountaineering expedition – a party of Japanese women – was allowed into Bhutan in April 1983. At present, barely half a dozen peaks have been made available and the number of expeditions in any year is very limited.

Chomolhari-Laya Group from the Tremo La East to the Toma La

CHOMOLHARI (Jomolhari)
Height: 7,315 metres.
Lat./Long.: 27°49′42″ 89°23′21″
First ascent: 1937 via Southwest
  Ridge

Lying a little east of the main route from India to Lhasa this fine peak was a familiar sight to the early

▲ *Chomolhari (7,315m) as seen from the plains of Tuna, on the northern Tibetan side. The border between Tibet and Bhutan runs along the highest visible ridges (Fosco Maraini)*

Everest expeditions as they approached the Tibetan frontier. In the course of travelling to and from Lhasa in 1936–37, F. Spencer Chapman had plenty of opportunity to study the peak and formed the opinion that the long southern snow and ice slope could be climbed by a small party, once one could get on it. He was well placed to obtain the necessary permission from Tibet and Bhutan, and the foot of the glaciated ridge which leads to the long final slope was reached four days after arrival at Phari. The party consisted of Chapman, C. E. Crawford and three Sherpas. Throughout the time they were on the mountain they were hampered by fine snow which fell every day, always by midday, lying deep and limiting visibility to a few yards.

During the next three days they worked their way up a series of steep, sharp snow and ice crests to the more level rounded saddle leading to the final 900-metre slope. The saddle was crossed by several almost continuous lines of crevasses, and just where the angle increased it seemed they would have to cut steps along the crest of a long, steep knife-edge of blue ice. By keeping to the west they managed to avoid this by cutting steps up an amphitheatre, through blocks of ice that had fallen from the ridge. All this was most exhausting but, pitching their tents at 6,100 metres, they felt pleased with their progress. However Crawford and two of the Sherpas were unable to continue and Chapman was left with a young porter named Pasang Dawa. About 300 metres above camp, a precipitous and much broken icefall was passed by means of a fallen flake that formed a natural bridge. Shortly afterwards they were pinned down for two hours by a blizzard accompanied by peals of thunder. Just above, an outcrop of

ice offered an uncomfortable campsite.

The pair set off next day at 4 a.m. and, keeping to the west, worked their way up above the steep slopes on the Tibetan side. The climbing was ideal and most of the new snow had either blown or slithered away. As they approached the west ridge the peaks of Sikkim and Nepal swung into view, but the actual top of the mountain was still some 150 metres above and separated from them by a long undulating and extremely sharp ridge. At midday they shook hands on the triple snow ridge of the summit.

Already the weather was beginning to deteriorate and Chapman made haste back to the main ridge, anxious to regain camp before stopping for any length of time. As they were about to descend the long slope, Pasang slipped and shot past Chapman, pulling him head-first on his back down the slope. Bumping over ice outcrops they fell over 100 metres before Chapman, fighting for breath, managed to drive in his axe, just as Pasang was about to disappear over the edge of the great drop into Tibet. Nevertheless they were back in camp by 3 p.m., not suspecting that far worse was yet to come.

Not realizing how exhausted they were, Chapman decided to move the tent down to a more comfortable spot. After descending about 100 metres, another blizzard started; as they could not now locate the route there was no alternative but to retrace their steps upwards to the old site. Each step was a nightmare, and the night that followed exceedingly uncomfortable as everything was sodden. Pasang was now a passenger, completely demoralized by the fall and suffering from snow-blindness.

Each of the following five days of agonizing descent they were stopped before midday by fresh

snow. It was difficult to find a route; they were soaking wet all the time and, as they had no matches, they could eat only snow mixed with barley-meal. Where the blizzard had cleared the steeper places Chapman had to cut steps, knowing that Pasang was unlikely to hold him. At one point Chapman fell into a crevasse from which he escaped only after three-and-a-half hours' very hard step-cutting. However, the route through the amphitheatre was reversed without mishap, Chapman lowering Pasang on the rope then cutting steps for himself. Next day they were off the snow but a walk of 25–30 kilometres over several high passes had to be endured before they reached the security of the Phari bungalow.

1970. Second ascent, by South Ridge

Four members of an Indo-Bhutanese expedition led by N. Kumar climbed the south ridge. The second summit team disappeared, possibly having fallen down the west face.

GANGCHEN TAG (Kangcheta)
Height: 7,000 metres
Lat./Long.: 28°05' 89°35'

MATSA GANG (Masa Gang, Masang Gang)
Height: 7,200 metres (probably less)
Lat./Long.: 28°07' 89°42'
First ascent: 1985 via Northeast Spur

An expedition from Kyoto University Alpine Club, led by Ryohei Hori, established base camp three kilometres southeast of the Toma La in mid-September. From there they attacked the northeast spur which necessitated some steep snow and ice climbing before they could reach the fore-summit. A third camp was placed between that and the main top which was reached by three parties on successive days. Their altitude measurements indicate a height for this peak of only about 6,800 metres.

JITCHU DRAKE (Tserim Kang)

Height: c.7,000 metres (probably less)
  South peak, 6,793 metres
Lat./Long.: 28°05' 89°50'
First ascent: 1988 via South
  Face/Southeast Ridge
(Tserim Gang (or Takaphu) is now
  given as a different peak of 6,532
  metres)

The first mountaineering expedition allowed into Bhutan was the Japanese women's group in spring 1983, led by Junko Tabei, the first woman to climb Mount Everest. They attempted the long southeast ridge and reached a height of 5,200 metres, above which the route became too steep and difficult for them. At about the same time an Austrian expedition was attempting the southwest ridge. The ice above their second camp (5,600 metres), on the up to 70° knife-edge ridge, was the most difficult part of the climb. On 15 May a tiny tent was placed on an ice ledge hacked out of the ridge at 6,100 metres and two days later five members reached the lower south summit.

In May 1984 a Japanese party led by Kuniaki Yagihara ascended to a col at 5,300 metres, cutting short the long route from the end of the southeast ridge attempted by the Japanese women the year before. Between 7–20 May they worked on the long, sharp snow ridge, with five members finally reaching the south summit. Four months later two members of an Italian expedition attempting the same ridge were hurled 750 metres down the east face when a section of the crest collapsed.

In May 1988 Doug Scott's party made an alpine-style ascent of the main peak in eight days. Because of severe snowstorms and mist the climb took twice as long as expected, forcing them on half rations. The assault started from their second camp (6,100 metres) below the icy slopes of the south face. Bad weather forced them to move from the middle of the face towards the southeast ridge where they had difficulty finding a campsite. Next day they made little progress; then it snowed all night and much of the next day. However on 31 May the weather was perfect. Leaving camp at 2.30 a.m. after eight hours they reached the south summit, below which they found the last shreds of the Japanese fixed ropes. On the top part of the ridge they had to climb over loose, aerated snow full of holes through which they could see down the 1,200 metres high east face. Then they traversed the 275 metres of ridge leading to the higher peak, past huge unstable cornices.

The Bhutanese side of the frontier peak Jeje Kangphu in northwest Lunana (August Gansser. Courtesy Swiss Foundation for Alpine Research)

▼

Gieu Gang (Gyu Kang)

Height: c.7,200 metres
Lat./Long.: 28°01' 89°28'

Luana Group from the Toma La East to the Gonto La

TSENDA

Height: c.7,100 metres
Lat./Long.: 28°09' 90°01'

TERI KANG

Height: 7,000 metres
Lat./Long.: 28°08' 89°54'

JEJE KANGPHU

Height: 7,300 metres (possibly 7,100
  metres)
Lat./Long.: 28°09' 90°13'

KANGPHU GANG

Height: 7,200 metres
Lat./Long.: 28°10' 90°17'

TABLE MOUNTAIN (Zongophu Gang)

Height: 7,000 metres
Lat./Long.: 28°10' 90°18'

GANG CHHEN (Kang Chen)
Height: 7,200 metres
Lat./Long.: 28°10' 89°56'

CHOMOLHARI GANG
  (Chomolhari Kangri)
Height: 7,000 metres
Lat./Long.: 28°11' 90°20'

led by Michifumi Ohuchi, first attempted the south ridge in autumn 1985. From camp at 5,220 metres the upper part of the ridge appeared to be very difficult. A reconnaissance of the west ridge showed it to be no easier so they

Chomolhari Kangri from the south. The summit rises from the vast plateau which has very steep walls (Michael Ward)

Telephoto shot of Gangkar Puensum at sunrise from base camp (Steven Berry)
▼

Bumthang Group from the Gonto La East to the Kuru Chu

GANGKAR PUENSUM
  (Kangkar Pünzum Rinchita)
Height: 7,541 metres (subsidiary
  peaks, 7,532 metres and 7,516
  metres)
Lat./Long.: 28°06' 90°25'

This peak lies in a remote and virtually unmapped region of northern Bhutan. A Himalayan Association of Japan expedition,

returned to their first choice. After traversing a snow dome to a col, followed by a level section of saw-tooth ridge (the 'Dinosaur'), there were two steep rock steps before Camp III could be placed at 6,880 metres. Illness then forced a retreat. An American expedition which had permission at the same time for the southeast and east ridges was diverted into a valley from which the peak could not be reached. The following year an Österreichischer Alpenverein expedition, led by Sepp Mayerl, fared no better on the south ridge, being hampered by severe monsoon weather.

In autumn 1986 a British expedition, led by Steven Berry, was defeated principally by constant bitterly cold winds. The walk-in started from Bumthang on the main east-west route across Bhutan and it was not until the sixth day, when they reached base camp (5,050 metres), that they had their first spectacular view of the peak. During the following week, advanced base camp was set up (5,500 metres) and four of the team began climbing and fixing rope to Camp I. The route largely followed that of previous attempts, across two steep rock sections – the first at the top of the 'Ramp' and the second at the top of the Japanese gully – before gaining the south ridge proper. This avoided the lower part of the Japanese gully threatened by séracs, which caused an accident to one of the 1985 Japanese party. The ridge was followed to Camp I which was set up at 6,250 metres.

Heavy snowfall between 4–7 October meant a withdrawal to base camp to conserve supplies on the mountain. Once this had cleared the skies remained clear but it was extremely windy and cold, making climbing very difficult. However, Camp I was re-occupied by 13 October. The route then crossed the top of the snow dome (6,700 metres) and the heavily corniced knife-edge 'Dinosaur' ridge to the foot of the first rock buttress where Camp II was placed. Even on the days when climbing was possible the strong winds made fixing rope on the ridge a dangerous business. After ten days they were ready to go for the summit. Because of the wind problem the plan was to traverse across the face below the left side of the ridge and then climb alpine-style up the face. On 23 October Jeff Jackson and Steven Monks began the task of fixing rope across the face but steep hard ice and the wind caused them to give up after only 120 metres. It was clearly time to abandon the climb.

For the time being permits are no longer available for this peak, partly because the local people believe that the gods have been angered by the four attempts on it made so far.

Gangkar Puensum – Ginette Harrison on 'Dinosaur Ridge' between Camps I and II (Steven Berry)

P.7239

*Location: 2 km northeast of Gangkar
    Puenzum
Lat./Long.: 28°07' 90°26'*

P.7239

*Location: 6 km south-southwest of
    Gangkar Puenzum, on its southern
    spur
Lat./Long.: 28°02' 90°24'*

KULA KANGRI (Künla Kangri, Gulha Kangri)

*Location: lies north of the main range,
    in Tibet
Height: 7,554 metres (Chinese figure,
    7,538 metres), three subsidiary
    peaks
Lat./Long.: 28°12' 90°32'
First ascent: 1986 via West Ridge*

After several years of negotiation with the Chinese, Kobe University received permission for an expedition to this peak. A three-man reconnaissance party in April 1985 explored the northern approaches and noted two possible routes – the east and west ridges. After long discussion they decided on the west ridge which, although steep and difficult, is short and not avalanche prone like the east ridge.

The following year the Kobe University Scientific and Mountaineering Expedition to Tibet, with twelve Japanese and five Chinese climbers, reached base camp on 17 March. It was some twenty kilometres from there, up the Kula Kangri glacier, to Camp I at the foot of the west ridge. The start of the ridge was barred by a steep 400-metre high ice wall (up to 70°) which took five days. Above that the ridge rose in steps with many steep cliffs and a number of crevasses. On 11 April Camp III was set up at 6,800 metres. Some 300 metres higher a 70-metre rock face was turned on the Bhutan side. The final camp was pitched at 7,100 metres. On 21 April in fine weather four Japanese climbers ascended a 40° ice slope leading to the summit ridge and reached the tiny summit platform in just over six hours. Two more Japanese made the ascent next day.

▲
The Tibetan side of Kula Kangri from the northern shore of Lake Puma Yumco (Pomo Tso) (G. Sherriff)

KARJIANG
Location: just northeast of Kula Kangri
Height: South peak 7,221 metres, central peak, 7,216 metres

1986. First Ascent of Central Peak

Starting from Moinda a party from the Himalayan Association of Japan approached the higher south peak but found it too difficult. They then turned to the central peak which was reached twice.

MELUNGHI KANG
Height: c.7,000 metres
Lat./Long.: 28°06′ 90°31′

CHUMHARI GANG
Height: c.7,000 metres
Lat./Long.: 28°08′ 90°24′

CHURA GANG
Height: 7,000 metres
Lat./Long.: 28°05′ 90°42′

Note: Other peaks which may be over 7,000 metres include Kangri, Takka Khon, Tsulim Khon, Tsunga Ri and Tsenda Gang.

Bibliography

Berry, S. (1988), *Thunder Dragon Kingdom*. Crowood Press, [Gangkar Puensum].

Berry, S. (1988), 'Kingdom of the thunder dragon', *HJ*, 44, pp. 40–7.

Chapman, F. (1940), *Helvellyn to Himalaya* (London: Chatto & Windus).

Gansser, A. (1964–5), 'Geological research in the Bhutan Himalaya', *MW*, pp. 88–97.

Gansser, A. (1968–9), 'Lunana', *MW*, pp. 117–31.

Hirai, K. (1987), 'Ascent of Kula Kangri from Tibet', *HJ*, 43, pp. 1–6.

Kohli, M. (1985), 'Mountaineering in Bhutan (1)', *AJ*, 90, pp. 18–20.

Mould, P. (1985), 'Mountaineering in Bhutan (2)', *AJ*, 90, pp. 21–2.

Olschak, B. (1966–67), 'Bhutan, paradise of the Himalaya', *MW*, pp. 80–7.

Steele, P. (1970), *Two and Two Halves to Bhutan* (London: Hodder & Stoughton).

Turner, R. (1966–67), 'Expedition to Bhutan', *MW*, pp. 88–105.

Tyson, J. (1978), 'Exploring Bhutan's north-west', *AJ*, 83, pp. 183–90.

Ward, M. (1965), 'Bhutan Himal', *AJ*, 70, pp. 106–19.

Ward, M. (1966), 'Bhutan Himal: some further observations', *AJ*, 71, pp. 281–4.

Ward, M. (1966), 'Some geographical and medical obervations in North Bhutan', *Geographical Journal*, 132, pp. 491–506.

Ward, M. (1985), 'The eastern Himalaya: an introduction', *AJ*, 90, pp. 10–17.

Ward, M. (1972), *In This Short Span* (London: Gollancz).

Sikkim Himalaya

Sir Joseph Hooker, the great mid-nineteenth century naturalist, was responsible for opening up the delights of travel in the little Himalayan kingdom of Sikkim. His well-known account of his travels, *Himalayan Journals*, contains many pages of vivid descriptions not only of the flora but also the people and the scenery, as he ascended towards the higher regions. In the alpine zone, where he spent six months, he climbed to around 5,500 metres and ventured several times to the tops of passes leading into Tibet. His itineraries included an almost complete circuit of Kangchenjunga, which took him to within twenty-two kilometres of the peak, and observation of Pauhunri from the Dongkya La. There were a dozen or more expeditions to the mountains of Sikkim during the latter part of the century, including the survey work done by Captain H. J. Harman around 1880. He attempted some of the high peaks, including Chomiomo (6,829 metres). The most important of these expeditions was that led by Douglas Freshfield in 1899.

Freshfield's party included the geologist and explorer E. J. Garwood, who was to make the map, Vittorio and Erminio Sella to act as photographers, the Alpine guide Angelo Maquignaz from Valtournanche, and the pundit Rinzin Namgyal. They reached the 'Green Lake' by the Zemu glacier on 20 September, 1899. From here, Freshfield hoped to examine the Nepal Gap and the northern side of the Zemu Gap but the weather was bad. He therefore withdrew and went round to the north via the Theu La and on 6 October crossed the Jongsong La into Nepal. Here, instead of the expected easy descent, he encountered the great expanse of the Kangchenjunga glacier which took some days to descend. The Sellas took some fine photographs of the western side of the main peaks, but Freshfield scarcely mentioned them in his book about the expedition. His route now led away into Nepal and after a long detour he crossed back into Sikkim over the Kang La on the Singalila ridge about ten kilometres south of Kabru.

However, the man who did the most pioneer mountaineering in Sikkim was the shy Scottish scientist Dr Alexander Mitchell Kellas. 'Perhaps no climber has enjoyed himself more among the Sikkim Himalaya than Dr A. M. Kellas of Glasgow', wrote Kenneth Mason. His first visit was in 1907 when he concentrated on the Zemu glacier area and twice tried to reach the Nepal Gap. His 1909 trip included two attempts on Pauhunri. On the opposite side of the country he crossed the Jongsong La, reached about 6,700 metres on the west ridge of Jongsong Peak, and made his third attempt to reach the Nepal Gap. The following year he investigated the pre-monsoon conditions, finally reaching the Nepal Gap except for a small rock wall at the summit which, typically, he did not bother to climb. After ascents of two 6,000-metre peaks he crossed to the northeast and ascended Pauhunri and Chomiomo. During his 1912 expedition he climbed Kangchengyao (6,889 metres). Throughout most of his Sikkim climbs Kellas made scientific observations on physiological reactions to altitude, about which he wrote valuable papers.

(Royal Geographical Society Collection)

Alexander Mitchell Kellas (d.1921)

Dr Kellas was born in Aberdeen and, through his professional interest in chemistry, became an authority on the effect of high altitude on the human system. While a university student he spent much time in the Scottish mountains and later visited Switzerland before commencing his visits to the Himalaya. His most successful expeditions were carried out in the Sikkim Himalaya but he also visited Nanga Parbat and Kamet, on which he reached a height of 7,200 metres in 1920. He published several important papers on the effects of altitude and addressed himself to the question of whether Mount Everest could be ascended without the use of supplementary oxygen. Kellas also obtained some of the earliest photographs of the Mount Everest region, and was chosen to accompany the first expedition to the mountain in 1921. However, he died of a heart attack on the approach march through Tibet. He was of a most retiring disposition and sadly wrote practically nothing about his climbing experiences.

Kangchenjunga Himal (northern section)

PATHIBHARA (Pyramid Peak)

Height: 7,123 metres Northeast peak: 7,100 metres
Lat./Long.: 27°49'15" 88°10'30"
First ascent: uncompleted ascent in 1949

In 1936 C. R. Cooke, F. S. Chapman and J. B. Harrison made an attempt on the northeast ridge and reached the summit of Sphinx, beyond which they considered the ridge would be too long and too difficult for them at that time. In 1939 the Germans, Paidar and Schmaderer, with the Swiss E. Grob established a camp on the Langpo La with the intention of following the northeast ridge, but the monsoon forced them to give up. These attempts were made from the Sikkim side.

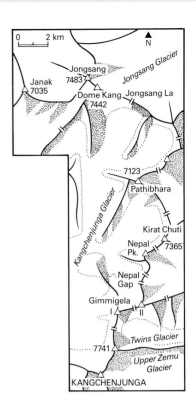

Pathibhara (Pyramid Peak) from the east. Taken from the Theiu La, a distance of over 20 kilometres (Harish Kapadia)

In 1949 René Dittert and his companions approached from the Nepal side up the labyrinthine Ginsang glacier and placed a camp on the Langpo La, beyond Sphinx and three kilometres from Pyramid Peak. Bad weather then intervened for nearly a week but at last a camp was set up at 6,700 metres on the northeast ridge and the route prepared to the top of Sphinx. After dropping about 100 metres to the col separating them from Pyramid Peak first cornices, then séracs forced the climbers to turn to the fluted slopes above the West Langpo glacier. When they arrived on the summit crest about eighty metres from the top, Dittert and Pargätzi found their way barred by a barrier of vertical spikes of snow and ice.

As they would have had to hack their way through, besides having a long way to return to their tent, they decided not to continue. Japanese climbers in 1964 were also unable to reach the summit on account of cornices.

KIRAT CHULI (Tent Peak)
Height: 7,365 metres
Lat./Long.: 27°47'10" 88°11'55"
First ascent: 1939 via South Ridge

After Dr Kellas' approach in 1910 the peak was not visited again until 1936. Members of Paul Bauer's expedition attempted the south ridge from Nepal Gap, over Nepal Peak. Conditions on the steep ridge were good but progress over the ridge towers was not fast. By

1 p.m. they had only reached about 6,700 metres. As Bauer was unwell only Karl Wien and Adolf Göttner (both to die on Nanga Parbat the following year) were able to continue. They bivouaced in an ice grotto but next day snow conditions were poor and it took four hours to travel several hundred metres to the gap beyond the central summit. It was clearly too late to attempt Kirat Chuli. After an hour's rest they continued towards the northeast summit, but just below the top, great sections of wind-slab snow broke away and there was no question of continuing. In the autumn of 1937 John Hunt reached only the southwest summit of Nepal Peak; his companion was unwell and it was too

Nepal Peak (left) and Kirat Chuli (Tent Peak) from the east, as seen from the Theiu La some 20 kilometres away (Harish Kapadia)

windy. Two years later E. Grob, L. Schmaderer and H. Paidar completed the traverse of Nepal Peak and the connecting ridge to reach Kirat Chuli.

NEPAL PEAK

Height: 7,180 metres (now given as 6,910 metres)
Lat./Long.: 27°46'37" 88°10'30"
First ascent: 1939 via South Ridge from Nepal Gap

Kangchenjunga seen during the ascent of the couloir between Camps II and III on Nepal Peak, November 1937 (John Hunt)

Nepal Peak was reconnoitred from the west by the 1899 Freshfield expedition. The southwest peak was climbed via the south ridge in 1930 by Erwin Schneider, a member of G. O. Dyrenfurth's international expedition. The central peak was climbed by the south ridge in 1936 by the Germans K. Wien and A. Göttner during an attempt on Kirat Chuli. The highest point was reached in 1939 from Nepal Gap by the Swiss-German party, E. Grob, H. Paidar and L. Schmaderer.

GIMMIGELA I (Twins I)

Height: 7,350 metres
Lat./Long.: 27°44'27" 88°09'42"

In early 1937 the Germans L. Schmaderer and H. Paidar and the Swiss E. Grob spent about six weeks on the Zemu glacier investigating the approaches to Kangchenjunga, during the course of which they attempted Gimmigela and Kirat Chuli. Like Bauer's party they were thwarted by soft snow and wind-slab. In the autumn C. R. Cooke and John Hunt also went up the Zemu glacier. From the Nepal Gap glacier they could see that there was no way of reaching Gimmigela I from that side. Cooke then examined the Twins glacier approach to the col on Kangchenjunga's north ridge. This north col lies midway between Gimmigela I and the junction ('Zuckerhutl', 7,741 metres) of the northeast spur of Kangchenjunga climbed by Bauer's expedition in 1931. Cooke just failed to reach the col which lies above an imposing 600-metre high wall of rock and ice.

In 1963 four Japanese climbers attacked from the western (Nepal) side of the peak. They had to abandon their attempt less than 150 metres from the summit because of avalanche danger and bad weather.

GIMMIGELA II (Twins II)

Height: 7,005 metres
Lat./Long.: 27°44'38" 88°10'57"

In 1936 three members of Paul Bauer's Siniolchu expedition climbed to the east ridge from the Nepal Gap glacier in an attempt to follow the ridge to the summit of Gimmigela II and on to Gimmigela I. Snow conditions were unfavourable and they did not get as far as Gimmigela II. Bauer meanwhile went up to Nepal Gap, not liking the look of the north ridge of Gimmigela II which rises sharply from this point. The following year C. R. Cooke and John Hunt reached the same spot and, despite Bauer's misgivings, considered that the north ridge would be feasible.

The unclimbed North Ridge of Gimmigela (Twins) II

▼

William Woodman Graham (Royal Geographical Society Collection)

▲

▼

The southeastern aspect of the Kabru massif seen from Darjeeling, a distance of about 60 kilometres. Kangchenjunga rises to the right of the picture (C. Reginald Cooke)

Kangchenjunga Himal (Singalila section)

The Kabru massif stands on a multi-summited ridge over 7,000 metres high. The summit area consists of a large ice-field about two-and-a-half kilometres long by nearly one kilometre wide which is pock-marked all over by 'wind tables', slabs of hard snow about three metres across supported on a short pedestal of snow. The peak first sprang to prominence when W. W. Graham claimed an ascent in 1883. He was, by his own admission, the first man to visit the Himalaya with the main object of climbing mountains 'more for sport and adventures than for the advancement of scientific know-ledge'. Numerous eminent mountaineers and other experts argued the pros and cons of his case for many years but it is now accepted that he was probably not even on the right mountain. His casual

account was quite at fault in some statements, he frequently mixed up the points of the compass, and misread his own position on the map. But as Sir Martin Conway said: 'All this implies no attack upon Mr Graham's veracity. He carried no instruments and made no observations for position. He merely believed that the peak climbed was Kabru.'

KABRU SOUTH (Kabru I)

Height: 7,317 metres
Subsidiary peaks: P.7080; P.7060
Lat./Long.: 27°36'30" 88°06'49"

In 1951 a Swiss climber Georg Frey reconnoitred this area and was killed attempting a peak east of the Ratong La.

Karbu South summit (C. Reginald Cooke)
▼

KABRU NORTH (Kabru II)

Height: 7,338 metres
Subsidiary peaks: North, P.7290;
* West, P.7279*
Lat./Long.: 27°37'03" 88°07'32"
First ascent: 1935 via Southeast Ridge

In October 1907, in a remarkable and little known ascent, the Norwegians C. W. Rubenson and Monrad Aas came within a stone's throw of the summit of Kabru. They made their way easily up the Rathong glacier to a height of nearly 6,000 metres and camped at the foot of the formidable Kabru ice-fall under the slopes of Kabru Dome. After five days of cutting steps through the maze of ice needles and crevasses they found a spot halfway up the ice-fall for another camp. The next part of the route was not as difficult but was exposed to falling blocks of ice.

They decided to make their assault from this point and climbed to the south ridge between Kabru Dome and the summit. Once on the ridge they found the time too short to continue and returned to camp. Next day, camp was transferred to a spot at about 6,700 metres.

After a very cold night they set off at 8.30 a.m. on 20 October with an icy wind blowing from the west (the prevailing wind). Slowly they cut steps up the hard snow of the south face, making for the saddle between the two peaks in an effort to reach the southern one which they believed to be the higher. The increasing strength of the wind made this impossible, so they bore off to the right and got under the shelter of the north peak. This proved to be much steeper and they had a couple of hours' hard work over rock and ice. 'Our

only watch being lost earlier in the day, we only had a hazy idea as to the time, but by the westering sun we knew only too well that evening was fast approaching, and had to hurry as fast as possible.'

Thinking they had the summit in sight they pressed on but, on reaching what appeared to be the top about 6 p.m., another snow ridge appeared, although only a few metres higher. The sun had set by now and they were confident of success but prudence dictated retreat. They had a fine view of the broad rounded ridge leading to the south peak which appeared easily climbable from that direction. They turned and began the descent. Going down a very steep slope Rubenson, who was behind, slipped and shot past his companion on his back. Aas managed to hold him but the rope nearly broke,

four of the five strands parting. Had they fallen they would have plunged off the slope to the névé, some 500 metres below.

In 1935 C. R. Cooke and G. Schoberth also made a post-monsoon attempt on Kabru by Rubenson's route. They, too, found the ice-fall to be the key to the climb. As a direct ascent was out of the question they by-passed the lower part by a detour on the shoulder of Kabru Dome. Even so they had two weeks of difficult climbing before they found themselves at last on the easy névé leading to the summit 900 metres above. After a reconnaissance from the south ridge they placed their final camp (6,850 metres) at the foot of the small ice-field which comes down from between the north and south peaks. The choice of route was either up the 450-

metre high ice-fall or a steep snow-slope and 300 metres of rocks; they decided on the latter. They set out twice but Schoberth was suffering badly from a cough, so turned back at the foot of the rocks. Cooke climbed on alone over the first band and then diagonally eastwards over the next to the south-east rib. Above some steep rocks the upper slopes appeared very steep and heavily corniced at the top so he doubled back to gain the summit ridge a little further south. Three rounded tops appeared in line. Cooke traversed the first, rounded the second and quickly

The Kabru party. Standing from left: Ang Thari, Gostav Schoberth, Jingmey, Ang Tsering, Pasang Kitar, Reggie Cooke, Pasang Phutar. Squatting: Sirdar Ang Tharkay (C. Reginald Cooke)

found himself on the last one, looking down a tremendous abyss to the Talung glacier. Descending by a shorter route he slipped and nearly came to grief just as Rubenson had done. On the hard snow he was unable to brake properly and his slide was only halted by cannoning into a bulge of rock.

KABRU III

Height: 7,353 metres
Lat./Long.: 27°37'52" 88°07'12"

KABRU IV

Location: this peak appears as an ice gendarme high up on the east face of the Kabru massif
Height: 7,395 metres
Subsidiary peaks: South, P.7245; North, P.7129, P.7149 and P.7278

In 1953 John Kempe and Gilmour Lewis ascended the Yalung glacier and established their top camp at 6,920 metres halfway between Talung Peak and the Kabru massif. From here a two hour climb brought them to the northern shoulder of the Kabru ridge and they were able to look down on the Talung glacier on the eastern side. Their aneroid barometer indicated a height of 7,315 metres. They decided to turn back but could have traversed to the highest point without difficulty.

1974: Talung Glacier Approach

An Indian expedition explored the very difficult approaches to the Talung-Kabru ridge from the eastern Sikkim side.

TALUNG

Height: 7,349 metres
Subsidiary peak: South, 7,181 metres
Lat./Long.: 27°39'15" 88°08'01"
First ascent: 1964 via Southwest Flank

After taking part in the 1954 Kangchenjunga reconnaissance, John Kempe, John Tucker and Gilmour Lewis made an attempt on Talung Peak from the Yalung glacier. They were prevented from reaching the top by a cut-off which barred access to the upper part of the north face. The route they should have taken lay slightly farther to the west. Kempe and Lewis probably reached a hump about 120 metres below the south peak.

In 1964 members of an international expedition ascended the Yalung glacier and placed three camps up the southwestern flank, the highest being about 200 metres below the Talung south col. The first assault nearly ended in catastrophe with one climber immobilized with chest pains, while lower down another had to be evacuated with a poisoned foot. After a storm and more illness in the party, two pairs set off in a lightning attack on the summit, with Franz Lindner and Tenzing Nindra arriving on top mid-afternoon.

Talung Glacier Approach

In 1974 an Indian party found all the eastern approaches from the Talung glacier subject to avalanche danger.

ZEMU PEAK (Zemu Gap Peak)

Height: 7,780 metres (possibly 7,730 metres)
Lat./Long.: 27°41'15" 88°11'00"

The long unclimbed east-southeast ridge of Kangchenjunga rises at over 7,000 metres above the Zemu Gap. Zemu Peak is the pronounced dome approximately halfway along the ridge.

Zemu Peak from the north. This is the pronounced dome on the eastern ridge of Kangchenjunga, about halfway between the Zemu Gap and the south summit (Harish Kapadia)

▼

Janak Himal

Dome Kang

Height: 7,442 metres
Lat./Long.: 27°52'40" 88°09'04"
First ascent: 1930 by Traverse from
  Jongsong Peak

G. O. Dyrenfurth traversed to the summit from Jongsong Peak on 8 June.

JANAK (Outlier)

Height: 7,035 metres
Lat./Long.: 27°52'20" 88°05'37"

JONGSONG PEAK

Location: lies on the Tibetan frontier
Height: 7,483 metres
Lat./Long.: 27°52'52" 88°08'08"
First ascent: 1930 via North Ridge

In the course of his first major climbing expedition in 1909, Dr Kellas ascended to a col (6,550 metres) on the west ridge after crossing the Lhonak glacier. Next day he climbed the ridge to over 6,700 metres in dense mist and stormy weather. The next year he reconnoitred the summit of Jongsong Peak from a height of 6,860 metres on Langpo Peak to the southeast. The first ascent was made by two members of G. O. Dyrenfurth's international expedition in 1930.

1983. Ascent from East

An Indian Army expedition ascended the South Lhonak glacier and made a route up the east side. In the same year a Slovene-Nepalese party came up from the south, finding the Ginsang glacier 100 metres deeper than fifty years before and no longer an easy approach. They reconnoitred from the Jongsong La. The south face appeared to be safe, but the south-east ridge would require fixed ropes and camps.

Günter Oskar Dyrenfurth (1886–1975)

Dr Dyrenfurth was born in Germany and became Professor of Geology at Breslau. He spent a number of years working on a geological map of Switzerland. Shortly after Hitler's arrival in power he moved to Zurich and took Swiss nationality. In 1930 he led his first international expedition to the Himalaya, which attempted Kangchenjunga and other peaks. Dyrenfurth himself reached the summit of Jongsong Peak, at that time the highest climbed summit. His second expedition in 1934 was to the Karakoram where he and his party between them climbed Baltoro Kangri V and all the peaks of Sia Kangri. Although his climbing career ended when he suffered a severe accident on the Lauteraarhorn in 1946, his interest in the mountains did not diminish and in 1952 he published the original edition of his standard history of the 8,000-metre peaks, *To the Third Pole*. This was followed in 1960 by *Der Dritte Pol*, a major history of Himalayan exploration and climbs. He continued to contribute to Himalayan history through his annual 'Himalayan Chronicles'. Anders Bolinder, who worked closely with Dyrenfurth on these in the latter years, was impressed by his single-minded doggedness and incredible vitality, as well as his rare ability to work with younger men. He also wrote several other books in German about his Himalayan expeditions.

Members of the Dyrenfurth 1930 International Expedition: their main objective was Kangchenjunga. From left to right–standing: Hermann Hoerlin, Erwin Schneider, Uli Wieland, Günther Dyrenfurth, Marcel Kurz, G. W. Wood Johnson; sitting: Dr Richter, Heddy Dyrenfurth, C. Duvanel, Frank Smythe (Alpine Club Collection)

P.7044

Lat./Long.: 27°52'19" 88°05'30"

P.7451

Lat./Long.: 27°52'45" 88°08'17"

Dongkya Range

Pauhunri

Location: lies on the Tibetan frontier
Height: 7,128 metres

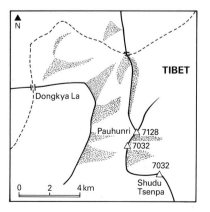

Lat./Long.: 27°57'13" 88°50'53"
First ascent: 1910 via Northeast Face

Dr Kellas wrote very little about his climbs. The following is taken from his laconic notes sent to Captain Farrar, editor of the *Alpine Journal*, ten years afterwards, about his 1909 expedition to Sikkim:

>   *19th August.* Cross Donkia La (18,131 ft).
>   *20th August.* Move up to high camp on Pawhunri (19,000 ft).
>   *21st August.* Mr Righi [his companion] being indisposed, make attempt on Pawhunri with 2 coolies. Reach 21,700 ft., but driven back by snowstorm. Snow very deep and powdery.

And again later:

>   *8th October.* Camp on Pawhunri (19,300 ft).
>   *9th October.* Ascend Pawhunri to 23,000 ft. Forced to retreat after sunset by deep snow and high wind. Reach camp after dark.

>   *10th October.* Recross Donkia La. . .

Although he does not say so, all his attempts were made from the Tibetan side. He was more forthcoming about his 1910 expedition, contributing a lengthy article to the *Alpine Journal* on climbing in Sikkim and Garhwal. After exploring in the Kangchenjunga region he set out for Pauhunri on 11 June accompanied by four porters and two days later was encamped on the snowline at 5,500 metres. The following day they climbed to 6,300 metres but were driven back by a high wind which whirled the fine snow into dense clouds. Camp was next moved up to 6,100 metres and on 16 June three of them reached the summit. Kellas says they took nearly six hours to ascend, but did not hurry, keeping close to the edge of the western cliffs until about 300 metres from the top, when they

▼

Peaks of the Pauhunri group (7,128m) as seen from the southwest from the hills above Samdong (Fosco Maraini)

made a bee-line for the summit through snow nearly a foot deep. The summit, which was corniced to the east, was some distance from, and much higher than, the top of the western face. He noted that, had they brought a spade, they might have dug a big hole on the top and brought up a tent to carry out experiments and take photographs.

1983. Northwest Face
Members of an Indian Army expedition made the first ascent from inside Sikkim.

P.7032 ('Pauhunri South')
Height: 7,032 metres
Lat./Long.: 27°56'38" 88°50'28"

P.7032 (Shudu Tsenpa)
Height: 7,032 metres
Lat./Long.: 27°55'42" 88°51'41"

Bibliography

Cooke, C. (1936), 'The ascent of Kabru', *HJ*, 8, pp. 107–17.

Dyrenfurth, G. (1931), 'The International Himalayan Expedition, 1930', *HJ*, 3, pp. 77–91, [Dome Kang].

Hechtel, R. (1965), 'Talung Peak', *AAJ*, 14, pp. 280–8.

Hunt, J. and Cooke, C. (1938), 'A winter visit to the Zemu glacier', *HJ*, 10, pp. 49–70.

Kefford, M. (1987), 'Kirat Chuli 1985', *HJ*, 43, pp. 112–14.

Kellas, A. (1912), 'The mountains of Northern Sikkim and Garhwal', *AJ*, 26, pp. 113–42.

Lindner, F. (1964–5), 'Talung Peak', *MW*, pp. 67–74.

Raeburn, H. (1921–22), 'Southerly walls of Kangchenjunga and the Rathong Pass', *AJ*, 34, pp. 33–50).

Rubenson, C. (1908–9) 'Kabru in 1907', *AJ*, 24, pp. 63–7; 310–21.

Eastern Nepal Himalaya

The modern frontiers of Nepal were drawn at the conclusion of the Nepalese War of 1814–16 which was brought about by the frequent Gurkha raids on territories controlled by the East India Company. (British direct rule of India only began in 1858 as a result of the Indian Mutiny.) Prior to the war, the first rough map of the country was made by Charles Crawford during the period 1801–03. In 1804 he surveyed a small part of eastern Nepal in the region of the Kosi and noted the great height of the snow peaks. In 1809–10 W. S. Webb observed the position and height of Dhaulagiri from survey stations in the plains and calculated its height quite close to today's official figure. During the campaign of 1814–16 some other great peaks were noted and then the frontiers were closed.

The Survey of India, led by Sir George Everest, were able to calculate accurately the positions and heights of peaks observed from the Indian plains but over a century passed before the King of Nepal gave permission for the government of India to send a party to survey his country. Even then, no British officer was allowed to accompany them. One notable journey previously was that made in 1873 by the pundit Hari Ram who crossed the western border at Bargaon and traversed northern Nepal as far as the Kali Gandaki between the Dhaula and Annapurna Himal. After Hari Ram, Captain Henry Wood was allowed into Nepal in 1903 to observe the principal peaks and to check their names. One lone surveyor, Natha Singh, made a hurried visit to the upper Dudh Kosi in 1907 and sketched the southern slopes of Everest, including the end of the Khumbu glacier. About this time the Nepalese government was actually prepared to allow a mountaineering expedition to visit Mount Everest but at the last moment the British government deemed it inadvisable. Otherwise, apart from one or two unauthorized incursions across the border by travellers and mountaineers (particularly from Sikkim), Nepal remained unknown to outsiders until 1949.

Kangchenjunga Himal (northern section)

KANGBACHEN
Height: 7,903 metres
Lat./Long.: 27°43'00" 88°06'48"
First ascent: 1974 via West Ridge

The 1949 Swiss Himalayan expedition reconnoitred the Ramtang glacier approach on the western side of the peak. Quite apart from a very dangerous ice-fall the upper part of the route looked extremely problematical. In 1965 a party of Yugoslavian climbers reached the western summit ridge but had to turn back still nearly two kilometres away. A further camp was made at the top of a traverse of the north face. The summit ridge was gained at 7,550 metres where the Sherpas turned back and the two Yugoslavs bivouaced, only to suffer serious frostbite.

A post-monsoon assault on the northwest face in 1973 by Japanese climbers reached 6,550 metres, but all four summit bids were repulsed by heavy snowfalls. The summit was eventually reached by Polish climbers on 26 May 1974. After gaining the ridge west of P.7532 (Kangbachen Southwest) they traversed across to the west ridge and made an alpine-style push to the top involving three bivouacs. The worst obstacle on the route was a 150 metres high system of sérac barriers and pinnacles between Camps III and IV, on which it took six days to place 200 metres of fixed rope. More ascents, by much the same route, were made by members of a Yugoslavian expedition a few months later.

P.7532 (Kangbachen Southwest, Yalung Peak)
Lat./Long.: 27°42' 88°05'

P.7385
Location: between P.7532 and P.7468 (Jannu East Peak)
Lat./Long.: 27°42'27" 88°05'17"

Kangchenjunga Himal (Kumbhakarna section)

JANNU (Kumbhakarna)
Height: 7,710 metres
Lat./Long.: 27°40'58" 88°02'45"
First ascent: 1962 via South Ridge

Jannu is an impressive massif; seen from the south the summit, supported by its southwest and southeast ridges, resembles the back of a huge chair. Thus the upper snow plateau embraced by the these ridges was christened 'Throne' by French climbers. The first reconnaissance of the mountain was made in autumn 1957 by Guido Magnone and two companions. They went up towards the head of the Yalung glacier and inspected the eastern side, finding ridges plastered with ice, hanging glaciers, and séracs discharging thousands of tons of ice at an alarming rate. They next tackled the southwestern approach up the Yamatari glacier, only to be further demoralized. Between two vertical rock walls a terrifying icefall, broken into two sections, cascaded down to the glacier from an upper plateau over 1,250 metres above. Nevertheless they prospected a possible route up the lefthand rock ridge (southwest spur). Their last disappointment was their view of the northern face. They could not discern a single weak point along this great mountain wall – a continuous succession of steep hanging glaciers and vertical walls overhung by snow cornices, and falling for over 2,500 metres.

Two years later a French team, led by Jean Franco, arrived to attempt Magnone's route from the Yamatari glacier. After the whole route had been swept by a huge avalanche just after their arrival in mid–April, they opted for the much longer southeast ridge route. An easy glacier led eastwards towards a point on the ridge at 6,500 metres, which they named 'Tête du Butoir'. Above 5,800 metres the climbing became extremely difficult with ice couloirs of more than 60°, and over 1,500 metres of rope were fixed. Camp IV lay below the Tête du Butoir, beyond which was the 'Arête de la Dentelle', an extraordinarily difficult,

Jannu–on the Tête de la Dentelle (Brian Hall)
▼

lacy ice ridge. Camp V was placed on the Throne plateau and the whole of the next day was occupied with a 300-metre ice slope and nearly vertical rocks leading to the crest of the ridge. Franco, Magnone and Robert Paragot then established Camp VI on the ridge at 7,350 metres. With Franco becoming snowblind only the other two were able to continue, which they did all day but made only another seventy-five metres.

In 1962 the French, this time led by Lionel Terray, placed Camp VI slightly lower down the south ridge, on a broad and comfortable site much easier to reach. This was made possible by an alteration in the ridge itself. Beyond this point it consisted of a series of steps, steep on one side and overhanging on the other. Rope fixing on the horizontal sections was extremely difficult. Eventually the climbers reached the base of the great black gendarme which bars the way. As before, this took several hours to turn on the western side, by a delicate traverse across rock and ice, a chimney and a very steep spine of snow which ran up to rejoin the ridge. Ahead stood four snow towers and a final long and narrow couloir. Next day the route was prepared as far as the rocks at the bottom of the couloir. The four climbers then descended, leaving Terray, Jean Ravier and Sherpa Wangdi at Camp VI.

Terray's assault team reached the farthest point in a couple of hours and succeeded in climbing two-thirds of the remaining route, but with only Terray using oxygen and in heavy snow this was as much as could be done safely. The third team consisting of Robert Paragot and Paul Keller, René Desmaison and Sherpa Gyalzen Mitchu covered in less than two hours what had taken two-and-a-half days to prepare, but they were still separated from the terminal arête by a snow spur. Progress was frustatingly slow, fixing rope on the steep slope. Emerging on a subsidiary top they saw the true summit, still some fifteen metres higher, at the far end of a 100-metre long ridge, marvellously narrow and with a little cornice running along its crest. After a few metres they were forced to continue sitting astride the ridge itself. Their arrival on top was greeted with applause from Camp VI, to which they returned in darkness after sixteen hours' climbing. The following day the rest of the team reached the top, making it one of the most successful Himalayan expeditions up to that time.

1976. North Face

A very strong New Zealand party experienced bad weather in 1975, during their autumn attempt which reached a height of 7,300 metres on this cold and difficult

One hundred metres below the summit ridge of Jannu (Brian Hall)

▶

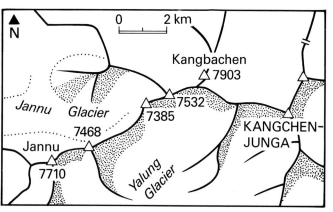

3,200-metre high face. First the route had to be forced up a 900-metre rock buttress beside an ice-fall to the snowfield above. A 200-metre high, nearly vertical, gully led to a system of ice gullies and an ice spur at 6,100 metres. Then vertical rock rose to steep ice and snow before the jagged summit ridge could be gained. Two members launched an alpine-style assault, with Geoff Wayatt reaching a col (7,170 metres) just below the summit ridge after two bivouacs. Both men suffered serious frostbite. Meanwhile the rest of the team attempted a safer route to the left. A gale cut short a summit bid by Brian Pooley and Lynn Crawford after they had reached the ridge.

The following March to May a sixteen–man expedition from Japan succeeded in getting four teams of thirteen Japanese and three Sherpas to the summit. The route taken followed closely that of the New Zealanders. The four teams rotated the tasks of route-finding, preparation and load carrying, and made continuous progress. Camp V was established on 24 April at the foot of the red tower on the shoulder of the east ridge at 7,150 metres. The last obstacle was a vertical chimney. During the period 11–14 May the top was reached four times, a change in the weather curtailing the chances of the remaining three members. The route was repeated by a Dutch team in 1987 but this success was marred by the loss of two members while descending only a few metres above Camp I. Frenchmen Pierre Beghin and Erik Decamp made an alpine-style ascent of the New Zealand-Japanese route, reaching the summit on 25 October.

1983. Southwest Spur

In 1979 and 1981, Czechoslovakian climbers were the first to attack this route, which runs up a 2,000-metre high buttress to the final summit tower. On the second occasion the party split at the top of the buttress, one traversing the Throne glacier to the French south ridge route, while the rest just failed to make a route up the difficult summit face. A French team completed the route, finding snow slopes and a chimney above the Czech high point.

1984–5. Winter Ascent and Route Variation

South Korean Kim Ki-Heyg and two Sherpas reached the summit via a spur on the south face, leading to the south ridge.

P.7468 (Jannu East Peak)

Location: 1½ km from Jannu on East Ridge
Lat./Long.: 27°41'18" 88°03'40"

Mahalangur Himal (Barun section)

BARUNTSE

Height: 7,129 metres
Subsidiary peaks: Central, 7,066 metres; North, 7,059 metres
Lat./Long.: 27°52'19" 86°58'55"
First ascent: 1954 via South Ridge from the East

Sir Edmund Hillary led a New Zealand expedition to the Barun glacier in 1954. Apart from survey work, twenty-three peaks were climbed, including Baruntse. This was a very severe ice climb and was made by Colin Todd and Geoff Harrow on 30 May. While crossing a level corniced stretch just below a great step in the ridge a section about sixty metres long broke away at the touch of an ice-axe. Progress now became very slow, cutting steps across an exceedingly steep face of snow. As the day was well advanced George

Lowe and Bill Beaven decided to return to the last camp, but Todd and Harrow carried on. The route grew more difficult; snow fell during the afternoon and a wind got up. Just as their companions were becoming seriously concerned the pair were found not far above camp, lost and exhausted. They had not reached the top until 4.30 p.m. and during their descent had found the many hundreds of steps cut along the steep corniced ridge filled with snow. Lowe and Beaven repeated the climb two days later.

1964. North Face Attempts

There were four Japanese attempts, and one French, on the north face in 1964. The Japanese were defeated by a huge cornice only fifty metres below the summit.

1980. East Ridge

Three Spanish climbers and an American made a new route and the second ascent of the peak. The principal difficulties were above 6,050 metres, with a 50°–65° ice slope to reach the east ridge. They continued over mixed ground, then ice, then ice and snow. The climb ended on the north ridge. At the same time, two Frenchmen disappeared high on the north ridge.

Doug Scott tackling the steep ice cliff on Baruntse (Terry Mooney)

1980. Winter Ascent

Four members of a Hokkaido expedition and two Sherpas reached the summit two weeks after setting up base camp.

1983. North Ridge

This was first attempted, via the west face, in 1980 by American climbers who were turned back by severe winds and incipient cold injuries only 100 metres below the north summit. The Dutch climbers Ubbink and Edwin van Nieuwkerk completed the climb in an alpine-style ascent.

CHAMLANG

*Height: 7,319 metres (The 8 km long
exposed ridge between P.7319
(highest point) and P.7235 (east
peak) does not drop below 7,000
metres. Apart from the main
summits there are several minor
points on the ridge)*
Lat./Long.: 27°46'30" 86°58'57"
First ascent: 1962 via South Ridge.

The New Zealand Alpine Club
expedition to the Barun valley in
1954 had permision to climb
Chamlang and Baruntse. The
expedition approached from the
south and split into three groups
for exploration and topographical
surveys, going up the Choyang,
Iswa and Barun valleys. George
Lowe and three others inspected
the southeastern flanks of the
mountain and were impressed by
its seemingly impregnable faces.
Two near-fatal accidents involving
Edmund Hillary and Jim McFarlane
left the expedition short of time
and climbers, and all their remaining resources were devoted to an
ascent of Baruntse. The following
year, the New Zealander Norman
Hardie surveyed the western approaches and thought that a small
party would be able to climb the
peak from the Hongu Khola.

In 1962 the Hokkaido University expedition went up the Hongu
Khola and made a route to the top
of a glacier flowing west from the
southern ridge. Camp III (6,250
metres) was pitched on the hard ice
of the knife-edge ridge. The summit assault was made from a snow
cave at 6,525 metres by Soh Anma
and Sherpa Pasang Phutar III over
hard ice.

1981. North Face and P.7010

Reinhold Messner and Doug Scott
made the first approach from the
north, up the Chamlang glacier, to
camp under the north face. They
climbed the face below the lowest

point and waded through snow to one of the minor summits.

1986. West Ridge

A Japanese group climbed this knife-edged ridge which was particularly difficult above 6,100 metres because of unconsolidated granular snow. Osamu Kushimi and Wangar Sherpa climbed the final 800 metres in seven hours.

CHAMLANG CENTRAL

Height: 7,180 metres
First ascent: 1984 by Traverse from
*   East Peak*

Climbed by Doug Scott and party.

Chamlang East

Height: 7,235 metres
Lat./Long.: 27°47′12″ 87°00′58″
First ascent: 1984 via North
*   Face/Northeast Ridge*

An international party, led by Doug Scott, started from the Lower Barun glacier and climbed steep ice leading to P.6705, followed by difficult ice left of the rocks on the steep northeast ridge which was gained after two

bivouacs. An hour's traverse took them to the central peak. The second rope had to make a difficult retreat after snowblindness and injury struck the party.

P.7316 ('Chamlang South')

Lat./Long.: 27°46′20″ 86°58′57″

P.7290

Location: east of Chamlang East

Mahalangur Himal (Makalu section)

KANGCHUNGTSE (Makalu II)

Height: 7,678 metres
Lat./Long.: 27°54′57″ 87°04′44″
First ascent: 1954 via South Ridge

At the end of the ill-fated 1954 New Zealand expedition to explore Chamlang and Baruntse, Edmund Hillary's party decided to reconnoitre the northern approaches Makalu. Three camps were established on the Chogo glacier. From there, Hardie, Todd and Lowe reached a saddle due north of

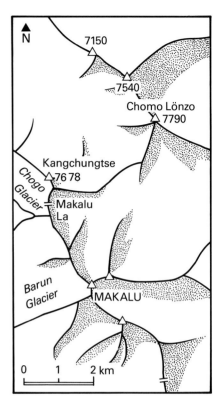

Kangchungtse, while Harrow and Evans reached a height of about 7,000 metres on the glacier terraces leading to the Makalu La at the foot of the south ridge. Later that year Jean Franco's French Makalu reconnaissance expedition set up a

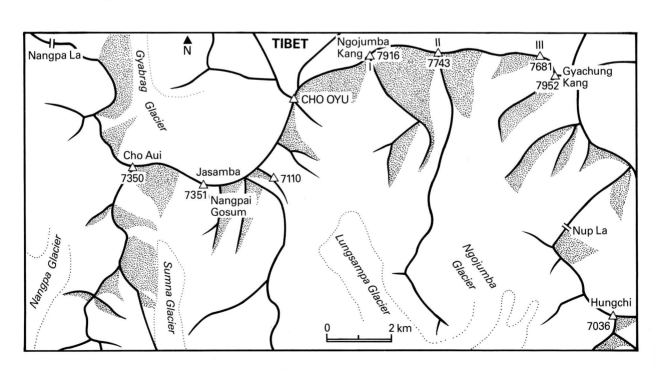

similar chain of camps. Their highest was on the Makalu La, which was reached on 15 October. Repeated attempts were made between 18 and 26 October to establish a higher camp on Makalu itself in cold and stormy weather. One day, however, was fine so Franco, Lionel Terray, Gyaltsen Norbu and Pa Norbu climbed Kangchungtse via the Makalu La. Starting from camp at 7,000 metres they reached the col in three hours where they rested for an hour. The distance to the summit was not far, but the ridge was fairly broken. They therefore ascended the vast but easier snow slopes on the Tibetan side of the ridge. In two hours they arrived at a secondary ridge leading to a forepeak and an hour later, at the end of a delicate and airy snow scallop, the summit.

1976. Northwest Ridge

This route was climbed by an expedition of the Seppyo Alpine Club of Japan. Satoshi Nara and Sherpa Lakpu Norbu reached the summit. It had been attempted by a Japanese group in 1972.

1979. East Ridge

All eight members of an international expedition, led by German Gerhard Lenser plus eight Sherpas, climbed this route between 9–17 October from the north col.

CHOMOLÖNZO

Location: in Tibet
Height: 7,790 metres
Subsidary peaks: Northwest, 7,540
*   metres; Northwest II, 7,150 metres*
Lat./Long.: 27°55'47" 87°06'44"
First ascent: 1954 via West Ridge

Jean Couzy persuaded Lionel Terray to make an attempt on this peak on 30 October at the end of the French reconnaissance of Makalu. The leader, Jean Franco, had ordered the mountain to be cleared because of the incessant gales and had asked Couzy and Terray to recover the tent and equipment from Camp V (7,510 metres) on the Makalu La. At dawn on the col the wind had abated to half strength. They left the Sherpas to wait there for them and set off on a long descent eastwards down gentle slopes to a col at about 7,200 metres on Chomolönzo's southerly ridge. Using oxygen they started up the

The peaks of Chomolönzo seen from the west during the ascent of Shartse (Kurt Diemberger)

technically easy ridge. The wind had now got up again and they could hardly stand. Terray wrote later, 'As soon as a gust died down a little we ran uphill as hard as we could go until the roar of the next gust could be heard coming, whereupon we huddled down with our backs to the storm, forcing our ice axes into the snow for purchase.' Near the summit they had to shelter behind a cornice to unfreeze the valves on their oxygen sets. The top was reached about noon and they were able to study the whole of the route on the north face of Makalu. After returning to the Makalu La they packed up and arrived in Camp III soon after nightfall. Terray considered it was one of the toughest and most memorable days he had ever experienced.

Mahalangur Himal (Khumbu section)

SHERATSE CHULI (Shartse, Peak 38)
Height: 7,591 metres
Lat./Long.: 27°57'21" 86°57'56"

SHARTSE (Shartse II Junction Peak)
Height: 7,459 metres
Lat./Long.: 27°57'56" 86°59'00"
First ascent: 1974 via South Ridge

A German expedition with the Austrian Kurt Diemberger ascended the Barun glacier to investigate the Shartse approach to Lhotse. They found the east ridge to be far too steep, with wild looking towers, but similar problems on the south ridge appeared to ease above 6,700 metres. After reaching the Barun La, four more camps were placed on the south ridge over a period of three weeks; storms then buried most of them. Later, Hermann Warth and Diem-

▲
The northern cliffs of Chomolönzo from the 1921 Everest expedition's camp at Pethang Ringmo

berger, supported by Sherpa Nawang Tenzing, re-climbed the ridge between 19–22 May, a bivouac tent serving as Camp VI at 7,100 metres, before going on to the top. In 1984 a Korean party made a variation by climbing to the south ridge via the southwest face.

P.7199
Location: Shartse area
Lat./Long.: 27°57'12" 86°59'30"

NUPTSE
Height: 7,855 metres
Lat./Long.: 27°58'02" 86°53'14"
First ascent: 1961 via South Ridge

The first attempt on this peak was made by a British party from the south. The first choice of route was the south [southeastern] ridge but from Tyangboche the climbers had observed a ridge directly below the summit which would cut out the need for a long high-level traverse. Upon reconnoitring the southeastern ridge from the Lhotse and Lhotse-Nup glaciers it was found to be very formidable in its upper reaches. Moving around to the Nuptse glacier the 'Central' [south] ridge showed great promise; the only apparent difficulty lay above the ridge, a rock band above which was an overhanging snow-field. Accordingly, base was set up on the tangled Nuptse glacier from which a series of easy snow slopes mounted to the ridge. Progress along the ridge was easy enough, apart from a stiff chimney at about 5,800 metres. Above Camp III the route became more difficult as the ridge steepened and the climbers were forced first on the eastern, then the western side. A temporary camp was eventually sited in a notch on the ridge after some more difficult climbing. Farther on, the best route offered was a traverse well below the crest and the permanent Camp IV was soon in place at the end of the ridge where it joined into the face.

The next camp was on a platform cut out at the top of a steep ice slope, followed by one at the bottom of the first snow-field. From there the rock band took several days to force, but Camp VII was eventually pitched on a very restricted spot just below the

upper snow-field. Above this, a couloir led to a saddle just left of the summit. This part of the route was hard work but after three days Dennis Davis and Sherpa Tashi found themselves sitting in sunshine on the saddle with the summit only 200 metres above them. They decided to grab the opportunity, instead of waiting for the others, and by four o'clock were on the top, looking down on the fantastic southeastern ridge twisting and turning towards Lhotse. Other members of the group made the ascent the next day. In 1975 a British-Nepalese attempt on the 1961 route ended in disaster with the deaths of three members and a Sherpa.

1979. North Face

Climbed by Alan Rouse, Brian Hall, Georges Bettembourg and Doug Scott alpine-style. Doug Scott and two companions had attempted it the year before but abandoned the climb in waist-deep

snow on top of steep rock. After an initial ice-fall they bivouaced at the foot of the prominent snow and ice spur. Next day they climbed up 300 metres and dumped their gear. On 18 October they set out with three days' food, reached the top of the spur and a further 300 metres on found a snow terrace suitable for a second snow cave. The top was reached next day in the afternoon after climbing steep snow arêtes. Violent winds and fresh snow gave cause for concern during the descent, but this was accomplished safely.

1981 South Face Attempt

A Canadian attempt in 1981 on a south face–west ridge route ended after a massive rock-fall wiped out their advanced base camp. They had climbed a 900-metre high buttress on the western section of the south face, which gave difficult mixed climbing over steep rock steps and unstable ice and snow mushrooms.

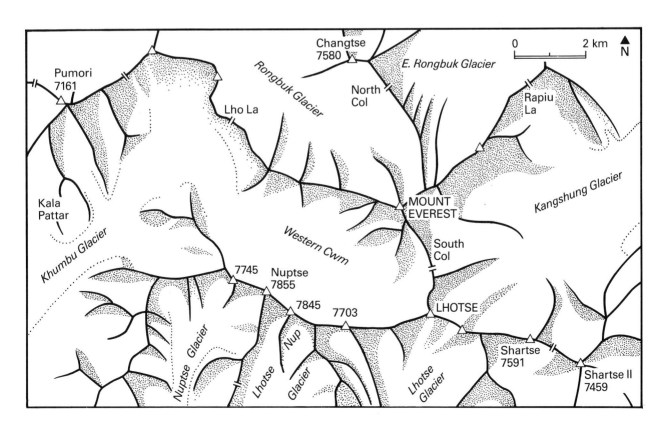

1987 South Spur Attempt

The Italians Enrico Rosso and Manoni Fabrizio reached 6,700 metres in bad weather on a line which was technically difficult and exposed. This new route had been attempted twice previously by the American Jeff Lowe.

NUPTSE WEST

Location: between the northwest and main summits
Height: 7,784 metres
First ascent: 1988

Climbed by a South Korean party on 22 December 1988. This was the first time the first ascent of a major summit had been made in winter.

NUPTSE NORTHWEST

Height: 7,745 metres
First ascent: 1977 via Northwest Ridge.

A party of Japanese climbed the long northwest ridge which overlooks the lower part of Everest's Western Cwm. Their route started up a spur on the right side of the main ridge. After camping close to the crest of the ridge, just below a snow dome, the sharp corniced ridge was followed to the top.

NUPTSE CENTRAL

Height: 7,845 metres

No attempts have been made east of Nuptse main summit.

NUPTSE EAST

Height: 7,703 metres

PUMORI

Height: 7,161 metres
Lat./Long.: 28°00' 53" 86°49' 41"
First ascent: 1962 via Northeast Ridge.

In Sherpa dialect, 'pumori' means an unmarried daughter; the mountain was named by George Mallory to remind him of his own daughter. The first attempt was made in 1953 by Hamish MacInnes and John Cunningham just after the first ascent of Everest. They established a base near the Khumbu glacier and although visibility was very poor they decided the best route was up a small ridge facing the Khumbu icefall. This led to a col with an east slope to the summit; a camp was placed on the ridge below the col. However, as the snow was not consolidated and the avalanche danger was increasing they decided that an alpine-style attempt would have to be made. Next morning the weather was fair and they climbed steadily until 3 p.m. in difficult snow conditions. Finally, deteriorating weather and the constant avalanches forced retreat. Their high point was about 6,700 metres. In the autumn a much larger Indian party commenced their ascent from the Khumbu base camp without any acclimatization and probably followed the Mac-Innes route, reaching much the same height. They noted a possible route from the col on the northeast ridge.

In December 1961, a three-man German-Swiss party, led by Gert Mehl, went to Nepal to make a film on the theme: 'The Sherpa as porter and climber'. Without permission they made an attempt on Pumori, climbing the east face directly under the summit to join the northeast ridge at about 6,500

▲

The magnificent North Face of Nuptse (Ed Webster/Mountain Imagery)

metres. The highest point reached was perhaps fifty metres below the summit. Shortly after beginning the descent Werner Stäuble and Sherpa Phurba Lobsang fell to the glacier at the foot of the east face. Some doubt was cast by the leader of the successful 1962 expedition, Gerhard Lenser, on the height reached, but later it was reported that this had been confirmed by another of the Sherpas, Anullah, in conversation with Charles Wylie at the British Embassy in Kathmandu.

The successful German-Swiss expedition of 1962 arrived at base camp on the north side of the Khumbu glacier on 4 April and spent ten days settling in. By 21 April they had established Camp I (5,500 metres) at the foot of a fierce 700-metre high rock wall and a week later placed a second camp on a strip of ice on this wall. Another week of difficult climbing brought them to the col above the wall, at the foot of the northeast ridge (6,220 metres). Bad weather and need for rest sent them down to base for ten days but they were back and ready to start by 15 May. By noon they had covered half the distance up the ridge. On 16 May they climbed an ice wall (about 45 metres high) and the rest of the ridge, to the foot of the final 500-metre ice slope and their second bivouac. The final slopes took five hours to the summit.

1972. South Face
In 1971 an expedition from Fujiomiya attempted the very steep rock and ice south face, but did not get far on account of bad weather and avalanche danger. The following year a Groupe de Haute Montagne party placed their first camp on the moraine which descends from Kala Pattar, choosing to ascend the spur which comes lowest. It has four rocky steps separated by ice or snow, and very steep corniced ridges; a final

rock wall of fifty metres leads to the summit slope. The first step was turned on the right. The harder, second step started with seventy-five metres of very difficult mixed climbing, followed by a 150-metre high overhanging amphitheatre, then up ice and rock. The third step was Grade IV+ rock, leading back to the corniced, broken ridge with vertical walls of rotten snow. This section took three days and brought them to the fourth step which for some time seemed unscalable, with extremely difficult and partly artificial climbing. At the top of the ridge, four days of storm and new snow buried their 3,000 metres of fixed ropes. After a few days the last part of the face was ascended easily enough. French climbers made an alpine-style ascent of the face in 1982.

1973. South [Southwest] Ridge
A Japanese expedition climbed this route during April from Kala Pattar. After fixing 350 metres of rope on the ice wall they reached the col on the ridge. More rope was fixed on the difficult rock ridge leading to Camp III (6,530 metres). The summit was reached after a bivouac only eighty metres below the top. In October 1978 Swiss climbers made a variation up part of the buttress. Two American climbers made a winter ascent of the route in 1984, but disappeared during the descent.

1974. West Face
Another Japanese group climbed this difficult and previously untried face. Two camps were set up on the face, the higher at 6,650 metres. The climb to the top from here, and return to camp, took over thirteen hours.

1981–82. East Face in Winter
Four Americans chose a new route several hundred metres to the right

of the major ice-fall on the east face. One camp was on the face and another where they joined the northeast ridge at 6,650 metres. The route was of moderate but sustained difficulty and required seven days on the final push which was completed by Ned Gillette, James Bridwell and Jan Reynolds.

1983. East Face (2)
Craig Linford and Donald McIntyre put up a route to the right of that done the year before. Most of the climbing was on 40°–55° water ice, and was done alpine-style. They finished the route at 6,435 metres.

1983. South Face Solo Winter Ascent
American Jeff Lowe climbed the face between 16–18 December.

1984 and 1986. East Face (3) and (4)
In 1984 an international group made a route to the left of the 1981–82 American ascent. Two years later the Japanese H. Aota and Y. Sasahara made an alpine-style ascent by a new route.

1986. South Face Scottish Route
Sandy Allan and Rick Allen made a route up the spur left of centre of the face. After climbing a steep ice couloir for some 300 metres (Grade IV–V), where they lost their bivouac tent, the pair gained an ice arête, which was ascended for two days (III–IV). Descent was made via the west face.

P.7290
Location: cast of Chamalang East

CHO AUI (Nangpai Gosum II)
Height: 7,350 metres
Lat./Long.: 28°04' 14" 86°38' 10"
First ascent: 1986 via Northwest Ridge

The Himalayan Association of

Japan expedition approached the mountain, which lies on the Tibet-Nepal border west of Cho Oyu, through Shikar [Xigar] and up the Gyabrag glacier. From a glacier camp (6,100 metres) they reconnoitred and prepared the route. Beyond the ice-fall there was a difficult ice face which took them to the northwest ridge, where they fixed rope and placed a camp. After a rest four of them set off for the summit but had to bivouac at 7,200 metres, completing the ascent the next day. Six others repeated the ascent two days later.

P.7186

Location: east of Cho Aui
Height: 7,186 metres
Lat./Long.: 28° 04' 26" 86° 38' 29"

JASAMBA (Nangpai Gosum I)

Height: 7,351 metres
Lat./Long.: 28° 04' 53" 86° 36' 23"

NANGPAI GOSUM III

Height: 7,110 metres

GYACHUNG KANG

Height: 7,952 metres
Subsidiary peak: Southeast, 7,850 metres
Lat./Long.: 28° 05' 53" 86° 44' 32"
First ascent: 1964 via West Flank/Northwest Ridge

The 1964 Japanese expedition approached via the Ngojumba glacier. Their route lay up an ice couloir on the west flank of the south face to the frontier summit ridge, where Akio Otaki fell to his death on the Gyachung Kang glacier on the Tibetan side. From the top camp two Japanese and Pasang Phutar III experienced great difficulties, especially a very steep and sharp rock ridge, before they were able to stand on the top.

1986. South Face/Southwest Ridge

Members of a Franco-Nepalese expedition made the second ascent of the peak via the buttress and ridge which form the western edge of the south face.. After an awkward glacier approach, the face began with a 800 metre high ice slope and a narrow snow ridge. Next the rock barrier was climbed by a series of chimneys.

The second assault pair succeeded in climbing an overhanging dihedral, just below the easier summit slopes; two other pairs completed the climb. In the autumn a Spanish group attempted a route farther left, but were defeated by the weather conditions at about 7,100 metres.

HUNGCHI

Height: 7,036 metres
Lat./Long.: 28° 02' 05" 86° 45' 31"

▼

South Face of Gyachung Kang from summit of Gokyo Peak (A. R. Allan)

NGOJUMBA KANG I
Height: 7,916 metres
Lat./Long.: 28°06'21" 86°41'05"
First ascent: 1982 via South Face

The south face was first attempted in October 1982 by a mixed party led by Guy Cousteix. After establishing three camps they abandoned the climb at about 7,000 metres because of deep snow. Three weeks later a South Korean-Nepalese party climbed the face direct with four high camps.

1988. Winter Ascent
South Koreans Yu Wang-Yul and Choi Mi-Ho made the first winter ascent on 11 February (third ascent of the peak).

NGOJUMBA KANG II
Height: 7,743 metres
Lat./Long.: 28°06'22" 86°42'22"
First ascent: 1965 from the South

A Japanese party from Meiji University ascended the Ngojumba glacier south of this difficult minor summit on the ridge between Gyachung Kang and Cho Oyu. Naomi Uemura and Pemba Tenzing climbed to the summit in twelve hours from camp at 6,800 metres. Several expeditions have climbed this peak in recent years in an effort to traverse the nearly five-kilometre long east ridge of Cho Oyu.

1987. South Face, South Ridge
From the Lungsampa glacier, the Yugoslavians Boris Kovačevič and Branko Puzak climbed the face in deep snow and on hard ice (50°–65°). On 11 November they reached the summit from their fourth camp at 7,200 metres. Two other climbers also succeeded two days later.

1988. Winter Ascent
On 11 February by South Koreans Yu Wang-Yul and Choi Mi-Ho.

NGOJUMBA KANG III
Height: 7,681 metres
Lat./Long.: 28 06'22" 86°42'45"

CHANGTSE (Zhangzi, Everest North Peak)
Location: in Tibet
Height: 7,580 metres
Lat./Long.: 28°01'31" 86°54'51"
First ascent: 1982 via Northeast Ridge

In mid-August, at the end of the 1935 Everest reconnaissance expedition, Eric Shipton and his companions tried an ascent, but the snow was so bad that the attempt was abandoned at just over 7,000 metres.

A German expedition approached the long northeast ridge via the East Rongbuk glacier, using yaks but no porters. From Camp II (6,100 metres) they climbed 600 metres up a snow and ice slope, placing Camp IV at 6,900 metres. From there the summit was reached on 14 October by Udo Zehetleitner; other members made another ascent two day later.

1983. Alpine-style Ascent
Chilean climber Gino Casassa, member of an Everest expedition, made an unauthorized ascent of the German route solo on 14 May, in a 19-hour round trip from camp at 6,100 metres.

1986. East Ridge
This was climbed by members of a large Sino-Japanese expedition.

KHARTA CHANGRI
Location: in Tibet northeast of Mount Everest
Height: 7,056 metres
Lat./Long.: 28°06'49" 86°59'58"
First ascent: 1935 from Northwest

This climb was made by Edwin Kempson and Charles Warren, members of Eric Shipton's Everest reconnaissance expedition, from the Kharta Changri glacier.

KHARTAPHU
Location: in Tibet northeast of Mount Everest
Height: 7,227 metres
Lat./Long.: 28°03'48" 86°58'45"
First ascent: 1935 from the West

Climbed by Shipton, Kempson and Warren from a side glacier leading off the East Rongbuk glacier.

Khartaphu from East Rongbuk Glacier (Nikola Kekus)

P.7011
Location: in Tibet 1 km southeast of the Lhakpa La
Lat./Long.: 28°02'02" 86°58'19"
First ascent: 1935

This peak was shown on the Jacot-Guillamod map of the 1921/24 Everest survey (see H. Ruttledge, *Everest 1933*, Hodder & Stoughton, 1934) as an unnamed peak of 6,965 metres. It was climbed by Bill Tilman and Edmund Wigram from the Lhakpa La during the 1935 Everest reconnaissance expedition.

P.7013

Location: in Tibet 1½ km west of
  Khartaphu
Lat./Long.: 28°04′01″ 86°57′42″

This location does not seem to correspond with any high peak on the Jacot-Guillamod map.

P.7018

Location: in Tibet 7½ km west of
  Khartaphu
Lat./Long.: 28°04′03″ 86°57′12″
First ascent: 1935

This point corresponds with the unnamed 22,580 ft (6,882 metres) peak on the Jacot-Guillamod map above Camp II on the East Rongbuk glacier. It was climbed by Eric Shipton and two companions.

P.7071 ('Kellas Rock Peak', Lixin Peak)

Location: in Tibet 8 km west of
  Kharta Changri
Lat./Long.: 28°06′45″ 86°55′02″
First ascent: 1935

This peak corresponds with the unnamed peak 23,180 ft (7,065 metres) on the Jacot-Guillamod map. It was climbed by Eric Shipton and his companions.

P.7023

Location: in Tibet 7 km north of Cho
  Oyu
Lat./Long.: 28°08′59″ 86°40′32″

P.7308

Location: In Tibet 5½ km north of
  Cho Oyu
Lat./Long.: 28°08′21″ 86°40′34″

PALUNG RI

Location: in Tibet c.8 km northwest of
  Cho Oyu
Height: 7,013 metres
Lat./Long.: 28°07′45″ 86°38′31″

▼

Kellas Rock Peak (Lixin Peak) from East
Rongbuk Glacier (Nikola Kekus)

Rolwaling Himal

GAURISHANKAR

Height: 7,134 metres (South summit
  7,010 metres – maybe only 6,983
  metres)
Lat./Long.: 27°57′57″ 86°20′07″
First ascent: 1979 via West Face

In 1952 Tom Weir and other Scottish climbers studied the south face and east ridge, both of which appeared hopeless. Later they inspected the northern side of the west ridge which looked possible. Two years later Raymond Lambert's Franco-Swiss team found the south, east and north ridges to be either corniced or with gaps and towers, with unclimbable faces in between. Lambert considered the peak unclimbable above 5,500 metres. Another British party in 1955 looked at the north ridge which was only accessible through closed Tibetan territory. A Japanese expedition in

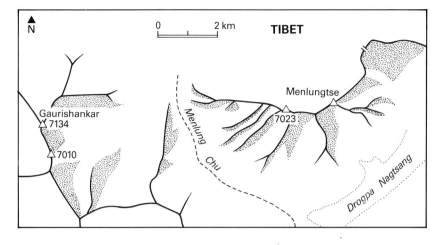

1959 found this to their cost when, at one stage, they were trapped on the north face by bad weather and armed Tibetans.

In 1964 there was a British attempt by a group which included Dennis Gray, Ian Clough and Don Whillans. After retreating from the knife-edge west ridge, the climbers forced their way over to and up the very steep and icy northwest face, reaching a height of about 7,045 metres. They were forced to re-treat after avalanches swept away their fixed ropes.

Don Whillans on Gaurishankar in 1964 (Dennis Gray)

After this no expeditions were permitted until 1979. Shortly be-fore departure a joint American-Nepalese party was informed that the northwest ridge was now in Tibet; consequently they were faced with the exceedingly difficult west face or southwest ridge. After a difficult approach, by way of the Rongshar gorge and Chumul Chu, base camp was set up on 6 April at

Gaurishankar from the west (Dennis Gray)

about 5,000 metres, and after reconnoitring they decided to attack the west face where a steep ice rib led to some ice fields and rock bands beneath the summit. The most worrying feature was a hanging glacier high up on the face. The first camp on the face was put in a small crevasse at 6,100 metres. Then a delicate traverse had to be made to the left to a niche, before ascending an ice runnel, above which a bivouac site ('Camp III') was found at 6,500 metres.

The weather now changed from blizzards to beautiful clear days and climbing conditions were perfect. The next section consisted of an ice chimney (70°+). The lead climbers were becoming exhausted by now and a summit bid had to be made quickly. The co-leader Pertemba decided to give Dorje a chance of getting to the top. So on 8 May John Roskelley, who had pioneered much of the route, and Dorje climbed quickly up the prepared route to the last ice field, towards the ramp cutting the final rock band. After an overhang (A3) the climbing was still steep but the pair soon ascended the last slope and shortly afterwards reached the top.

Spanish climbers attempted a new route, left of the American one, on the west face, up a series of ice spurs and rock walls. At 6,300 metres they traversed to the summit ridge but, having overcome all major difficulties, were prevented by illness from reaching the top. A Japanese attempt in 1983 to repeat the American route failed at the final obstacle, a 50-metre vertical rock wall.

1979. Southwest Ridge

Peter Boardman's party climbed the southwest ridge and summit plateau to reach the south summit. The following year an Austrian team, led by F. Huber, reached 5,795 metres on the southwest

ridge before very strong winds destroyed most of their tents and equipment.

1983. South Face

A Polish attempt on the south face was defeated by the danger of avalanche. Members of a Yugoslav party climbed the south face to the southwest ridge, then joined Boardman's route which was followed to the south summit.

1984. Variation Finish to West Face Route

American climbers made a variation finish to the American route, ascending directly to the summit above 6,345 metres, to the right of the 1979 route.

1984. South Summit via Southeast Ridge

In 1980 a pre-monsoon Japanese-Nepalese expedition reached 6,400 metres on the very long southeast ridge which required fixed rope all the way. They were defeated by tiredness and changing weather. Members of an Australian group on the same ridge reached a subsidiary peak (Tseringma) beyond which they had neither the time nor the equipment to reach even the south summit. In 1984 Japanese climbers completed the ascent of the southeast ridge to the south summit.

1985. Alpine-style Attempt

Japanese climbers K. Sakai and T. Orizumi attempted an alpine-style ascent, but Sakai fell to his death from a height of 5,900 metres.

1986. Winter Ascent

On 16 January South Korean Choi Han-Jo and Sherpa Ang Kami (his second ascent) reached the summit after a winter ascent of the west face route and variation finish.

1986. Southwest Face Attempt

Spanish climbers attempted a line left of the Roskelley route, reaching 6,100 metres. They withdrew in the face of bad weather and avalanches on the faces.

MENLUNGTSE (Jobo Garu, Qiao Ge Ru)

Location: in Tibet
Height: 7,181 metres
Lat./Long.: 27°58'16" 86°26'15"

After the 1951 reconnaissance of Everest's Western Cwm, Eric Shipton and his companions explored the surrounding country using Namche Bazar as their base. On their last trip they left Namche on 4 November, ascended the Nagpo Dzangpo (the next valley west of the Bhote Kosi to which Shipton refers) and split into three groups.

Shipton and Michael Ward continued northwestwards up the Pangbuk valley. Climbing a small peak to the east of the glacier they had a splendid view of the frontier range and a lofty snow saddle, the Menlung La. Immediately below the saddle on the western side was a wide glacier (the Drogpa Nagtsang) and beyond, towering in lofty isolation, a superb peak, Menlungtse. Descending to the glacier they could not tell whether they were still in Nepal but continued, turning northwards to skirt the western flanks of Menlungtse. Shipton then realized they were above the ravine of the Menlung Chu, a river whose lower end had been reached by the 1921 Everest expedition. They could see that Menlungtse was isolated in a glacier basin like Nanda Devi and, in Shipton's words, 'on every side its colossal granite walls were pale and smooth as polished marble'. They were now joined by Bill Tilman and Tom Bourdillon. Reluctant to retrace their steps they descended the Menlung Chu into

Tibet to join the great river Rongshar which cuts its way right through the Himalayan barrier. By following this they were able to cross back into Nepal. However, it was a narrow squeak as the *dzongpen* (headman) at the frontier fort sent men to capture them; but human nature prevailed over Communist principles and the soldiers were content with a small bribe instead.

In 1984 Chris Bonington approached the Chinese authorities for permission to organize an expedition to attempt Menlungtse. At last everything was fixed for 1987 and he set off with his companions, fellow-Briton Jim Fotheringham and Norwegians Odd Eliassen, Bjorn Myhrer-Lund, Torgeir Fosse and Helge Ringdal. Entering Tibet from Nepal they travelled north to the town of Tingri before turning south for Menlungtse and base camp on the western side of the mountain. This was reached on 25 March after a long march using yaks to cross a snow-blocked high pass.

On the southern side of the peak all four ridges appeared steep and difficult but not without hope. They commenced fixing rope up the steep granite slabs at the start of the central buttress of the south face. After four days they had moved up stores and equipment and reached the rocky crest. The ridge turned into a terrifying pile of shattered blocks, but conditions improved after several rope-lengths. After descending to pick up gear they reached their high point by late afternoon. Overnight the weather began to change and by the time they got to the upper snowfields it was snowing and blowing hard, and they found themselves exposed to an electrical storm in which Jim Fotheringham was struck. During the night Eliassen and Myhrer-Lund's tent was torn to shreds. Retreat was imperative.

Determined to find a better route they went to examine the southeast ridge (which leads straight to the summit), but one look was enough to convince them that it would be even more difficult and lengthy. Returning to their original route they placed the rest of their fixed rope to give themselves a higher starting point. After two days they were chased down by another storm but next morning the weather seemed to improve and after four days they had regained their highest point of 6,100 metres. The weather deteriorated once more, however, this time for good, and they were lucky to descend without incident.

MENLUNGTSE WEST

Location: in Tibet
Height: 7,023 metres
Lat./Long.: 27°58'07" 86°25'15"
First ascent: 1988 via West Face

In 1988 Chris Bonington took another party to Menlungtse. The difficult west peak was climbed by Andy Fanshawe and Alan Hinks alpine-style between 19–24 May. The route up the 2,000-metre high west face commenced with complicated but easy ground, leading to a long 55° ice-field and a final 300 metres on the granite headwall. The first attempt ended just below the final headwall when the climbers ran out of energy after five days. Following a brief reconnaissance of the east ridge, a second assault was launched on the west face with food for only four days. The pair started in the early hours of 19 May. A couloir was climbed to 5,800 metres where they made camp. After a rest day the previous highest bivouac was reached without great difficulty up pitches of 55° névé, green ice and some deep soft snow. Near midnight their tent was almost buried by an avalanche but they managed to find their ropes next day. On 23 May, and now out of food, they attacked the difficult granite headwall which provided some fine climbing and interesting route-finding. Once off the face they

▲

Menlungtse West–West Face. The 1988 British route takes the square-cut ice face left of the prominent snowy rib before breaking through the rockwall at its narrowest point. The higher east summit is about two kilometres behind (Andrew Fanshawe)

made for the summit in failing light up a broad open slope, arriving on top at 10.30 p.m. Unfortunately, the two-kilometre traverse to the main peak was out of the question, this being the only realistic means of reaching it.

NYANANG RI
Location: in Tibet
Height: 7,071 metres
Lat./Long.: 28°18′53″ 85°47′53″

In 1982, during 4–7 May, Doug

Scott, Alex MacIntyre and Roger Baxter-Jones climbed the south ridge and traversed clockwise round the summit to the northeast ridge; they did not go to the top.

PHOLA GANGCHEN (Molamenqing)
Location: in Tibet; satellite of Shisha Pangma
Height: 7,661 metres (7,703 metres per Chinese survey)
Lat./Long.: 28°21′17″ 85°48′45″
First ascent: 1981 from East

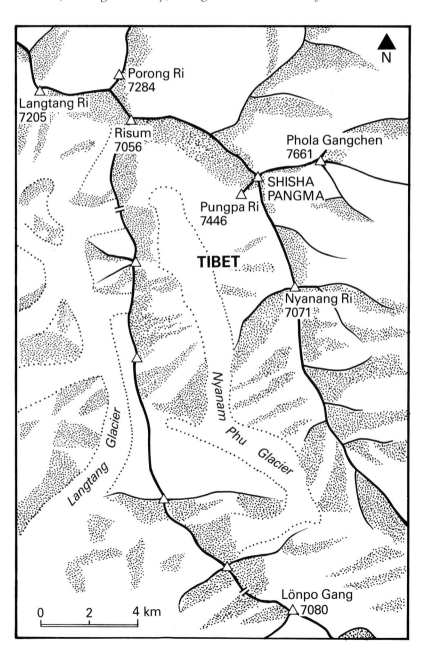

A New Zealand expedition approached via the Yambu Kangala glacier east of Shisha Pangma. Their original objective was the north ridge but its approaches were threatened by ice cliffs. Instead they chose a safer route which traversed Shisha Pangma between the north face and north peak, thence across snowfields westwards to Phola Gangchen. The route was not technically difficult but very long, requiring five camps; all load carrying was done by the climbers. Three groups reached the top over a period of one week. The weather was quite stormy throughout.

PORONG RI
Location: In Tibet, about 8 km northwest of Shisha Pangma, to which it is connected by a ridge
Height: 7,284 metres
Lat./Long.: 28°23′40″ 85°43′15″
First ascent: 1982 via north ridge

Minoru Wada and Yukio Eto, members of a 14-man expedition from Japan's Oitaken Mountaineering Club, reached the summit on 14 May via the north ridge, Wada falling to his death during the descent.

1982. East Ridge
Members of the same expedition climbed the peak by the east ridge on 17 May.

PUNGPA RI
Location: In Tibet, 1½ km southwest of Shisha Pangma
Height: 7,446 metres
First ascent: 1982 via Southwest Couloir and Ridge

After an attempt on Nyanang Ri, Doug Scott, Roger Baxter-Jones and Alex MacIntyre moved up to a camp under Shisha Pangma. From here they made the first ascent of Pungpa Ri, which is really the southwest shoulder of Shisha

Pangma and separated from it by a saddle at 7,300 metres. The three climbed a 45° couloir and bivouaced at 6,700 metres. Next day they ascended the south ridge (Grade IV) in a strong wind to a second bivouac, completing the ascent and descent next day.

Pamari Himal

Labuche Kang (Choksiam)
Location: in Tibet
Height: 7,367 metres (7,312 metres or 7,316 metres on some maps)
Lat./Long.: approx. 28°20' 86°20'
First ascent: 1987 via West Ridge

This peak lies somewhat to the north of the main frontier chain of the Himalaya but is much nearer to that range than it is to the Transhimalaya. It may belong to the Pamari Himal, which lies between the Tamba Kosi and the Sun Kosi, and which is also referred to as the Lapchi Kang. The peak was first approached during the 1986 post-monsoon period by the four members of a joint Chinese-Japanese reconnaisance party. They climbed to a col at 6,200 metres and found a reasonable route on the west ridge. The north face and north ridge were considered unsuitable. A year later a much larger Tibetan-Japanese expedition, with nine members from each country, started from the village of Langgoloz and placed an advanced base camp twenty-one kilometres up the valley at 5,300 metres. The first camp (5,600 metres) was on a snow plateau and the second (6,150 metres) on the hanging glacier on the northwest face, from which the west ridge was gained using a considerable amount of fixed rope. The expedition survived the great October blizzard which swept the Himalaya, and the third camp was set up

on the west ridge on 25 October. Next day, four Japanese and four Tibetans (one a 17-year-old woman) reached the summit after fixing more ropes. They were followed twenty-four hours later by another party.

Langtang Himal

GANG BENCHEN (Kangpenqing)
Location: in Tibet
Height: 7,211 metres (previously 7,415 metres)
Lat./Long.: 28°33'30" 85°32'15"
First ascent: 1982 via North Face

Japanese climbers approached via the small glacier north of the peak. Camp II (6,700 metres) was placed on the snow face above the ice-fall. From Camp III at 7,100 metres, eight members reached the top in two-and-a-half hours on 21 April in fine weather. Three other climbers repeated the ascent the next day. The route was not difficult.

LANGTANG LIRUNG (Ganchen Ledrub)
Height: 7,234 metres

Lat./Long.: 28°15'22" 85°31'10"
First ascent: 1978 via East Ridge

H. W. Tilman and P. Lloyd travelled along the southern flanks in 1949 and noted that the south side, defended by a great cirque, looked quite impregnable. Tilman and Tenzing went up the Lirung glacier but reached only a subsidiary ridge beyond which lay a high glacier bay and the frontier ridge. Later they were stopped by border guards from approaching from the north.

During the period 1961–64, three attempts were made to climb the relatively easy but hazardous east ridge, at the cost of the lives of two Japanese, two Italians and a Sherpa. The highest point reached was about 6,100 metres. This route was not completed until 1978 when the summit was reached on 24 October by Seishi Wada and Pemba Tsering from Camp IV at 6,650 metres.

1986. West Ridge
In 1964 a small Australian party made an autumn attempt on the long, safe but technically difficult west (southwest) ridge, which leads to the west shoulder. At about 6,500 metres they came to a

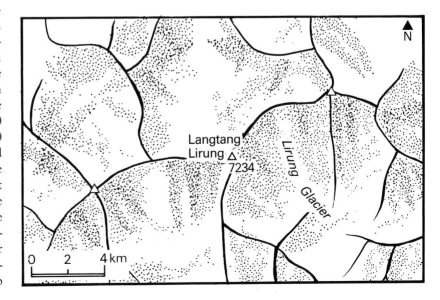

▲

South Ridge of Langtang Lirung (Nikola Kekus)

150-metre high rock tower, looking like a pile of stacked plates. From the top the ridge ahead looked easy enough, but higher up were a lot of sharp edges and ice cliffs. With the weather beginning to turn the party decided reluctantly to give the mountain best.

The 1986 South Korean expedition placed three camps up as far as 6,000 metres during the last week of September. Their progress was hampered by bad weather. They reached 6,500 metres in an effort to establish another camp, but eventually started for the summit from Camp III. After eighteen hours' climbing they bivouaced at the foot of a 80° snow wall. Next day they climbed the wall and set up a camp at 7,000 metres on the last pitch of the west ridge. The top was gained in four hours from there.

1988. Winter Ascent
A Polish expedition put three members on the summit via the southeast ridge on 3 January.

1980–86. South Face Attempts
The first attempt on the south face was made in 1980 by a mainly British expedition. The height of the face and its logistical problems prevented a full alpine-style ascent. The team managed to put two camps on the face before giving up. The route followed a series of snow and ice gullies, a rib and airy rock buttresses, before the steep ice arête which leads to the summit 900 metres above. The ice arête was threatened by avalanches. In 1984 an eight-man Canadian group tried to repeat this route. Their highest point was 6,350 metres before an avalanche wiped out the top camp. In 1986 the Americans

Daniel Newell and Elliot Spake, with Sherpa Gyalgen, were killed in an avalanche while on a buttress leading to the northeast ridge.

LANGTANG RI
Height: 7,205 metres
Lat./Long.: 28°22'55" 85°41'01"
First ascent: 1981 via Southwest
  Ridge

An attempt in 1955 by Raymond Lambert (Swiss) and Jules Détry (Belgian) was abandoned because of dangerous ice cliffs and cornices. A Japanese attempt in 1971 on the southeast ridge failed at about 6,000 metres because of faulty stoves. The first ascent was made by four members of a Japanese–Nepalese expedition.

TSOGAKA
Location: near Langtang Ri
Height: 7,193 metres
Lat./Long.: 28°23'00" 85°41'15"

Jugal Himal

LÖNPO GANG (Big White Peak)
Height: 7,080 metres (now given as
  6,979 metres)
Lat./Long.: 28°11'45" 85°48'00'
First ascent: 1962 via South Face

Monica Jackson and two companions were the first climbers to investigate the southern approaches to this peak. In 1955 they went up the easiest of the southern glaciers, the Phurbi Chachumb, and reached a col on the Tibetan border north of Phurbi Chachu (6,658 metres). They found that on the Tibetan side the Jugal peaks fall in sheer precipices. Most of the peaks appeared to be difficult but Lönpo Gang looked feasible for a strong party. Two years later the leader of a British party, Captain Crosby Fox, and two Sherpas were swept into a crevasse by an avalanche near their Camp IV at 5,650 metres. In 1958 a Japanese party made the same approach but soon realized that they had neither enough supplies nor enough personnel for a serious attempt on the peak.

After two further attempts, a strong Japanese expedition arrived in April 1962. They went up the glacier and crossed a ridge to the head of the Dorje Lakpa glacier. This long route required five camps as far as a high pass on the ridge. Camp VI was pitched at the head of the Dorje Lakpa glacier and Camp VII right under the south face. On 2 May Yasuhisa and Morita started at 5 a.m. to prepare the route to the summit, fixing ropes on the 70° ice wall, which they traversed to the centre. This was the limit of the 1961 attempt. Higher up they came to a knife-edge ridge near the Tibetan frontier, before returning to camp. Next day they made good progress and reached the top at 2 p.m.

1987. West Face, Southwest Ridge

From the Langshisha glacier a Korean team made the ascent of this peak by a new route. Between Camps I and II, 600 metres of rope were fixed on a steep ridge away from avalanche danger. After snowy weather more rope was fixed on the knife-edge southwest ridge and Camp III set up at 6,680 metres. The Koreans Lee Jeong-Hoon and Kim Soo-Hyeon with Sherpas Da Gombu and Ang Temba reached the summit early on 27 September. The climbers encountered many crevasses, but the slope was not over steep.

P.7013

Location: near Langtang Ri
Lat./Long.: 28°23'09" 85°42'42"

P.7050

Location: near Langtang Ri
Lat./Long.: 28°23'01" 85°41'20"

RISUM

Height: 7,050 metres
Lat./Long.: 28°22'24" 85°43'25"

Bibliography

Allan, S. (1988–89), 'Pumori–the Scottish route', *AJ*, 93, pp. 48–50.

Boardman, P. (1981), 'British-Nepalese Gaurishankar expedition, 1979', *HJ*, 37, pp. 15–18.

Bonington, C. (1988), 'Menlungtse 1987', *HJ*, 44, pp. 32–9.

Carrington, R. (1980), 'Jannu-alpine style' *HJ*, 36, pp. 18–22.

Clough, I. (1965), 'Gauri Sankar, 1964', *AJ*, 70, pp. 96–105.

Culbreth, W. (1985), 'Gaurishankar's west face', *AAJ*, 27, pp. 81–3.

Cullinan, P. and Brammer, G. (1981), 'Australian Gaurishankar (Tseringma) expedition', *HJ*, 37, pp. 19–21.

Day, H. (1988), 'British Xixabangma expedition 1987', *HJ*, 44, pp. 24–31.

Fanshawe, A. (1988), 'Of mice and Menlungtse', *Mountain*, 123 (September/October), pp. 20–5.

Gicquel, M. (1974), 'South face of Pumori', *HJ*, 32, pp. 6–12.

Gregory, A. (1956–7), 'The Merseyside Himalayan expedition, 1955', *AJ*, 61, pp. 54–9.

Lambert, R. (1955), 'Expédition au Gaurisankar', *AAJ*, 9, pp. 113–16.

Lenser, G. (1962–63), 'Pumori–the daughter mountain', *MW*, pp. 127–32.

Lowe, G. (1955), 'The Barun expedition, 1954', *AJ*, 60, pp. 227–38. See also, *MW*, pp. 97–110.

Lynam, J. (1988), 'Zhangzi–Autumn 1987', *HJ*, 44, pp. 15–23.

MacInnes, H. (1955), 'Creagh Dhu Himalayan expedition, 1953', *AJ*, 60, pp. 58–61.

Marmier, J. (1987), 'Gyachung Kang 1986', *HJ*, 43, pp. 10–16.

Olech, K. (1975), 'The first ascent of Kangbachen', *AJ*, 80, pp. 29–36.

Paytubi, J. (1988), 'Data about Pumori', *HJ*, 44, pp. 177–9.

Read, A. (1980), 'The Nepalese–American Gaurishankar expedition', *AAJ*, 22, pp. 417–26.

Rouse, A. (1980), 'Jannu', *AJ*, 85, pp. 77–83.

Scott, D. and MacIntyre, A. (1984), *The Shishapangma expedition*, Granada. Includes Nyanang Ri and Pungpa Ri.

Searle, M. (1983), 'Langtang Lirung south face, 1980', *AJ*, 88, pp. 106–10.

Sigayret, H. (1984), 'French expedition to the southwest ridge of Jannu–spring 1983', *HJ*, 40, pp. 42–7.

Sighele, G. (1976), 'French expedition to Pumori, 1975', *HJ*, 34, pp. 22–6.

Simonetta, W. (1988), 'Kangchungtse expedition 1987', *HJ*, 44, pp. 172–3.

Sprang, G. (1988), 'Jannu–North Face 1987', *HJ*, 44, pp. 169–70.

Stark, E. (1955–56), 'Jugal Himal', *HJ*, 19, pp. 75–81.

Takahasi, A. (1965), 'Ascent of Big White Peak', *HJ*, 25, pp. 43–50.

Taylor, P. (1967), 'Langtang Lirung, 1964', *HJ*, 27, pp. 141–3.

Walmsley, J. (1961), 'Nuptse', *AJ*, 66, pp. 209–34.

Yashima, H. (1988), 'Cho Aui expedition 1986', *HJ*, 44, pp. 163–5.

Central and Western Nepal Himalaya

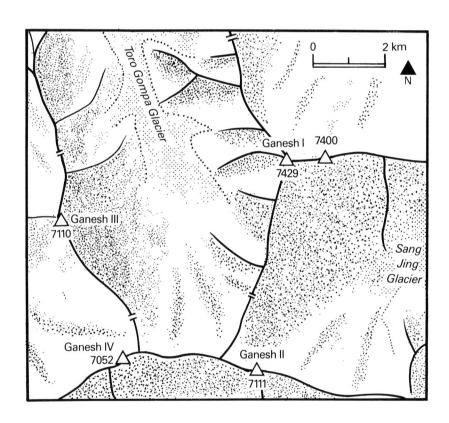

Ganesh Himal

Ganesh I (Yangra)
Height: 7,429 metres
Subsidiary peak: East, c.7,400 metres
Lat./Long.: 28°23'30". 85°07'38"
First ascent: 1955 via Southeast
Face/Ridge

Continuing their 1950 trip to the Langtang Himal, H. W. Tilman and his companions approached the Ganesh Himal from the southeast. Their first climb was Paldor (5,928 metres), a southern outlier, but they were not given any views of the high peaks. Proceeding northwestwards towards a large glacier they were rewarded with the sight of a great mountain completely filling the head of the valley. The southwest ridge seemed to offer a straightforward way to the top. Tilman went up the middle of the Sang Jing glacier until the whole glacier bay came into view – a cirque of four monstrously steep and broken ice-falls. Later with Lloyd he discovered that the southwest ridge sprang from a high col but a possible route leading to it was threatened by the rotting face of one of the ice-falls. Lastly Tilman and Tenzing went up to attempt the col but the high temperatures of the monsoon had made it impossibly dangerous.

Three years later a four-man New Zealand party led by Athol Roberts applied for permission to climb in the Burhi Gandaki area and arriving feeling fit and confident they set about tackling the highest peak within reach. Although troubled by poor snow and ice conditions and altitude sickness, they reached a height of about 6,100 metres on the northwest ridge. Beyond that they could see a 450-metre section of serrated ice towers, while the last 900 metres included a vertical rock step and crown of ice.

▲ *Ganesh Himal from the south (Nikola Kekus)*

In 1954 a Japanese expedition was refused access to Manaslu by local inhabitants and diverted their vast stores of equipment and food to the Toro Gompa glacier on Ganesh. They had no information about the peak except what could be gleaned from Namgyal, the sirdar of the New Zealand expedition. Short of time the Japanese decided to try the northwest ridge but on closer inspection found that Namgyal's version of it was far from accurate. The lowest saddle on the frontier ridge was a crest barely wide enough to stand on, while the Tibetan side was a sheer ice precipice which could not be traversed. Above the saddle they could see why the New Zealanders had turned back. Further reconnaissances failed to discover an alternative route from the Toro Gompa glacier. Frustrated they spent another ten days on the New Zealand route, reaching about 6,400 metres. Further on there did not appear to be any campsite.

The following year a Franco-Swiss expedition, led by Raymond Lambert, was beset by bad weather, poor snow conditions and the severe illness of one member, who had to be evacuated. Very slowly they managed to place three camps up the southeast face which is crossed by subsidiary ridges. On 24 October Lambert, Claude Kogan and Eric Gauchat, a brilliant young climber, left Camp III and climbed the slope to the saddle between the main and east peaks in six hours. An hour later they were on the pointed top of the main peak where cornices threatened to plunge them down the Tibetan side. On descending, and against Lambert's orders, Gauchat went on ahead but slipped on the smooth slopes swept clean by the high wind they had experienced all day. Unable to descend in the fall line his companions had to make a considerable detour next day to

reach his body which lay in a most dangerous area.

(Courtesy Eyre & Spottiswoode)

Claude Kogan (1919–59)

Claude Kogan was one of the most distinguished women climbers of her generation with a fine record of climbs in the Alps, Caucasus, Greenland and the Andes, as well as in the Himalaya. Small and slightly built, she was a designer of swimsuits in her own factory in Nice. In 1951 she was a member of the Franco-Belgian expedition to Alpamayo in the Cordillera Blanca, where she climbed Quitaraju with Nicole Leininger. The following year she made the first ascent of Salcantay in the Cordillera Vilcabamba with Bernard Pierre. In 1953 the latter took her on his expedition to Nun, After most of the climbers had been caught in an avalanche she and Pierre Vittoz made the ascent together. Her second Himalayan expedition was an attempt on Cho Oyu in 1954 with the Swiss climber Raymond Lambert; they were only some 500 metres from the top when the weather defeated them. She achieved her second Himalayan summit in 1955 when she climbed with Lambert and Eric Gauchat to the top of Ganesh I. That same year she became the first woman to give a talk to the members of the Alpine Club. She returned to the Himalaya in 1959 as leader of an international all-women expedition to Cho Oyu. With Claudine van der Stratten and Sherpa Angnorbu she became trapped in the highest camp during several days of severe storm and they were all carried away by an avalanche.

1960. East Peak

On 31 May P. J. Wallace with Pa Norbu and Gyalzen reached the east peak via a variant of the 1955 route, following one of the southeast ridges from the Sang Jing glacier.

1985. West Ridge Attempt

A 1985 Korean-Nepalese attempt on the steep and difficult west ridge ended when a Sherpa dropped a load of pitons 1,000 metres down the mountain.

GANESH II
Height: 7,111 metres
Lat./Long.: 28°20'25" 85°07'07"
First ascent: 1979 via North Face

A Japanese-Nepalese group ascended the Sang Jing glacier to the col between Ganesh II and V and immediately realized that the east ridge, which was their objective, was twice as long as expected. In addition it was heavily corniced with a sharply curving knife-edge. They got to a high point of 6,500 metres after climbing a series of dangerous ice towers covered in breakable crust.

The attack was transferred to the north face after a dangerous traverse across a terrace on the northeast face. After climbing a knife-edge buttress they reached the snow plateau between the north and northeast spurs where a camp was placed (6,400 metres). The route continued up a steep ice wall between hanging glaciers to another camp (6,900 metres) on the north spur. Next day the summit was easily reached up a broad ridge.

1980. Southeast Face Attempt

This was attempted in October by a small Swiss-Nepalese party led by Peter Molinari. They started up the southeast face towards the south ridge but found the route was difficult and the rotten ice would not take ice screws. They reached a height of 6,100 metres.

1984. South Face

The first attempt on the dangerous south (southwest) face had been made alpine-style the previous year by members of a Polish expedition. After six days of difficult climbing (up to Grade V) they ran out of equipment at the foot of a big tower on the southeast ridge, 300 metres below the summit. Shortly after commencing the descent, one of the trio was killed while abseiling. One of the others made a daring solo descent, and the third was eventually rescued by his companions. The British climbers Rick Allen and Nick Kekus followed the Polish route, with variations. In deteriorating weather they reached the summit and then bivouaced in a snow cave on the west ridge a few metres lower. Unstable snow and strong winds forced them to abseil blindly down the face, the descent taking three days.

West Ridge Attempts

The west ridge was attempted in 1984 by the Swiss and again two years later by Koreans, bad weather intervening on both occasions.

GANESH III (Salasungo)

Height: 7,110 metres
Lat./Long.: 28° 22' 20" 85° 03' 33"
First ascent: 1981 via North Ridge and via Northeast Spur and North Face

This peak was attempted unsuccessfully six times prior to the first ascent. In spring 1953 New Zealanders reached 5,500 metres on the north ridge. A year later the Japanese tried the west ridge.

There were no more attempts until spring 1971 when the Japanese reached 5,400 metres on the northeast spur. There were two Japanese expeditions in 1980: an attempt on the south ridge in the spring and one on the northeast spur in the autumn. Six months later another Japanese expedition reached 6,800 metres on the south ridge, only a little higher than their predecessors. In the end the mountain was climbed by two routes simultaneously in September–October 1981. German Hermann Warth and three Sherpas ascended the north ridge to 6,300 metres where they met up with a Japanese group who had come up the northeast spur. From there they joined forces and took the same route on the north face to the summit.

Ganesh II South Face (Nikola Kekus)

GANESH IV (Pabil)

Height: 7,052 metres
Lat./Long.: 28°20'30" 85°04'40"
First ascent: 1978 via South Face and
Southeast Ridge

A Japanese-Nepalese expedition made the first ascent by climbing the south face, finishing up the southeast ridge. The summit was reached by four parties.

1980. South-Southwest Spur

From camp at 5,800 metres, the Frenchmen Erik Decamp, Guy Dufour and Alain Richier made an alpine-style ascent with four bivouacs. They climbed the south-southwest spur to the southeast ridge and south face.

1981. Winter Attempt

An American-Nepalese party was defeated by storms on the south face; their high point was probably no more than 5,500 metres. Conditions obliged them to climb directly up the centre of the face where they encountered steep, hard ice.

Kenyan climber Iain Allan tackling an ice-fall. Beyond rises Chamar (7,187m) in the remote Sringi Himal (John Cleare)

Serang (Sringi) Himal

CHAMAR

Height: 7,187 metres
Lat./Long.: 28°33'19" 84°56'43"
First ascent: 1953 via Northeast Ridge

After their attempt on Ganesh I the 1953 New Zealand expedition moved northwestwards and turned their attention to Chamar, an ice sheathed giant near the Tibetan frontier. It was the last week of May with the onset of the monsoon imminent. Access to the glacier running down from the east face proved to be the first problem. Over the next two weeks they set up camps on the glacier and the dangerous, avalanching ice face. Camp V was on the summit ridge at 6,700 metres and the final section of the route resembled the ridge of a huge roof, overhung with waves of cornices. For half of the distance Maurie Bishop had to cut a way up a near vertical ice step followed by the reluctant Namgyal. The following day two more members and another Sherpa also reached the summit as the monsoon was breaking. They got back to Camp V safely but next day were faced with the descent of the dangerous face in cloud and new snow. Responding to shouts for support, Bishop and three Sherpas started up from Camp IV only to be avalanched back to their starting point. The trio, one snowblind, inched their way down during the rest of the day, and all the next. The last day on the mountain was fine and they reached the safety of the easy glacier below. There do not appear to have been any more attempts on Chamar apart from one by a Japanese-Nepalese expedition in 1983. They reached about 7,000 metres on the original route.

P.7183 ('Chamar South')

Lat./Long.: 28°32'48" 84°56'56"

Mansiri (Manaslu) Himal

HIMAL CHULI

Height: 7,893 metres
Lat./Long.: 28°26'08" 84°38'32"
First ascent: 1960 from Western Saddle

Apart from exploratory visits in 1950 and 1954, the first attempt on the peak in 1955, by climbers from Kenya, was made from the southwest and it had to be abandoned before any serious climbing had been done. Among other difficulties, the joint leader Arthur Firmin sustained a serious leg injury in a fall into a crevasse above base camp. Despite immediate evacuation he died before reaching hospital.

A 1958 Japanese reconnaissance party approached the peak from the northeast, up the Shurang

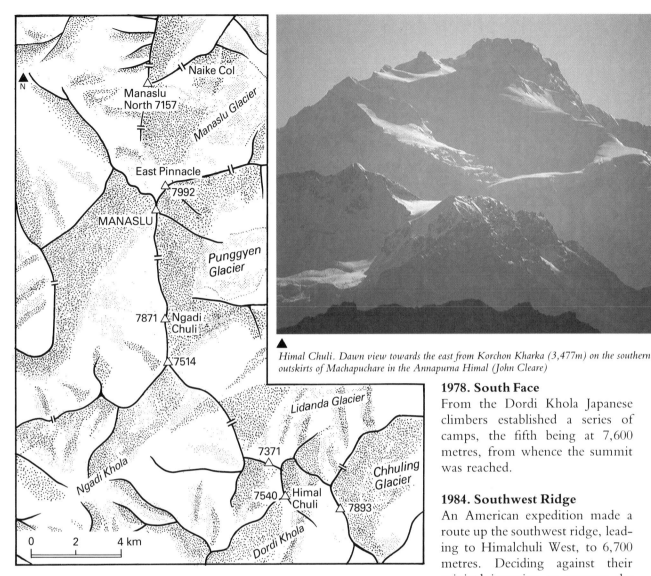

Himal Chuli. Dawn view towards the east from Korchon Kharka (3,477m) on the southern outskirts of Machapuchare in the Annapurna Himal (John Cleare)

Khola to the Lidanda Nokkoshi (pass). From there they followed a spur leading to the northeast ridge of Himalchuli, reaching 6,250 metres at the base of a steep gendarme. The following year a full climbing party trying the route found that, from the shoulder of Rami Peak, they were forced to descend a 300-metre ice cliff to a snowfield above the Chhuling glacier in order to reach the summit pyramid. Delayed by snowstorms and hard ice, an assault was launched from camp at 7,100 metres. Steep (60°) slopes and terribly hard ice allowed the summit pair to reach only 7,400 metres

before having to turn back.

Also in 1959, a party returning from a reconnaissance of Dhaulagiri II examined the western side of the peak from the Ngadi Khola, finding a feasible route. Apart from an avalanche accident, the 1960 Japanese group made steady progress up to the broad snow col between the west and main peaks, where they placed their sixth camp. The assault pair, Hisashi Tanabe and Masahiro Harada, using oxygen, climbed hard for eight hours before arriving on the long, horizontal snow ridge which forms the summit. The worst obstacle was a very steep ice wall.

1978. South Face

From the Dordi Khola Japanese climbers established a series of camps, the fifth being at 7,600 metres, from whence the summit was reached.

1984. Southwest Ridge

An American expedition made a route up the southwest ridge, leading to Himalchuli West, to 6,700 metres. Deciding against their original intention to traverse the south face, they contoured around the west peak, entering the upper cwm from the north. The final assault started up the first bulges of the west face and traversed towards the northeast skyline. The summit was reached by R. Jackson, D. Langmade, M. Yager and Sherpa Pema Dorje. The southwest ridge was first tried in 1975 by the Japanese.

1985. Southeast Ridge

From their third camp at 6,700 metres Japanese climbers traversed the four kilometres long snow plateau to the summit, which proved to be harder work than the first part of the route. This route had been attempted in 1979 by an American team via the south ridge, after the east ridge had been found to be a series of loose rock gendarmes. The great distance involved could not be covered in the severe snow conditions they encountered.

HIMAL CHULI WEST
Height: 7,540 metres
Lat./Long.: 28°26′07″ 84°37′07″
First ascent: 1978 from the East

In 1978 members of a Japanese expedition tackled Himal Chuli main peak from the head of the Dordi Khola. Two of the group diverted from camp at just under 7,000 metres to climb the west peak.

HIMAL CHULI NORTH
Height: 7,371 metres
Lat./Long.: 28°26′59″ 84°36′23″
First ascent: 1985 via North Face

This peak was climbed by Korean Leë Jae-Hong and four Sherpas. Lee Jae-Hong reached the summit half an hour before the others,

Chamar and other summits of the remote Sringi Himal are seen due east from near base camp (4,575m) on the east flank of Himalchuli–across the deep gorge of the Burhi Gandaki near Namrung (John Cleare)

having bivouaced 400 metres above their camp.

1985. Southwest Ridge
Five days after the first ascent, the Polish climbers Zdzistaw Jakubowski and Jerzy Klincewicz made a route up the southwest ridge to the southwest face, followed by a traverse to the east ridge. The summit was reached on 1 November from their second bivouac at 6,600 metres.

MANASLU EAST PINNACLE
Height: 7,992 metres
Lat./Long.: 28°33′16″ 84°33′52″

MANASLU NORTH
Height: 7,157 metres
Subsidiary peak: North Peak II, 7,157 metres
Lat./Long.: 28°36′14″ 84°32′40″
First ascent: 1964 via Northeast Ridge

A small Dutch-Austrian group ascended from the Manaslu glacier to the east. The route went by way of the Naike Col and the ice-fall above. On 25 October, Fons Driessen, Jan De Lint and the Austrian Hubert Schriebl, with two Sherpas, climbed the steep summit ridge to the top.

1979. North Peak II from North
A Czechoslavakian team, led by Vladimir Krupicka, reported the existence of a second north peak. From the Larkya glacier (between the north and northeast ridges) they established five camps as far as 6,425 metres on the north ridge, despite bad weather. Two pairs reached the top on 16 and 18 October.

1983. South Ridge
A joint British Services expedition made the second ascent of this peak by a new route. From the Manaslu glacier they climbed to a col (Manaslu North Col) and reached

the top via the long and technically difficult south ridge.

NGADI CHULI (Peak 29, Dakum, Dunapurna)

Height: 7,871 metres
Lat./Long.: 28°30'13" 84°34'09"
First ascent: Possibly 1970, via East Ridge and Face

Japanese climbers reconnoitred the western approaches in 1961 but failed to discover a route. In 1963 another party established several camps on the eastern side of the mountain, and suggested a route from the northeast via the Punggyen glacier. In 1969 Osaka University made its third attempt, starting up the south side of the east ridge, but was defeated by a steep ice face at 7,350 metres. There was no place to bivouac and some big crevasses lay across the route close to the top.

A possible first ascent by H. Watanabe and Lhakpa Tsering occurred in 1970. The climbers ascended the east ridge and face. After being out of sight for two hours very near the summit they reappeared and suffered a fatal fall near their camp at about 7,400 metres. Polish climbers who achieved the ascent in 1979 considered, in view of the topography of the mountain, that the 1970 pair could not have reached the summit.

1979. West Buttress
Polish climbers R. Gajewski and M. Pawlikowski succeeded in forcing a route to the summit. The first obstacle was a 700–metre high headwall (Grade V, A2). The route then continued up difficult ice left of the crest. Higher up a face of a 100 metres was followed by a traverse across ice-fields to the foot of the highest rock pinnacle on the ridge. The last pitch was mixed Grade V climbing.

P.7036
Lat./Long.: 28°31'40" 84°31'21"

P.7514 (Ngadi Chuli south shoulder)
Location: 2 km south of Ngadi Chuli
Height: 7,514 metres
Lat./Long.: 28°29'14" 84°34'01"

Peri Himal

HIMLUNG
Height: 7,126 metres
Lat./Long.: 28°46'19" 84°25'19"
First ascent: 1983 via East Ridge from South

In 1963 a seven-man Japanese expedition had only five days of fine weather out of forty-six on the mountain, which lies on the Nepal-Tibet border. The following year, a Dutchman and an Austrian approached from the southeast over the Larkya La.

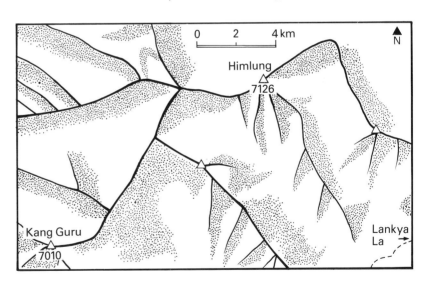

They found the routes to the west and east ridges were constantly avalanched and the very long south ridge too difficult for a small party. The northeast ridge was attempted from southeast of the peak by a Japanese-Nepalese team in spring 1982 and again in spring 1983. Hampered by heavy snowfall and

winds they reached 6,700 metres before giving up. A third joint team made the first ascent via the east ridge, again from the south in the post-monsoon period.

1987. South Ridge Attempt
A four-man American group set up base camp on the Himlung glacier, then ascended the Ratna ice-fall to 5,185 metres. After heavy snowfall they decided to move left to the 'Wishbone' couloir, by means of which they were able to reach the western spur of the south ridge at 5,640 metres. Two more days were required to reach the actual south ridge, over brittle ice and steep rock. They abandoned the climb at just over 6,100 metres on account of the difficulty and condition of a member of the party.

P.7038
Lat./Long.: 28°44'06" 84°22'04"

P.7098
Lat./Long.: 28°45'25" 84°24'58"

P.7139
Lat./Long.: 28°44'14" 84°25'12"

RATNA CHULI
Height: 7,035 metres
Lat./Long.: 28°51'53" 84°22'02"

KANG GURU (Naurgaon Peak)

Height: 7,010 metres (now given as 6,981 metres)
Lat./Long.: 28°39'27" 84°18'05"
First ascent: 1955 via West Face/Northwest Ridge

In 1950 H. W. Tilman's party attempted the west face but were stopped by difficult ice at about 6,280 metres. Five years later H. Steinmetz and two other Germans reached the top on 2 July via the west face and northwest ridge.

1981. Southwest Ridge

A Japanese expedition made the third ascent of this peak by a new route. They gained the ridge from the south side at about 5,200 metres after climbing up loose rock. Nearly 2,500 metres of rope were fixed on the ridge. The 'Blue Pinnacle' was turned on the south side, despite avalanche danger. Higher up they encountered an enormous crevasse above which an ice wall led to the 'Balcony'. From there, on 27 April, Y. Segi, D. Yamamoto, H. Sugita, Sherpa Nawang Choklang and Sherpa Ang Temba climbed a broad snow face to the summit.

1984. West Face Climbs

A pre-monsoon Korean expedition reported climbing the west face to the southeast ridge which was joined at about 6,000 metres. Another Korean group climbed the west face to the west ridge at 6,570 metres, reaching the summit on 19 September.

1988. East Face

N. Mason, J. Diplock and J. Holmes with four Sherpas climbed the face on 23 October with one bivouac, having fixed ropes to 6,100 metres. The route was seriously menaced by rock fall.

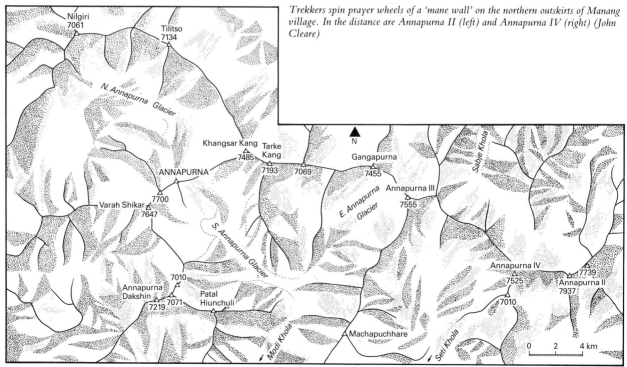

Trekkers spin prayer wheels of a 'mane wall' on the northern outskirts of Manang village. In the distance are Annapurna II (left) and Annapurna IV (right) (John Cleare)

Annapurna Himal

Annapurna II

Height: 7,937 metres
Lat./Long.: 28°32'05" 84°07'30"
First ascent: 1960 via West Ridge from the North

In 1953 Basil Goodfellow and Frank Yates spent a fortnight early in the year surveying and photographing the southern approaches to the Annapurna Himal. Annapurna II was seen to carry very little snow on its south and southwest faces which rise from the glaciers in grey-black rock slabs. The west ridge appeared to slope up easily at about 40° but a long traverse of the summit ridge would be necessary if tackled from the east. Members of a German expedition in 1955 had a closer view of the peak from Annapurna IV and decided that the best route would be along the west ridge; the south ridge appeared to be impossible.

The 1960 British Indian Nepalese Services' Himalayan Expedition was led by J. O. M. Roberts with, among others, Richard Grant and Chris Bonington. The expedition approached the range from the north, up the Sabje (Sabcho) Khola and established a base camp (about 4,500 metres) at the foot of the north face of Annapurna IV. Camp III was placed on the western shoulder ('Dome') of Annapurna IV, Camp IV under the summit, and the last two on the main ridge leading to Annapurna II. The connecting ridge, over three kilometres long, is narrow and corniced and the slope falls away to the south at an angle of about 45°. Grant and Bonington were given the task of establishing the route and by the end of April they had got as far as Camp IV, but the weather worsened with regular afternoon snow, high winds and low temperatures. After a week's rest the final advance was set in motion. They had hoped to place the final camp at 7,600 metres, but when Grant and Bonington reached the intended site they found it to be lower than Camp V; they had still well over 700 metres to climb, up the triangular summit mass of rock and snow.

The assault was set for 17 May but the day before was unsettled and the summit trio retreated to Camp V in case of trouble. However the morning dawned fine, so Grant, Bonington and Sherpa Ang Nyima set off. The route up the summit pyramid followed a 45°–50° rock rib, stepped in places by boulders and perched slabs, giving severe rock-climbing. In places snow overlying ice had to be climbed over. The snowy top was reached late afternoon.

1973. North Face

The Shinshu University Alpine Club's 1971 attempt on the north face ended in tragedy. On 4 May M. Sato and Sherpa Girme Dorje reached 7,800 metres on the northeast ridge but had to turn back as Sato was exhausted. By 9 p.m. he was unable to descend further so his companion anchored him to an ice axe and went back to camp. Shortly afterwards Sato was found to have disappeared, probably having fallen down the south side of the ridge. Two years later another Japanese group followed much the same route. Their top camp was sited at 7,300 metres between Annapurna II and IV and their route finished up the west ridge. On 6 May three climbers set off but two of them stopped early with 600 metres still to go. Katsuyuki Kondo kept going and reached the summit at 8.30 p.m. in bright moonlight before returning to the bivouac.

1983. South Face/Spur

This route was accomplished by a five-man team from Australia, led by T. Macartney-Snape. The climb lasted from 20 August to 8 October. They were held up by two big snowstorms during September, and one member was injured in two separate rock falls. On 6 October L. R. Hall, A. Henderson, G. Mortimer and Macartney-Snape left camp at 7,100 metres, and bivouaced at 7,600 metres for two nights, reaching the top on the eighth. There have been several other attempts to make routes on the south face.

ANNAPURNA III

Height: 7,555 metres
Lat./Long.: 28°35'01" 83°59'31"
First ascent: 1961 via Northeast Face

Very little information about this peak was available to the Indian team led by Mohan Kohli in 1961. Neither Bill Tilman nor Jimmy Roberts, who had both led expeditions to the range, had been able to discern a possible route. The mountain bristled with gendarmes and cornices and was guarded lower down by some nasty icefalls. Kohli's party started early and were at the foot of the mountain by 4 April. Preliminary reconnaissances suggested that there was a way to the upper part of the mountain via the eastern glacier and ice-fall which led to a col at about 5,150 metres. This would avoid the great 2,500-metre high north ice-fall, which was avalanched almost hourly. Beyond the col was a series of ice terraces which offered access to an upper shelf – the last point of take-off for the summit. On 22 April Kohli, P.C. Chaturvedi and two Sherpas completed the crossing of the ice terraces and reached the upper plateau, but found themselves cut off from the main peak by a huge glacial trough nearly a kilometre wide, which necessitated a detour of three kilometres to the east.

They were now ready to go for the summit. Another camp was established beyond the glacier trough and six climbers prepared to make an early start on 26 April. The first obstacle was a large crevasse, then the route steepened in knee-deep snow. By 10.30 a.m. they were still 600 metres from the top, at which point one member had to drop out. The going continued to be very slow and at 4 p.m. they had to turn back within 200 metres of success. After a break of several days at base camp, Kohli left for the summit again, with Sonam Gyatso, Sonam Girmi having started the day before with two Sherpas to remake the track and move the top camp up to 6,800 metres. On the morning of 6 May they set off on soft snow and after seven hours reached the east saddle, which connects with the summit ridge, with 250 metres still to go. The snow gave way to hard ice and the slope steepened to nearly 70° as the weather deteriorated. Struggling on grimly they gained the highest point at 4.15 p.m.

1970. South Face/West Ridge

A Japanese women's expedition made the second ascent of the peak and the first from the south via the Modi Khola. The most difficult climbing was between 5,900 and 6,800 metres where ropes were fixed. The summit team, Junko Tabei and Hiroko Hirakawa, with two Sherpas, made the summit from Camp V (6,800 metres) on 19 May, despite extremely cold conditions.

1977–79. South Face Variations

Both the 1970 Japanese and 1977 Italian routes went through a long unstable ice-fall to converge below the high saddle (6,860 metres) between Gangapunra and Anna-

purna III. The eight-man American team of 1978 chose a rock buttress at the side of the ice-fall, leading to the upper face. Over 1,700 metres of fixed rope were placed up to Camp III at the base of a steep mixed couloir. At the second attempt three climbers, Werner Landry, Edward Connor III and Greg Sapp, managed to climb the couloir and the 40° face to reach the summit ridge at 7,300 metres seventeen hours after setting out. They decided not to risk going to the top which was still five hours away. In 1979 a British team climbed a combination of the Italian and American routes.

1980. East Ridge from North

Swiss climbers used a couloir slightly north of the route used in 1961 to gain access to the upper part of the mountain. From camp on the great plateau Jean-Pierre Rieben and Temba Sherpa climbed the east ridge to the top in eight-and-a-half hours, returning via the Indian northeast face route.

1981. Southeast Buttress Attempt

A British group was the first to approach this area of Annapurna III, up the Seti Khola. After reconnoitring it, the buttress was climbed to within 150 metres of the obvious step and equipment dumped. Later the previous high was reached in two days, followed by three more of hard climbing (Grade V, V+). At about 6,500 metres they decided to go down as the ridge ahead looked dangerous and would require another four to six days to complete.

In 1983 British climbers were unable to reach a sick companion attempting the east ridge from the south. In 1986 an Italian climber was killed on the southwest buttress, a route which had been considered twice before but never attempted. The great central

couloir of the southwest face remains unclimbed.

ANNAPURNA IV

Height: 7,525 metres
Lat./Long.: 28°32'14" 84°05'02"
First ascent: 1955 via North
*   Face/Northwest Ridge*

One of the earliest expeditions into Nepal was that led by H. W. Tilman in 1950. The aim was to build up a nucleus of experienced Himalayan climbers. Dismissing the idea of an attempt on Makalu as too serious for his party, he examined instead the northern side of the Annapurna Himal and selected Annapurna IV as the most suitable. Charles Evans and the New Zealander W. P. Packard made the first attempt and were below the final shoulder at about 7,300 metres when they had to turn back before an impending storm. Next day another pair retreated with numbed feet. On the third day the climbers got to within 200 metres of the top before exhaustion forced them to give up.

Further attempts on the route were made by the Japanese, but it fell to a German expedition, led by Heinz Steinmetz, to make the first ascent. They found the ice bulge above Camp I less formidable than in earlier years, but even so it was not suitable for porters, who were sent down.

An ice corridor offered a good line to the big snow plateau leading to the western shoulder ('Dome') which was reached in a few days. The climbers were then tent-bound for two days of storm but at the end of May they were poised for a summit bid. On 30 May Jürgen Wellenkamp, Harald Biller and Steinmetz left their camp (at about 6,500 metres) with bivouac equipment and food for three days. Good conditions compensated for the time required for the quite technically difficult summit ridge and by noon they had the summit pyramid in sight. Dumping their bivouac equipment they struck out for the top but the distance was deceptive and they did not arrive until 5.30 p.m. It was pitch dark by the time they got back to the dump and they dug into the wall of a crevasse for the bitterly cold night.

1976. South Face

The Germans Pit Schubert and Heinz Baumann completed this route but were lucky to survive. From base camp the party ascended a difficult ice-fall where much rope was fixed. More ropes were fixed on steep rocks above the second camp. Contrary to the general wishes, Schubert and Baumann decided to climb the remaining 2,500 metres of face directly upward alpine-style. They set off on 10 May, radio contact was lost and on 20 May they were given up for dead. Meanwhile they had surmounted the rock and another ice-fall to make camp at 5,660 metres. Having sorted out what they needed for what looked like a quick ascent they continued and by 13 May had reached about 6,800 metres. The top seemed quite close but avalanches, route-finding and weather problems slowed them down, and food and fuel ran out. It took five more days to finish the climb, Schubert by now having badly frozen feet. As they descended the weather turned bad and avalanches almost dragged them from the face. Lower down the fixed ropes had been removed as the rest of the expedition retreated; even base camp had been evacuated before they arrived.

1981. Winter Ascent

A Canadian group climbed the normal route as training for the Canadian Everest expedition.

1987. Central Rib of North Face

An American team, led by S. Brimmer, ascended the Subje Khola. The approach to the rib was complicated, going around, across and into crevasses. Several séracs also had to be climbed on

▲ *The southern aspect of Annapurna Dakshin seen from Pun Hill (Gordon Larkins)*

the way to the rock wall at the base of the rib. Rope was fixed up the steep rock wall to its junction with a long, steep snowfield. Sheer rock and narrow loose ledges made the siting of Camp II very difficult; eventually it was placed at 5,950 metres. The route zig-zagged along the very exposed rib to a 30-metre high vertical ice wall, the last barrier to the upper snowfields and summit plateau. On 10 October, three-and-a-half weeks after reaching base camp, T. Schinhofen and Sherpa Pemba Norbu got to the top at 3.15 p.m. from the third camp at 6,955 metres.

ANNAPURNA DAKSHIN
(Annapurna South, Moditse)
Height: 7,219 metres
Subsidiary peaks: Central, 7,071
  metres; North, 7,010 metres
Lat./Long.: 28°31' 04" 83°48' 30"
First ascent: 1964 via North Ridge

During their visit to the Annapurna area in 1953, Basil Goodfellow and Frank Yates noted that there might be a route up the east flank of the south ridge. However in 1964 the second Kyoto University expedition to the Himalaya made their base camp higher up in the Annapurna sanctuary, and attacked the peak from the east. Their first choice of route, the southeast ridge (to the central summit) from the col between Annapurna Dakshin and Patal Hiunchuli, proved to be impossible, so they tackled a steep ice and snow spur ('Sérac Ridge') leading to the north ridge. Eventually Camp V was placed at 6,600 metres on a small snow terrace, the last spot for a tent below the main ridge. The first assault team lost so much time step-cutting and clearing the final cornice that it was 3.40 p.m. when they reached the central summit; they decided there was insufficient time to continue.

Next day two parties made good progress to the ridge. S. Uyeo and Sherpa Mingma Tsering gained the highest point after three hours, but the other pair were unable to reach the northern summit which lies in the opposite direction.

1970. South Face
Four Frenchmen from Chamonix climbed the middle of the exposed 3,000-metre high face. The route was a zigzag which involved climbing directly up portions of very steep séracs; higher up they were able to gain a spur on the face. The summit pair had a hard fight to gain the summit ridge: the final 100 metres became perpendicular and a terrible wind blew from the north. Too late to reach the summit that day, and unable to descend in darkness, they bivouaced and reached the top at 6 a.m. on a beautiful morning.

1972. Southeast Ridge
Three Japanese reached the central summit via the southeast ridge.

1976. East Face
A British Forces expedition from Hong Kong made a route to the southeast ridge. The face climb consisted of a stepped ridge of snow and ice to Camp IV (6,250 metres) below an ice cliff thirty metres high. A further 300 metres brought them to the ridge and a bivouac at 6,860 metres, whence the summit was reached despite a strong wind.

1978. Southwest Ridge
Climbers from Meiji University followed the very steep rocky ridge on which other Japanese had given up in 1974 at 6,100 metres. Above Camp III (6,400 metres) they left the ridge and climbed on the south face, on 60°–70° slopes. Two parties reached the top.

1979. West Face
Polish climbers made an alpine-style ascent with four bivouacs. Two others on the north face disappeared.

GANGAPURNA
Height: 7,455 metres
Lat./Long.: 28°38' 18" 83°57' 00"
First ascent: 1965 via East Ridge from
  the South

Günther Hauser's German expedition climbed the peak from the East Annapurna glacier via the south flank and east ridge. From a very low base camp five camps were needed. The chief difficulty was a 400-metre, 55° snow and ice face between Camps IV and V. All eight climbers and three Sherpas got to the top.

1972. West Ridge
A Japanese party from Nagano climbed this ridge from the south. On 15 October two members and Sherpa Girme Dorje reached the summit from Camp IV. Next day the higher camp failed to make radio contact with Camp II. Two Sherpas sent to investigate reported that the camp and its occupants had disappeared, as subsequently they did also.

1981. South Face
A four-man Canadian party was reduced to two when one member succumbed to mountain sickness at 6,400 metres after surmounting the lower ice slope. The other pair, James Blench and John Lauchlan, turned the upper rock band in three days by a ramp and gully system of tricky mixed climbing and brittle ice. On the fourth day a short rock pitch led them out of the exit gully to the summit snow slopes, and eventually the top.

1983. North Face to East Ridge
A party of Yugoslavian climbers ascended the east side of the north

face by a route 1,300 metres high to reach the east ridge at just over 7,000 metres. In all, over 1,200 metres of rope were fixed. It was decided that the assault should be made from Camp II (6,100 metres). On the east ridge the wind was so strong that at times the climbers had to crawl.

KHANGSAR KANG
(Roc Noire)
Height: 7,485 metres
Lat./Long.: 28° 36′ 50″ 83° 52′ 29″
First ascent: 1969 via East Ridge from the South

In 1964 Japanese climbers led by S. Shima reached about 7,140 metres. Five years later members of a German expedition led by L. Greissl reached the top on 13–14 May.

▲

The northern side of Gangapurna (A. R. Allan)

Roc Noire seen from first bivouac on the North Face of Gangapurna (A. R. Allan)

▼

▲
The Nilgiri peaks (Kurt Diemberger)

NILGIRI NORTH

Height: 7,061 metres
Lat./Long.: 28°41'21" 83°44'48"
First ascent: 1962 via North Face and
Northwest Ridge

A Dutch party led by C. G. Egeler, with Lionel Terray as climbing leader, travelled up the Kali Gandaki to the northern approaches to the peak. The ascent was accomplished without incident, Terray and four others completing the climb.

1981. Traverse from Tilitso West

A Japanese team climbed the north ridge of Tilitso West, from which a narrow ridge leads for four kilometres west to Nilgiri North over two subsidiary peaks. From a bivouac beyond the top of Tilitso West the assault team continued along the ridge, followed by their support party, and were held up on 6 May by a blizzard. Next day Etsuo Hino and Toyohumi Miyazaki got to the top of Nilgiri North in fourteen hours.

P.7010

Location: south of Annapurna IV
Lat./Long.: 28°31'28" 84°04'42"

P.7069

Location: east of Tarke Kang
Lat./Long.: 28°36'19" 83°54'58"

P.7739

Location: northeast of Annapurna II
Lat./Long: 28°32'05" 84°07'18"

TARKE KANG (Glacier Dome)

Height: 7,193 metres
Lat./Long.: 28°36'25" 83°53'28"
First ascent: 1964 via South Ridge

Japanese Mitsuhiro Nishimura and Sherpa Dorje ascended the south ridge from the west to the summit plateau.

1981. North Face

This enormous ice wall was climbed in October by the Italians C. Schranz, M. Roncaglioni and G. Tagliferri with Sherpa Gombu. After a long glacier approach Camp III was established at the foot of the north face (about 5,500 metres). Camp IV was placed inside a large sérac on the face (6,100 metres) and the ascent completed next day.

1983. West Ridge

This was climbed by the Austrians R. Mayr, F. Kleissl and O. Ölz, with Sherpas Ang-Nima and Gyaltzen. The route went up a 300-metre high ice gully, then over ice slopes to the ridge between Tarke Kang and Khangsar Kang, followed by a long snow slope. Descending alone Ölz had to bivouac and was avalanched, but escaped more or less unscathed.

1983. West Ridge

Three Austrians and two Sherpas made the ascent in one day, taking twelve hours. The route followed was from the south, first up a 300-metre high ice gully, then over ice slopes to the west ridge.

TILITSO (Tilicho)

Height: 7,134 metres
Lat./Long.: 28°40′58″ 83°48′50″
First ascent: 1978 via North Ridge

After climbing Nilgiri North in October 1962, a Dutch expedition, with Lionel Terray, visited Tilitso and reached the east col as the weather was beginning to turn very wintry. The peak was then taken off the permitted list until 1978 when it was climbed by a French expedition in October. From base camp to Camp I (6,150 metres) took a week, 700 metres of rope with the climbers having to fix up a very difficult spur leading to the northwest shoulder. On 10 October Emin, the sirdar, broke trail in deep snow as far as 6,645 metres which allowed his companion, Emanuel Schmutz, to reach the summit by mid-afternoon.

1982. Winter Ascent

A three-man Sherpa party, the first all-Sherpa expedition, climbed the north ridge, using two camps above Tilitso Lake, between 17–26 January.

There have been several recent attempts on the north ridge route, the most successful getting to within a 100 metres of the top before being forced back by bad weather.

P.7700

Location: mid-way on ridge between Annapurna I and Varah Shikar

On the north face of Annapurna a well-defined spur rises to a subsidiary peak (7,700 metres) on the ridge between Annapurna and Varah Shikar. In 1984 a French party, led by H. Sigayret, reached about 7,200 metres before a fatal accident caused the expedition to be called off. After a dangerous glacier approach the route started on the west side of the spur and proceeded over a combination of rock, ice and snow on ice. Ropes were fixed more on account of the hardness of the ice than the steepness. The final obstacle above the high point was a fifty-metre high sérac. Two camps were placed on the spur, at 6,100 and 6,900 metres.

VARAH SHIKAR (Fang)

Height: 7,647 metres
Lat./Long.: 28°34′41″ 83°48′12″
First ascent: 1980 via West Ridge from the South

The Fang is a sharp rock and ice tooth crowning three jagged ridges and sérac-covered faces. Its south face rises steeply about 4,900 metres. In 1975 an Austrian expedition attempted Annapurna I by a route leading up the west ridge and over Fang, but abandoned it after Franz Tegischer was killed by an avalanche at Camp II (5,500 metres).

In 1979 Italian climbers attempted the southeast ridge. The route followed a steep rock, mixed rock and ice cliff 900 metres high. They reached the heavily corniced crest of the ridge at 6,360 metres, but the snow was unstable and the weather unsettled.

The first ascent was made the following year by an Austrian expedition. They climbed a 2,450-metre high face which they considered was steeper and more difficult than the Matterhorn North Face. Above, the climbing on the sharp ice ridge and steep flanks required great concentration, particularly with the constant threat of lightning. It took two weeks to overcome the chief climbing difficulties. After a break caused by deep, fresh snow the ascent was completed without incident.

Dhaulagiri Himal

CHUREN HIMAL WEST

Height: 7,371 metres
Subsidiary peak: Central, c.7,320 metres
Lat./Long.: 28°43′55″ 83°12′45″
First ascent: 1970 via Southeast Flank/Buttress

In 1954 a British party led by J. O. M. Roberts reconnoitred the Dhaulagiri range and were able to observe this peak from the north during their ascent of Putha Hiunchuli.

After climbing in the Mukut Himal in 1962, a Japanese expedition put a couple of camps up the mountain from the north but gave up on account of monsoon storms and lack of time. The 1969 Italian expedition ascended the Ghustung Khola and reconnoitred the east and west ridges, deciding eventually to tackle the latter by way of the difficult rock of the southern spur. After placing their highest camp on the west ridge, the attempt was called off at 6,600 metres. A Japanese group in 1970 climbed the central and western summits via the southeast flank and buttress.

1975. West Ridge

Two Japanese groups made this ascent in pre- and post-monsoon expeditions.

CHUREN HIMAL EAST

Height: 7,371 metres
Lat./Long.: 28°44′37″ 83°13′47″
First ascent: 1970 via East Ridge

South Korean Kim Ho Sup and Rinsing Angyal claimed the first

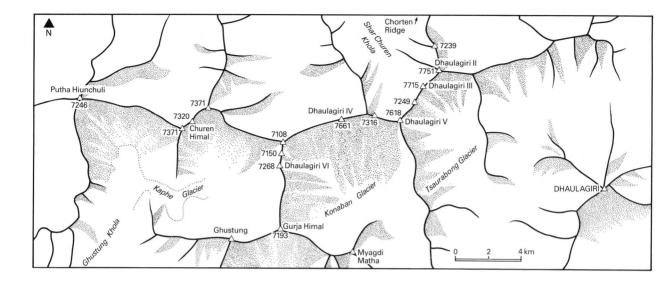

ascent of the peak on 29 April 1970 via the east ridge. The Japanese climber T. Serizawa, who reached about 7,150 metres on the same route, questioned the Korean claim. During the period 1977–82 there were three expeditions which attempted routes from the north and on the southeast ridge.

1987. South–East Ridge Attempt

Eight Korean climbers found the final summit ridge of knife-edge ice too difficult. The weather was deteriorating and they were tired after a month on the mountain. A Korean and a Sherpa reached a height of 7,200 metres on 11 May.

1988. Southeast Face/Southwest Ridge

South Koreans Shin Jang Seop and Lee Heung Sik made the second ascent of the peak on 7 May.

DHAULAGIRI II

Height: 7,751 metres
Lat./Long.: 28° 45' 46" 83° 23' 22"
*First ascent: 1971 via West Flank and
    Southwest Ridge*

In 1954 J. O. M. Roberts led a party to the Dhaulagiri Himal and observed the northern aspects of the main range from the Barbung

Khola, a distance of about fifteen kilometres. The next four expeditions (British, South Korean, and two Japanese) failed to surmount the 5,200-metre high Chorten Ridge which guards the north-western approach. However in 1963 Walter Gstrein and Ernst Kulhavy, members of an Austrian expedition, discovered a way which gave access from the village of Mukut across the ridge to a basin at the foot of the upper slopes. In bad weather the climbers spearheaded the attack to about

7,000 metres, at which point Sherpa Dorje had to be evacuated with frostbitten toes. The general condition of the porters and imminence of the monsoon prevented a further attempt.

The second Austrian expedition in 1971, led by Franz Huber, crossed the Chorten Ridge and set up camp in the basin. They safely negotiated the two-kilometre long traverse under giant ice overhangs and, after two attempts, set up camp at 6,000 metres, remaining there for a week because of bad

▲ *Dhaulagiri II from camp on Dhaulagiri (Kurt Diemberger)*

weather. In 1963 the ice barrier, which cuts off the summits of Dhaulagiri II and III at a height of 6,000–7,000 metres, had defeated the climbers, but this time, after a thorough study of the eventual route from the Chorten Ridge, they were able to surmount this obstacle by way of an ice gully. On 18 May the two teams (Adolf Huber and Sherpa Jangbu; Adolf Weissensteiner and Ronald Fear) proceeded without further difficulty through knee-deep snow up to the corniced southwest ridge and the top.

1978. East Ridge from South

The first attempt on this route was made by a Japanese expedition in 1975, from the Tsaurabong glacier. From a glacier camp they followed a small feeder ridge dropping down from the first peak on the east ridge at about 6,700 metres. The route then traversed the south side of the ridge under a rock wall over steep snow and hard ice. From now on the weather was good only in the mornings. They had difficulty finding a site for another camp, so decided to try from Camp III. The assault team passed the prepared part of the route and continued on the south face up to 7,300 metres, but going on would have meant one or two bivouacs and they were recalled. The successful 1978 Japanese group followed the same route, the leader Yoshio Ogawa and Shoji Koiko reaching the summit with one bivouac from the fifth camp.

1979. Traverses

A large Japanese expedition led by Michiko Takahashi, the only woman in the team, climbed the east ridge of Dhaulagiri II and the south ridge of Dhaulagiri V, putting camps on both summits. Parties then traversed from one to the other, via the top of Dhaulagiri III, in both directions.

P.7239

Location: 2 km from Dhaulagiri II on the North Ridge

DHAULAGIRI III

Height: 7,715 metres
Lat./Long.: 28°45′16″ 83°22′46″
First ascent: 1973 via Southwest Face from North

A German group led by K. Schreckenbach crossed the difficult Chorten Ridge and then had to wait out heavy snowfall for ten days. Then after two days of very slow and strenuous progress Camp III was made in a snow cave at 5,850 metres. A forced climb was made to a height of 7,000 metres, where the climbers made another snow cave camp at the foot of the steep west ridge flanked by ice. A hurricane-type storm piled up huge amounts of snow on the ridge making it impossible to climb. However, as the sky above was cloudless and the snow condition good Schreckenbach, Saler and Habert climbed the rocky southwest wall in the fall line from the summit, which they reached just after midday. The storm continued to rage around them and they stayed on top only ten minutes before descending to spend a cheerless night in the snow cave without food or drink.

1973. West Ridge

K. Hiller, P. von Gizycki, K. Sussmilch and Sirdar Norbu, members of K. Schreckenbach's expedition, reached the summit three days after the first ascent, having climbed the west ridge in windless weather.

1979. Traverses

Members of a large Japanese expedition traversed the peak in two directions en route to Dhaulagiri II and V.

DHAULAGIRI IV

Height: 7,661 metres
Lat./Long.: 28°44′10″ 83°18′55″
First ascent: 1975 via West Ridge from the Kaphe Glacier

The early expeditions attacked Dhaulagiri VI from the Kaphe glacier, under the impression they were attempting this peak which was hidden from them. This error was avoided in 1970 when an Austrian party, led by R. Hoyer, gained the west ridge from the Konaban glacier. They placed three camps along the ridge, which they compared to the Peuterey ridge of Mont Blanc, to a height of 6,900 metres. Sometime between 9–11 November five climbers and a Sherpa were overwhelmed at or above the top camp, and no trace of them was found despite ground and air searches. Japanese attempts on the Austrian route in 1971–72 were thwarted, by bad weather and the death of a climber from pulmonary oedema respectively. This route claimed another victim the following year when a British climber, A. Dewison, fell while descending from camp at about 6,750 metres.

Two groups in 1973–74 attempted a completely different route by approaching the mountain from the north. The 1973 Austrian expedition, led by Adolf Huber, crossed the Chorten Ridge and ascended the Shar Churen Khola over seemingly endless slopes of snow and ice. Above their camp at 6,800 metres rose a very steep, mixed face, 400 metres high, which appeared to be the only way to the knife-edged, corniced summit ridge. On reaching the ridge further progress was found to be impossible so they descended to try farther east. The ridge was reached twice more but shortage of supplies and then a bad storm defeated them. Next year a Royal Air Force expedition had reached only 5,250 metres when falling ice hit a group ferrying loads. Two Sherpas were killed instantly and another died later.

Ironically, perhaps, the first ascent was made from the direction of the original attempts, that is, from the upper Kaphe glacier towards Dhaulagiri VI. In 1970 Japanese climbers got as far as 'Gama Peak' north of Dhaulagiri VI; two years later their compatriots pressed the attack on over Gama Peak and Junction Peak. In 1975 more Japanese climbers followed this route and succeeded in putting a camp (about 6,950 metres) beyond the west col. The first attempt failed at about 7,200 metres, after which S. Kawazu and E. Yasuda set off on 9 May from a bivouac some 100 metres higher. They were seen at 4 p.m., just below the top, and later radioed that they had reached the summit just before 6 p.m. and were bivouacing. Next morning there was no sign of them and searchers later found their bodies roped together and lying beneath the south face of the peak.

1975. West Ridge from Konaban Glacier

A post-monsoon Japanese expedition led by K. Takahashi approached the mountain by climbing the southeast ridge of Myagdi Matha (6,273 metres) into the inner basin of the Konaban glacier. From here they gained the ridge at the west col and completed the route which had defied four earlier parties.

P.7108 (Junction Peak)

Lat./Long.: 28°43'20" 83°16'40"
First ascent: 1972 via Traverse from Dhaulagiri VI to IV

This peak was climbed up the south ridge as part of a traverse from 'Gama Peak' during a Japanese attempt to reach Dhaulagiri IV.

1975. West Ridge

This route was followed by Japanese climbers en route to Dhaulagiri IV, on which the summit pair died during their descent.

P.7150 ('Gama Peak')

Location: just south of Junction Peak on the ridge leading to Dhaulagiri VI
First ascent: 1970 from South Col

Climbed by K. Nakajima and G. Nakeyama, members of a post-monsoon group attempting Dhaulagiri IV.

P.7316

Location: on the ridge between Dhaulagiri V and VI at the top of the spur dividing the Churen Khola and Shar Churen Khola
Lat./Long.: 28°44'16" 83°20'19"

DHAULAGIRI V

Height: 7,618 metres
Lat./Long.: 28°44'04" 83°21'56"
First ascent: 1975 via South Ridge from Tsaurabong Glacier

Both 1971 Japanese expeditions suffered fatalities. The Kenryo Alpine Club gave up their attempt on the southwest face when H. Tezuka, K. Aoki and T. Yanagisawa fell to the Konaban glacier from a height of 7,000 metres. They were descending because Yanagisawa was unwell; a fourth climber behind them witnessed the accident. In the autumn the Kyusho University Alpine Club were attempting the south ridge when two members and two Sherpas were swept down 600 metres in an avalanche just above Camp II. Fukashi Chiiwa was buried and suffocated, but the others survived.

No such disasters befell the large 1975 Japanese expedition which was very carefully planned. From the Tsaurabong glacier they tackled the southeast face and fixed

rope on the 50° snow and ice, up to 'White Peak' on the end of the south ridge. After two camps and fixed rope on much of the narrow, icy ridge, Masaaki Moriaka and Sherpa Pemba Tsering reached the top on 1 May.

1979. Traverses

Members of a large Japanese expedition climbed the south ridge and camped on the summit during traverses of the peak to and from Dhaulagiri II.

P.7249

Location: 2 km north of Dhaulagiri V
Lat./Long.: 28°44'45" 83°22'34"

DHAULAGIRI VI

Location: the name given to the peak at the eastern head of the Kaphe Glacier, obscuring the higher Dhaulagiri IV
Height: 7,268 metres
Lat./Long.: 28°42'30" 83°16'32"
First ascent: 1970 via West Spur and South Ridge

The first two parties to tackle this peak were led by Jimmy Roberts who was misled into thinking that he was on the much higher Dhaulagiri IV, which in fact lies some six kilometres behind it. In 1962 the climbers made an ascending traverse of the southwest face from the upper Kaphe glacier. Two Sherpas reached 6,400 metres and reported that the proposed finish up the northwest corner looked feasible; but the climb was abandoned because of the apparent danger of ice avalanches sweeping the traverse. In 1965 they followed the same route up to 5,800 metres, then tried to gain the south ridge by climbing the ice shoulder on the southwest flank of the summit pyramid. The weather deteriorated and snow conditions on the steeper slopes were difficult, tedious and dangerous. Subsequent heavy snowfalls confirmed the expedition's decision to pull out. In 1970 the aim of the Kansai Mountaineering Club was to climb Dhaualgiri IV via Dhaulagiri VI. From the upper Kaphe glacier they made a difficult rock and ice route up the west ridge which descends from the south shoulder. On 16 April, Camp VI was established at 7,000 metres on the plateau of the main south ridge and next day four members climbed to the summit. The longer than expected distance from there to the top of Dhaulagiri IV – and a steep ice cliff near the col on its southwest ridge – compelled them to give up at that point.

1983. Southwest Buttress
The Canadians D. Griffith, P. Carter, A. Sole and R. Rohn made a new route alpine-style in six days from base camp at 4,100 metres. The route followed an elegant and objectively safe ice buttress. The climbing was over deep snow and hard ice in unsettled weather.

GURJA HIMAL (Sauwala)
Height: 7,193 metres
Lat./Long.: 28° 40′ 26″ 83° 16′ 37″
First ascent: 1969 via West
*   Face/Ridge*

During his 1962 reconnaissance and attempt to reach Dhaulagiri IV, Jimmy Roberts and two Sherpas climbed Ghustung North (6,529 metres) which is three kilometres west of Gurja Himal. From there they were able to study the whole of the western side of the peak.

The 1969 Japanese post-monsoon expedition camped on the Kaphe glacier near a previous British camp. After gaining an upper snowfield they were able to see the west side of the peak, but the going was hard in deep snow. The first team reached 6,900 metres before fatigue drove them back. Two days later,

▲

Gurja Himal–southern outlier of the main Dhaulagiri chain–seen here from due east on Pun Hill above the Ghora Pani La

T. Saegi and Sherpa Lhakpa Tenzing followed their tracks, and then up a snow and ice ridge to reach the summit.

1972. Northwest Spur, North Ridge
Members of a French expedition reached the summit by both a new route and the Japanese one. The new route followed the Japanese approach to Dhaulagiri IV, then via a rock band to the upper snow basin and the foot of the northwest spur. From there, on 21 October, S. Sarthou and B. Mathieu reached the summit with one camp, descending by the Japanese route which had been prepared.

1985. West Ridge

A Japanese-Nepalese expedition made a new route with three high camps finishing up the northwest face. During the descent the leader fell and later died. In the same year a Rumanian was killed on the south face of Konaban while attempting a route from the south.

PUTHA HIUNCHULI (Dhaulagiri VII)

Height: 7,246 metres
Lat./Long.: 28°44'56" 83°8'55"
First ascent: 1954 via Northeast face

J. O. M. Roberts and Ang Nyima ascended this peak during a reconnaissance of the Dhaulagiri massif.

1972. South Ridge/Face

Two Japanese parties climbed this route during pre- and post-monsoon expeditions.

Nalakankar Himal

GURLA MANDHATA (Naimona'nyi, Namunani)

Location: in Tibet
Height: 7,728 metres (7,694 metres according to latest Chinese survey)
Lat./Long.: 30°26'18" 81°17'57"
First ascent: 1985 from the North

In the summer of 1905 T. G. Longstaff accompanied C. A. Sherring, of the Indian Civil Service, on his trip to Tibet, the reason for which was to see that the Treaty of Lhasa, recently negotiated by Francis Younghusband, was being upheld as regards the Bhotias for whom he was responsible. Leaving Sherring to his official business, Longstaff set out to explore the vast and isolated massif of Gurla Mandhata, a mountain famous in religious and epic literature, the topography of which was completely unknown, although the positions and heights of four peaks had been fixed by intersection by the Indian Survey. On 18 July Longstaff and his two Alpine guides plus six porters left with a week's provisions. They made directly for the foot of the first western spur, toiling up stony slopes towards the snowline and eventually stopping to camp at about 5,500 metres, where the porters turned back.

The next day turned into a rest day but on 20 July they got off at 2 a.m. and were soon ascending a steep snow dome. Working their way towards the northern side they saw another great shoulder, the main western ridge. On gaining the first top they were disappointed to discover that a tremendous drop separated their outlier from the

(Alpine Club Collection)

Thomas George Longstaff (1875–1964)

Tom Longstaff had a medical degree but never practised, being of independent means. Instead he devoted his active life to travel and climbing, and became the leading mountain explorer of his era. As his fascinating memoirs (*This My Voyage*) show, he ranged across the mountains of the northern hemisphere, from Canada to the Himalaya, over a period of thirty-five years. He was a pioneer of the light climbing expedition, and was quick to take advantage of the latest equipment. After a successful, guideless visit to the Caucasus in 1903, he paid his first visit to the Himalaya in 1905 where he attempted to penetrate the Nanda Devi sanctuary by way of the col which bears his name, south of Nanda Devi East. In the same year he reached 7,000 metres on Gurla Mandhata and visited the Api region in northwest Nepal on the trail of Henry Savage-Landor. Two years later he became the first man to reach the summit of a mountain over 7,000 metres when he climbed Trisul near Nanda Devi. One of his major contributions to geography came in 1909 when he ascended the Bilafond glacier, crossed the Saltoro Pass and explored the Siachen glacier in the Karakoram, discovering the group of high peaks now known as Teram Kangri. Longstaff also took part in the 1922 Everest expedition and made several tours to arctic Spitsbergen, Greenland and Baffin Island. He served as Honorary Secretary of the Royal Geographical Society, receiving the Founder's Medal in 1928. He was President of the Alpine Club in the period 1947–49.

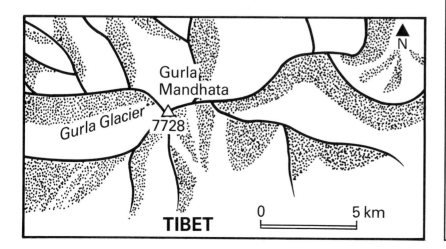

main peak. They were now obliged either to transfer to the main ridge or advance up the glacier in between; Longstaff chose the former. Accordingly they descended to re-provision and move camp.

The main ridge was similarly stony and waterless and they did not reach snow until a height of about 5,800 metres, where they camped. Next day with the weather fine they followed the easy ridge on good snow. By mid-afternoon they were at about 7,000 metres but the top was a long way off and clouds were gathering. Deciding to descend the southern slope of the ridge to a suitable bivouac spot, they had gone only thirty or forty metres when the slope avalanched under the top man, Henri Brocherel. He shot down, sweeping Longstaff from his feet. Alexis Brocherel grabbed Longstaff but was dragged down in turn. Riding the snow wave they shot over several outcrops until the slide stopped on a gentler

▲

Isolated giants on the Tibetan plateau. Gurla Mandhata seen from the southwest; to the left in the distance is the holy mountain Kailas

slope; they had fallen over 900 metres in a minute or two.

Still in the mood to continue, next day they advanced up the higher Gurla glacier, making for the final ridge a little to the south of the highest point. The heat was extreme and by 3 p.m. two of them were unable to continue and a cold bivouac in a snow cave ensued. Making an early start next morning they climbed the last ice-fall for over an hour before being halted by a long crevasse with an overhanging wall on the far side. This was impassable in the dark and by 4 a.m. Longstaff was so cold that he could not go on. Henri was keen to carry on, alone if need be, but Longstaff could not countenance his solo return through the ice-fall later in the day and felt

compelled to order retreat. Descending they found no one waiting for them, and all their equipment still high on the mountain; thus they had to endure several days of considerable hardship before meeting up with some of their porters.

The next recorded visit to the peak was made in 1936 by the Austrian mountaineer Herbert Tichy and Kitar, a porter who had been on Nanga Parbat. In a secret attempt they reached about 7,165 metres before they were turned back by fresh snow and bad weather.

The 1985 Japanese-Chinese expedition established base camp at the tongue of the Zaromalangpa Glacier on 2 May, a reconnaissance having been made the year before. Just over three weeks later, Camp IV was placed at 7,420 metres, some 1,800 metres higher. The ascent was made from there the next day, and again two days later. Afterwards the team carried out scientific work.

Gurans Himal

API

Location: Yoka Pahar section
Height: 7,132 metres (East peak)
Subsidiary peak: West, 7,100 metres
Lat./Long.: 30°00'15" 80°56'00"
First ascent: 1960 via Northwest Face

This peak lies in the northwest tip of Nepal. The area was visited illicitly in 1899 by A. H. Savage-Landor who wrote an account (*Tibet and Nepal*, Black, 1905) of a peak over 7,000 metres high which he called 'Lumpa'. After overpowering the Nepalese frontier guards he penetrated the Nampa Khola and explored the glacier system at its head. He described how in the course of twelve hours, he had ascended and descended 3,000 metres wearing a straw hat and shoes, and carrying a 'cane'. In 1905 T. G. Longstaff managed to secure three days' grace from the Nepalese frontier guards, during which he located Savage-Landor's camps and cairn marking his highest point – actually about 5,000 metres – on a spur leading to no very high peak. This excursion took place to the north of Api.

The first photographic record of Api was made in 1936 by the Swiss geologists Arnold Heim and August Gansser, although they mistakenly called it Nampa, which is another high peak seven kilometres to the east of Api. Gansser's photograph showed a great ice cap rising gently from a height of about 6,100 metres. In 1953, with Nepal now open to foreigners, W. H. Murray and J. B. Tyson made a detailed reconnaissance of the western and northern approaches, and attempted to get on the northwest ridge. From the Api Khola the western approach was guarded by an ice-fall raked by avalanches. Having moved round to the north to the Nampa Khola their explor-

ation was hampered by the onset of the monsoon, and they got no further than Longstaff had done.

In 1954 Piero Ghiglione led an Italian party to explore the Api-Nampa-Saipal chain from the south, and to attempt the ascent of Api. Their Api base camp was set up in the Api Khola to the northwest of the peak on the same spot as Murray and Tyson had camped the year before. From the West Api glacier the best route appeared to be up steep grassy slopes to some rock buttresses and then on the first upper glacier, and from there up another glacier to the foot of the final crevassed, ice face which gives access to the twin peaks of Api. The younger members of the party were in too much of a hurry and disregarded Ghiglione's advice. G. Rosenkrantz succumbed to exhaustion and exposure during the summit attempt; later, B. Barenghi disappeared during a solo bid for the top. Sherpa Gyalgen made a valiant but unsuccessful attempt to rescue Rosenkrantz.

In 1960 the Doshisha Alpine Society expedition from Japan followed Ghiglione's route. The section between the second and third camps was threatened by ice blocks falling from the main peak and they had to traverse a steep slope over bad snow on top of ice. After returning to base camp the second part of the ascent was commenced on 7 May and the fourth camp quickly established on the north ridge at 6,600 metres. The two climbers set off at 5 a.m. on 10 May on a fine cloudless morning, but with a strong northwest wind behind them. The slope leading to the summit was very long, just as they had been warned. At times their crampons would not grip on the hard blue ice and every step had to be cut. Gradually they approached the huge summit cornice and gingerly made their way along it for a short

distance to the highest point of all just before noon. The climb was repeated next day.

1971 and 1973. West Ridge Attempts
Japanese attempts were abandoned at just over 6,000 metres as the route was difficult and dangerous.

1978. East Ridge
The Italian route gained the Api-Nampa col after Grade IV-V difficulties and 55°–65° ice. They then followed the east ridge, first sharp and corniced, then with great rock pillars. The top was reached on 16 October by C. Bianchi, M. Maggi, A. Rocca and V. Tamagni in terrible weather.

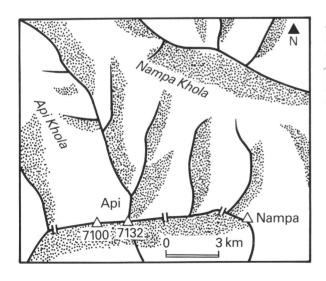

Distant view of the Api–Nampa range from the jeep track (unusable) near Baitadi (Crispin Agnew)

Above Camp III (6,220 metres) an ice nose led to a second glacier, then a 55° ice ramp to a third glacier. The 50° summit slopes were ice, the upper part rotten and covered with unstable powder snow. Three thousand metres of rope were fixed. The summit party were obliged to turn back because of bad snow and ice conditions, fatigue and frostbite.

1983. Northwest Ridge

Polish climbers made the third ascent of Api in winter. Camps I and II were placed on the route of first ascent. On 22 December T. Piotrowski, A. Bielún and Z. Terlikowski started up the northwest ridge, bivouacing at 5,800 and 6,000 metres. Bielún

1980. South Face Attempt

A British Army Mountaineering Association group reached a point about 125 metres from the top. The route followed more or less a difficult ridge, the main problem being a seventy-five metre high gendarme at about 5,360 metres.

South Face of Api seen during the last stages of the approach march (Crispin Agnew)

◀

The east ridge was ruled out because of the steep and rotten quality of the lower part; there was a similar problem in getting on the south ridge. Finally they tackled the west ridge and reached a height of about 6,300 metres from where the route to the top looked difficult but feasible. The death of one member and an early monsoon prevented any further advance.

The first ascent was made by a Japanese group by way of the south ridge, using four intermediate camps. The deputy leader and Sherpa Pasang Phutar III were the summit climbers.

1985. West Ridge, Southwest Face and Traverse

Six members of a Spanish expedition ascended the west ridge. Meanwhile, another group climbed the southwest face and descended the west ridge.

went on ahead and was seen for the last time as he reached the summit. Piotrowski also managed to get to the top but had to bivouac in a snow hole on the way down.

SAIPAL

Location: Saipal Himal section
Height: 7,031 metres
Lat./Long.: 29°53'14" 81°29'43"
First ascent: 1963 via South Ridge

In 1954 an Austrian team led by Rudolf Jonas reconnoitred the peak from their base camp at the foot of the 3,000-metre high south face, which was found to have steep ice slopes and adverse sloping strata.

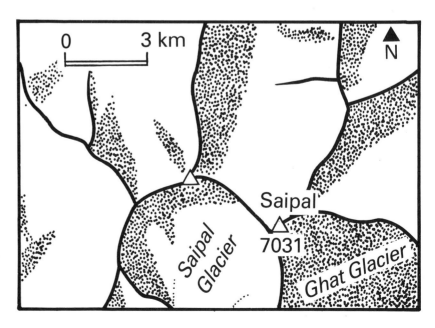

Bibliography

Agnew, C. (1981), 'Soldiers on Api', *AJ*, 86, pp. 167–71. See also, *HJ*, 40, 1984, pp. 65–9.

Allan, S. (1987), 'Gangapurna north face 1985', *HJ*, 43, pp. 125–6.

Allen, R. and Garin, R. (1986), 'Ganesh Himal', *HJ*, 42, pp. 26–34.

Azpiazu, J. (1988), 'Expedition to Annapurna II', *HJ*, 44, pp. 182–5

Bonicelli, A. and Calegari, N. (1975), 'Himal Chuli, 1974', *HJ*, 33, pp. 53–7.

Cleare, J. (1980), 'Himalchuli', *HJ*, 36, pp. 33–40.

Connor, E. (1979), 'Annapurna II attempt', *AAJ*, 22, pp. 59–61.

Consiglio, P. (1972), 'Churen Himal, 1969', *HJ*, 31, pp. 163–9.

Eidher, E. (1965), 'The 1963 Austrian Dhaula Himal Expedition', *HJ*, 25, pp. 63–66.

Fear, R. (1972), 'Dhaulagiri II', *AAJ*, 18, pp. 21–5.

Fukuzawa, K. (1972), 'Japanese Mt. Api Expedition, 1971', *HJ* 31, 150–2.

Gicquel, M. (1972), 'Annapurna South Peak (7,195 metres), south face, 1970', *HJ*, 31, pp. 181–5.

Goodfellow, B. (1954), 'North of Pokhara', *HJ*, 18, pp. 81–6.

Graf, L. (1972), 'Dhaulagiri IV, 1969', *HJ*, 31, pp. 153–6.

Hannigan, C. (1988), 'Winter on Annapurna IV', *AJ*, 88, pp. 177–8.

Hauser, G. (1966), 'German Himalayan expedition, 1965', *AJ*, 71, pp. 89–97.

Huber, F. (1972), 'Dhaulagiri 2', *AJ*, 77, pp. 168–9. See also, *HJ*, 31, 1972, pp.192–4.

Kameyama, Y. (1976), 'Dhaulagiri II – east ridge, 1975', *HJ*, 34, pp. 31–4.

Kearney, S. (1987), '1986 American Annapurna II Expedition', *HJ*, 43, pp. 121–3.

Kekus, N. (1985), 'Annual leave – Ganesh II south face', *AJ*, 90, pp. 71–3.

Miyazaki, E. (1971), 'Japanese Women's Annapurna III Expedition, 1970', *HJ*, 30, pp. 127–8.

Miyoshi, K. (1972), 'Gangapurna northwest ridge, 1971', *HJ*, 31, pp. 145–9.

Muraki, F. (1955), 'Uprising of the faithful (Ganesh Himal)', *MW*, pp. 129–32.

Nishamae, S. (1976), 'First ascent and tragedy on Dhaulagiri IV, 1975', *HJ*, 34, pp. 35–8.

Nomura, T. (1971), 'First ascent of Dhaulagiri VI, 1970', *HJ*, 30, pp. 141–6.

Noshi, T. (1975), 'Gangapurna 1974', *HJ*, 33, pp.46–8.

Piotrowski, T. (1985), 'Winter expedition to Api', *HJ*, 41, pp. 55–60.

Prochazka, V. (1972), 'Czechoslovac expedition to Annapurna', *HJ*, 31, pp. 195–9.

Roberts, J. (1955), 'Round about Dhaulagiri', *AJ*, 60, pp. 248–56.

Roberts, J. (1960), 'Annapurna II, 1960', *AJ*, 65, pp. 143–50.

Roberts, J. (1963), 'Dhaula Himal', *AJ*, 68, pp. 188–97.

Roberts, J. (1966), 'With the Royal Air Force on Dhaulagiri IV', *AJ*, 71, pp. 75–88.

Rutland, R. and Rutland, L. (1982), 'Annapurna III south face', *HJ*, 37, pp. 29–32.

Sahashi, T. (1975), 'Putha Hiunchuli, 1972', *HJ*, 33, pp. 49–52.

Sanchez, J. (1987), 'Tilicho Peak, 7,132 metres: north face, northeast ridge', *HJ*, 43, pp. 127–8.

Schreckenbach, K. and Gizycki, P. (1975), 'Dhaulagiri III', *AJ*, 80, pp. 198–201.

Sigayret, H. (1985), 'Nameless peak – Annapurna massif route in sketches', *HJ*, 41, pp. 45–9. (P.7700 between Annapurna I and Fang.)

Steinmetz, H. (1957), 'German Nepal Expedition 1955', *HJ*, 20, pp. 71–77.

Sumiyoshi, S. (1971), 'Peak 29 expeditions by the Osaka University Mountainering Club, 1961–70', *HJ*, 30, pp. 147–53.

Takahasi, M.(and others) (1972), 'Churen Himal, 1971: Tokyo University Ski Alpine Club Expedition', *HJ*, 31, pp. 174–80.

Tilman, H. (1951–52), 'Annapurna Himal and south side of Everest', *AJ*, 58, pp. 101–10.

Tsoukias, M. (1987), 'Annapurna South: east face 1985', *HJ*, 43, pp. 123–5.

Tyson, J. (1953–54), 'Exploring the Api and Nampa group', *AJ*, 59, pp. 421–7.

Uyeo, S. (1965), 'Ascent of Annapurna South Peak (Ganesh)', *AJ*, 70, pp. 213–17.

Yager, M. (1985), 'Himalchuli', *AAJ*, 27, pp. 84–8.

Yagihara, K. (1979), 'Dhaulagiri IV, 1975', *HJ*, 35, pp. 175–80.

Yakushi, Y. (1970), 'Gurja Himal: first ascent, 1969', *AJ*, 75, pp. 17–24. See also, *HJ*, 30, 1971, pp. 95–100.

Yamamoto, R. (1972), 'First ascent of Churen Himal', *AJ*, 77, pp. 105–9. See also, *HJ*, 31, 1972, pp. 170–3.

Zaharias, Z. (1985), 'Australian Army Nilgiri North (7,061 metres) Expedition, 1983', *HJ*, 41, pp. 50–4.

Kumaun and Garhwal Himalaya

The crest zone of the Great Himalaya passes southeastwards, in an almost straight line, through the Kumaun–Garhwal Himalaya. On this line stand the mountain groups of Satopanth and Chaukamba, at the head of the Gangotri glacier, and Nanda Devi. North of the Great Himalaya is the Zaskar range, unofficially regarded as the boundary between India and Tibet. The aspect is more Tibetan than Himalayan. Here lies Kamet, the first of these peaks to be approached.

Prior to the Nepalese War of 1814–16 the King of Nepal controlled much of the territory which includes the Kumaun–Garhwal Himalaya, and it was the interference of his Gurkhas with the affairs of the East India Company which led to the eventual campaign. During the period 1808–14 attempts to extend route surveys into the area were frequently frustrated, but in 1812 William Moorcroft and H. Y. Hearsey carried out a daring and successful journey. Disguised as fakirs, they took with them a pundit, Harbeh Dev, who counted their paces while Hearsey recorded their direction with a compass. After making the first crossing of the Niti La (east of Kamet) by

Europeans they reached Lake Manasarowar near Kailas where they solved some questions regarding the great rivers of India. Returning over the Niti La they were briefly imprisoned until released by special order of the King of Nepal. Their subsequent report and route map aroused considerable interest amongst geographers. Moorcroft's later and more famous travels were in the Karakoram and he died in Afghanistan in August 1825.

The survey of the Kumaun–Garhwal Himalaya began in 1815 as soon as the Gurkhas had withdrawn, but it was a slow process. The detail mapped was scanty – little more than the principal rivers and routes – but by 1819 the heights of the main peaks were being computed. One notable traveller of this period was G. W. Traill, the first Deputy Commissioner of Kumaun. In 1830 he crossed the main Himalayan axis between Nanda Devi and Nanda Kot, from the Pindari glacier to Martoli, by way of the difficult saddle still known as Traill's Pass. It was not crossed from north to south until Hugh Ruttledge did this in 1926, nearly a hundred years later.

The detailed exploration and

survey of the region proceeded in the 1840s and 1850s, though not always without difficulty. One of the most active survey assistants was W. H. Johnson (later to fall from grace as a result of his visit to the Kun Lun) who succeeded in establishing a survey station near the Nela pass (northwest of Kamet) after others had failed. The geologist and botanist Richard Strachey made interesting explorations in the middle of the century, as did also two of the Schlagintweit brothers, Robert and Adolphe, before the official survey parties arrived. Strachey was the first to determine the approximate heights of the peaks in the Kamet group, while the Schlagintweits traversed the range on the Tibetan side. However, much of the work done in this region was patient and painstaking rather than spectacular, for it was to be many years before anyone succeeded in penetrating the ring of high peaks surrounding Nanda Devi.

Because of the apparently insignificant face which the Kamet group presents from the Indian side, it attracted no attention until 1848 when Richard Strachey determined the height and position of its four peaks.

In 1855 two of the Schlagintweit brothers, Robert and Adolphe, approached from the northern side and claimed to have reached a height of over 6,700 metres on Kamet, but most probably on Abi Gamin which stands in front of Kamet on the Tibetan side. Little was known of the higher topography until the Survey of India worked there from 1875 to 1877, when I. S. Pocock set up his plane-table at just over 6,700 metres on the eastern slopes of Abi Gamin.

The first mountaineering for pleasure expedition was mounted by W. W. Graham in 1883. Apart from his explorations in Sikkim, he went up the Rishiganga in an attempt to reach Nanda Devi, and attempted the southwest ridge of Dunagiri, probably reaching about 6,200 metres, although he claimed to have got higher. Longstaff's expeditions of 1905 and 1907 were much more important, particularly the latter when the party climbed Trisul, the first 7,000–metre peak to be ascended. Most of the activity in the region in the years leading up to the outbreak of the First World War was concentrated on Kamet, by such well-known figures as C. F. Meade and A. M. Kellas, and another equally good climber, A. M. Slingsby who was killed in the war.

The Nanda Devi group remained one of the least known and inaccessible parts, protected from prying eyes by the gorge of the Rishiganga and the surrounding ring of high peaks. The early Indian surveyors were unable to penetrate the area and no fewer than eight attempts, by such men as Longstaff, Bruce, Ruttledge and Somervell, were made to reach the Inner Sanctuary. It was not until 1934 that Eric Shipton and Bill Tilman were able to force a way up the gorge of the Rishiganga and reconnoitre Nanda Devi at close quarters.

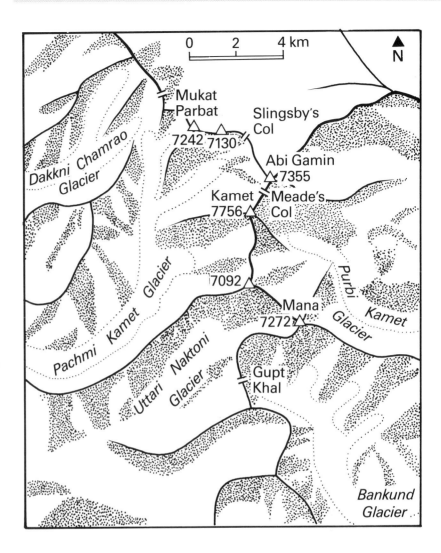

Kamet Group

ABI GAMIN (Eastern Abi Gamin)

Height: 7,355 metres
Lat./Long.: 30°55′57″ 79°36′09″
First ascent: 1950 via Northeast Ridge from Tibet

All the early approaches to this peak were made with the objective of finding a route up Kamet, from which it is separated by the high gap (7,138 metres) known as Meade's Col. In 1855 the Schlagintweit brothers made a valiant attempt from the northern, Tibetan side. They described their climb in a letter to King Friedrich Wilhelm IV of Prussia: 'We camped at a height of 19,326 ft [5,891 metres] on the moraine of the glacier. The night was bitterly cold and stormy, but next day was clear, so we attempted an ascent of the Eastern Peak . . . The ascent on frozen snow was very steep. At 2 p.m. we realized we could go no further.' According to their calculations they had reached a height of 6,785 metres. The peak was eventually climbed from the north by members of a small Anglo-Swiss party.

1953. Southwest Ridge

During an ascent of Kamet Indian climbers ascended Abi Gamin from Meade's Col.

The Schlagintweit Brothers – Adolphe (d.1857), Hermann (d.1882) and Robert (d.1885)

The brothers were born in Munich between 1826 and 1833 and grew up in a cultured atmosphere. After some climbs in the Alps they went out to India in 1854 at the invitation of the East India Company to continue the scientific survey begun in 1846 by Captain Elliot. After travelling through India they arrived in Calcutta in March 1855 where they installed equipment for meteorological observations and geothermal measurements. Then they began their series of Himalayan journeys. Hermann went into Sikkim along the Singalila Ridge, while his brothers travelled to Garhwal. Here Adolphe made what was possibly the second crossing of Traill's Pass. From Milam (northeast of Nanda Devi) they crossed into Tibet in disguise but were caught and escorted back. They managed to escape at night, however, and eventually reached Gartok. It was on this journey that they made their attempt on Abi Gamin. In the summer of 1856 Hermann and Robert made a trek northwards from Leh, crossing the western end of the Transhimalaya mountains. The cold and other privations were severe. High passes had to be crossed and there was little firewood, water or fodder. Hermann and Robert returned to Europe in May 1857, but Adolphe stayed behind and crossed the Karakoram and the Aksai-chin before reaching Yarkand. Towards the end of August he arrived in Kashgar where he was brutally murdered. In 1888 a monument was erected there in his honour by the Russian Geographical Society. Most of the journeys made by the brothers were over ground already covered, although they did add to the knowledge of the extreme northeastern corner of Ladakh. Nevertheless, their studies included geology, climatology, ethnology and magnetology; as well as astronomy, the meaning of Tibetan words and observations of some of the *great* peaks. In all this, their work was a valuable basis for future research.

▲
Kamet and Abi Gamin from a peak (c. 6,500m) on the ridge between the East Kamet Glacier and the Banke Plateau (Frank Smythe)

KAMET
Height: 7,756 metres
Lat./Long.: 30° 55' 13" 79° 35' 37"
First ascent: 1931 via Northeast Face

This peak was visited for the first time in 1848 when Richard Strachey determined its height. Seven years later Adolphe and Robert Schlagintweit, who were engaged as surveyors, made an attempt on Abi Gamin from Tibet, believing it to be Kamet. The peak was surveyed in the 1870s by I. S. Pocock.

Between 1907 and 1914, seven

small parties visited the mountain and explored both east and west sides. T. G. Longstaff, C. G. Bruce and A. L. Mumm reached over 6,100 metres under the southwest ridge of Abi Gamin on the eastern side and thought the route too prone to avalanches. In 1911 A. M. Slingsby's party got to about 6,700 metres on the west flank of Abi Gamin from Slingsby's Col between Abi Gamin and Mukut Parbat. In 1912 and 1913 both Slingsby and C. F. Meade reached 7,000 metres by Slingsby's route, and Meade also managed to gain the col (Meade's Col, 7,140 metres) between Kamet and Abi Gamin from the eastern side by a variant of Longstaff's route. After the First World War Dr Kellas made his third visit to the peak in 1920 and reached Meade's Col, although he could not persuade his porters to pitch a tent there because of the excessive cold.

The first ascent in 1931 was a minor landmark in mountaineering history, as it was the highest summit to be reached at that time, but nowhere near the height record already achieved on Everest in 1924 when Lt. Col. E. F. Norton climbed to a height of 8,572 metres without oxygen. The victorious party was led by Frank Smythe and included Eric Shipton. They were accompanied by ten Sherpas and everything was well organized. Camps I and II were on the north side of the Purbi Kamet glacier and Camp III on the upper shelf of the glacier. The hardest part of the route was a 300-metre high rock wall above this camp, which was followed by an ice dome. The climbers set up their fifth camp at 7,100 metres on a large snowfield just below Meade's Col.

On 21 June, Smythe, Shipton and R. L. Holdsworth, with Sherpas Lewa and Nima Dorje, made their bid for the summit, following not the actual northeast ridge but rather the northeast edge of the face beneath. Progress was fast until the slope steepened, with a thin layer of snow on ice, about 125 metres below the summit ridge. Here Nima Dorje dropped out. The others pressed on slowly, cutting steps, and reached the top at 4.15 p.m. after more than eight hours. The second ascent of the peak was made by three other members of the party two days later.

1955. North Ridge

Indian climbers made the third ascent from Meade's Col but kept to the ridge above Smythe's route.

1979. East Face

An Indian group ascended from southeast of Meade's Col.

1983. West Face Attempt

An Indian expedition made a route along an ice-fall and up very steep rock to just over 7,000 metres before being turned back by a blizzard. The route looked hazardous.

1985. West Ridge from the South

A joint Indian Army–French Army expedition ascended from the Pachmi Kamet glacier. They attacked the southern flank of the west ridge and made a *direttissima* line up the face to the ridge crest at 6,900 metres. Over 3,000 metres of rope were fixed. The route was partly up steep ice grooves and was Grade V–VI. Wind was a problem on the west ridge, but eventually a large party reached the summit after three weeks on the mountain.

MANA

Height: 7,272 metres
Lat./Long.: 30° 52' 52" 79° 36' 57"
First ascent: 1937 via South Ridge

During the course of survey work in 1937, R. Gardiner and R. C. A. Edge discovered and crossed the Gupt Khal, a pass which had eluded Frank Smythe in 1931. Gardiner noted that the east ridge might be feasible from the Bankund glacier. Later that year Smythe completed the ascent of the south ridge solo, from a plateau at the head of the Uttari Naktoni glacier, his companion, P. R. Oliver, becoming exhausted at about 7,000 metres. An earlier attempt on the east ridge from the Bankund reached only Deoban (6,852 metres). Smythe then crossed to the west side of the peak by the Gupt Khal (Zaskar Pass), ascending the south ridge after an abortive attempt on the northwest ridge.

1966. Northwest Ridge

The first part of this route was a 60° wall of ice more than 600 metres high, threatened by hanging glaciers. Above was a plateau of deep snow. Two hours after the assault party had started the weather deteriorated, but they reached the summit in eight hours. The top part of the route included a rock face where sixty metres of fixed rope had been placed beforehand.

1988. North Face

This was climbed from the Purbi Kamet glacier by members of the Indo-Tibetan Border Police.

MANA NORTHWEST

Height: 7,092 metres
Lat./Long.: 30° 53' 51" 79° 35' 46"

MUKUT PARBAT

Height: 7,242 metres (east peak, 7,130 metres)
Lat./Long.: 30' 57' 08" 79° 34' 13"
First ascent: 1951 via Northwest Ridge

A four-man New Zealand expedition included two climbers who were to become very well known two years later – Edmund Hillary and George Lowe. Together they reconnoitred first the Purbi Kamet glacier, which was found to offer a very broken approach to the northwest ridge. The full expedition now concentrated on the Dakkni Chamrao glacier. Without undue difficulty they surmounted the ice-fall leading to the ridge and cramponed over gentle ice slopes to the crest. On 11 July the four men and Pasang Dawa Lama set off up the exposed ice and snow of the northwest ridge, which was swept by an icy wind. By midday they still had 370 metres to climb and the route ahead was a knife-edge of ice. H. E. Riddiford, F. M. Cotter and Pasang decided to carry on. Despite the debilitation caused by dysentery, Riddiford managed to cut step after step up the sensational ridge for three hours. On reaching the summit plateau it was another two hours' plod through soft snow before the top was gained at six o'clock.

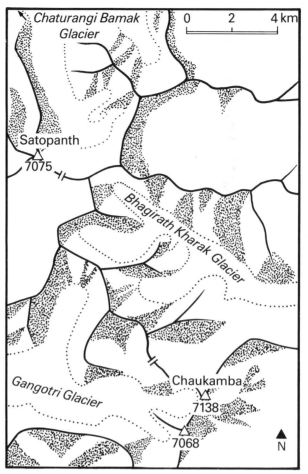

Gangotri Group

CHAUKAMBA I (Badrinath Peak)

Height: 7,138 metres
Lat./Long.: 30°44′59″ 79°17′28″
First ascent: 1952 via Northeast Face

In May 1936 Major Gordon Osmaston led a survey party to the Gangotri glacier. No one had explored the final kilometres leading to Chaukamba and it was a great thrill to find that the topography differed greatly from the existing map.

A 1938 Austrian expedition, led by Rudolf Schwarzgruber, made a reconaissance lasting nearly a month, during which they explored the peak from the north, west and east. The west and east sides offered no promise but the party reached about 5,800 metres on the north face, from the Bhagirath Kharak glacier, en route

to the northeast ridge. The route appeared easy but an ice avalanche falling nearby made them decide to give up.

The following year, André Roch led a small Swiss party to the area, one of his objectives being the ascent of Chaukamba. After fine ascents of Dunagiri and two other peaks, the attempt on Chaukamba ended in tragedy. Roch followed the Austrian approach and made camp at about 5,750 metres in an apparently safe spot. However during a midday rest an avalanche carried away the whole camp; as a result one Sherpa died later and a local porter was buried. (A 1976 party found debris and human remains from the Roch expedition.)

The 1952 Franco-Swiss expedition again used the northern

approach. From Camp III at 5,950 metres, Lucien Georges and Victor Russenberger made the climb to the summit. The chief difficulties were the threats of avalanches between the lower camps and the deep snow on the northeast face.

CHAUKAMBA II (Chaukamba Southwest, Badrinath II)

Height: 7,068 metres
Lat./Long.: 30°43′56″ 79°16′53″

SATOPANTH

Height: 7,075 metres
Subsidiary peak: West, 7,045 metres
Lat./Long.: 30°50′34″ 79°12′53″
First ascent: 1947 via North Ridge/North Face

In 1938, Rudolf Schwarzgruber's Austrian party retreated from the northeast ridge because of deep

First view of the head of the Gangotri Glacier, looking towards Chaukamba (Gordon Osmaston)

Nanda Devi Group

DUNAGIRI
Height: 7,066 metres
Lat./Long.: 30° 31' 57" 79° 50' 02"
First ascent: 1939 via Southwest Ridge/Face

In 1883 W. W. Graham claimed to have reached a height of around 6,900 metres on the southwest ridge, but this was almost certainly an overstatement, the reality being nearer 6,200 metres. Longstaff reconnoitred the Dunagiri and Bagini glacier approaches in 1907. Fifty years after Graham's attempt, P. R. Oliver and D. Campbell reached about the same point, being unable to find a route up the southwest ridge from the Tolma valley. During a survey in 1936 with Gordon Osmaston, Eric Shipton and Angtharkay reached 6,700 metres on the same ridge but ran out of time. A later reconnaissance of the north flank showed this to be unpromising. The next year, Frank Smythe and P. R. Oliver got as far as Shipton had done, but then failed because of the weather and lack of time.

It was left to André Roch and two other Swiss climbers to make the first ascent of the southwest ridge at their second attempt. The difficulties began above the point reached by W. W. Graham, with a fifty metre high wall. A rope was fixed up this obstacle; above was a steep slope dotted with rock up which they moved rapidly. Progress slowed down considerably as next they tackled a very steep snow slope. By 11 a.m. the climbers had gained the top of the buttress, the junction with the

snow, although they considered it was a possible route. Then they reached about 6,100 metres on the northwest ridge.

André Roch and his companions had unexpected success in 1947 on the north ridge which merges into the face at 6,500 metres. From camp on the Chaturangi glacier they reconnoitred the foot of the northwest ridge, finding impassable walls of red and green gneiss. Not fancying the Austrian route, a rocky couloir, they switched their attention to the north ridge. Camp II was pitched on the little peak (5,800 metres) at the foot of the ridge. Next day Roch and his three companions followed a rocky ledge on the eastern side of the crest, overlooking the Sunalaya glacier some 1,200 metres below. They continued up the ridge, first

on one side then on the other, to a dome. From there the slope rose to the summit at an average of 45°. On the final stretch, 150 metres below the summit ridge, it became much steeper and there seemed to be considerable avalanche danger. Roch climbed the slope to test it, followed shortly afterwards by the others. From there it took a further one-and-a-half hours to cover the short distance to the highest point at the eastern end of the summit ridge because of cornices and wet snow on the southern side.

1983. Northwest Ridge
Three Japanese climbed this ridge as far as the western summit of Satopanth. The higher peak looked to be a long way off and the weather was threatening, so they decided to descend.

snow ridge which leads to the summit. The apparently easy ridge was covered with loose, powdery snow and corniced on both sides; in places they progressed on their knees, at others they had to best-ride crumbling masses. It was extremely exposed and where the angle increased the snow was so deep that they could hardly move. By 2 p.m. they were all exhausted and had reached only a height of 6,800 metres, still some way from the top.

▲
The southwest ridge of Dunagiri seen from camp at 6,100 metres (Frank Smythe)

After a week's rest at base camp they set off for the second time at 6 a.m. on 5 July. In two-and-a-half-hours they reached their previous high point, but ahead of them were several gendarmes and a long sharp crest with cornices. In the last part

the ridge steepened in two steps, then eased off and at noon they were standing on the highest point.

1975. Southwest Face
The British climbers Joe Tasker and Dick Renshaw climbed this difficult 1500 metres high face alpine-style. The crux came at 6,400 metres, over steep rock requiring some artificial aid, and difficult mixed terrain. The ascent lasted seven days and the descent,

by the same route, four more. In 1981 Polish climbers attempted the southeast face, up the 50°–60° ice left of the Tasker-Renshaw route. They reached the southwest ridge before bad snow conditions stopped them.

1976. North Ridge
Members of a Japanese expedition abandoned a short-cut route, through an ice-fall, to P.6093 because of falling ice blocks and gained the ridge lower down via a big gully. The entire route was thus longer and more difficult but less dangerous. Fixed ropes and ladders were required to overcome steep ice walls, rockfaces and several gendarmes. Two parties reached the top. At the same time, three Americans and a Mexican died in a fall from the southwest ridge.

1977. East Ridge Attempt
A Japanese attempt on the east ridge in 1977 nearly succeeded.

HARDEOL (Tirsuli South)
Height: 7,151 metres
Lat./Long.: 30° 33' 41" 80° 00' 48"
First ascent: 1978

After their successful ascent of Nanda Devi East, the 1939 Polish Himalayan Expedition moved up the Milam glacier to inspect the Tirsuli massif. From this eastern side they could see the high snow basin which lies between the south and east peaks and the avalanches which sweep the face beneath. For this reason they ruled out any attempt on Hardeol from this direction. Nevertheless, subsequent parties did attempt this east face. In 1967 an Indian expedition reached about 6,200 metres before giving up in the face of heavy snowfall, avalanches and blizzards. In 1974 a joint Indian-New Zealand all-women expedition had reached only 5,500 metres before two members were injured in an avalanche. The following year an attempt on the west face, by an Indo-Tibetan Border Police team, was abandoned at about 6,400 metres, because of blizzards, before the climbers had reached the col separating Hardeol from Tirsuli West. The peak was climbed on 31 May 1978 by a group from the Indo-Tibetan Border Police led by S. P. Mulasi.

TIRSULI (Tirsuli East)

Height: 7,074 metres
Lat./Long.: 30° 34′ 59″ 80° 01′ 22″
First ascent: 1966 via East Face

During their reconnaissance of the eastern side of the Tirsuli massif, the 1939 Polish Himalayan Expedition noted the great rock spur leading to the snow ridge which makes three leaps up to the east peak. A careful examination through binoculars convinced them that the east peak might be climbed by this route and a way found to the upper névé leading to Hardeol. In the event they were unable to get to the ridge and so,

moving northwards, they started up the east face where A. Karpinski and S. Bernadjikiewicz camped (at about 6,400 metres). The following morning the rest of the party found this camp buried under an immense avalanche. Apart from a few pathetic remnants, nothing was left. The 1964 Indian group led by M. S. Kohli managed to reach 5,650 metres before heavy snowfall and avalanches forced them to give up, having lost half of their equipment. Next year K. P. Sharma's Indian party attained about the same height on the east ridge. The third Indian expedition, led by C. Mitra in 1966, did, however, manage to establish a line of camps on the east face. From Camp V (6,650 metres) N. Mallik, S. Chakravorty and two Sherpas reached the summit on 9 October.

TIRSULI WEST

Height: 7,035 metres
Lat./Long.: 30° 34′ 45″ 80° 00′ 14″

During their reconnaissance of Hardeol, the 1939 Polish Nanda Devi East expedition came to the conclusion that the only route from the east would be via Tirsuli East. Nearly thirty years later, in 1968, an Indian team reached about 6,250 metres on the west ridge, but the rest of the route appeared to be too difficult.

Nanda Devi

Height: 7,816 metres
Lat./Long.: 30° 22′ 32″ 79° 58′ 22″
First ascent: 1936 via south ridge

As the highest peak in this region, Nanda Devi natually aroused considerable interest amongst surveyors, travellers and mountain-

▼ *The east faces of Hardeol and Tirsuli seen from the Milam Glacier. Tirsuli West lies behind Tirsuli main peak (Harish Kapadia)*

eers. But, true to the legend of its namesake (the Princess Nanda who fled there to preserve her virginity), the mountain defied all human attempts to reach its foot until some fifty years ago. It stands within a wall of high peaks over 100 kilometres in circumference which enclose a hidden world of high pastures and glaciers known as the Sanctuary. The only approach on foot is up the terrific gorge cut by the Rishiganga river, with precipitous cliffs from 1,500 to 2,500 metres high on each side.

Neither the early surveyors nor the first climbers were able to penetrate the Sanctuary. W. W. Graham made a brief foray up the Rishiganga in 1883. Longstaff was also unsuccessful in 1907, although two years before he had reached a col to the east from which he could observe the south face of Nanda Devi. During the period 1926–32, Hugh Ruttledge (leader of the 1933 and 1936 Everest expeditions) made three reconnaissances but failed to find any practicable route into the Sanctuary from the north or south. One of the cols he visited, the Sundardhunga Khal (5,820 metres) was eventually used by Shipton and Tilman to exit from the Sanctuary in 1934, but they considered it was not passable in the opposite direction.

In 1934 Eric Shipton and Bill Tilman, in one of their remarkable, low-budget expeditions, succeeded in forcing a way through the Rishiganga gorge early in June. In a week of trial and error, creeping along walls of crumbling rock, they made a route which not only got them into the Sanctuary but which was also just feasible for a much larger expedition to follow. They mapped the Uttari Rishi glacier and reconnoitred the north faces of the Nanda Devi peaks without finding a suitable route. In mid-July they withdrew on account of the monsoon. Return-

ing in September they completed their survey of the southern basin of the Sanctuary, climbed Maiktoli and then reached about 6,535 metres on the rocky, 'coxcomb' crest of Nanda Devi's south ridge.

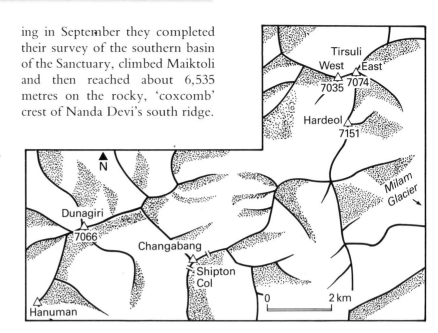

Nanda Devi from south glacier: the route of first ascent follows the ridge running diagonally across the face
▼

(Audrey Salkeld Collection)

Eric Earle Shipton (1907–77) and Harold William Tilman (1898–1978)

The names Shipton and Tilman recall one of the greatest mountain partnerships of all time, but whereas Shipton never left the mountains, Tilman later became more interested in ocean sailing. Their climbing career together began in 1930 with a brilliant traverse of the two highest peaks of Mount Kenya. Although both engaged in growing coffee in Kenya at that time they came of different backgrounds. Tilman had been through the Royal Military Academy at Woolwich. Shipton had already travelled a fair amount, having been born in Ceylon, had climbed in the Alps and spent some time at university. After their climb on Mount Kenya, Tilman bicycled across Africa while Shipton began his Himalayan career. He was on Frank Smythe's successful 1931 expedition to Kamet and the two major expeditions to Everest in 1933 and 1936. In 1934 the pair carried out their most remarkable joint venture when they went up the Rishiganga gorge and surveyed

the Nanda Devi sanctuary. They were together the following year on a small reconnaissance expedition to Everest and again in 1937 when they explored the glaciers and peaks adjacent to the Shaksgam river in the Karakoram. In 1938 they went to Everest again. Tilman also visited the Assam Himalaya just before the war, while Shipton was surveying in the Karakoram again. In 1947, during Shipton's second tour as British Consul-General at Kashgar, they made attempts on Bogdo Ola and Muztagata. Following the opening of Nepal, Tilman explored the Langtang Himal in 1949 and the Annapurna Himal in 1950, finishing up with a reconnaissance of the southern approaches to Everest. As a result of his report of a possible route via the Western Cwm, Shipton established the existence of the South Col route in 1951. Their remarkable exploits in Asia were now over. Shipton became intensely involved with expeditions to Patagonia and Tierra del Fuego, crossing the ice-caps and climbing various peaks including the legendary Mount Burney. Tilman also visited the southern Patagonian ice-cap, sailing there in his boat 'Mischief'. Apart from this he made several voyages to the arctic and antarctic regions, often landing to explore some mountain or other. Both wrote a number of entertaining books about their adventures. Shipton was married with two sons, and became a distinguished President of the Alpine Club; but Tilman remained a misogynist all his life, which ended when he disappeared at sea.

Satisfied that this ridge offered the best route, they made a hazardous exit via the Sundardhunga Khal.

Two years later, an Anglo-American expedition succeeded in climbing the Shipton-Tilman route on the south ridge. The ridge was difficult from the start, with poor rock and great exposure on both sides. The weather was foul and the climbers could find no decent campsites. After sixteen days they managed to establish Camp III at 6,470 metres, at the one place where the ridge eased off to a snow saddle. Following a bad storm they pushed the route to the next camp (6,650 metres) up a sloping nose of ice which proved to be a severe trial. The first assault had to be called off at around 7,300 metres when Charles Houston became unwell; the rest of the party had to go up and bring him down the ice nose. In a final desperate bid Bill Tilman and Noël Odell, who were the only pair still capable of making an attempt, climbed from a bivouac near the previous high point. The very steep part of the route where the ridge merges into the summit face was first over good rock, then soft, knee-deep snow. The final obstacle was a rock wall followed by a snow gully, finishing up a difficult snow arête. The ascent had taken nine hours. The whole climb was made without the use of crampons and with very few Sherpas.

◀

Members of the successful 1936 Anglo-American expedition to Nanda Devi. From the left: (back) W. F. Loomis, C. S. Houston, N. E. Odell, H. A. Carter; (front) H. W. Tilman, T. G. Brown, P. Lloyd, A. B. Emmons

1976. Traverse from East Peak

Nanda Devi is joined to its east peak by a long and difficult ridge. In 1951 Frenchmen R. Duplat and G. Vignes were last seen close to the summit of Nanda Devi in the

early afternoon, having climbed the south ridge. It was their intention to traverse the three kilometre-long ridge to the east peak. R. Dubost and Tenzing Norgay climbed the latter, but found no trace of the missing pair.

In 1975 members of an Indo-French team climbed Nanda Devi and the east peak, but failed to complete the traverse of the ridge because of bad weather. The following year a large Indo-Japanese expedition traversed the south face of Nanda Devi and placed a camp on the ridge at 7,260 metres. The same day, just after 5 a.m., two climbers left their camp under the summit of Nanda Devi East. The principal difficulties began five hours later on a 200-metre high hump at the lowest part of the ridge. This section took another five hours. The main peak camp was reached shortly afterwards.

1976. Northwest Face and North Ridge

An Indo-American expedition, led by H. Adams Carter and W. F. Unsoeld, had success and poignant tragedy. After a complicated approach the northwest face was climbed with two intermediate camps between 29 July and 22 August; the climbers were hampered by the monsoon conditions. The north buttress above was steep with holdless slabs and shallow awkward chimneys before a final snow slope. During the second summit assault, Unsoeld's daughter, Nanda Devi, collapsed at Camp IV and died in her father's arms shortly afterwards. She was buried high on the mountain by her three companions.

1978. North Ridge Attempt

In May a Czechoslovakian team attempted the entire north ridge, but only reached a fore-summit (7,055 metres) before the early

arrival of the monsoon prevented any further progress.

1981. Northeast Face

A Czechoslovakian group climbed the prominent ridge on the face in the post-monsoon period. The route had been tried in 1978 by two British climbers who encountered bad snow conditions.

▲

NANDA DEVI EAST
Height: 7,434 metres
Lat./Long.: 30° 21′ 58″ 79° 59′ 30″
First ascent: 1939 via South Ridge

Nanda Devi (right) from the northeast with Nanda Devi East and the connecting ridge. The wall of the Sanctuary is seen running left from Nanda Devi East (Nikola Kekus)

Tom Longstaff paid his first visit to the Himalaya in 1905, with the guides Alexis and Henri Brocherel, and started by exploring the eastern approaches to Nanda Devi. The Pachu glacier was followed to its head, directly under the northeast ridge of Nanda Devi East. Then he crossed, by a difficult snow pass, into the next valley to the south, the Lawan Gad. The Lawan valley was also explored to its head where they reached a high col ('Longstaff Col') at a height of 5,910 metres, one of the few points where Nanda Devi's protecting

ring sinks below 6,100 metres. From here Longstaff obtained good views of Nanda Devi's south face and the southern glaciers of the 'Inner Sanctuary'. He also reconnoitred the south ridge of Nanda Devi East but had insufficient food for a serious attempt.

In 1934, after penetrating the Nanda Devi basin, Shipton and Tilman were able to examine the great north faces of Nanda Devi and Nanda Devi East and the precipitous rock wall between them. The first ascent of the peak was made in 1939 by a Polish party, led by A. Karpinski, via the south ridge from Longstaff Col. Camps were established along the ridge until bad weather drove everyone back to base. Three attempts were needed before Camp V was pitched on 30 June at 7,000 metres. Next day the four climbers were storm-bound. On 2 July J. Bujak and Dawa Tsering set off, followed by S. Bernadzi-kiewicz and J. Klarner. Not long after Bernadzikiewicz had to descend and was accompanied by Dawa. The others continued and reached the summit at 5.20 p.m., returning to camp late that night by the light of a full moon.

1981. Southwest Face

An expedition of Indian para-troopers, led by Major K. I. Kumar, made base camp at 4,950 metres in the Nanda Devi basin and set up four camps on the southwest face (ridge) between 10 September and 3 October. On 4 October P. Lal and Phu Dorjee were returning from the summit of Nanda Devi East when they fell to

their deaths. Also during descent, Daya Chand, a member of the third summit group, slipped and was killed. Later, two more members perished on the southwest ridge of Nanda Devi itself.

TRISUL

Height: 7,120 metres
Lat./Long.: 30° 18' 46" 79° 46' 38"
First ascent: 1907 via Northeast Flank

The first reconnaissance of the western and southern approaches to this peak was made by T. G. Longstaff in September, 1905. Earlier in the year he had explored the approaches to Nanda Devi and then accompanied C. A. Sherring on a long tour through southern

Tibet, in the course of which he made an attempt on Gurla Mand-hata. To the south, his exploration of the Bidalgroar glacier corrected the existing map of the Kail Ganga.

Two years later, Longstaff returned with a strong party – C. G. Bruce, A. L. Mumm, three Alpine guides, and a party of Gurkhas. The month of May was spent exploring the Dunagiri region, but on 2 June Longstaff, Mumm, the guides and four Gurkhas were back at Dibrugheta. From the Rishi-ganga valley they gained the Trisul glacier which gives access to the eastern side of the mountain. From a camp on this glacier, at a height of 5,300 metres, Longstaff, A. and H. Brocherel and Karbir reached

the summit in ten hours on 12 June. This was the first ascent of a 7,000–metre peak, the height of which was accurately known, and about the ascent of which there was no doubt. The party was quite well acclimatized after a month spent for the most part above 4,500 metres, with two nights at over 6,100 metres. There have been numerous subsequent ascents of the Longstaff route. During the second American ascent, on 21 September 1975, Bruce Carson died when a summit cornice collapsed, precipitating him down the 900 metres of the vertical south face.

1976. West Face

A Yugoslavian expedition ascended the Nandakini valley and turned north to make base camp under Nanda Ghunti (6,309 metres). By means of an unpleasant couloir they crossed to the Ronti glacier and pitched camp on 1 May at 5,200 metres at the bottom of the face. The route followed the central ice rib, above which ropes were fixed on water ice, mostly 55°, with some vertical steps. After ten stormy days, a height of 6,400 metres had been reached (Camp III). On 13 May Camp IV was set up and ropes fixed between III and IV. After another stormy day 15 May was warm and cloudless. A. Grasseli and S . Marenče climbed the easy ridge to reach the top at 9 a.m.

1978. South Ridge

A Japanese group climbed this long but easy route from the Trisul glacier, with three camps.

1981. West Face Variation

Where the Yugoslav route went up a sheet ice ridge, the solo German climber, Anton Freudig, found a better route some 300 metres to the left, rejoining the ridge above Camp III. The west face offers many possibilities for interesting and difficult routes.

1987. West Face Alpine-Style and Traverse

All six members of a Yugoslavian team made the ascent between 28 and 30 May. Four of them traversed the peak to Trisul II and III, while the other pair made a paraglide descent of 3,100 metres to base camp.

Trisul seen from the northwest from Nanda Ghunti (6,309m) (André Roch)

▼

Bibliography

Agrawal, M. (1971), 'Ascent of Trisul, 1970', *HJ*, 30, pp. 197–200.

Bajaj, J. (1982), 'Eagle's nest atop Kamet and Abi Gamin', *HJ*, 38, pp. 57–63.

Berrill, K. (1952), 'Abi Gamin, 1950', *HJ*, 17, pp. 80–96.

Bhuyan, R. (1974), 'Kamet 1972', *HJ*, 32, pp. 93–6.

Birnie, E. (1932), 'First ascent of Kamet', *HJ*, 4, pp. 27–34.

Blake, S. and Bujak, J. (1941–42), 'Polish ascent of Nanda Devi, East Peak, 1939', *AJ*, 53, pp. 31–45.

Carter, H. (1979), 'Nanda Devi from the north, 1976', *HJ*, 35, pp. 186–90.

Clarke, M. (1980), 'Nanda Devi via the south ridge', *HJ*, 36, pp. 54–7.

Gombu, N. (1966), 'Second ascent of Nanda Devi', *AAJ*, 15, pp. 90–2.

Greenwood, R. (1952), 'Trisul 1951', *HJ*, 17, pp. 112–14.

Inada, S. (1980), 'A month on Trisul', *AJ*, 85, pp. 193–7. (See also, *HJ*, 36, 1980, pp. 58–61.

Jayal, N. (1956–57), 'Kamet 1955', *MW*, pp. 143–6.

(Kellas, A.) (1920–21), 'Dr.Kellas' expedition to Kamet in 1920', *AJ*, 33, pp. 312–19.

King, T. (1980), 'Nanda north face', *HJ*, 36, pp. 44–53.

Kumar, N. (1964–65), 'Nanda Devi', *MW*, pp. 52–5.

Kunaver, V. (1988), 'Trisul's Ales' Kunaver memorial route', *AAJ*, 30, pp. 37–40.

Languepin, J–J. (and others) (1952), 'The French on Nanda Devi', *HJ*, 17, pp. 60–3.

Lohner, A. (and others 1949), 'Swiss Garhwal expedition of 1947', *HJ*, 15, pp. 18–45.

Meade, C. (1920–21), 'The Schlagintweits and Ibi Gamin (Kamet)', *AJ*, 33, pp. 70–5.

Mitra, C. (1967), 'The first ascent of Tirsuli', *HJ*, 27, pp. 67–75.

Noyce, W. (1943–44), 'Towards Trisul', *AJ*, 54, pp. 166–71.

Oliver, P. (1934), 'Dunagiri and Trisul, 1933', *HJ*, 6, pp. 91–105.

Oliver, P. (1934), 'Trisul, 1933', *AJ*, 46, pp. 142–6.

Osmaston, G. (1939), 'Gangotri triangulation', *HJ*, 11, pp.128–39.

Reichart, L. and Unsoeld, W. (1977), 'Nanda Devi from the north', *AAJ*, 21, pp. 1–23.

Riddiford, H. (and others) (1952), 'New Zealand expedition to the Garhwal Himalaya, 1951', *HJ*, 17, pp. 42–59.

Roch, A. (1940), 'Dunagiri, Gauri Parbat, Rataban and Chaukhamba [Badrinath Peak], 1939', *HJ*, 12, pp. 30–51.

Roch, A. (1940), 'Garhwal 1939: the Swiss expedition', *AJ*, 52, pp. 34–52.

Roskelley, J. (1987), *Nanda Devi – the tragic expedition* (Harrisburg, PA: Stackpole Books).

Ruttledge, H. (1933), 'Nanda Devi', *HJ*, 5, pp. 28–32.

Sandhu, B. (1976), 'Ascent of Nanda Devi and Nanda Devi East, 1975', *HJ*, 34, pp. 59–66.

Sandhu, B. (1982), 'Men and women's ascent of Nanda Devi', *HJ*, 38, pp. 64–7.

Sandhu, B. (1987), 'Indo-French mountain round-up', *HJ*, 43, pp. 38–44.

Schwarzgruber, R. (1939), 'German Garhwal–Himalaya Expedition, 1938', *AJ*, 51, pp. 79–84.

Shipton, E. (1935), 'The Nanda Devi basin', *AJ*, 47, pp. 58–75.

Shipton, E. (1937), 'Survey in the Nanda Devi district', *AJ*, 49, pp. 27–40.

Slingsby, C. (1913), 'An attempt on Kamet', *AJ*, 27, pp. 326–8.

Šmída, V. (1982), 'Nanda Devi's northeast face', *AAJ*, 24, pp. 77–82.

Smythe, F. (1931), 'The Kamet Expedition, 1931', *AJ*, 43, pp. 289–308.

Smythe, F. (1938), 'Garhwal, 1937', *AJ*, 50, pp. 60–81.

Tilman, H. (1935), 'Nanda Devi and the sources of the Ganges', *HJ*, 7, pp. 1–26.

Tilman, H. (1937), *The ascent of Nanda Devi* (Cambridge: Cambridge University Press).

Western Himalaya

Nun Kun Massif

The peaks of Nun Kun lie about 100 kilometres east of Srinagar. The northern approach is by way of the Zoji La, on the ancient caravan road from Srinagar to Leh and Central Asia, said to have been used by Genghis Khan. The three principal peaks are Nun, Kun and Pinnacle Peak (6,930 metres). Between Nun and Kun is a high névé plateau ending in a broken ice-fall to the northwest. The topography of the massif was not shown correctly on the existing maps when, in 1898, C. G. Bruce and a brother officer, Major F. G. Lucas, took a party of Gurkhas to Suru for training in mountain exploration and climbing. This expedition carried out the preliminary reconnaissance of the group, finally crossing the Sentik La on the western ridge of Nun to descend the Barmal glacier.

Much of the early exploration in the Punjab Himalaya was carried out, over a period of many years, by the brothers Arthur and Ernest Neve, who had established a mission hospital in Kashmir by the 1880s. In 1902 Arthur Neve and

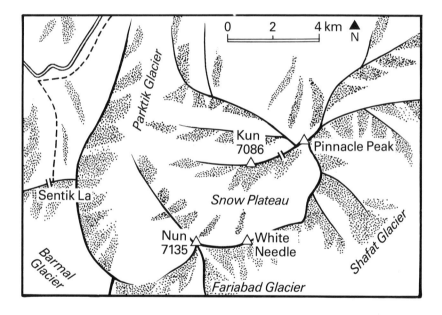

the Rev. C. E. Barton ascended the Shafat glacier, examined the eastern flanks of Nun and repeated Bruce's crossing of the Sentik La. Neve visited the region again in 1904, when he made a sketch of the topography correcting the old map, and a third time in 1910, climbing D41 and taking observations with a clinometer lent him by the Survey of India.

In 1903 the Dutch mountaineer H. Sillem, during his round the world climbing trip, made an expedition to the area with his wife, camping in the Shaphat valley. He then spent three weeks in the region of the Nun Kun plateau, or snow basin, the upper snow-field which he discovered. He photographed the snow plateau between Nun and Kun, and reached a height of 6,400 metres on Nun. In 1906 the American couple, Dr William Hunter and Mrs Fanny Bullock Workman, made a complete tour of the massif and an inaccurate survey, so that the map they produced could not be accepted by the Survey of India.

Arthur Neve (d.1921)
Neve went out to Kashmir in 1882 and, with his brother Ernest, established a mission hospital in Srinagar four years later. Between them they visited almost every valley in Kashmir, Baltistan and Ladakh in the course of their work, and climbed most of the high peaks in the Pir Panjal. Arthur Neve was one of the first Europeans to visit Nanga Parbat, going up the Rupal valley to Tarshing in 1887, which was a fairly hazardous trip on account of robber bands. In the early 1900s he visited the Nun Kun massif more than once and correctly identified its topography. He also paid several visits to the Karakoram. In 1909 he accompanied T. G. Longstaff and A. M. Slingsby in the search for and exploration of the Siachen glacier, which included the discovery of the Teram Kangri group. He returned home to serve during the First World War, and died shortly afterwards as a result of his work among the wounded.

KUN

Height: 7,086 metres
Lat./Long.: 34°01'48" 76°04'22"
First ascent: 1913 via Northeast Ridge

In 1913 the Italian mountaineer Mario Piacenza, well known for his exploits in the Alps and Caucasus as well as journeys in Iran and Turkestan, led an expedition to the region. His companions were Count Cesare Calciati, Lorenzo Borelli, Erminio Botta and two guides. After preliminary explorations the expedition ascended the Shaphat glacier to the plateau where they placed their fourth camp between the striking pyramids of Nun and Kun. Piacenza, Borelli and two of the others reached the summit of Kun via the northeast ridge at their second attempt. 'It was atrociously cold,' wrote Borelli, 'the wind cut our faces; and we put on more and more clothes until we looked like onions.' In only the second recorded attempt on the peak, in 1971, an Indian Army team put seventeen climbers on the summit during 25–27 June.

1978. Southeast Ridge

From a camp on the plateau Czechoslovakians Jan Jursa and Jan Matúš climbed this route, Jursa alone continuing along the sharp snow ridge above the saddle. The ascent took nearly ten hours.

▼

Northwest side of Kun (Nikola Kekus)

1981. West Ridge/Face

After an unsuccessful attempt to climb the west face in 1979, Japanese climbers returned to it in 1981. After ferrying loads up the Parktik glacier for nearly two weeks they established themselves at the foot of the face at 5,850 metres. Kunihiko Kondo and Minoru Nagoshi started up the face on 24 June finding much rotten rock; they reached the summit on the twelfth day.

NUN

Height: 7,135 metres
Lat./Long.: 34°00' 76°02'
First ascent: 1953 via the West Ridge

Until 1934 no one had attempted any climb on this peak. However in this year J. B. Harrison and James Waller organized a holiday trip to the massif solely for the purpose of finding out why Nun had remained inviolate. They approached via the Shaphat glacier, finding the cairned campsite from

the 1906 Workman and 1913 Italian expeditions. For their reconnaissance they continued southwestwards, towards the Fariabad glacier, and stopped again on the site of a Workman camp under the southern slopes of 'White Needle', a prominent point on the east ridge of Nun. They were now at a height of about 6,100 metres and were disappointed to find that the lip of the high snow basin was still some 300 metres above them, with an approach by a steep snow-covered ice slope. The wall seemed far away but they reached it and easily crossed the bergschrund. However the ice slopes were so awkward that they did not feel competent to tackle them. Next day they tried a different approach through a crevassed area and then thigh-deep snow. Eventually the crest of the ridge was reached just in time to catch a glimpse of the high cwm and the encircling peaks before cloud closed in for the day. Turning leftwards they struggled to the top of White Needle but were unable to see anything of the route ahead.

Waller returned in 1937 to try the west ridge but had to give up with bad toothache after getting a good view of the ridge which looked promising. The first serious attempt on this route was made in 1953 by an expedition led by Frenchman Bernard Pierre. The party, which included Pierre Vittoz who had reconnoitred the peak the year before, went up the Krish Nai valley and placed their base camp at the foot of a glacier which rose gently to the pass at the base of the west ridge. From the pass they could see that the ridge rose in two great leaps, then lost itself in the southwest face, while another rib above the precipices of the northwest face led straight to the summit. Between them was a hanging glacier.

Although the two steps on the ridge appeared formidable, especially the upper one which culminated in a large tower, they decided to carry on.

The first tower, some 200 metres high, was turned on the left through an ice gully, beyond which were easy slopes of broken rock and névés leading to a ramp of very steep ice where a rope was fixed. They continued over difficult mixed terrain until the summit of the upper tower was gained; it was by now nearly five o'clock.

Nun from advance base camp with White Needle Peak on right of picture (Steven Berry)

The other side of the tower was a steep, thin ice ridge which proved to be extremely hazardous and definitely unsuitable for regular passage. Retreating, they were lucky to find a large glacier ledge on the northern side of the tower.

In breaking weather a camp was made on a ledge of ice on the other side of the main tower and the route prepared as far as the hanging glacier at 6,150 metres. After a hold-up a major assault was launched, remaking the camps and route as far as the foot of the snow face which falls from the summit, where the final camp was installed. The weather seemed set for a summit bid, but soon deteriorated and after twenty-four hours they began to descend, only to be caught in a snow slide. No one was seriously injured but the main climbing party was reduced to Pierre Vittoz and Madame Claude Kogan.

With support from Bernard Pierre these two forced their way back up the route as fast as possible to find that the top camp had disappeared under an enormous ridge of fallen séracs. After an uncomfortable night they set off in calm and radiant weather. Haunted by the memory of the avalanche and the prospect of another they avoided the direct line and tried to make a safe route, but found themselves wallowing in wind crust lying on bottomless powder snow. Further on they encountered great bands of wind-blown snow but eventually reached firmer snow on a slope which led to the crest of the ridge. Their troubles were not over yet as the whole ridge was unstable and they had to cut their way through snowdrifts to a final rock tower and the little snow crest of the summit.

1971. East Ridge
The east ridge was climbed in 1971 when an Indian military academy expedition made a new approach from the north. Camps were established at 6,700 metres and after waiting out a day of storm a group reached the top using much fixed rope; two cadets were badly frost-bitten.

1976. Northwest Ridge
This was climbed by members of a Czech expedition in October.

1977. West Face
Galen Rowell and others climbed this face largely alpine-style. They followed the Czech route for a short distance, then veered right to the unclimbed west face. At 6,700 metres progress was slowed by a long traverse on 55° ice. The summit was reached by two parties, the second having a lucky escape from a serious fall while descending in the dark.

1978. North Ridge
Members of a 27-man team of the Indian Border Security Force climbed the north ridge, six of them also skiing down the northeast face.

1982. Direct West Ridge Variant
P. Lev, G. Ball, P. Stettner and J. Glidden gained the west ridge high up, directly from the plateau up the extreme right side of the west face. Climbing alpine-style, a long day took them across the 45° snow face, above which they wound their way through rock outcrops and snow gullies; then up the ice head-wall to the upper bowl between the west ridge and the French route. Next day, Lev and Ball turned back after a couple of pitches while the others continued up the knife-edge summit ridge.

Bibliography

Harrison, J. (1935), 'A visit to Nun Kun, 1934', HJ, 7, pp. 53–66.

James, R. (1947), 'Short expedition to the Nun Kun massif', HJ, 14, pp. 19–32.

Needle, R. (1982), 'The lure of Nun', HJ, 38, pp. 119–23.

Neve, A. (1902–3), 'A first exploration of Nun Kun', AJ, 21, pp. 304–11.

Neve, A. (1904–5), 'Nun Kun revisited', AJ, 22, pp. 348–52.

Pierre, B. (1954), 'Nun-Kun', AAJ, 9, pp. 29–31.

Schauer, R. (1980), 'Sixth ascent of Kun (7,087 metres)', HJ, 36, pp. 122–5.

Ungerholm, S. (1976), 'Second Swedish expedition to the Himalaya, 1975', HJ, 34, pp. 142–5.

Vittoz, P. (1954), 'Ascent of the Nun (23,410 ft)', MW, pp. 82–92.

Nanga Parbat (subsidiary peaks)

Forepeak
Height: 7,910 metres
First ascent: 1971

Climbed by members of a Czecho-slovakian expedition.

P.7817
Location: north of main summit
First ascent: 1978

Climbed by members of a Czecho-slovakian expedition after climbing the Diamir face.

P.7785
Location: lies north of P.7817

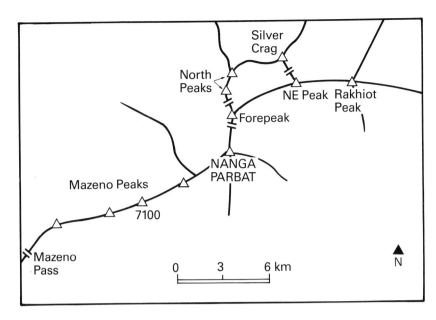

Nanga Parbat's west ridge. From base camp (about 3,580 metres) they opened up a route as far as the site of Camp IV at about 6,100 metres. From there to the col there appeared to be no difficulties. The weather during their visit was very bad.

1986. Northwest Face Attempt

The Spanish climbers J. L. Zuloaga, K. de Pablo and A. Posada climbed alpine-style between 29 July and 6 August. Bad weather stopped them 200 metres from the top: thirty-six 60-metre abseils were made during descent. The difficult rock and ice route started from a height of 4,300 metres.

Northeast Summit (Dyrenfurth's NE-Zacken)

Height: 7,530 metres
First ascent: 1971

Climbed by members of a Czechoslovakian expedition.

SILVER CRAG (Dyrenfurth's Silberzacken)

Location: This point lies north of the Silver Saddle
Height: 7,597 metres

RAKHIOT PEAK

Height: 7,070 metres
First ascent: 1932

Climbed by P. Aschenbrenner and H. Kunigk, members of Willi Merkl's expedition.

MAZENO PEAK

Location: On the ridge leading west from Nanga Parbat to Mazeno Pass
Height: perhaps 7,100 metres
Subsidiary peaks, possibly four: 7,070 metres, 7,100 metres, 7,120 metres, 7,060 metres.

The southern approach to this peak was reconnoitred by a Bavarian expedition in 1964. From the Rupal valley the best chance appeared to be to gain the prominent col on

Bibliography

(Bayerische Karakorum-Expedition 1964) (1966), 'Kampf um die Mazeno-Peaks', Österreichische Alpenzeitung, 84 Jahrgang, Folge 1347, pp. 57–61.

Orolin, M. (1972), 'Second Czechoslovak Tatra expedition to the Himalaya – Nanga Parbat 1971', *HJ*, 31, pp. 267–74.

Greater Karakoram

The first travellers to provide accurate information about the western Himalaya and the Karakoram were William Moorcroft and his companion George Trebeck. Between 1820–25, from his base at Leh, Moorcroft explored much of Ladakh and placed the Karakoram and Saltoro passes on his map. Several travellers made important journeys in the region in the 1830s, including H. Falconer who was probably the first to discover the Biafo glacier; the most important of all was G. T. Vigne.

Born in 1801 Vigne was educated at Harrow and for a few years practised law, while in addition to playing cricket for the M.C.C. he was a keen hunter and talented artist. But he soon tired of life in England and in 1830 set off on his travels. Between 1835–40 he made a detailed exploration of the Vale of Kashmir and discovered the great peaks of the Karakoram. In 1835 on his first trip, and not long after sighting Nanga Parbat, Vigne entered Baltistan and from the top of a small glacier 'gazed down upon the sandy plains and green orchards of the [upper] Indus. . . . To the north, wherever the eye roved, there arose with surpassing grandeur a vast assemblage of enormous summits.'

In the course of four subsequent expeditions Vigne explored the area around Gilgit, several of the major passes and the Hispar-Biafo glaciers. He was no mountaineer and suffered great hardships on the glaciers. Nevertheless he demonstrated quite conclusively that there was no pass by which British India could be invaded from the north. His classic book, *Travels in Kashmir*, was the first comprehensive account of the region and thus of great assistance to the officers of the Great Trigonometrical Survey a few years later.

The opening up of the great peaks discovered by Vigne was principally the work of a slightly built but very tough young officer, Henry Haversham Godwin-Austen. He joined the survey in 1857, the year in which the first observations of the Karakoram peaks were made from Kashmir. After several years' topographical survey work there he was sent to Baltistan in 1860 and carried out his most famous journeys the following year. In the course of his work he frequently climbed to over 6,000 metres, although he had no equipment or formal knowledge of mountaineering. His explorations included the Chogo Lungma, Kero Lungma, Biafo, Panmah and Baltoro glaciers.

H. H. Godwin-Austen (Royal Geographical Society Collection)

One of Godwin-Austen's first goals was the investigation of the Muztagh Pass, the most westerly of the three passes over the range. After marching up the Panmah glacier his party spent an uncomfortable night on the ice before tackling the pass next day. Progress was slow on account of snow softened by the sun and the numerous crevasses. When they were still some way from the top of the pass the weather clamped down and they were only just able to get back to camp. The expedition then turned its attention to the Baltoro glacier which leads to ten out of the world's thirty highest peaks. Here Godwin-Austen sketched the topography of K2, and from the flanks of Masherbrum was able to establish that it stood on the Karakoram watershed. A few years later he contracted fever while working on the northeast frontier; he was invalided home but lived until 1924. He came to be regarded as the greatest of the Kashmir surveyors and the first mountaineer in the Karakoram.

Just prior to the arrival of the first mountaineering expedition in the summer of 1892 another fine piece of exploration was carried out by Lt. George Cockerill as a result of the peace arising out of the Hunza-Nagir campaign of 1891, which enabled the government to reconnoitre and map the western Karakoram and Hindu Kush. Cockerill explored the Shimshal as far as the Shimshal pass and discovered the Momhil, Malungutti, Yazghil, Khurdopin and Virjerab glaciers, along with Disteghil Sar, the highest peak west of K2.

The exploration of the Karakoram continued right up to the outbreak of the Second World War. In 1947 India and Pakistan gained their independence and the area once more became highly sensitive politically. The two countries fought over the partition of Kashmir and the Chinese made territorial demands in the north. In 1984 India gained military control over the eastern Karakoram and even today gunfire still breaks out occasionally on the Siachen glacier.

(Royal Geographical Society Collection)

Kenneth Mason (1887–1976)

Lieutenant Colonel Mason was born in Sutton in Surrey. After passing through the Royal Military Academy at Woolwich he was commissioned and soon went out to India where he joined the Survey of India. Between 1910 and 1913 he worked on the triangulation of Kashmir and linked up with the Russian surveys coming south from the Pamirs. In the Karakoram he completed some of the earlier surveys with important work at the western end of the range and, in 1926, the exploration of the Shaksgam valley. For this he was awarded the Founder's Medal of the Royal Geographical Society in 1927. In the same year he was a leading figure in the founding of the Himalayan Club and its first Honorary Secretary; he also edited the *Himalayan Journal*. In 1932 he retired from the Indian Service and became Professor of Geography at the University of Oxford, a chair which he held until 1953. In 1955 he published his book, *Abode Of Snow*, still the most authoritative one volume work on the historical and geographical background to the entire Himalayan chain, with a remarkably comprehensive summary of climbing and exploration. Mason was the first to admit that he was never an expert climber in the modern sense. Despite this he had great practical experience of the mountains as well as an unrivalled knowledge of the Himalaya, its peoples and its history.

Batura Muztagh

The Batura Muztagh extends from Koz Sar, south of the Batura glacier, to the gorge of the Hunza river.

In 1925 the Vissers explored and mapped the Batura and Pasu glaciers. The principal peaks of the group are located on a difficult ridge sometimes called the Batura 'Wall'. A detailed study of the region, with revision of heights and peak names has been made recently by the Polish mountaineer Jerzy Wala and his new map was published in 1988 by the Klub Wysokogórski 'Trójmiastro', Gdańsk. The ridge continues towards Shispare.

Transferring from Rakaposhi, Mathias Rebitsch's 1954 German-Austrian expedition first approached the Batura peaks from the south up the Baltar glacier. They explored the eastern and northern branches, finding themselves in each case in a rocky cirque allowing no access to the high peaks. After attempting a smaller peak they followed their scientific party round to the Batura glacier to investigate the northern approaches to the peaks. They could see at once that the only access to the upper snow slopes of the two highest summits lay up a 2,000-metre high ice-fall. Although the ice-fall was constantly in motion its ascent was accomplished without accident. Bad weather intervened and conditions became chaotic.

As a consolation prize, Dolf Meyer and Martl Schliessler climbed the nearest peak to Camp IV (6,200 metres), calculating it to be 7,300 metres high. However, according to their map, the peak climbed appears to be P.6845 on the ridge running east from Batura IV (previously Batura II).

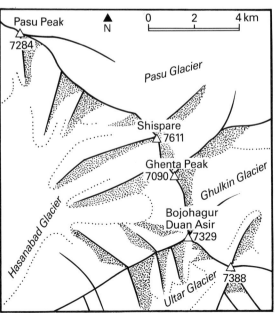

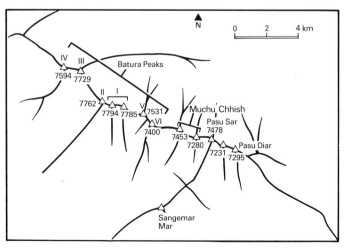

The Batura Wall from the south–the Batura summits run from left to right towards the Ultar massif (A. V. Saunders)

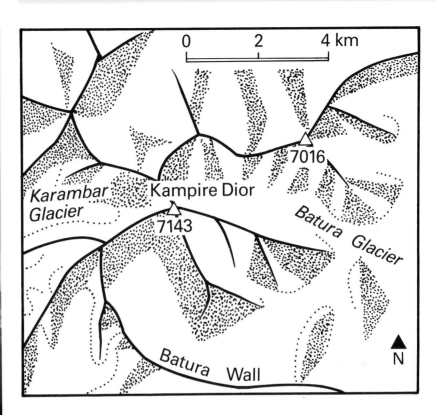

KAMPIRE DIOR (Karambar Sar)

Location: about 20 km northwest of the main Batura peaks
Height: 7,143 metres
Lat./Long.: 36°37'32" 74°19'10"
First ascent: 1975 via South Ridge, West Ridge

In 1959 members of a German expedition made a thorough reconnaissance of the area and concluded that the best approach would be via the Karambar glacier. Both the west and south ridges were found to be long and prone to avalanches in bad weather; the apparently technically easier south ridge had two problematical sections.

The Hiroshima Yamano-kai expedition led by Keiji Enda ascended the Karambar glacier. They gained the south ridge and traversed two peaks, placing their fourth camp at 6,400 metres. Next day four members started at 3 a.m., traversing to the west ridge and fixing ropes on the way. They reached the summit in six hours.

P.7016 (Schneider's P.6931)

Location: 4 km northeast of Kampire Dior
First ascent: 1986 via North Ridge from West

This peak actually lies on a separate spur system, just south of P.6931, and is largely hidden. The Italians started by attacking the south face. Bad weather hampered the climb which consisted of a 45°–50° slope of snow and ice as far as 6,600 metres, then steeper rock. The first assault, on 29 July, came to an abrupt end at about 6,600 metres

because of the weather and difficulties encountered. The climbers then rounded the southwest spur and made their way up the glacier to the west side of the north ridge. The snow saddle (6,800 metres) on the ridge was reached easily, and next day they were on top by 10.30 a.m. During the descent from the ridge, Mancinelli's leg was broken by a falling rock. His companions succeeded in getting him down to the last camp and he was evacuated by helicopter three days after the accident.

BATURA VI (previously Batura II, Peak 31)

Height: 7,594 metres (previously indicated as c. 7,600 metres)
First ascent: 1978 via Southwest Face

The Himalayan Association of Japan expedition, led by Mitsuaki Nishigori, set up camp on the Baltar glacier south of the peak. An attempt was made on the southern spur to a height of 6,250 metres, but the route was too long. They then made four camps up the southwest face, three members making the ascent on 6 July.

BATURA III
Height: 7,729 metres (previously indicated as 7,710? metres)

P.7,640
Location: approximately halfway between Batura III and Batura II

BATURA II (P.c.7,700)
Height: 7,762 metres

BATURA I
Height: 7,795 metres (previously 7,785 metres)
Subsidiary peak: West, 7,794 metres (previously P. c.7,700 metres)
Lat./Long.: 36°30' 39" 74°31' 26"
First ascent: 1976 via South Face/East Ridge

In 1959 three British and two German climbers perished in an attempt on this peak. They were last seen by their companions in the ice-fall, which Mathias Rebitsch had climbed five years earlier. However a reliable hunter reported seeing two heavily laden figures moving slowly on the shoulder of the peak, at a point which had been considered as a possible campsite, and only some 450 metres from the top. No trace of the climbers was found by the rescuers and it seems likely that they died in an avalanche.

In 1976 a D.A.V. expedition were refused permission to use the northern approach and camped on the east branch of the Baltar glacier. The route went over the top of a minor peak ('Saddle Peak', 6,050 metres) to the Batura Saddle. From Camp III (6,300 metres) the route led diagonally up along the whole summit wall below great ice terraces. Camp V was placed on a prominent shoulder at 7,200 metres. On 30 June the assault

party of three set off in cloud but got separated; shortly afterwards the wind got up and it began to snow. Hubert Bleicher continued easily up the 35°–40° slope, passing a rock spur at 7,500 metres, and reached the summit about 3.30 p.m. where he was joined soon after by Herbert Oberhofer.

1980. South Ridge Attempt
Two Japanese climbers attempted the south ridge from the Muchichul glacier. Eventually Takenaka made a solo attempt but gave up some 300 metres from the summit, exhausted by the deep snow. .

1981. Winter Attempt
Austrian climbers got two-thirds of the way up the 3,660-metre high south face. The route followed a difficult buttress and corniced ridge. Using snow cave camps they carried on and climbed steep bare ice along the knife-edge ridge to a height of 6,300 metres. Bad weather, avalanche danger and climbing difficulties forced a retreat.

1983. Second Ascent and New Route
Austrian climbers made a new line to the left of that taken by the Germans in 1976.

1988. West Peak Attempt
A Polish-German team failed to reach Batura I West before making the third ascent of the main peak by the 1983 route.

HACHINDER CHHISH ('Teigni')
Height: 7,163 metres
Lat./Long.: 36°27' 74°29'
First ascent: 1982 via East Face

The 1964 Canadian party led by E. F. Roots set out to locate and climb this peak which had been reported but not precisely identified. After two weeks' explor-

ation, camp was established on the Muchichul glacier. Reconnaissances of three sides of the massif revealed no route safe for porters or camps early in the season. Moreover, from all directions the upper 1,200 metres of very steep rock would require considerable time and equipment.

A seven-man Japanese expedition in 1978 started from the Baltar glacier west of the peak. Since a big couloir looked dangerous they climbed the neighbouring rock buttress. After three weeks, Camp VI was placed at 6,500 metres. An attempt on the south ridge was made by T. Kamei and H. Midorokawa but they soon ran out of food and rope. During the descent Kamei fell to his death descending a fixed rope which had been cut by rock-fall.

The 1982 Japanese expedition from Kanazawa University returned to the Muchichul glacier to attempt the east face. The route consisted of the lower face (1,200 metres), the steep upper wall (900 metres) to the forepeak and the knife-edge ridge to the summit. The first section was climbed by way of a wide couloir to a level snow ridge leading to the upper wall. This was a steep snow slope, then a smooth snow ridge, and finally steep icy rock below the forepeak. A heavily corniced ridge led to the summit, which was gained by a final icy gully running up to the summit cornice.

SIA CHHISH
Location: southwest of Hachinder Chhish
Height: probably 6,500 metres
First ascent: 1983 via West Spur and North Ridge

This peak was climbed by the Italians G. Mallucci, E. de Luca and G. di Federico, who reported its height as 7,040 metres.

BATURA V (P.c.7,600)

Height: 7,531 metres
First ascent: 1983 via South Face

An expedition, led by Władysław Wisz, climbed the 3,500-metre high south face, a route comparable in difficulty to the great north faces of the Alps. Nearly 2,500 metres of rope were fixed on the face. On 29 August the Poles Zygmunt A. Heinrich and Paweł Mularz, and the German Volker Stallbohm set off from camp at 6,400 metres for an alpine-style assault on the summit, which was reached after two bivouacs. Three others also got to the top.

BATURA VI

Height: 7,400 metres (not previously indicated)

MUCHU CHHISH (P.c.7,500)

Height: 7,453 metres

MUCHU CHHISH EAST

Height: 7,280 metres (not previously indicated)

PASU SAR (P.c.7,500)

Height: 7,476 metres

P.7,291

Location: approximately halfway between Pasu Sar and Pasu Diar

PASU DIAR (previously Pasu Peak 55)

Height: 7,284 metres (or, 7,295 metres)
Lat./Long.: 36°28′51″ 74°36′53″
First ascent: 1978 via Southeast Ridge

This peak was first attempted by Japanese climbers in 1974. In 1978 a Pakistani-Japanese team ascended the Pasu glacier to the east of the peak. The ascent of the ice-fall was the most difficult and dangerous part of the entire climb. The route then led up a gentle ice slope to the ridge which connects Pasu Diar and Shispare. From here the icy summit pyramid rose steeply. On 3 July seven members climbed the steep ice as fast as possible and arrived on the sharp, rocky summit at 1.15 p.m. The second ascent was made in 1985 by the same route.

Sangemar Mar

Location: on spur southwest of Pasu Diar
Height: 7,050 metres, or, 6,949 metres
Lat./Long.: 36°27′ 74°34′
First ascent: 1984 via Southwest Ridge

Climbers from Osaka University fixed 3,000 metres of rope up the ridge, the first part of which was 40°–50° ice. From the third camp (6,400 metres) six members set off on 11 July and reached the top at 2 p.m.

SHISPARE (Peak 33)

Height: 7,611 metres
Subsidiary peak: Northwest, 7,100 metres
Lat./Long.: 36°26′30″ 74°40′52″
First ascent: 1974 via Southeast Ridge from the north

The Polish-German Academic Expedition ascended the Pasu glacier. Reconnaissance revealed the best route to be the ridge dividing the Pasu and Ghulkin glaciers, accessed along the vast buttress which slopes down to the glacier. The first part presented great technical difficulties and 1,500 metres of rope were fixed. The crest of the ridge was reached after ten days. From here two kilometres of ice ridge were traversed to the snow plateau between Shispare and P.7090 on the ridge leading to Bojohagur Duanasir. Janusz Kurczab left the group and climbed P.7090 which the team named 'Ghenta Peak' (Bell Peak). From the snow plateau the route led up a 45° slope. Later, an avalanche struck the second assault party, killing one member.

P.7090 ('Ghenta Peak')

Location: 2 km southeast of Shispare
First ascent: 1974 from the north

Climbed during ascent of Shispare from the north.

BOJOHAGUR DUANASIR (Ultar I)

Height: 7,329 metres
Subsidiary peak: South, 7,250 metres
Lat./Long.: 36°24′10″ 74°41′43″
First ascent: 1984 via Southwest Ridge

In 1982 six Japanese climbers attempted the south side from the Ultar glacier which was reached from the Hunza valley. The weather was poor and they did not get far above the southwest col (5,957 metres). Three members were hit by rock-fall. Two years later Tsumeo Omae led another Japanese expedition which approached the peak from the west via the Hasanabad glacier. After climbing a spur they reached the southwest ridge and established their fourth camp at 6,900 metres. The route then traversed a 7,250-metre forepeak to the summit which was reached on 28 and 30 July. A British expedition led by Tony Saunders, was attempting the mountain at the same time from the Ultar glacier, but failed at about 6,800 metres.

ULTAR SAR (Bojohagur Duanasir II, Ultar II)

Height: 7,388 metres
Subsidiary peak: West, 7,350 metres
Lat./Long.: 36°23′ 74°43′

In 1986 a Pakistani-Japanese expedition first attempted the north face from the Ghulkin glacier. Above the ice-fall, after an avalanche had hit a tent and equipment and food were lost, they decided to withdraw. Then they transported everything round to the south face, and gained a plateau at about 5,000 metres. Two routes on the rock face were tried from there, but the route was too dangerous because of falling stones and ice. The high point was 5,500 metres.

Hispar Muztagh

The Hispar Muztagh extends from the gorge of the Hunza river, north of the Hispar glacier, to the head basin of the Biafo glacier.

The Hispar glacier was discovered in 1861 by H. H. Godwin-Austen during his exploration of the great glacier region comprising the Chogo Lungma, Kero Lungma, Biafo, Panmah and Baltoro. He was the first to ascend most of these glaciers. In 1892 Martin Conway's expedition spent the best part of a month exploring and mapping the Hispar and Biafo glaciers, including the first crossing of the Hispar pass. The Workmans followed in Conway's footsteps in 1908 but added little to the knowledge of the area. The next important expedition was that of the Vissers in 1925. At that time the glaciers descending the northern flanks of the Hispar Muztagh had not been mapped, although the Malangutti glacier had been visited and sketched by George Cockerill. The Vissers' explorations included the Khurdopin and Yazghil glaciers. The Malangutti glacier was mapped as well.

In 1938 Michael Vyvyan explored the Khunyang glacier which previously had not been penetrated far enough to view the great eastern bay of the head basin. In the course of this work he approached Disteghil Sar, Khunyang Chhish and Pumari Chhish. He also located the pass leading to the Yazghil glacier, which it was thought would make

a direct route to the Shimshal river. The following year Fountaine and Secord, members of Shipton's survey party, crossed the col at the head of the Khunyang glacier but were forced to abandon any attempt to reach the final col over the main watershed because of the danger of ice avalanches.

P.7010 (Lupghar Sar West II)

(*Note:* The Lupghar peaks are not to be confused with the lower peaks of the Lupgha group, north of the Batura glacier.)

Members of the 1986 Bizkaiko Expedizioa from Spain explored the Baltbar valley which leads to the southwestern aproaches to Lupghar Sar West. Its unclimbed western summit (P.7010) offers a magnificent route on its southwest spur.

LUPGHAR SAR WEST

Height: 7,199 metres
First ascent: 1979 via Southwest Ridge

A D.A.V. group led by H. Gloggner ascended the left branch of the Gharesa glacier to reach the foot of the southwest ridge. In deep snow a route was made over a forepeak and along a corniced ridge which steepened to a rock band and another ridge. After a break for bad weather Gloggner and his brother left camp for a summit attempt. They climbed four rope-lengths over terribly rotten rock before bivouacing on the snow slope leading to the final buttress. Next day they climbed unroped over rotten slabs and blocks insecurely held by a mortar of ice. The climb took so long that

Members of the 1925 Visser expedition. Standing: four Indian survey assistants and the guides Franz Lochmatter and Johann Perren. Seating (left to right): Khan Sahib Afraz Gul Khan, Dr Philips, C. Visser, Mrs Jenny Visser-Hooft, Baron B. Ph. van Harinxma thoe Slooten

Philips Christiaan Visser (1882–1955)

Dr Visser was a distinguished Dutch diplomat and mountaineer. Initially he entered the family business in Schiedam and climbed extensively in the Alps between 1902 and 1913. At the outbreak of the First World War he was climbing in the Caucasus. His diplomatic appointments included countries in the Middle East, South Africa and the USSR. In 1912 he married Jenny van't Hooft who henceforth accompanied him on all his mountain expeditions until her death in 1939. He is principally remembered

in the history of mountaineering for his four Karakoram expeditions (1922, 1925, 1929–30, and 1935) while Consul-General at Calcutta. In 1922 the Vissers visited the northern glaciers of the Saser group and reconnoitred Saser Kangri. In 1925 they carried out a much more ambitious programme, exploring the northern flanks of the Batura and Hispar Muztaghs. The expedition was described in Jenny Visser-Hooft's book, *Among the Kara-Koram Glaciers In 1925.* Dr Visser's own writings were strictly scientific.

they were obliged to bivouac on the summit. The ascent was repeated six weeks later by three Japanese climbers who then traversed eastwards to Lupghar Sar Central.

LUPGHAR SAR CENTRAL

Height: c.7,200 metres
Lat./Long.: 36°21' 75°02'
First ascent: 1979 by traverse from
 Lupghar Sar West

Climbers from Hosei University followed the first ascent route to the summit of Lupghar Sar West. Then they traversed for one-and-a-half kilometres along a knife-edge snow ridge to the central peak, which took them three hours. They reported that the three main peaks are nearly the same height, the central peak possibly being the highest.

LUPGHAR SAR EAST

Height: c.7,200 metres

In 1986 a Japanese expedition approached from the north up the Momhil glacier, hoping to try the east ridge but found dangerous hanging glaciers on the proposed route. The alternative was the northeast ridge from the col between Lupghar Sar East and Dut Sar (6,858 metres). The route to the col lay up a couloir, but they were defeated by the final 150-metre high snow wall.

MOMHIL SAR

Height: 7,343 metres
Lat./Long.: 36°19'03" 75°02'10"
First ascent: 1964 via Southeast Face,
 South Ridge

An Austrian group, led by H. Schell, ascended the central branch of the Gharesa glacier to the south-eastern flank of the mountain. The weather was extremely bad and it took over a month to reach the col between Momhil Sar and Trivor.

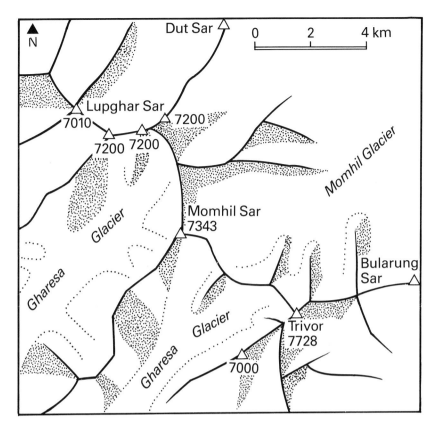

(This was the 1960 route of ascent to Trivor.) However the east ridge above the col was too difficult without much route preparation. Eventually the whole party traversed a long steep ramp across to the south ridge which was followed to the summit.

1980. West Buttress Attempt

From the left branch of the Gharesa glacier members of a Spanish expedition from Córdoba reached a foresummit on the west buttress after some very difficult, and partly vertical, ice climbing. Pneumonia and frostbite forced a retreat at 5,400 metres.

TRIVOR

Height: 7,728 metres
Lat./Long.: 36°17' 75°06'
First ascent: 1960 via Northwest Ridge

The Anglo-American party led by Wilfrid Noyce ascended the central branch of the Gharesa glacier with two intermediate camps. The

route to the col on the ridge between Trivor and Momhil Sar was made by Don Whillans and Ali Gohar; Camp III was set up here. A long horizontal stretch followed but, even so, it was no place for inexperienced porters. The next camp was placed at the end of this section above a little col. The far side the rocky ridge reared up towards a two-headed tower, beyond which was very steep snow up to a rock castle. This part was pioneered by Whillans and Noyce over two separate days. Whillans was now running a fever, so Noyce and the American Jack Sadler went up to put up a camp under the rock castle. Next day they continued, avoiding two enormous ice bulges, to a small col at about 6,830 metres. They then got on steeper, more broken ground below a triangular hanging glacier and were forced to spend the night in a crevasse, where they were just able to erect a tent. After a day's delay caused by a snowstorm they set off at 5.45 a.m. Cramponing up hard snow beside a rock rib brought them to a second rib, then a jumble of unstable blocks. They trudged on towards the summit ridge, and eventually got to the top of the final sharp cone at 2.45 p.m. After another night in the crevasse camp they descended to Camp IV and the expedition was over. Don Whillans' adventure was not over, however, for he rode his motorcycle back to England, a six-week journey made using only the map in the back of his diary.

TRIVOR SOUTHWEST
Height: c.7,000 metres

BULARUNG SAR
Height: c.7,200 metres
Lat./Long.: 36°18'12" 75°09'00"

MALANGUTTI SAR
Height: 7,025 metres (previously 7,320 metres)
Lat./Long.: 36°22' 75°10'
First ascent: 1985

The peak was attempted in 1984 by a Japanese party led by Yoshiro Kasai. Three members of another Japanese expedition and Ang Nima Sherpa made the first ascent the following year.

DISTEGHIL SAR
Height: 7,885 metres (central peak, 7,760 metres)
Lat./Long.: 36°19'35" 75°11'20"
First ascent: 1960 via South Face, West Ridge

A British-Italian group, led by Alfred Gregory, reconnoitred this peak in 1957 from the Khunyang glacier. They selected a route which led to a col west of the summit. The climbing was on a steep face and the weather eventually made conditions impossible. Their high point was about 6,700 metres.

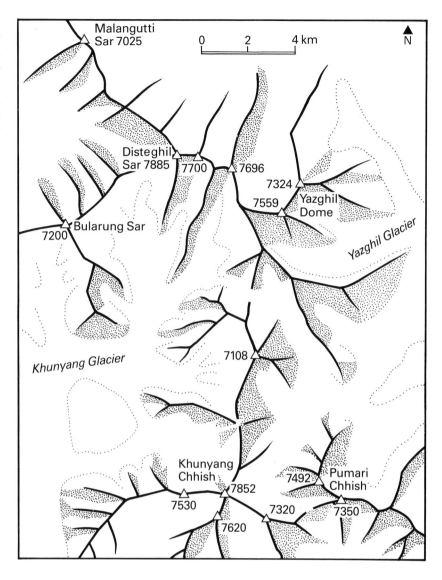

Two years later, a Swiss expedition led by Raymond Lambert were prevented from attempting the British route by the threat of avalanches. Instead they decided on the longer but less dangerous southeast ridge. Bad weather, however, forced their retreat after reaching 7,000 metres.

The 1960 Austrian expedition led by W. Stefan preferred to try the British route which winds up the south face. They reached the west ridge at 7,000 metres. As the weather appeared to be breaking, Günther Stärker and Dieter Marchart made a dash for the summit, arriving at a little col between two peaks; they climbed both to be sure. The storm broke and they had several days of struggle under frightful conditions back to base camp. The second ascent of this route was made by a Spanish group in 1982.

DISTEGHIL SAR EAST
Height: 7,696 metres
Lat./Long.: 36°19'09" 75°13'10"
First ascent: 1980 via East Face

After baggage and porter trouble the 1980 Polish expedition proceeded with reduced equipment up the Khunyang glacier. With four intermediate bivouacs they gained the col between Disteghil Sar East and Yazghil Dome South. After a day spent climbing the latter peak they made the first ascent of Disteghil Sar East, climbing its 600-metre high east summit face, the bottom part of which they likened to the north face of the Matterhorn. They had to descend by moonlight.

1983. Different East Face Approach

Italian climbers ascended the east face from the col leading to Yazghil Dome North.

YAZGHIL DOME NORTH

Height: 7,324 metres
First ascent: 1983 via Southwest Ridge

From a camp in the col between Disteghil Sar East and Yazghil Dome South, the Italian climber Cristiano Casolari worked his way around the latter peak to the col between it and Yazghil Dome North, continuing up snow and difficult mixed terrain.

YAZGHIL DOME SOUTH

Height: 7,559 metres
Lat./Long.: 36° 18′ 75° 15′
First ascent: 1980 via Southwest Face

On 21 July members of a Polish expedition left their depot (5,100 metres) on the upper Khunyang glacier and crossed the south ridge of Disteghil Sar to the col between that peak and Yazghil Dome South with four bivouacs. On 25 July they climbed Yazghil Dome South by its southwest face. Deep snow and miserable weather plagued them but it cleared while they were on top.

KHUNYANG CHHISH

Height: 7,852 metres
Lat./Long.: 36° 12′ 75° 13′
*First ascent: 1971 via South Face,
   South Ridge*

The British-Pakistani expedition of 1962 was abandoned after the death of E. J. E. Mills and M. R. F. Jones. They had overcome the greatest obstacles on the route up the southwest side and were pre-paring the route along a narrow ridge at about 6,100 metres when the snow avalanched. They fell 1,500 metres to the Pumari Chhish glacier.

Three years later, a large Japan-ese group spent five days trying to find a route on the western side of the peak before switching to the 1962 route. Difficult rock, ice walls and sharp ridges with complicated cornices and crevasses used up all their fixed ropes. On the last day of the climb, at 7,200 metres, a narrow snow ridge suddenly col-lapsed sending Takeo Nakamura to the Khunyang glacier below.

Disteghil Sar seen from the north at the head of the Malangutti Glacier (John Hunt)
▼

The others immediately abandoned the ascent.

In 1971 a thirteen-man Polish expedition climbed a direct route up the south face from the Pumari Chhish glacier to reach the south ridge which was followed to the summit. Four members reached the top after a most uncomfortable bivouac seventy-five metres below the summit.

1988. North Ridge

In 1980 three British climbers succeeded in climbing the northwest spur to gain the north ridge at about 6,900 metres before being defeated by bad weather. A French attempt in 1982 was also unsuccessful. Between 22 June and 11 July 1988, a five-man British party set up three camps to a height of 6,200 metres with breaks for bad weather. The final assault was made by Keith Milne and Mark Lowe. Climbing over the forepeak ('Sod's Law Peak') they continued in good weather and light winds, reaching the summit after two bivouacs.

KHUNYANG CHHISH EAST
Height: 7,320 metres

KHUNYANG CHHISH NORTH
Location: about 5 km north of the Khunyang massif
Height: 7,108 metres
First ascent: 1979 via North Ridge

A Japanese expedition from Hokkaido University climbed the north ridge from the col leading from the Khunyang glacier to the upper Yazghil glacier. Eight members reached the summit.

KHUNYANG CHHISH WEST
Height: c.7,350 metres

KHUNGYANG CHHISH SOUTH
Height: c.7,620 metres

PUMARI CHHISH (Peak 11)
Height: 7,492 metres
Lat./Long.: 36°12'45" 75°15'12"
First ascent: 1979 via North Ridge

The 1974 Ö.A.V. expedition, led by A. Furtner, approached this peak from the north, up the Yazghil glacier but were unable to get within three kilometres of their objective. The glacier was found to be impassable, either on its chaotic surface or on the dangerously friable and difficult rock slopes alongside.

The Hokkaido Alpine Association expedition of 1979 approached from the west via the Khunyang glacier and the col north of Khunyang Chhish North, leading to the upper Yazghil glacier. They found that the 700-metre high icefall leading to the col averaged 60°. From there they made camp at the foot of the north ridge of Pumari Chhish. Another steep snow slope led to a forepeak at 6,900 metres.

In all, nearly 2,300 metres of fixed rope were needed. From base camp to summit was a distance of nineteen kilometres.

PUMARIKISH SOUTHEAST
Height: c.7,350 metres

YUKSHIN GARDAN SAR
Height: 7,530 metres
Lat./Long.: 36°15' 75°23'
First ascent: 1984 via South Ridge

A Japanese expedition in 1981 ascended the Khunyang glacier to the col leading to the upper Yazghil glacier and placed their third camp southwest of the peak. They made a summit bid to 6,800 metres, hampered by bad weather, having found the glacier approach too long.

In 1984 two expeditions set up base camps on the Yazghil glacier; an Austrian team went for the south ridge and a Japanese one tried the north ridge. The Austrians made their way up the broken glacier. From their third camp (5,050 metres) they ascended 800 metres up a 40° ice face and

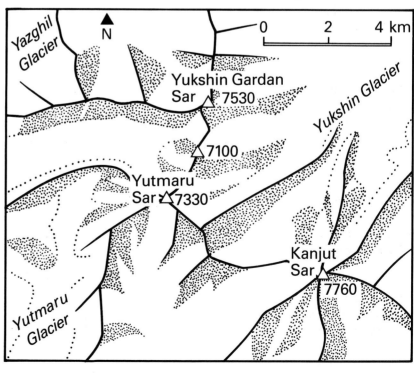

crossed an eight-kilometre long snow basin to camp under a col on the south ridge. The final camp was placed in the col (at about 6,600 metres) right beneath the summit face. Bad weather caused the first and second assaults to be called off, but after a two-week delay four Austrians started for the summit on 26 June in excellent weather. Steep snow led to an ice-covered buttress and a narrow gap, after which a 60° ice couloir was descended for 150 metres before a 45° slope led to the top. This was not reached until 4.30 p.m., and a cold bivouac ensued.

1984. North Ridge Attempt

K. Otaki's Japanese expedition spent a month on this route but gave up because of brittle, vertical rock above 6,500 metres.

1984. South Ridge Variation

After abandoning their attempt on the north ridge the Japanese expedition led by K. Otaki made two alpine-style attempts on the south ridge. The second party went up the Upper Yazghil glacier and gained the ridge south of P.7100. Then they traversed the east side of this and completed the route of first ascent.

P.7100 ('Yukshin Gardan Sar South')

Location: on ridge between Yukshin Gardan Sar and Yutmaru Sar
Lat./Long.: 36° 14' 75° 23'

YUTMARU SAR

Height: c.7,330 metres
Lat./Long.: 36° 14' 75° 22'
First ascent: 1980 via West Ridge, North Ridge

Japanese climbers ascended the North Yutmaru glacier. Despite injury and bad weather, the col on the west ridge was gained. The climbers then crossed the great snowfield on the northwest face

and placed their fourth camp below the north ridge. The second summit attempt succeeded, despite a bivouac at 6,800 metres.

1981. Southeast Ridge Attempt

French climbers found the southeast ridge objectively too dangerous. They tried a spur leading to the west ridge of Kanjut Sar, hoping to descend from there to the col on the southeast ridge of Yutmaru Sar, but the bottom of the spur was constantly swept by falling séracs.

KANJUT SAR

Height: 7,760 metres
Lat./Long.: 36° 12' 21" 75° 25' 40"
First ascent: 1959 via South Ridge

The ten-man Italian expedition, organized and led by Guido Monzino, ascended the very crevassed but fairly level Khani Basa glacier and set up base camp (4,900 metres) below the south face. After three camps had been established, the last at 6,000 metres on the south ridge, the climbers were pinned down by a snowstorm in Camps II and III, following which they retired to base camp before continuing the assault. On 9 July the team began opening up the route again and a week later were re-established on the south col. Work began on making the route up the broad snow ridge and after a couple of days Jean Bich and Camillo Péllissier were in position at Camp VI (7,000 metres) ready for the final assault.

After leaving camp at about 5 a.m. on 19 July, Péllissier soon realized that Bich was feeling unwell, with a numbed hand and stomach pains, and after an hour he had to give up. Péllissier decided to continue slowly. He climbed a rock step and steep snow slope to a snow gully which looked as if it would lead to the summit crest. The gully, which reminded Péllissier of

couloirs on the Matterhorn, was quite steep and he was acutely aware that he would have to descend the same way. The crest, which seemed so near, was in fact still a long way off. On reaching the ridge he was faced with a treacherous corniced slope. Although the major difficulties were over, it took all his reserves of strength and determination before he was able to stand on the distant summit.

1981. West Face

Japanese climbers ascended the Yutmaru glacier to the foot of the west face. They climbed the centre of the face, first passing rocky pinnacles by means of a very technical rock traverse. There followed an exposed horizontal ridge. A 45° snow slope rose to the big snowfield under the rocky summit face. The top was reached twice after suffering avalanche damage and bad weather.

Panmah Muztagh

In 1861 H. H. Godwin-Austen crossed the Skoro La to the Braldoh valley, and explored and mapped the glacier region comprising the Chogo Lungma, Kero Lungma, Biafo, Panmah and Baltoro, being the first to ascend most of these glaciers.

In 1929 Ardito Desio, a member of the Duke of Spoleto's expedition, explored and mapped the Panmah glacier. Eric Shipton's 1937 'Blank on the map' expedition surveyed the Skamri ('Crevasse') glacier which drains the northern flanks of the Panmah Muztagh. Four months were spent among the Hispar, Biafo, Panmah and Chogo Lungma glaciers, their branches and tributaries, and a detailed map made of most of the

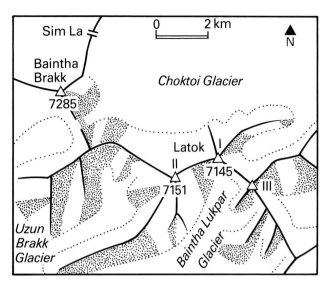

area. Passes were crossed at the heads of the Nobande Sobande and Choktoi glaciers of the Panmah complex into the Lukpe Lawo ('Snow-Lake'), and this area also was mapped.

Watercolour of the Panmah Glacier (1872) painted by H. H. Godwin-Austen in 1872 (Royal Geographical Society Collection)

▼ *Baintha Brakk from the east (Paul Nunn)*

BAINTHA BRAKK (OGRE)
Height: 7,285 metres
Lat./Long.: 35° 56' 54"N 75° 45' 11"E
First ascent: 1977 via West Ridge

British climbers, led by Don Morrison, reconnoitred the south and north faces in 1971, and found a feasible route on the latter. Bad weather prevented them getting very far. There was also an attempt by Japanese climbers in 1974. Morrison led another attempt in 1975. The 1976 Japanese party approached from the Uzun Brakk glacier to the left side of the southwest face. They gained the col and climbed the big snow band which separates the upper and lower rock walls. Their permit expired, however, before they could complete the climb.

The first ascent was made in 1977 by Chris Bonington and Doug Scott. The route gained the west col from the south. Earlier, Scott and Paul 'Tut' Braithwaite had traversed eastwards not far

above the glacier to attempt the south rock pillar. From the col the west summit was reached by two routes, the west ridge and the southwest ridge; from there a ridge leads to the main peak. Shortly after beginning the abseils down the face of the main summit, Scott sustained fractures to both legs during an involuntary pendulum. Bonington also injured himself during this descent. When they eventually reached the lower camps they had a long wait for assistance to arrive.

1983. South Pillar

The south pillar was climbed in 1983 by members of a French expedition, but they did not complete their ascent of the mountain.

LATOK I

Height: 7,145 metres
Lat./Long.: 35°55′43″ 75°49′24″
First ascent: 1979 via South Face

In 1975 a Japanese Alpine Club expedition gave up an attempt on the southern side because of tre-

mendous avalanches and rock-fall. In 1976 the Shensu Club started from the south side up the couloir which leads to the col between Latok I and Latok III, which is east of the main peak. The climb was abandoned at 5,700 metres because of falling séracs. In 1977 Italian climbers decided that the south wall was not accessible, neither was the Japanese couloir. In 1978 an American group attempted the rocky north ridge which rises 2,440 metres. They reached about 7,000 metres before having to retreat on account of one member being ill and a storm which lasted five days. The climb was hard and sustained.

The Japanese made the first ascent in 1979 from the southern Baintha Lukpar glacier. Their route ascended the buttress left of the couloir previously tried. It was hard work fixing the route on the buttress. Finally, three members took thirteen hours to reach the top in bad snow from the highest camp. The climb was repeated three days later.

LATOK II

Height: 7,151 metres (possibly 7,108 metres) (south summit, 7,080 metres)
First ascent: 1977 via Southeast Buttress

A Japanese expedition abandoned an attempt on the west ridge in 1975 because of avalanches and rockfall. Two years later British climbers, attempting the same route, probably reached the Japanese high point, before learning of the death of Don Morrison in a crevasse accident. The climbers reported that there appeared to be a lot of difficult climbing in the upper sections of the ridge, with steep rock, ice and gendarmes for about 600 metres. In 1987 a strong British party was defeated on the west ridge by bad weather having reached 6,860 metres.

In 1977 an Italian expedition led by Arturo Bergamaschi succeeded in making a route from the south. The route consisted of a series of ice walls and mixed ground to a small gorge ending in a chimney, followed by snow slopes and rocks to 6,680 metres. The summit party was delayed by storm and did not arrive on the south summit until 7.45 p.m. Another three hours were needed to gain the highest point.

CHANGTOK I (Chiring)

Height: 7,091 metres
Lat./Long.: 35°56′ 76°10′

In 1986 a Japanese expedition was called off when one member was killed after falling into a crevasse. The base camp was on the Chiring glacier and the highest point reached was about 5,600 metres.

CHANGTOK II

Height: 7,045 metres

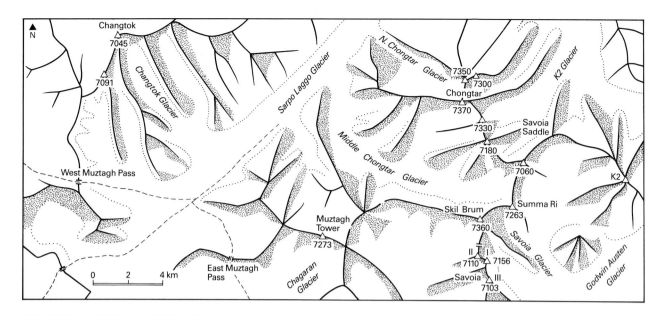

▲ *Baintha Brakk and the Latok group (Paul Nunn)*

Baltoro Muztagh

The Baltoro Muztagh extends from the West Muztagh pass, north and east throughout the length of the Baltoro glacier, to its head southeast of the Gasherbrum group.

The Baltoro glacier was explored and mapped in 1861 by H. H. Godwin-Austen. He was the first to discover the Baltoro approaches to K2 and to sketch its topography. Francis Younghusband crossed the Mustagh (East Mustagh) pass to the Baltoro glacier in 1887. In 1902 Oscar Eckenstein's expedition to K2 made a valuable contribution with their exploration of the Godwin-Austen glacier. The first climbing expeditions to the Baltoro were those of Conway in 1892 and the Duke of Abruzzi in 1909. Apart from exploring and attempting to climb K2, the Duke's party mapped the whole region on a large scale, including the Broad Peak and Gasherbrum groups.

MUZTAGH TOWER

Height: 7,273 metres (West Summit, 7,270 metres)
Lat./Long.: 35°50' 76°22'
First ascent: 1956 via Northwest Ridge

This peak, observed and named by W. M. Conway in 1892, was rightly considered inaccessible until the developments in climbing

though difficult, are by no means vertical. The two summits are about 300 metres apart, connected by a knife-edge col only a few metres lower.

The first attempt on the peak was made by a small British party consisting of John Hartog, Ian McNaught-Davis (joint leaders), Joe Brown and Tom Patey. They approached the western side of the peak up the unknown Chagaran glacier and after two weeks had established camp above the first of the difficulties. A long, easy snow slope led to the northwest ridge where a col was defended by a

the final overhangs, and was approached by a long traverse across 40° ice.

After a ten-day delay caused by bad weather, the route to the col was made safe for the Balti porters and Camp III on the col stocked for the assault. Progress up the continuously steep, difficult and exposed ridge was slow, and ropes had to be fixed. Eventually a platform was constructed out of ice and rocks for the little tent which constituted Camp IV, less than halfway up the ridge. The guy-ropes were simply attached to boulders hanging over the edge; a

attitudes and techniques after the Second World War. Its faces are plastered with ice and hanging glaciers where they are not too steep for snow and ice to lie. Nevertheless its tower-like appearance is deceptive, for it is in fact wedge-shaped and its ridges,

▲

The upper Baltoro Glacier and the Muztagh Tower (centre) (Ned Gillette)

severe 365-metre high wall of ice. The key to this section turned out to be a vertical chimney, of some twenty-five metres, up through

wind would have carried it away.

On a cold, clear morning, McNaught-Davis and Brown set out for the summit. They were soon held up by an overhanging barrier which had to be turned by a severe traverse on the west face and a gully filled with deep loose snow. The ridge continued to demand the utmost care and finished with a twenty-five metre crawl up a knife-edge to the west top. The time was already 6 p.m. An attempt to reach the higher summit demonstrated how dangerously exhausted they were. Struggling back they bivouaced a hundred metres down the ridge. Lower down, the dangerous gully was now frozen and comparatively safe. Here they met the others on their way up. Hartog and Patey succeeded in crossing to the east summit, but failed to get back to camp the same night; after bivouacing in a small crevasse below the band of overhangs Hartog suffered severe frostbite to his feet. Further weakened by stomach trouble he managed to get himself down the rest of the way to base camp on the Muztagh glacier before collapsing. The second ascent of this route (as far as the west summit) was not made until 1984.

1956. Southeast Ridge

A week after the British ascent four members of a French expedition led by Guido Magnone made another route up the southeast ridge, also extremely difficult. Then they helped with the evacuation of the injured Hartog who wrote later: 'The kindness of the French remains for me one of the noblest deeds in the history of mountaineering – the conversion of rivalry to great friendship and affection.'

1976. Southwest Ridge Attempt

A fourteen-man Japanese expedition reached just over 7,000 metres in June.

CHONGTAR NORTH

Height: 7,350 metres (northeast peak, 7,300 metres)

CHONGTAR

Location: in China, west of Savoia Saddle
Height: 7,370 metres
Lat./Long.: 35°54' 76°24'

CHONGTAR SOUTH (Mount Spender)

Height: 7,330 metres

This peak was attempted by an American expedition in 1985. They approached via the Sarpo Laggo and North Chongtar glaciers. After selecting a route along the west-southwest ridge, they were stormbound for a week. A lightweight attempt by three members reached 7,000 metres, too late in the day to complete the ridge to the summit.

P.7180 (Chongtar South II, Savoia Kangri II?)

Location: in China, west of Savoia Saddle and south of Chongtar South

P.7060 (Savoia Kangri III, Summa-Ri North)

Location: in China, southwest of Sovoia Saddle

SUMMA-RI (Savoia Kangri I)

Location: on border with China
Height: 7,263 metres
Lat./Long.: 35°51' 76°27'

SKIL BRUM

Height: 7,360 metres
Lat./Long.: 35°51' 76°25'
First ascent: 1957 via Southwest Face

In 1957 two members of the successful Austrian Broad Peak expedition, Markus Schmuck and Fritz Wintersteller, climbed this peak. In ten hours they crossed sixteen kilometres of the Godwin-Austen and Savoia glaciers and climbed snow slopes on skis to camp at 6,100 metres. From there they ascended the southwest face to the summit, first on hard snow then in deep powder.

SAVOIA I

Location: south of Skil Brum
Height: 7,156 metres
Lat./Long.: 35°49' 76°25'

In 1982 a group of Czech climbers started from the Savoia glacier up a prominent ridge on the 1,800-metre high east face, but were stopped by strong winds after 600 metres. The highest point reached was where the ridge abuts the true face, the link being a very delicate, thin ice ridge.

SAVOIA II

Height: 7,110 metres (possibly 7,170 metres)

SAVOIA III

Height: 7,103 metres

SKYANG KANGRI (Staircase Peak)

Height: 7,544 metres (southwest peak, 7,500 metres)
Lat./Long.: 35°54'40" 76°34'48"
First ascent: 1976 via East Ridge

In 1902 a curiously assorted party went out to this region with K2 as its principal objective. They were led by the eccentric Oscar Eckenstein, an engineer who designed the basic modern crampons and ice axe. He was accompanied by Aleister ('Great Beast') Crowley, a third Briton, two Austrians and one Swiss. Among their achievements was the ascent of the Skyang La (Windy Gap) and the assessment that Skyang Kangri could be climbed easily from it; overall, however, the results of the expedition were disappointing.

The first attempt on the peak was made by the large Abruzzi expedition of 1909. During the very thorough reconnaissances of K2, a camp was pushed up above the Skyang La, only to find a huge cleft cutting across the whole slope and barring any further progress. Despite the efforts of his guides, the Duke of Abruzzi was obliged to give up at a height of about 6,600 metres.

The east ridge, as the route from the Skyang La is called, rises (from south to north) to a point east of the main peak. The remainder of the route (east to west) is across a one-kilometre wide gentle looking saddle. In 1975 an Austrian group, half of them teenagers, and half female, made the first attempt on the peak since 1909. At a height of just over 7,000 metres, the leader

Ferdinand Deutschmann continued climbing alone when his companion Valentin Caspaar became exhausted. Deutschmann was never seen again. After waiting in camp for two days, Caspaar was descending alone when he was swept down 450 metres by a wind-slab avalanche. Three days later a companion got him down to the Skyang La and he was eventually evacuated by helicopter.

In 1976 a Japanese expedition started from the upper Godwin-

Austen glacier and attacked the east ridge, which rises like a five-stepped staircase. On the lower part of the second step they came to what was probably Abruzzi's crevasse. On this occasion there was an ice bridge. Between the second and third steps the route went through the séracs of a hanging glacier. The third and fourth steps were ice walls. From Camp IV above the fourth step the first assault pair had to turn back on account of fatigue. Two days later, on 11 August, Yoshioki Fujioji and Hideki Nagata got to the final ridge and had to tunnel through hanging cornices just below the summit.

HRH Prince Luigi di Savoia, Duke of Abruzzi
▼

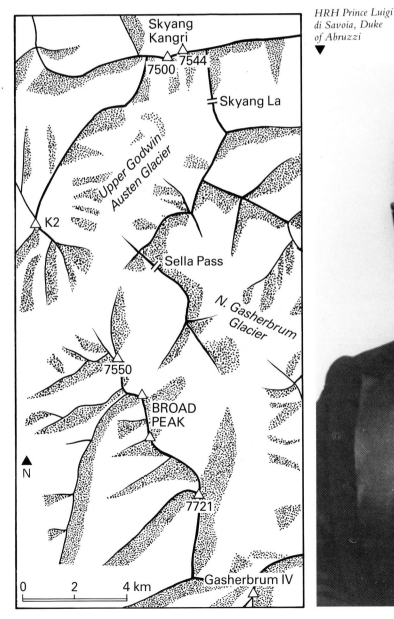

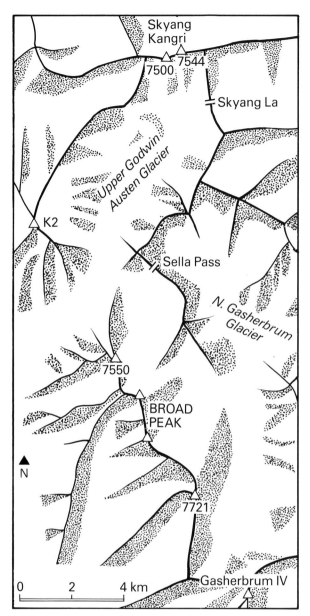

1980. West Face Attempts

Alpine-style attempts were made by the Americans Jeff Lowe and Michael Kennedy. The west face rises over 1,800 metres from the upper Godwin-Austen glacier and consists principally of 600 metres of moderate snow and ice/mixed climbing, followed by a rock head wall. First they tried the prominent buttress in the centre of the face, but retreated after their second bivouac at the start of the upper buttress (at about 6,600 metres).

The limestone rock was very soft, crumbly and without cracks. Their second attempt was made on the south buttress, starting from a height of 5,800 metres. The major difficulty of the route, a 300-metre high rock band (pitches of F8/F9) was surmounted on the second day, but a storm came on that night. They decided to traverse to the east ridge and bivouaced at about 7,070 metres. As Lowe was by now seriously unwell, they were obliged to retreat by abseiling

diagonally into a long gully on the right side of the south face. A traverse across very avalanche-prone slopes brought them eventually to the 'Cat's Ears' (part of the first step). They got back to advanced base camp after seven days on the mountain, partly without food.

BROAD PEAK NORTH
Height: 7,550 metres
Lat./Long.: 35°49′ 76°33′
First ascent: 1983 via North Ridge

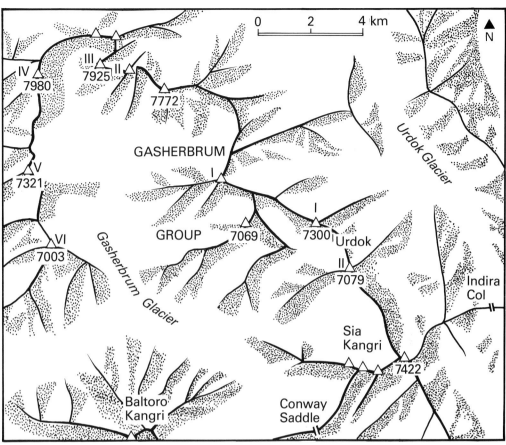

Broad Peak–north, central and main peaks seen from K2 (Kurt Diemberger)

The Italian Renato Casarotto made a solo attempt in 1982 on the north buttress, but had to give up owing to bad weather after being on the wall for twenty-four days. The following year, Casarotto succeeded in soloing the north spur between 22 and 28 June. This elegant route rises 2,450 metres up very difficult ice, rock and mixed terrain. Casarotto's highest bivouac was at 7,500 metres when he was overtaken by darkness. Without any equipment at all he was forced to stand up for eight hours, moving only to massage his hands and feet.

BROAD PEAK SOUTH

Height: 7,721 metres (possibly 7,470 metres)
Lat./Long.: 35° 46' 76° 35'

GASHERBRUM II EAST

Height: 7,772 metres
Lat./Long.: 35° 44' 76° 40'
First ascent: 1983 from the Gasherbrum La

In 1983 a Polish expedition from Kraków climbed this peak during an acclimatization trip up the southeast ridge of Gasherbrum II. From the Gasherbrum La they ascended the long ridge, first reaching the distinctive snow pyramid at 7,200 metres. On their second trip they continued on to the prominent P.7772, clearly visible from base camp.

GASHERBRUM III

Height: 7,952 metres
Lat./Long.: 35° 45' 36" 76° 38' 33"
First ascent: 1975 via East Face

In 1958, after the Italian ascent of Gasherbrum IV, Riccardo Cassin reconnoitred the northwest spur of Gasherbrum III solo, starting from their Camp IV on the upper plateau at the head of the South Gasherbrum glacier. Cassin reached a height of about 7,300 metres. Although the upper snow slopes appeared moderately easy, there seemed to be a belt of fairly formidable rocky precipices all around them.

In 1975, two men and two women, members of a Polish expedition, climbed the peak. From the col separating Gasherbrum II and III they were unable to overcome the 100-metre high rock band at the start of the east ridge, and turned instead to the central couloir on the east face. Above this was a snowfield and a gully which led to the summit ridge, a knife-edge of loose rock.

1985. Southwest Ridge Attempt

A Scottish Mountaineering Club party tackled the long rocky southwest ridge which rises from the top of the dangerous 800-metre high ice-fall between Gasherbrum III and IV. Only two climbers were left to make the final assault. They bivouaced at 7,400 metres on a very exposed patch of snow. Higher up they had to climb in roped pitches, and this slowed them down considerably. They reached 7,700 metres below a step just under the summit tower. Time and weather compelled retreat.

P.7600 and P.7300

Location: on ridge between Gasherbrum III and IV

GASHERBRUM IV

Height: 7,925 (or 7,980 metres)
Lat./Long.: 35°45'38" 76°37'02"
First ascent: 1958 via Northeast Ridge

This famous and beautiful peak, described in 1892 by Martin Conway, was first approached in 1934 when G. O. Dyrenfurth's party tackled the lower part of the South Gasherbrum glacier in an attempt to reach Gasherbrum I (Hidden Peak). A further stretch of the glacier was covered by the 1956 Austrian expedition to Gasherbrum II. Riccardo Cassin's 1958 Italian expedition worked their way up to the topmost basin between Gasherbrum III and IV during June and July, having overcome two major ice-falls. The climbers then discovered a hitherto

unknown hanging valley leading easily and safely to the northeast col, which was reached on 8 July.

The view up the northeast ridge revealed a series of obstacles and a vertical drop of some 800 metres high up on the ridge. Another camp was placed only 100 metres above the col and between 10 and 14 July Walter Bonatti and Carlo Mauri laboriously overcame the 'Ridge of the Cornices' and four towers as far as the 'Snowy Cone'. The distance to the top, however, remained immense; another camp was required. The onset of the monsoon then held up the advance and the climbers took the opportunity to have a rest.

After restocking, Camp VI (7,350 metres) was pitched in a most precarious position about halfway up the ridge, below the final tower. On 4 August Bonatti and Mauri left at daybreak, passed the previous high point, and continued over more difficult ground, but had to return to camp when still a long way from the top. Next day they rested and their support team brought up supplies and mail from home. Then they tried again. By 7.30 a.m. they were already on new ground and the difficulties had eased but the narrow ridge, composed of unsteady slabs of rock, was exceedingly dangerous. Just past a tiny col they climbed a hard chimney to emerge as it were on top of the world as the view opened suddenly before them. When they got to the apparent summit they found this point to be a forepeak with the true summit still 300 metres away along a nasty looking ridge. The final pyramid gave the hardest climbing of the entire route, over Dolomite-like gables and turrets.

Bonatti and Mauri began the descent in a race against a storm which had sprung up; with much difficulty they reached the safety of their tent after thirteen hours

away. Next day the descent to the lower camp was accomplished in what Bonatti described as: 'The most horrid hours I have ever lived on a mountain.'

1980. South Face and East Face Attempts

American climbers abandoned their route on the south face at 6,850 metres when they encountered thin, loose snow over very loose rock. Moving to the east face they made several attempts, but had to retreat because of avalanches and bad weather.

1985. West Face

This had been attempted by several parties. In 1978 British climbers attempted this 3,000-metre high face via the central rib and a steep snow and ice face. The high temperature caused a rapid snow melt which released fusillades of rockfalls. Above 7,000 metres the route looked very hard and out of the question in the conditions. In 1981 three Japanese were killed when a huge sérac collapsed. The following year another Japanese group reached a high point of 6,500 metres. In 1983 two Americans made an alpine-style attempt and got to the top of the Black Towers, the prominent feature which had stopped all previous parties, before being defeated by the weather. The climb was completed in 1985 by Robert Schauer and Wojciech Kurtyka who climbed the west face to the summit ridge. As they were exhausted, however, they did not follow the apparently easy traverse to the summit. They descended the north ridge.

1986. Northwest Ridge

This route was attempted twice by American groups in 1983 and 1984. The first expedition was defeated by bad weather after two summit attempts had reached over 7,000 metres. Next year the climb-

▲ *The beautiful West Face of Gasherbrum IV: the Northwest Ridge route takes the lefthand skyline (Randy Leavitt)*

ers got to over 7,300 metres but ran out of steam in rapidly deteriorating weather. The route was completed, to make only the second ascent of the peak, by two Australians and an American.

1986 and 1988. South Ridge/ Southwest Ridge Attempts

Two British expeditions, led by D. Lampard, reached 7,300 and 7,000 metres on these difficult routes.

GASHERBRUM V

Height: 7,321 metres (east peak, c.7,300 metres)
Lat./Long.: 35°42' 76°36'

Three members of a Japanese ex-

pedition reported having climbed this peak on 1 August 1978 but later stated that they had only been to the lower east peak. Next day the leader Ryuichi Babaguchi set off ahead of another pair. After they had reached the top (of the east peak presumably) they found that Babaguchi had fallen to his death in a crevasse.

P.7100

Location: on ridge between Gasherbrum IV and V

GASHERBRUM VI

Height: 7,003 metres
Lat./Long.: 35°41' 76°37'
First ascent: 1985

The Italian Maria Luisa Ercalani reported having climbed this peak from the Abruzzi glacier in June 1985. The likely route of ascent involves considerable objective dangers and steep ice.

GASHERBRUM I (Hidden Peak) South

Height: 7,069 metres
Lat./Long.: 35°41' 24" 76°42' 00"
First ascent: 1980 via Southwest Ridge and Traverse

A lightweight expedition, consisting of two Frenchmen, Maurice Barrard and Georges Narbaud, followed a line slightly to the right of the 1936 French route on Hidden Peak. The ascent of Hidden Peak

South was over serious mixed terrain. Above a 450-metre high S-shaped couloir, very steep slopes ended at cornices leading to the summit. Then the climbers descended the moderate northwest slopes to climb the southwest face of Hidden Peak itself.

URDOK I

Height: 7,300 metres
Lat./Long.: 35°41' 76°44
First ascent: 1975

The 1975 Austrian Hidden Peak expedition climbed this peak from their Camp III (6,400 metres) after their ascent of Gasherbrum I.

URDOK II

Height: 7,079 metres

Siachen Muztagh

In 1909 T. G. Longstaff, acompanied by Arthur Neve and A. M. Slingsby, ascended the Bilafond glacier to its head, crossed the Bilafond La (Saltoro Pass) and discovered the great Siachen glacier. To the north of the glacier they found the group of peaks which they named Teram Kangri. No peaks had been triangulated in the area at that date, and the topography was unknown. In 1911 and 1912 the Workmans visited and explored the whole of the Siachen glacier. They were accompanied by Alpine guides and surveyors. They also explored the Teram Shehr glacier and crossed the Sia La. Teram Kangri I and III were triangulated in 1911 by the Survey of India. Teram Kangri II was triangulated in 1912 by the surveyor accompanying the Workmans.

The north face of Gasherbrum V as seen from the ice-fall between Gasherbrum III and IV, at about 6,500 metres (Fosco Maraini)

In 1929 Ardito Desio, a member of the Duke of Spoleto's expedition, made a rapid route reconnaissance up the Shaksgam and over the difficult Singhi glacier which blocked the valley. He reached the western side of the Kyagar glacier, which had held up Kenneth Mason in 1926. He did not cross it but tied his route-map to Mason's 1926 hill stations on the other side. In 1935 the Vissers' survey of the Shaksgam valley was completed which included the side valleys, for example, the twenty-nine kilometre–long Singhi valley.

SIA KANGRI I (Queen Mary Peak)

Height: 7,422 metres
Lat./Long.: 35° 39' 51" 76° 45' 43"
First ascent: 1934 by traverse from Sia Kangri II

The peak was climbed by two members of G. O. Dyrenfurth's international expedition from the Conway Saddle.

1981. From Kondus Glacier

An Indian Army expedition ascended the Siachen glacier and camped on the col just above the Kondus glacier opposite Conway Saddle. Sia Kangri I was reached via Sia Kangri II East Peak, south of the great plateau.

▲

The northern aspect of Gasherbrum VI. In the foreground is part of Camp I (c. 5,600m) of the successful 1958 Italian expedition to Gasherbrum IV (Fosco Maraini)

1985. Ski Ascents

Sia Kangri I and the west and central summits of Sia Kangri II were ascended on skis from Conway Saddle.

1986. South Face

Members of an Indo-American expedition found themselves in the middle of an artillery battle as fighting flared up between Indian

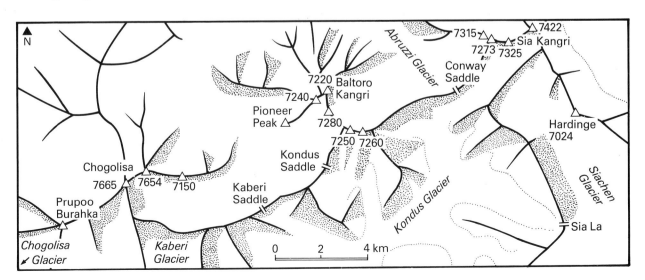

▲

Sia Kangri from Conway Saddle in 1934 (André Roch)

later, Hans Ertl and a companion followed the ridge again and climbed the central and east peaks, as well as Sia Kangri I.

1974. Southwest Face to Central Peak

Four Austrians traversed north from below the Conway Saddle and climbed the southwest face. The main difficulties of the route were a partly overhanging ice wall (45 metres and a 300-metre high couloir.

P.7024 (Mount Hardinge)

Location: on a southern spur of the Sia Kangri massif and 5 km north of the Sia La
Height: also recorded as 7,093 metres

In 1979 a seven-man expedition from Japan attempted this peak from the Kondus glacier. From Camp III on the Sia La they crossed the Siachen glacier, placing their sixth camp on the southeast ridge. Two summit bids during 8–9 July failed at 6,650 metres because of bad rock.

SINGHI KANGRI (Singhi Ri, Mt. Rose)

Height: 7,202 metres
Lat./Long.: 35°35'56" 76°59'05"
First ascent: 1976 via Northwest Ridge

From the Siachen glacier a Japanese university party moved round to the Staghar glacier to climb the northwest ridge of the mountain. The summit was reached twice.

TERAM KANGRI I

Height: 7,462 metres
Lat./Long.: 35°34'38" 77°05'04"
First ascent: 1975 by traverse from Teram Kangri II

Between July and August a large Japanese expedition from Shizuoka University climbed the south ridge

SIA KANGRI II AND III

Height: east (II) peak, 7,325 metres; central peak, 7,273 metres; west (III) peak, 7,315 metres
First ascent: 1934 via South Ridge from Conway Saddle

In 1934 Professor G. O. Dyrenfurth led one of his international expeditions to the Baltoro glacier. From the Conway Saddle he, his wife and various others reached the depression between the central and western summits and climbed the latter. A few days

and Pakistani forces in this disputed region, currently held by India. The American climbers trying a route from the northeast withdrew but the Indians completed their route on the south face, despite being shelled at an altitude of 6,850 metres.

of Teram Kangri II and traversed to the main peak.

TERAM KANGRI II
Height: 7,402 metres
Lat./Long.: 35° 34' 05" 77° 05' 30"
First ascent: 1975 via South Ridge

All eighteen members of a Japanese expedition reached this summit en route to Teram Kangri I.

1978. South Face
An Indian Army expedition camped on the Teram Shehr glacier below the south face; the lower part of the route was a rocky rib. After several attempts three members reached the summit.

TERAM KANGRI III
Height: 7,382 metres (west peak, c.7,300 metres)
Lat./Long.: 35° 35' 50" 77° 03' 11"
First ascent: 1979

A Japanese expedition started at the foot of the gully on the eastern side of the south ridge leading to Teram Kangri I. From the ridge, two members reached the summit at the third attempt.

APSARASAS I
Height: 7,245 metres (south peak, 7,117 metres)
Lat./Long.: 35° 32' 23" 77° 09' 03"
First ascent: 1976 via West Ridge of South Peak

Members of Osaka University made the first ascent of this peak on 7 August. From the Teram Shehr glacier they ascended towards the west ridge of Apsarasas I South. This is a narrow snow ridge leading to a steep ice wall. After reaching the south peak the eight climbers waited out a week of bad weather. A further camp was placed beyond the south peak, from which four members reached the main summit.

1980. From Southeast
Ascent by an Indian Army expedition.

APSARASAS II
Height: 7,239 metres
Lat./Long.: 35° 32' 04" 77° 10' 18"

APSARASAS III
Height: 7,230 metres
Lat./Long.: 35° 31' 05" 77° 12' 30"

APSARASAS IV
Height: 7,221 metres
Lat./Long.: 35° 31' 12" 77° 12' 47"

APSARASAS V
Height: 7,187 metres
Lat./Long.: 35° 31' 12" 77° 11' 30"

APSARASAS VI
Height: 7,184 metres (east peak, c.7,000 metres)
Lat./Long.: 35° 31' 15" 77° 13' 11"

Rimo Muztash

The 7000-metre peaks of the Rimo Muztagh are located in the Rimo and Kumdan groups.

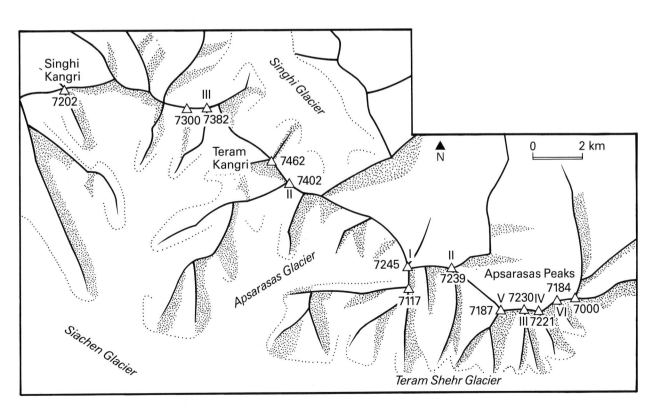

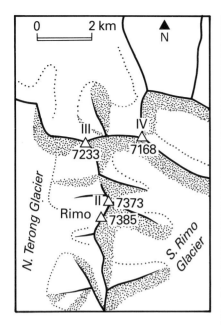

▲

Close-up of Southwest Face of Rimo III (Harish Kapadia)

RIMO I (Peak 51)

Height: 7,385 metres
Lat./Long.: 35°21'22" 77°22'09"
First ascent: 1988 via West Face

In 1985 two British climbers, Victor Saunders and Stephen Venables, starting from the North Terong glacier, climbed snow-slopes to the southwest spur (6,400 metres). After four days of hard mixed climbing they had reached 6,850 metres when the loss of their bivouac equipment forced a retreat. Two other climbers inspected the eastern side of the peak but found no line suitable for a fast ascent.

The following year an international expedition approached from the east via the Depsang Plain, finding the area occupied by military personnel. From the South Rimo glacier they attacked a snow and ice gully on the south face, but bad weather and fixing rope delayed them for three weeks. On 6 October they retreated from a height of 6,850 metres on account of deep snow, and avalanche and crevasse conditions. On their way out the Indian Army confiscated all their films.

The 'Painted Mountain' was climbed eventually by members of an Indo-Japanese expedition led by Hukram Singh. From camp on the hanging glacier, close under the summit on the western side, the top was reached on 28 August after nearly six weeks delay for bad weather. Two Indians and two Japanese made the ascent.

1988. South Face

One-and-a-half hours after the first ascent, two more members of the same expedition reached the summit via the south face, having fixed 2,000 metres of rope.

RIMO II (Peak 50)

Height: 7,373 metres
Lat./Long.: 35°21'24" 77°2'15"

RIMO III (Peak 49)

Height: 7,233 metres
Lat./Long.: 35°22'32" 77°21'38"
First ascent: 1985 via East-Northeast Ridge

This Indo-British expedition was the first to visit the Terong basin since 1929. From the glacier between Rimo III and IV, the British climbers J. Fotheringham and D. Wilkinson, ascended 800 metres of mixed ground to bivouac on the east-northeast ridge of Rimo III, about 500 metres below the summit. On the fourth day they climbed the ridge in deep snow to the summit.

RIMO IV (Peak 48)

Height: 7,168 metres
Lat./Long.: 35°22'38" 77°23'04"
First ascent: 1984 via West Face and Southwest Ridge

▲
Rimo I with the Southwest Ridge in foreground. The righthand skyline leads to Ibex Col. The first ascent of the peak in 1988 was made up this ridge (Harish Kapadia)

This peak was climbed alpine-style (between 7 and 9 August) by M. P. Yadov and G. K. Sharma, members of an Indian Army expedition. From the South Rimo glacier they climbed the west face to the southwest ridge and so to the top; the climb was repeated two days later.

CHONG KUMDAN I
Height: 7,069 metres ⁃
Lat./Long.: 35° 11' 77° 35'

CHONG KUMDAN II
Height 7,005 metres
Lat./Long.: 35° 11' 77° 33'

MAMOSTONG KANGRI I
Height: 7,516 metres
Lat./Long.: 35° 08' 54" 77° 34' 41"
First ascent: 1984 via Northeast Ridge

The peak was first reconnoitred in 1907 by Arthur Neve and D. G. Oliver when they explored the large Mamostong glacier. In 1984 an Indo-Japanese group ascended the glacier, getting their first sight of this peak with its sheer rock faces, crumbling rock ribs and hanging glaciers. Dismissing the south and east aspects as unclimbable, the party continued northeastwards over a col, crossed the Thangman glacier and reached a saddle on the northeast ridge. Good progress was made up ice of uncertain stability before bad weather intervened. Finally, five climbers left camp on the saddle on 13 September and reached the summit at eleven a.m. The climb was subsequently repeated twice.

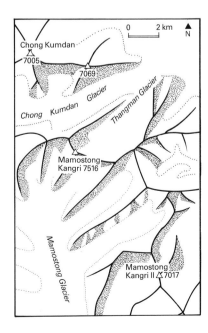

MAMOSTONG KANGRI II
Height: 7,017 metres
Lat./Long.: 35° 04' 43" 77° 38' 20"

Saser Muztagh

The 7,000-metre peaks are located in the Saser group, a great massif south of the Saser Pass, some of the peaks of which were triangulated before 1860. The group was not surveyed in detail during the early surveys of Kashmir by E. C. Ryall and it was not until Arthur Neve visited the Sakang and Phukpoche glaciers that any details were known.

In 1899 Neve visited the area and photographed the highest peak Saser Kangri. In 1909 he and A. M. Slingsby accompanied T. G. Longstaff, and in the course of their explorations ascended the Nubra valley to Panamik from where they reconnoitred the western approaches to the Saser group. They camped on the North Phukpoche glacier, but bad weather drove them back to Panamik.

One of the first mountaineers to visit the Karakoram after the First World War was Dr. Ph. C. Visser who, in 1922, made the first of four fine expeditions. With his wife and Alpine guides he visited the six small glaciers which drain northwestwards from the group, and also approached by way of the South Phukpoche glacier. Like Longstaff they were prevented by the weather from getting further than the head of the glacier.

A determined reconnaissance of the group was carried out in 1946 by J. O. M. Roberts and G. Lorimer, together with two Sherpas. Because of lack of time and support, Roberts could not hope to climb Saser Kangri but he examined it closely from the head of both Phukpoche glaciers, and

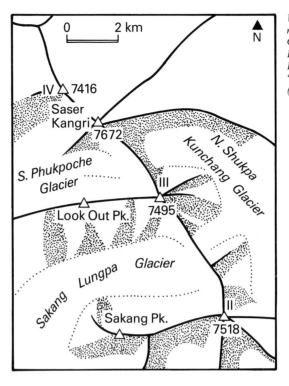

West side of Saser Kangri massif from South Phukpoche Glacier; left to right, Saser Kangri IV (7,415m), Saser Kangri I (7,672m) and 'Plateau Peak' (7,310m) (Harish Kapadia)

also the western side of the adjacent peaks from the Sakang glacier. Meanwhile Lorimer and Sherpa Sonam reconnoitred the northeast side of Saser Kangri which they reached via the Saser Pass after a long detour to the north. Roberts concluded that none of the group was climbable from the western side.

SASER KANGRI
Height: 7,672 metres
Subsidiary peak: Western foresummit, 7,620 metres
Lat./Long.: 34° 52' 02" 77° 45' 13"
First ascent: 1973 via South Ridge/Face

The first person to approach this peak was J. O. M. Roberts who, in 1947, reconnoitred the southern side and climbed Lookout Peak on the west ridge of Saser Kangri III.

In 1956 an Indian group, attempting this peak as part of the advance course of the Himalayan Mountaineering Institute, set up

camp on the South Phukpoche glacier below the west face. The two possible routes, to the north and south cols, were obviously difficult, but higher up the northern ridge looked less frightening than the southern. An attempt to reach the south col failed miserably. They then attempted to work their way round to the eastern side of the peak, but were unable to cross the ridge dividing the Sakang Lungpa and North Shukpa Kunchang glaciers. After an inspection of the formidable Saser Kangri II from a nearby 6,000-metre peak, members of the team climbed Sakang Peak, thought to be well over 7,000 metres high but now given as 6,943 metres.

In 1970 another Indian attempt followed an assessment of the chances in September 1969 by Major C. S. Nogyal. Again the approach was made to the west face which, contrary to expectations, was found to be constantly avalanching; any direct or southern route was out of the question. To the north of the peak the alterna-

tives were a difficult rock rib or a traverse across stretches of broken ice where rope would have to be fixed continuously. A last try was made by prospecting the west ridge of Saser Kangri IV, in an effort to traverse to the main peak, but this ridge was found to be dangerously corniced and to fall sharply on both sides.

India's then highest unclimbed peak was finally ascended by members of an Indo-Tibetan Border Police expedition. The long supply line went up the Shyok valley and thirty-five kilo-metres-long North Shukpa Kunchang glacier, approaching the peak from the southeast for the first time. After surmounting the ice-fall at the head of the glacier, they reached a large snowfield similar to Everest's Western Cwm. A mammoth ice wall blocked the way to the col on the south ridge and required over 1,200 metres of fixed rope. After a spell of bad weather the first summit party succeeded in making camp on the col at the foot of a rock band. Next day the four

gained the top of the rocky portion after three hours' struggle and continued up the steep ridge of snow-covered rock. Just below the summit they were obliged, by the strength of the wind, to crawl on all fours but managed to reach the top shortly afterwards. Two more ascents were made later.

1987. Northwest Ridge

Members of a large Indo-British army expedition made the first approach to the peak from the west, up the south Phukpoche glacier, using a common route with a party attempting Saser Kangri IV. After succeeding on the latter peak, the first assault team reached only the western forepeak of Saser Kangri I. After waiting for two weeks, a party of six left Camp III (6,500 metres) at 9 a.m. and reached the main summit in three hours. Three others made a remarkably fast ascent, going from base camp (4,950 metres) to the top in nine hours.

SASER KANGRI II (Shukpa Kunchang, K24)

Height: 7,518 metres (west peak, 7,518 metres)
Lat./Long.: 34°48' 77°48'
First ascent: 1985 to West Summit via Northwest Ridge

An Indo-Japanese team approached the peak from the west by way of the Sakang Lungpa glacier. Above Camp II (5,900 metres) 2,400 metres of rope had to be fixed up the almost vertical rock, snow and ice west face to the crest of the northwest ridge. After a halt for the weather, the summit was reached in just under twelve hours from Camp IV (6,650 metres). The peak has two summits for which the same altitude is given and they are separated by an almost level ridge about one kilometre long.

SASER KANGRI III

Height: 7,495 metres
Lat/Long.: 34°50' 77°47'
First ascent: 1986 via Northwest Face

An Indo-Tibetan Border Police team approached via the Shyok valley and North Shukpa Kanchang glacier. They climbed steep ice and rock, especially above Camp III (5,700 metres), to reach the northwest ridge. This was crossed at a saddle and the climb continued on the western side of the peak.

SASER KANGRI IV (Cloud Peak)
Height: 7,416 metres
Lat./Long.: 34°52' 77°45'
First ascent: 1987 via West Ridge

During an attempt on Saser Kangri I, members of a large Indian and British army expedition climbed this peak by two routes. The west ridge party fixed twenty rope-lengths up to Camp III (6,150 metres) on the southwest shoulder. From here, a British pair climbed a snow gully on the west face in eight hours to make the first ascent.

1987. South Ridge
While two British climbers were ascending the west ridge, three Indians spent the day fixing rope on the route to Saser Kangri I. They returned to camp by ascending Saser Kangri IV by its south ridge.

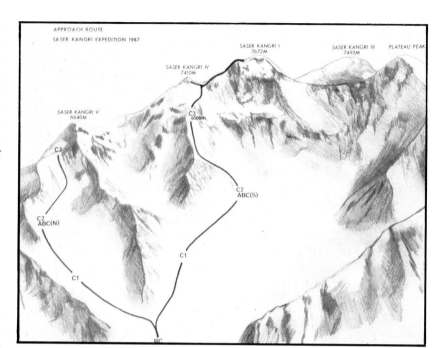

▲

Topographical diagram of the west side of the Saser Kangri massif showing the routes climbed by the 1987 expedition (Stephen Bell)

▶

Saser Kangri. Approaching Camp III (c. 6,700m) on the West Ridge during the first ascent from the west (Stephen Bell)

Bibliography

Anthoine, J. (1978), 'British Ogre Expedition 1977', *AJ*, 83, pp. 3–8 (see also, pp.116–17).

Bahuguna, H. (1971), 'The Indian Saser Kangri Expedition, 1970', *HJ*, 30, pp. 243–8.

Bonington, C. (1978), 'The Ogre', *AAJ*, 21, pp. 412–34.

Chadwick-Onyszkiewicz, A. (1977), 'Gasherbrum II and III, 1975', *AAJ*, 21, pp. 36–41.

Chamoli, S. (1987), 'Saser Kangri III, 1986', *HJ*, 43, pp. 84–91.

Cherian, K. (1987), 'Sia Kangri 1986', *HJ*, 43, pp. 80–3.

Child, G. (1987), 'Gasherbrum IV's northeast ridge', *AAJ*, 29, pp. 17–24.

Cohen, G. (1987), 'Attempt on Gasherbrum III, 1985', *HJ*, 43, pp. 101–11.

Duff, M. (1985), 'Second ascent of the Mustagh Tower', *AJ*, 90, pp. 74–6.

Edwards, J. (1960), 'Batura Muztagh Expedition,1959', *AJ*, 65, pp. 48–52. (see also, *MW*, 1960–61, pp. 87–107.

Fowler, M. (1985), 'Bojohagar', *AJ*, 90, pp. 77–83.

Fujii, M. (1983), 'Kanjut Sar west face', *AJ*, 88, pp. 179–80.

'German-Austrian Karakoram Expedition 1954', (1955), *MW*, pp. 19–33.

Hartog, J. (1956–57), 'The climbing of the Muztagh Tower', *AJ*, 61, pp. 253–70.

Horniblow, P. (1963), 'Khinyang Chhish, 1962', *AJ*, 68, pp. 100–7.

Kapada, H. (1986), 'Eastern Karakoram: a historical review', *HJ*, 42, pp. 144–53.

Kennedy, M. (1979), 'Latok I', *AAJ*, 22, pp. 24–8.

Kumar, N. (1981), 'Teram Kangri II expedition', *HJ*, 37, pp. 107–12.

Kurczab, J. (1975), 'Shispare climbed', *AJ*, 80, pp. 223–5.

Kurtyka, W. (1986), 'The shining wall of Gasherbrum IV', *AAJ*, 28, pp. 1–5.

Kurtyka, W. (1986), 'The abseil and the ascent', *HJ*, 42, pp. 120–6.

Kus, A. (1972), 'The battle for Khinyang Chhish', *AJ*, 77, pp. 21–5.

Kus, A. (1972), 'Khinyang Chhish climbed – Polish Himalayan-Karakoram Expedition, 1971', *HJ*, 31, pp. 283–9.

Longstaff, T. (1912), 'Mr. Collins' triangulation of Teram Kangri', *AJ*, 26, pp. 307–13.

Maraini, F. (1959), 'Italian expedition to Gasherbrum IV', *AJ*, 64, pp. 155–67, illustrated (see also, *MW*, 1960–61, pp. 72–86.

Milne, K. (1989), 'Kunyang Kish', *Mountain*, 126, pp. 22–7.

Noyce, W. (1961), 'Ascent of Trivor', *AJ*, 66, pp. 9–14, illustrated, (see also, *MW*, 1960–61, pp. 141–56).

Nunn, P. (1978), 'A hundred days in the Himalaya, 1977. Pt.1, Latok II', *AJ*, 83, pp. 114–20.

Onyszkiewcz, J. (1976), 'Polish ascents of Gasherbrum II and III, 1975', *HJ*, 34, pp. 93–6.

Payne, R. (1988–89), 'Karakoram lessons: the high-altitude expe-dition. British-New Zealand Gasherbrums Expedition 1987', *AJ*, 93, pp. 7–11.

Pischinger, R. (1965), 'First ascent of Momhil Sar', *AJ*, 70, pp. 69–73.

Prunes, J. and Bergamaschi, A. (1984), 'Climbs in the Disteghil Sar group', *HJ*, 40, pp. 130–4.

Roberts, J. (1947), 'Saser Kangri, eastern Karakorams, 1946', *HJ*, 14, pp. 9–18.

Roberts, J. (1947–48), 'Recon-naissance of Saser Kangri', *AJ*, 56, pp. 149–56.

Sandhu, B. (1985), 'First ascent of Mamostong (7,516 metres)', *HJ*, 41, pp. 93–101.

Saunders, A. V. (1986), 'Bojohagur 1984', *HJ*, 42, pp. 133–43.

Scott, D. (1979), 'A crawl down the Ogre', *HJ*, 35, pp. 241–50.

Sharma, G. (1985), 'Ascents in the Rimo group of peaks', *HJ*, 41, pp. 117–21.

Singh, H. (1986), 'Indo-Japanese expedition to Saser Kangri II', *HJ*, 42, pp. 97–108.

Singh, J. (1975), 'Homage to Saser Kangri, the "Yellow Mountain", 1973', *HJ*, 33, pp. 119–28, (see also, *AAJ*, 20, pp. 65–7).

Stefan, W. (1961), 'Disteghil Sar', *AJ*, 66, pp. 1–8 (see also, *MW*, 1962–63, pp. 60–9).

Stefan, W. (1975), 'Sia Kangri. 1974 diary', *AJ*, 80, pp. 151–3.

Thadani, K. (1982), 'Ascent of Apsarasas I in the Karakoram', *HJ*, 38, pp. 124–7.

Visser, P. (1923), 'The Sasir group in the Karakoram', *AJ*, 35, pp. 75–80.

Lesser Karakoram

The Lesser Karakoram comprises the ranges of shorter alignment, as opposed to the main crest system. Nearly all the peaks of the Lesser Karakoram lie to the south of the great glaciers.

Rakaposhi Range

RAKAPOSHI

Height: 7,788 metres
Lat./Long.: 36°08′39″ 74°29′22″
First ascent: 1958 via Southwest
*   Spur/Ridge*

In 1892 the first mountaineer to approach the peak was Martin Conway who viewed the mountain from the southern side, having penetrated the Bagrot Gah. Although the upper slopes appeared to be climbable, Conway considered that reaching the crest of any of the supporting ridges would be difficult and dangerous. Forty-six years later, C. Secord and M. Vyvyan started up the immense northwest ridge, reaching a forepeak at about 5,800 metres. After the Second World War, in 1947, Secord, H. W. Tilman and two Swiss climbers made an attempt on the southwest spur, but

abandoned their climb when blocked by a great gendarme at about 5,800 metres. From the top of the gendarme Tilman observed the 600-metre high steep wall of snow and ice which he christened 'Monk's Head'. It would be necessary to overcome this in order to gain the main southwest ridge, and it appeared to be a most formidable obstacle. Tilman tried to by-pass the Monk's Head via the Biro glacier, but the avalanche danger was too great.

In 1954 two parties visited Rakaposhi. An Austro-German group led by Mathias Rebitsch made a brief attempt on the southwest spur before giving up at around 5,200 metres. A Cambridge University expedition led by Alfred Tissières included George Band and several other strong young alpinists. They pushed beyond the gendarme on the southwest spur and actually climbed the Monk's Head before retiring. Beyond their highest point the route seemed reasonably easy, but they were not equipped to undertake such a long and difficult route.

In 1956 a four-man British-American party led by Mike Banks reached a high point (at about

7,170 metres), well up on the shoulder of the southwest ridge, but the effort involved was too much and they were unable to improve on this in two subsequent summit attempts. Banks returned two years later with a British-Pakistani Forces expedition and, with Tom Patey, reached the summit after placing the top camp 300 metres higher than in 1956, just below the snow plateau at the base of the summit pyramid. On the final day the pair set off in a blizzard and intense cold. The top was reached after five hours, both climbers suffering minor frostbite.

1979. Northwest Ridge

A Polish-Pakistani expedition had their base camp on the Biro glacier destroyed by the blast from a gigantic ice avalanche but managed to carry on. Camp I was set up at the foot of the northwest ridge, where the climbing difficulties began, and some 3,000 metres of rope were fixed. Four gendarmes were turned on the right and after three weeks the third camp was placed at 6,200 metres on the shoulder of the 'Nun's Head'. A slab traverse brought them to the snow terrace below the summit pyramid. The terrace was tra-

▲ *The northern flanks of Rakaposhi from the Hunza valley (Paul Nunn)*

versed to a col at the end of the southwest ridge, and so to the top. The ridge had been tried earlier in 1964 by an Irish party, but they found the route too long and very hard.

1979. North Ridge

In 1971 and 1973 Karl Herrligkoffer led expeditions to attempt the extremely difficult north ridge. The first group went up a steep glacial valley from Jul-Ghulmat and established a route up a broken ice-fall, then a 300-metre high ice wall, and over a number of dangerous gendarmes. A sharp rock ridge was extremely difficult, as was a 70° ice slope, but they reached the junction with the main ridge in eleven days. The route was open but some of the climbers were sick and the attempt was called off. Two years later the climb had to be abandoned because of lack of time and adverse weather conditions after overcoming all the major problems.

A Waseda University expedition climbed the ridge which had defeated Karl Herrligkoffer's German expeditions. Above 6,400 metres a 150-metre high rock band was passed by way of a couloir. The top camp was placed above an ice step at 7,300 metres. On 1 August E. Ohtani and M. Yamashita bivouaced at 7,600 metres and got to the top next day, where they found evidence of the Polish ascent. An alpine-style ascent of this route was made in 1984 by the Americans D. Cheesmond, B. Blanchard and K. Doyle.

1986. Northwest Ridge Variation

A Dutch expedition climbed a shorter route to the right of the 1964 Irish attempt, to reach the ridge at 6,000 metres, where they joined the 1979 Polish route.

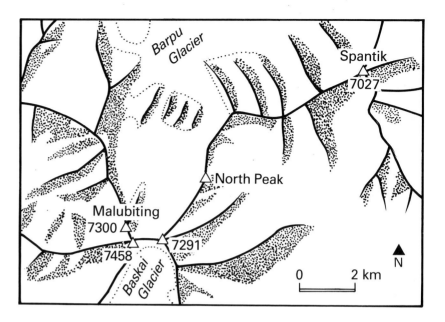

1985–87. East Ridge Attempts

So far, climbers have succeeded only in getting on the ridge at P.7010. In 1987 members of a Japanese expedition decided that the traverse to P.7290 seemed too difficult, despite excellent weather.

P.7290

Location: on east ridge of Rakaposhi, 2 km east of main peak
Lat./Long.: 36°09' 74°31'

P.7010 ('Rakaposhi East Peak')

Location: on east ridge of Rakaposhi, 2 km east of P.7290
Lat./Long.: 36°09' 74°32'
First ascent: 1985 via North Buttress

Members of an Austrian expedition trying to reach the east ridge of Rakaposhi made an alpine-style ascent with two bivouacs. Between 5,500–6,000 metres the route was up a 65° ice slope and a very exposed, sharp ridge. Four climbers reached the top. During the descent G. Fellner sustained fatal injuries after falling a hundred metres down an ice slope.

DIRAN (Minapin)

Height: 7,257 metres
Lat./Long.: 36°07' 14" 74°39' 44"
First ascent: 1968 via North Face, West Ridge

The German-Austrian expedition of 1954, led by Mathias Rebitsch, established that Diran could be climbed from the south over steep ice slopes and along the west ridge. In 1958 the first attempt on the peak ended in tragedy when the British climbers Ted Warr and Chris Hoyte vanished in a storm. They were last seen going strongly only 100 metres from the summit, having climbed the north face and west ridge. The following year German climber Rudolf Bardolej and the porter Kabul failed high on the British route on account of wind and Kabul's lack of fitness.

In 1964 an Austrian party reached only about 5,500 metres on the north face, being driven back by bad weather, deep snow and avalanche danger. The first Japanese expedition in 1965 reached the British high point before they too were defeated by strong wind and whirling snow. The successful Ö.A.V. party of 1968 were blessed with fine weather for their summit attempt which was made from a camp at 6,100 metres. There was first a steep step before the ridge flattened and led to the 400 metres of the 45° final slope and the surprisingly large summit plateau.

1979–86. North Ridge Attempts
Several expeditions have tried this route. The first was a Spanish party in 1979 but they reached only the col (5,020 metres). In June–July 1981 a Japanese expedition reached 5,650 metres, or possibly a little higher, before giving in to the weather. Two years later Swiss climbers gave up after encountering bottomless powder snow. In 1984 a French expedition abandoned their attempt because of dangerous séracs and avalanches. The next year another Spanish group also had to admit defeat after being on the mountain throughout June. Above the col they found the ridge as far as 5,300 metres steep, but uniform with some poor rock and cornices. For the next 800 metres it was much rougher with overhanging séracs. Then there was a series of snow and ice towers covered with powder snow. This unstable section continued for 300 metres and

they lacked sufficient rope to fix the route safely. Meanwhile, a bear had broken into their first camp and devoured thirty man-days of food. The second Japanese attempt, in 1986, was called off when one climber disappeared between the col and Camp III.

Malubiting West
Height: 7,458 metres
Lat./Long.: 36°00' 74°52'
First ascent: 1971 via Northeast Ridge (and under Central Peak)

In 1955 German climbers ascended from the Malubiting glacier on the eastern side of the peak to the southeast ridge, but bad weather prevented the possibility of an ascent. A British-Pakistani army team were in the Chogo Lungma area in 1959 and as part of their programme made an attempt on this peak. Two members gained the southeast ridge from the Malubiting glacier and the summit of Malubiting East (6,970 metres).

The 1968 Manchester Karakoram Expedition attempted Malubiting from the Baskai glacier, thus gaining the southeast ridge from the opposite side. The ridge to the east peak proved to be quite difficult, and one member of the

party was killed before they had completed much of it. In 1969 members of a Polish expedition attempted the north face, reaching about 7,100 metres, after having approached through the Polan La from the Chogolungma. After overcoming technical problems they withdrew on account of the weather and length of the route. They made the first ascent of Malubiting North (6,840 metres).

A 1970 Munich D.A.V. expedition reached the southeast ridge between the eastern and central summits, but found that from there they could not reach the col between the central and main (west) peaks as expected. They decided, therefore, to try the northeast face of the central peak but a lost crampon cut short the attempt.

In 1971 an expedition led by Horst Schindlbacher traversed the north peak from the Polan La and reached the col between the central and main peaks. They climbed the east ridge from the col on hard snow to make the first ascent.

1974. Barpu Glacier Approach
An Italian group found that the Malubiting group is unclimbable from this direct northern approach

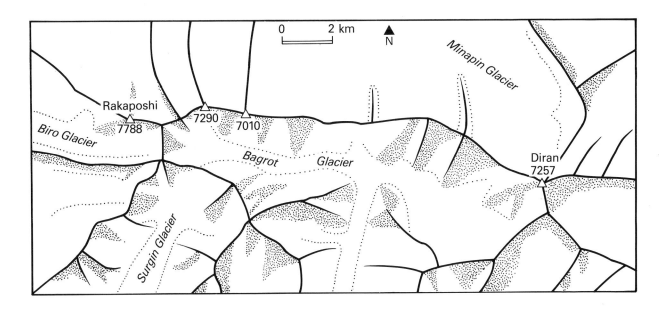

on account of enormous blocks of ice which fall day and night from an unbroken fifty-metre high band of vertical ice to the rocks below.

MALUBITING CENTRAL
Height: 7,291 metres
Lat./Long.: 36°00' 74°54'
First ascent: 1975 via West Wall

Japanese climbers reached the summit by the west wall, having approached via the northeast ridge and upper plateau. Previous expeditions had by-passed this summit in their attempts to reach the main peak.

MALUBITING NORTHWEST
Height: 7,300 metres
Lat./Long.: 36°01' 74°53'

SPANTIK ('Pyramid Peak', Ghenish Chhish. Also called Golden Parri by Conway and Yengutz Har by Shipton)
Height: 7,027 metres
Lat./Long.: 36°03'28" 74°58'45"
First ascent: 1955 via Southeast Ridge

In August 1903 Dr and Mrs Workman ascended the southeast ridge of this peak, over two minor points which they called Chogo and Lungma, to within an estimated 330 metres of the top.

In 1955 five German climbers led by K. Kramer reached the summit on 5 July via the same ridge. The climbers were hampered by bad weather, and the snow and ice conditions, so the relatively easy ascent turned into a considerable struggle. Four camps were set up, the highest on the summit ridge at 6,450 metres, some three kilometres beyond 'Lungma' across a high plateau. They were rewarded with a brief view from the top. The second ascent of the mountain was also made by this route in 1978.

▲

William Hunter and Fanny Bullock Workman

1978. South Ridge
The third successful expedition to Spantik climbed the south ridge in July-August. Near the top they crossed to the southeast ridge. The route had great avalanche danger.

1984. Southeast Ridge/ Southwest Ridge Variation
From a camp near the top of 'Mount Lungma' (6,400 metres), Dutch climbers used snowshoes to cross the intermediate plateau to the southwest ridge, which they ascended to the top.

▲ *The Northwest ('Golden') Pillar of Spantik (A. V. Saunders)*

1987. Northwest Pillar

British climbers Mick Fowler and Victor Saunders spent a total of nine days on the mountain. A 900-metre high snow buttress led up to the pillar which consisted of another 900 metres of steep mixed ground. The summit plateau was crossed in deep powder snow. They descended the prominent snow and ice spur falling from the southwest ridge two kilometres west of the Pillar.

MAKORUM

Location: south side of Hispar glacier
Height: historically, 7,239 metres
Lat./Long.: 36°03'25" 75°07'04"

This peak was listed by Kenneth Mason [*HJ* 10 (1938): 111] from a map by Afraz Gul. It appears to correspond with Makrong Chhish (6,608 metres).

Haramosh Range

HARAMOSH

Height: 7,409 metres
Lat./Long.: 35°50'29" 74°53'52"
First ascent: 1958 via East Ridge

The first reconnaissance of this peak, which rises above the Indus valley like a sphinx, was carried out in 1947 by the Swiss climbers H. Gyr and R. Kappeler. From the Haramosh La they gained a high pass (5,400 metres) to the east of the three northeastern forepeaks of Haramosh and found the connecting ridge was steep and inaccessible. Most of a Frankfurt expedition's efforts in 1955 were directed at Spantik and Malubiting, but two members, E. Reinhardt and J. Tietze, climbed to the upper Haramosh basin and decided that the northeastern route was possible but very long, and would require six or seven high camps.

Two years later there occurred on Haramosh a sequence of events making up one of the most harrowing of all climbing tragedies. The main aims of the expedition from Oxford University were to explore and survey the approaches. They were led by Tony Streather, a professional soldier from the Royal Military Academy, Sandhurst. The first two weeks were spent exploring the northern and western sides of the mountain without discovering any route.

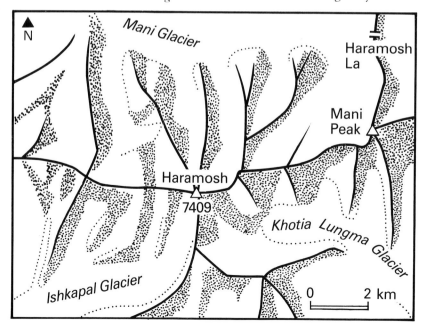

They then turned to the long east ridge which runs over the subsidiary Mani Peak (6,684 metres). By mid-September four camps were in place. On the 15th, B. Jillott, J. Emery, R. Culbert (from New Zealand) and Streather climbed to a point on the ridge near Mani Peak.

From here they could see the summit of Haramosh, some six and a half kilometres away, and the rest of the route which looked impassable on account of its steepness and broken snow formations. Suddenly, a patch of bad snow avalanched under Jillott and Emery, sweeping them down about 300 metres over an ice cliff

▲

Haramosh–the 'Cardinal's Hat', the highest point reached by the 1957 party (H. R. A. Streather)

▲

Haramosh, Bernard Jillot and John Emery seconds before the slope on which they were standing avalanched (H. R. A. Streather)

and into a snow basin. They managed to climb up to the bergschrund and traverse under the ice cliff, and by the afternoon of the 16 September were reunited with the others who had descended to assist them. Jillott and Emery were now without ice axes, so all four climbers tied on one rope; as a result the whole party fell twice, the second time back into the snow basin. Now they had no axes and were all very tired.

After spending the night in the bergschrund, Streather was the only fit member of the party. They made some slow progress upwards and, as there were no axes, climbed unroped. On the way they recovered Culbert's axe and began to traverse above the ice cliff. At the end of the traverse Culbert was unable to continue, being minus one crampon and with a frostbitten foot, so Streather gave him a rope. The inevitable happened, and both

men fell down into the snow basin again. Meanwhile, Jillott and Emery regained the crest and tried to descend to Camp IV for rescue supplies. Along the way, Jillott missed the route and walked over a vertical drop to his death. Emery was by now very weak and frostbitten, but managed to reach the camp where he was joined next day by Streather alone, having failed to extricate Culbert by himself. Next morning, Emery was almost helpless and Streather was hardly able to crawl out of the tent. Not knowing whether Culbert was still alive, Streather was forced to abandon him in the hope that he could get Emery down. More dead than alive they reached Camp III, where the last member of the group, Scott Hamilton, was waiting anxiously. Descending ever more painfully they were eventually met by their porters. Afterwards John Emery survived his extensive frostbite, qualified as a doctor and returned to serious climbing, but was killed descending the Weisshorn in 1963. Tony Streather was able to continue with his military and climbing careers.

In 1958 the Austrian climbers H. Roiss, S. Pauer and F. Mandl reached the top via the east ridge during a brief spell of good weather in the middle of the monsoon.

1978. West Ridge

The Japanese climbers Sumiya Isono, Ryo Nishikori and Kenji Shimakata reached the summit on 22 July.

1988. Southwest Face

On 29 July three Polish climbers reached the summit via the difficult 4,000-metre high southwest face, after fixing 2,500 metres of rope. Three others completed the climb two days later. Subsequently, three other members of the party completed the climb, while two more climbed a lower point, 'Sari Sumari', reported as about 7,000 metres but actually 6,700 metres.

Masherbrum Range

BALTISTAN PEAK (K6)

Height: 7,281 metres
Lat./Long.: 35°24'30" 76°33'
First ascent: 1970 via Southeast Ridge

Two parties reconnoitred this peak in 1961. An Austrian group found the east (Kondus) side unpromising, while a RAF expedition explored the northern and southwestern approaches. The north face, rising almost vertically for

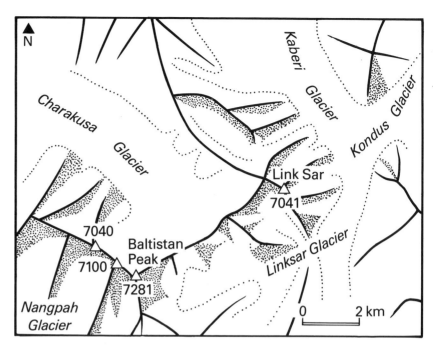

over 2,000 metres, was clearly out of the question. From the southwest the group reached a height of just over 6,000 metres. To gain the principal summit would have necessitated a high level traverse of three kilometres, including the climbing of difficult rocks at an altitude of about 7,300 metres. Three years later it was reported that a German expedition had reached 6,300 metres from the Link Sar glacier; subsequently it was shown that they were in fact on K7 which lies five kilometres to the north (that is, three km north-west of Link Sar).

In 1969 an Italian expedition attempted a route on the 2,000-metre high southwest wall to a forepeak (7,040 metres). Bad weather drove the summit pair back only 250 metres from the top.

The 1970 Ö.A.V. expedition discovered a new approach via the Nangpah glacier. From the basin a narrow hanging glacier on the southeast face rose to the 'K6 Shoulder' and ended on the southeast ridge. From a col, steep and dangerous ice couloirs and difficult rock led to Camp II (6,900 metres). After passing the shoulder to the

southeast ridge, a heavily corniced ridge led to the foot of the summit tower. Exhaustion, lack of equipment and bad weather then obliged them to wait at base camp for two weeks. Eventually they were in a position to fix a rope on the first vertical section of the summit tower (Grade V+, A2). Next day two pairs, in poor weather, struggled up a steep ice and rock couloir and climbed the final icy rock face to the summit.

BALTISTAN PEAK NORTHWEST

Height: 7,100 metres (northwest II peak (Cima Abruzzi), 7,040 metres)
Lat./Long.: 35°25' 76°32'

In 1969 an Italian expedition, led by Luigi Barbuscia, attempting the main peak climbed the 2,000-metre high west wall of the northwest ridge. Bad weather drove the leading pair back when they were close to the first forepeak (that is, P.7040) which they may have climbed. In 1975 a Japanese group approached the K6 group from the north and reached a col between

P.6900 and P.7040 (Cima Abruzzi). They attacked the ridge leading to P.7040, but after two bivouacs turned back at 6,900 metres.

LINK SAR

Location: at junction of the Kaberi and
  Kondus glaciers
Height: 7,041 metres
Lat./Long.: 35°26' 76°36'

In 1979 a Japanese university party ascended the Kondus glacier and reached 6,050 metres on the avalanche prone east face.

PRUPOO BURAHKA

Location: southwest of Chogolisa
Height: c.7,000 metres (possibly
  6,950 metres)
Lat./Long.: 35°34' 76°35'
First ascent: 1977 via Northwest Ridge

A large Japanese group went up the Chogolisa glacier and climbed the broad snow ridge on 14 July.

CHOGOLISA (Bride Peak)

Height: Southwest Summit, 7,665
metres; Northeast Summit, 7,654
metres
Lat./Long.: 35°36'44" 76°34'23"
First ascent: Northeast Summit, 1958
  via East Ridge; Southwest Summit,
  1975 via West Ridge

The first attempt on this peak was made on the northeast summit. In 1909, after his failure to climb K2, the Duke of Abruzzi had no intention of withdrawing without climbing something higher than anything previously attained. The season was not advanced and his party was strong and healthy. The northern flank of Chogolisa seemed to offer an easy, if tedious, route to the summit. The Duke pushed up a camp to the Chogolisa Saddle (between Chogolisa and Pioneer Peak) but then the monsoon arrived. In spite of this his porters managed to place another camp above the saddle at 6,600 metres on the long east ridge. From here the Duke and three guides made two determined assaults. On the first occasion they reached 7,100 metres, after making a route between a dangerous cornice and a gaping crevasse, when a storm broke. It was six days before the strong winds and heavy snowfall passed and they could try again.

Starting at 5.30 a.m. they made good progress and were at 7,000 metres after one and a half hours. Then they were enveloped in mist. Groping their way up the steep and treacherous ridge in soft snow, 'More than once they heard, terrifyingly close, the crack of snow detaching itself from the slope and slithering into the void. They could see no more than a few yards in any direction, but realized that bottomless gulfs were opening up around them.' About 11 a.m. they

▲ *Chogolisa from the northeast (Kurt Diemberger)*

reached a rock step (7,400 metres) which took them two hours to climb because of the altitude. Ahead another indeterminate snow-slope loomed up through the mist: the ridge was too dangerous to tackle blindly. After waiting for two hours in the hope that the weather would clear, the Duke reluctantly ordered retreat. He had come close to the summit; his only consolation was the new height record.

This route was attempted again in 1957 by the Austrians Hermann Buhl and Kurt Diemberger, after their ascent of Broad Peak. Travelling light, they moved their tent up to 6,750 metres under the southern slopes of P.7150. After a day of storm they made good progress, despite dangerous snow conditions. Traversing under P.7150 they followed the sharp, corniced ridge down to the Duke of Abruzzi's col, arriving there about 9 a.m. Above was a steep, mostly broad snow ridge leading to the summit. Continuing unroped they climbed swiftly until suddenly visibility deteriorated and a furious gale sprang up. Although the time was only one o'clock and they were only about 300 metres from the top, Buhl decided they must turn back before their tracks were covered. As Diemberger was leading the way down a quaking movement beneath his feet made him leap for safety. When Buhl did not appear Diemberger hastened back up the slope, finding Buhl's footsteps leading over the jagged edge of the broken cornice which had carried him down the north face to his death.

In 1958 an expedition from the Academic Alpine Club of Kyoto, led by T. Kuwabara, also followed this route, finding on the way the Austrians' half-buried tent. The Japanese then placed a further camp under P.7150, but their first attempt on the summit ridge got

▲

Hermann Buhl on Chogolisa a few hours before the fatal accident (Kurt Diemberger)

no farther than their predecessors' one. M. Fujihira and K. Hirai then attacked from a camp 200 metres below the southern side of the col on the ridge, using oxygen. Chest deep snow made progress slow and their oxygen ran out, but they persevered and reached the top of the ridge at 4 p.m. Above them was the forty metres of the summit rock pinnacle on which they could stand only one at a time. They arrived back in camp exhausted after eighteen hours.

1975. Southwest Summit

In 1975 an Austrian expedition led by E. Koblmüller climbed the slightly higher southwest summit which is separated from the northeast peak by a 900-metre long ridge. Until then the south side of Chogolisa was almost completely unexplored. Base camp was set up above the confluence of the Kondus and Kaberi glaciers, nearly twenty kilometres from the south face of the mountain. They ascended a giant ice-fall on the Kaberi glacier, above which rose a kilometre-high, 50° ice slope, to the col (6,750 metres) at the foot of the two-kilometre long west ridge. From the col, F. Pressl and G. Ammerer traversed the long flat stretch of the ridge and pitched a bivouac tent at just over 7,000 metres. Next day they reached the top in twelve hours. Two days later, another pair repeated the climb. Japanese climbers attempting the south ridge in 1980 were hampered by bad weather and finally had to abandon it when they diverted to assist some American climbers who had fallen from the Austrian route on the west ridge.

1983–4. Northwest Spur and Variation

The Germans A. Fischer, H. Wendlinger and G. Brosig made the ascent of the higher summit by a new route from the northwest. Climbing alpine-style they fixed rope on the upper part of the spur and bivouaced below the summit block on a small plateau. Next day the route led up steeply between séracs and debris; after great effort the top was reached at 7 p.m. The following year a mixed European party encountered much better conditions, climbing a snow gully left of the spur on skis. The whole team reached the summit, including a German woman, Alice Zebrowski. The descent was made on skis.

1984. Southwest Face

A French expedition, barred from normal access to the Kaberi glacier, had to make a difficult approach via the Chogolisa-Buesten glaciers over a high pass (5,500 metres). From camp on a plateau at the bottom, the south ridge was gained at 7,000 metres via the very steep snow slopes of the southwest face. B. Aucher, P. Dubois, J–M. Galmiche and E. Monier reached the summit safely, but Mlle Aucher and Philippe Dubois were killed in an avalanche while descending.

1986. Northeast Ridge

Spanish climbers ascended the ridge which separates the north and east faces of the northeast peak. They gained the ridge by climbing some 50°–60° slopes between ice séracs. The ridge continued at an angle of 40°–50° to a hollow at 6,300 metres, whence flatter slopes led to séracs at 6,950 metres. On the summit they found a Japanese doll left by the first climbers.

P.7150

Location: On east ridge of Chogolisa II; it was called 'Ridge Peak' by Hermann Buhl and Kurt Diemberger and 'Ice Dome' by the 1958 Japanese party
Lat./Long.: 35° 35′ 76° 35′

BALTORO KANGRI I
(Golden Throne)

Height: 7,240 metres (previously given as 7,312 metres)
Lat./Long.: 35° 38′ 50″ 76° 40′ 00″
First ascent: 1976

This peak was first seen by W. M. Conway's expedition in 1892. After travelling up the Baltoro glacier for several days they saw at the head of the valley 'an enormous mountain, not marked on any map. It was throne-like in form, and auriferous veins seemed to permeate its mass; we therefore named it the Golden Throne.'

▲ *W. M. Conway (1856–1937), c. 1895*

Conway laid siege to the mountain during the second half of August, putting a series of camps towards the southwest spur. With the weather threatening to break, they tackled the ridge and soon found themselves on hard ice. Conway's guide, Mathias Zurbriggen, led the way up the monotonous ridge, cutting steps continuously. Cornices forced them to keep to the right-hand slope and the heat of the sun made their progress even slower. At last, at 2.45 p.m., they reached what appeared to be the summit – 'But here a most unwelcome surprise awaited us. The summit of the Golden Throne was still some 1,300 feet [395m] above us, and the peak on which we stood was absolutely cut off from it by a deep depression, of whose existence we had been till now in ignorance.' Conway named his summit Pioneer Peak, the height of which he calculated to be 6,893 metres. In fact it is less than that. Nevertheless he had attained the greatest proven height to date.

The first attempt from the eatern side of the massif was made in 1963 by members of a Japanese expedition who probably only succeeded in reaching the summit of Baltoro Kangri III. In 1976 Japanese climbers Y. Toyama and G. Sueki met their support party on the top of

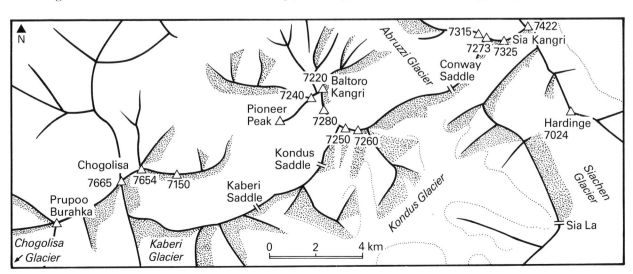

Baltoro Kangri III and then traversed Baltoro Kangri II to the main peak.

BALTORO KANGRI II

Height: 7,220 metres (or, 7,300 metres)
First ascent: 1976 via Traverse

Japanese climbers traversed Baltoro Kangri II from III on their way to Baltoro Kangri I.

BALTORO KANGRI III

Height: 7,280 metres (or, 7,310 metres)
First ascent: 1963 via East Ridge

In 1963 a large Japanese expedition ascended the upper Abruzzi glacier on the eastern side of the massif, placing their top camp just beneath the main ridge between Baltoro Kangri IV and V. In fine weather the summit pair, T. Shibata and S. Kono, were delayed by deep snow and a steep ice wall, forcing them to bivouac on the main ridge between III and IV. Next morning, after four hours' struggle on the steep snow flank, they reached the top of Baltoro Kangri III (and presumably no further), to be followed thirty minutes later by S. Shima and K. Fujimoto who had started only that morning.

BALTORO KANGRI IV

Height: 7,250 metres

There is no positive report of an ascent of this summit but it may have been climbed by the Japanese parties in 1963 and/or 1976.

BALTORO KANGRI V
(Baltoro Kangri east peak)

Height: 7,260 metres
Lat./Long.: 35°37' 76°42'
First ascent: 1934 via Northeast Ridge

Members of G. O. Dyrenfurth's international expedition made the ascent from Conway Saddle, keeping below the main ridge.

MASHERBRUM

Height: 7,821 metres (that is, the northeast summit)
Lat./Long.: 35°38'36" 76°18'31"
First ascent: 1960 via Southeast Face

In 1911 Dr and Mrs Workman went up the Hushe ravine and photographed the Masherbrum and Ghandogoro glaciers which flow from the south and southeast flanks of the peak. This was all the information that the first expedition in 1938 had to go on. The leader was James Waller, with J. B. Harrison, R. A. Hodgkin, T. G. Brown and J. O. M. Roberts. Looking across the Masherbrum glacier they could see a snow plateau at about 6,700 metres, above which rose the great snow and ice face enclosed by the southeast and east rock ridges. They made their way up the eastern arm of the Masherbrum glacier and after two weeks had established their fifth camp on the plateau, and were attacking the

▲ *North face of Baltoro Kangri seen from the Gasherbrum Glacier (André Roch)*

southeast face. From the highest camp at 7,500 metres a summit bid by Harrison and Hodgkin was defeated by storm and exhaustion, as a result of which they were severely frostbitten while descending in a blizzard.

In 1955 a Canterbury Mountain-

Bob Downes, came up in the second assault party, but died overnight with the sudden onset of pneumonia. In mid-August Don Whillans and Joe Walmsley made another valiant attempt, again reaching the summit couloir which was still full of dangerous snow.

storm which lasted several days, paradoxically the face was in better condition, as avalanches had removed much of the soft snow. The top camp was reopened but they found that their cache higher up had been swept away. Bell and Willi Unsoeld laboriously fixed a new tent and set out for the summit on the morning of 6 July. Hot sun and the steepness of the slope made for slow going in the couloir, but at 11 a.m. the narrow crest of the summit ridge was reached. Above, a step of rotten rock gave way to a knife-edge of snow and a second step split by a chimney. The final pitch was a gentle snow ridge which was reached at 3.15 p.m. Two days later, Clinch and Jawed Akhter Khan repeated the ascent, though not without experiencing their own adventures.

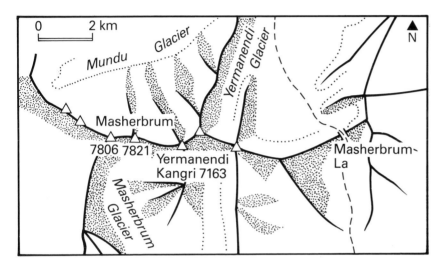

1985. Northwest Ridge/Face

In 1976 a fourteen-man Japanese expedition attempted the west and north ridges from the Mundu glacier. A semi alpine attempt in 1981 on the north face ended at about 5,500 metres when a serac broke off from an ice cliff, starting an avalanche down a ramp above five climbers. In 1985 the Japanese Kansai Karakoram Expedition started up the north ridge from the Yermanendu glacier. Frequent collapses of the upper glacier forced them to traverse to the northwest ridge where camps were established up to 7,200 metres. Rotten rock then necessitated another traverse right and they eventually climbed the northwest face to the col between the northeast and southwest peaks. All members reached the top on 23 July after nearly seven weeks on the mountain.

1985. Northwest Face

An Austrian party reached the summit the day after the Japanese by a completely different route.

eering Club party from New Zealand reached the mountain in mid-April, finding deep snow still covering the approaches. As a result it took them thirty-two days to accomplish what the 1938 party had done in five. The build-up was halted first by the death of a porter. By the end of May they were established on the Dome at 6,700 metres when another week was lost through porter sickness. After reaching the foot of the final face on 11 June, bad weather and the arrival of the monsoon squashed their remaining chances.

By contrast, two years later, a British party from the Rucksack Club gained the southeast face in two weeks and made good progress up to 7,300 metres. The first summit attempt was foiled by dangerous soft snow in the couloir between the northeast and southwest tops. Bad weather then kept the climbers pinned down for several days. The deputy leader,

Taking to a rock buttress on the left side they encountered very severe rock and had to retreat after climbing only some sixty metres in six hours.

The fourth expedition to attempt the southeast face was made up of Americans and Pakistanis, and was directed by Nick Clinch, with George Bell as climbing leader. From base camp on 1 June good progress was made, although after ten days they were hampered for the rest of the climb by intermittent cloud and snow. It proved to be hard work higher up and it was nearly the end of the month before the first summit bid. The slopes leading to the couloir were covered in soft heavy snow which required great effort to traverse, and by 2 p.m. the climbers had not reached the foot of the couloir. During the descent Dick McGowan was taken ill suddenly, but managed to get down to a lower camp safely. After a wild

North Face of Masherbrum from the Baltoro Glacier (H. Adams Carter)

From the Mundu glacier their route to Camp I at 5,500 metres was very technical (rock 5.9, ice 85°). This was followed by a ridge and slope (55°–60°) to Camp III at 6,300 metres. The first summit bid on 12 July got to 7,000 metres, followed by another ten days later. From a bivouac at 7,200 metres the route was mostly rock-climbing (5.7–5.8), with some ice couloirs. A. Orgler, M. Larcher and R. Renzler were the summit party.

MASHERBRUM SOUTHWEST

Height: 7,806 metres
Lat./Long.: 35° 38' 29" 76° 18' 23"
First ascent: 1981 via Southeast Face

In 1981 a Royal Air Force expedition attempted an alpine-style ascent of the southeast face. The approach from the south was up the Masherbrum glacier where the serious climbing began at base camp (4,100 metres). The route followed the line of the 1960 first ascent of Masherbrum to the top of the Dome. The climbers reached 7,130 metres before illness and bad weather stopped them.

In the same year this summit was tackled by a Polish expedition. They followed the same route on the steep southeast face. After a difficult ice section, three climbers reached the col between the two main peaks and bivouaced in a snow hole. Next day the final summit ridge was more difficult than anticipated, taking seven hours. Two of the climbers died in an impromptu bivouac halfway down the ridge, the third one miraculously surviving a fall later down the face.

P.7200, P.7200, P.7000

Location: on west ridge of Masherbrum

The more westerly P.7200 was climbed in 1988 by members of an Italian expedition, led by Augusto Zanotti.

YERMANENDI KANGRI

Location: on east ridge of Masherbrum
Height: 7,163 metres
Lat./Long.: 35° 38' 76° 19'

A four-man D.A.V. party in 1981 made a route across Masherbrum's

southeast face to the col between Masherbrum and P.7163 (Yermanendi Kangri). Volker Stallbohm visited the col, but could not find a route up the peak. Later they reached 7,400 metres in an attempt on the main peak.

Saltoro Range

DEPAK

Height: 7,150 metres
Lat./Long.: 35° 31' 76° 48'
First ascent: 1960 via North Face/ West Ridge

A small German-Austrian party attempted the Ghaint peaks from the north. Having reached what they thought was their summit they could see that a deep col separated them from 'Mount Ghent'. They named their peak Depak, an abbreviation for the title of their expedition.

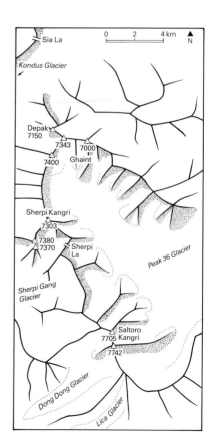

GHAINT I (Mount Ghent)

Height: 7,400 metres
Lat./Long.: 35°31'06" 76°48'07"
First ascent: 1961 via West Ridge

An Austrian expedition tackled the west ridge from the north after a very long approach up the Kondus glacier. During the second part of May the group experienced adverse weather conditions. At the fourth attempt the youngest member, Wolfgang Axt, succeeded in reaching the top of Ghaint I, climbing solo from the highest camp (6,400 metres) in the depression under the long west ridge.

GHAINT II (Ghent North)

Location: 2 km northeast of Ghaint I
Height: 7,343 metres
Lat./Long.: 35°31'44" 76°48'33"
First ascent: 1977 from West(?)

An Austrian expedition led by Wolfgang Axt made a number of ascents in this area, including the first ascent of Ghaint II. Base camp was on the Kondus glacier and four high camps were set up between 11 and 27 June. From Camp IV (6,675 metres) members made the ascent of Ghaint II from the western (?) side on 28 June.

1978. Northeast Ridge

H. Kobayashi's Japanese group set up five camps on the Kondus glacier between 27 May and 26 June. Camp VI was placed at just over 7,000 metres near the top of Depak. Three members made the ascent on 15 July, followed by five others over the next two days.

GHAINT III

Location: 2 km east of Ghaint II
Height: c.7,000 metres
Lat./Long.: 35°30' 76°49'

SHERPI KANGRI (Sherpi Kangri Rock Pinnacle)

Height: 7,380 metres (south peak, 7,370 metres)

Lat./Long.: 35°27' 76°47'
First ascent: 1976 via West Ridge

In 1961 Austrian climbers led by Erich Waschak concluded that the only approach to this peak would be from the south via Karmading and the Khorkondus valley; they also considered the eastern flanks more promising.

The 1974 Kobe University expedition managed to ascend three of the ice-falls of the Sherpi Gang glacier. After trying to reach the west ridge from the fourth ice-fall they abandoned their plan to climb the south and west ridges. They also gave up on the east ridge of the main peak and the south ridge of the east peak. British climbers in 1975 established camp under the south face, but soon realized that the difficulties were too great and the distance to the summit too far in the available time.

The following year members of the Japanese Alpine Club ascended the ice-falls of the Sherpi Gang

glacier and attempted the west ridge. Having gained the ice and rock of the sharp, steep ridge they crossed to the 'Eagle's Head', one of the hardest parts of the route. From there two members reached the summit in perfect weather.

SHERPI KANGRI EAST

Height: 7,303 metres
Lat./Long.: 35°27'54" 76°47'07"

Attempted by Japanese climbers in 1974 via the south ridge.

SALTORO KANGRI I

Height: 7,742 metres
Lat./Long.: 35°24'01" 76°50'55"
First ascent: 1962 via Southeast Face

During their 1911–12 reconnaissance, Dr and Mrs Workman examined the peak at close quarters, both from its northeastern and southwestern sides, and reached a height of perhaps 6,100 metres. They gave very few details about the mountain in their book, *Two Summers*. The first serious

▲ *Saltoro Kangri from camp on the Lica Glacier (John Hunt)*

attempt on Saltoro Kangri was made in 1935 by a small party comprising James Waller, John Hunt, J. S. Carslaw and R. Brotherhood. The first week was spent on a detailed reconnaissance of the west and south faces from the Dong Dong and Lica glaciers. With great difficulty the party then crossed a col at the head of the Lica glacier and set up an advanced base under the east face. In mid-June they began their attempt and in five days placed three camps up to a height of 6,770 metres. The next day they reached the crest of the south ridge at about 7,530 metres, but it was late, they were tired and the weather was deteriorating.

A joint Japanese-Pakistani expedition in 1962 approached from Peak 36 glacier and followed the 1935 route. They found snowshoes very helpful in the steep, deep snow. The assault team left camp (7,200 metres) and did not have great difficulties, but the continuous slope of deep snow slowed them down. Near the 'Gendarme', about one-and-a-half kilometres from the top, they had to bivouac without much equipment. Next day, after seven hours' struggle in deep snow, they climbed a shallow ice gully leading to the final ridge and summit.

SALTORO KANGRI II
(North)
Height: 7,705 metres
Lat./Long.: 35°24′24″ 76°50′50″

A 1975 Japanese attempt failed because of supply problems and avalanche danger. The following year a D.A.V. group reached the upper Peak 36 glacier. They were

East Face of Saltoro Kangri (John Hunt)

hampered by porter trouble and unsettled weather, but managed to reconnoitre a route on the east spur to 6,500 metres, apparently beyond the technical difficulties. Avalanches followed by fresh snow put an end to any hopes of a summit bid. In 1981 another D.A.V. party had such organizational problems that their programme was upset. From the Mahari-Lica glacier they advanced to the foot of the southwest face. Bad weather, logistical problems and lack of time prevented any ascent.

K12
Height: 7,428 metres (previously 7,468 metres)★
Lat./Long,: 35°18′13″ 77°00′55″
First ascent: 1974 via Northwest Ridge

In 1957 the Imperial College expedition led by Eric Shipton's party made a reconnaissance and survey of the area. From a peak (at about 6,850 metres) at the head of the Lolofond glacier they had a fine view of the north side of K12 and the colossal basin of the K12 glacier. Later, an attempt to cross from this basin westwards to the Bilafond glacier via the Grachma glacier was largely foiled by poor weather which hindered navigation.

A small international group in 1960 approached the peak from the west, up the Grachma glacier, the upper part of which rises close to the west face. It took them a long time to find a route through the final ice-fall, but eventually they were able to cross the pass west of K12 and descend northwards into the extensive snow basin first seen by Shipton's party three years previously. After some surveying, an attempt was made on the west ridge from the pass. Steps were cut up the steep ice and snow buttresses on the ridge to reach the snow apron which covers the upper southwest face. Stephenson gained a point close to 7,000 metres but, although the difficulties of the route had all been over come, he ran out of time.

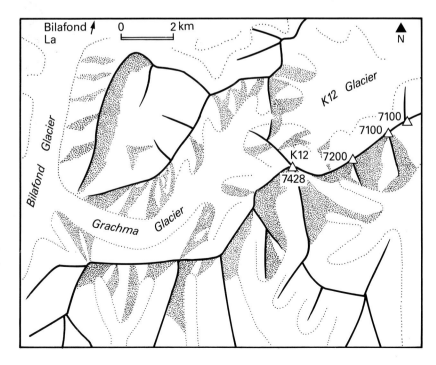

The first Japanese attempt in 1971 was nothing like as successful, but in 1974 they reached a col northwest of K12. Having achieved the ascent of the northwest ridge Shinichi Tagaki and Tsutomu Ito radioed news of their success from a bivouac where they were pinned down by the weather for a day. Resuming their descent on 1 September they slipped, and in their last radio message at 6.30 p.m. said that they were hanging from an ice piton. Rescuers reached the area two days later, but found no trace of them. The climb was repeated in 1975 by another Japanese team.

1984. West Ridge

This was climbed in October by three members of an Indian Army expedition which approached from the K12 glacier and gained the west ridge from its northern side. The climb to the ridge was very steep and difficult. From camp (6,550 metres) the assault party took seven hours to climb the knife-edge ridge on hard and brittle ice. It was extremely cold and windy.

(★ In his valuable article on Karakoram nomenclature (*HJ* 10 (1938): 115) Kenneth Mason classified two peaks in the Chumik group: ('K12') 24,370ft (7,428 metres) (Pk.8/52E, 1855–60) 24,503ft (7,468 metres) (Pk. 18/52E, Collins). It now appears that these peaks are one and the same. The height adopted by Survey of India now is 7,428 metres. K12 glacier is known locally as Gyong La II or G.II glacier.)

P.7200, P.7100, P.7100
Location: all on northeast ridge of K12

Peaks Lying North of the Greater Karakoram

KARUN KUH
Location: north of the Shimshal valley and the Hispar Muztagh and east of the Batura Muztagh
Height: 7,350 metres
Lat./Long.: 36°36'47" 75°04'48"
First ascent: 1984 via Southwest Ridge

The peak was attempted in 1983 by a mixed European-Pakistani foursome. They approached from Murkhan, twelve miles north of Pasu on the Karakoram Highway, and reached the Karun Koh glacier in two days. A possible route showed on the southwest ridge which has three rock towers halfway and a narrow corniced ridge above. Schauer and Saad Tarek reached 5,400 metres before conditions obliged to them to give up.

The following year, Chris Bonington and Alan Rouse, with two Pakistani climbers, followed the Austrian route, finding a safe passage to a glaciated shelf below the pinnacles. Bonington and Rouse tried to turn these but encountered hard, bare ice and made very slow progress. They then decided to examine the unexplored east side of the mountain. The southeast, east and north ridges appeared dramatically steep and narrow with séracs threatening the faces between. A last attempt on the southwest ridge was foiled by the weather.

A four-man Austrian party, who were on the mountain at the same time, were able to stay after Bonington's group had left. Having fixed rope on the pinnacles traverse they camped on the saddle above. After another break for weather they set out from the saddle, overcoming poor ice on the ridge, and reached the ramp above the rock section. From there the summit face, which was 45°–60° sheer ice in places, was climbed to the summit.

CROWN (in Chinese, Huang Guan Shan)
Location: in or on border with China (Sinkiang)
Height: 7,265 metres
Lat./Long.: 36°06' 76°12'

Crown seen from the southwest on the Skamri Glacier (Eric Shipton)

This peak lies north of the Skamri ('Crevasse') glacier and was reconnoitred by Eric Shipton's party in 1937; they went up a side glacier to the west of Crown. In 1987 the second Japanese expedition to attempt it approached via the Aghil Pass and Skamri glacier. Advanced base was established near the junction of this glacier and the Crown glacier and Camp I (5,100 metres) below the southeast ridge. Camp II was at 5,800 metres above a steep rock band and snow face. From Camp III (6,500 metres) the climbers made a short traverse on the east face and then ascended for 500 metres until stopped by a 100-metre high A-shaped rock wall which could not be overcome because of dangerous conditions. Shortly afterwards a British team, led by Captain Henry Morgan, ran out of time on the mountain, having got within seventy-five metres of the top.

Bibliography

Banks, M. (1956–57), 'Struggle for Rakaposhi', *AJ*, 61, pp. 449–57.

Brooke, F. (1958), 'The ascent of Rakaposhi', *AJ*, 63, pp. 159–68.

Chand, P. (1985), 'Ascent of K12 in the Saltoro hills', *HJ*, 41, pp. 90–2.

Cheesmond, D. (1985), 'North face of Rakaposhi', *AAJ*, 27, pp. 53–60.

Chorley, R. (1955), 'To the Monk's Head on Rakaposhi', *AJ*, 60, pp. 48–57.

Clinch, N. (1962–63), 'Masherbrum', *MW*, pp. 40–9.

Diemberger, K. (1958–59), 'Broad Peak-Chogolisa', *MW*, pp. 142–50.

Gizycki, P. (1972), 'Malubiting – the Munich Karakoram Expedition, 1970', *HJ*, 31, pp. 253–7.

Gyr, H. (1952), 'Karakoram expedition, 1947', *HJ*, 17, pp. 102–11.

Hall, B. (1981), 'British 1980 expedition to Baltoro Kangri', *AJ*, 86, pp 198–200.

Herligkoffer, K. (1975), 'Rakaposhi, 1973', *HJ*, 33, pp. 156–8.

Hewitt, L. (1956–57), 'The second attempt on Masherbrum', *AJ*, 61, pp. 29–37.

Hirai, K. (1979), 'Ascent of Sherpa Kangri', *HJ*, 35, pp. 254–7.

Hornbein, T. (1962), 'Ascent of Masherbrum', *AJ*, 67, pp. 9–25.

Hunt, J. (1936), 'Peak 36, Saltoro Karakoram 1935', *HJ*, 8, pp. 14–24 (see also, *HJ*, 9, 1937, pp. 127–43; see also, *AJ*, 47, 1935, pp. 282–7).

Irvin, R. (1957), 'Rakaposhi–almost', *AAJ*, 10, pp. 54–63.

(Japanese Railway Workers Karakoram Expedition) (1979), 'First ascent of Prupoo-Brukh', *AJ*, 84, pp. 118–22.

Jubany, A. (1987), 'Diran 1985', *HJ*, 43, pp. 155–7.

Koblmüller, E. (1972), 'Ascent of K6', *HJ*, 31, pp. 149–55; (see also, *HJ*,31, pp. 258–62).

Kodama, S. (1981), 'Rakaposhi from the north', *AJ*, 86, pp. 185–8.

Kumar, N. (1983), 'Indian Army expedition to the eastern Karakoram, 1981', *HJ*, 39, pp. 104–114.

Kus, A. (1970), 'Autumn under Malubiting: Polish Karakoram Expedition, 1969', *HJ*, 29, pp. 162–4.

Kus, A. and Gizychi, P. (1971), 'Two expeditions to Malubiting', *AJ*, 76, pp. 180–9.

Kuwabara, T. (1959), 'First ascent of Chogolisa', *AJ*, 64, pp. 168–74.

Mandl, F. (1960–61), 'Haramosh', *MW*, pp. 42–60.

Matous, R. (1984), 'Masherbrum and back again', *Ascent*, IV, pp. 9–20.

Noxon, J. (1964), 'Survey of the Ghondokoro and Chogolisa glacier area in the Karakoram range', *AAJ*, 14 pp. 121–3.

Patey, T. (1960–61), 'Rakaposhi', *MW*, pp. 32–41.

Pischinger, R. (1970), 'Diran 1968', *HJ*, 29, pp. 60–4.

Roiss, H. (1959), 'First ascent of Haramosh', *AJ*, 64, pp. 12–24.

Sander, R. (1956–57), 'Among the peaks of Chogo Lungma', *MW*, pp. 173–90.

Saunders, A. V. (1988–89), 'The Golden Pillar: the first ascent of the northwest pillar of Golden Peak (7,062 metres), Karakoram', *AJ*, 93, pp. 1–6; (see also, *HJ*, 44, 1988, pp. 135–41 and *AAJ*, 30, 1988, pp. 21–8).

Schindlbacher, H. (1975), 'Malubiting – snow peak above desert valleys', *AJ*, 78, pp. 53–6. (see also *HJ*, 32, 1974, pp. 79–81).

Schneider, H. (1960–61), 'German Karakoram Expedition, 1959', *MW*, pp. 108–25.

Shidei, T. (1968), 'Ascent of Saltoro Kangri', *AJ*, 69, pp. 73–80.

Shipton, E. (1958), 'Imperial College Karakoram Expedition, 1957', *AJ*, 63, pp. 185–93.

Smyth, A. (1962), 'Royal Air Force Karakoram Expedition, 1961', *AJ*, 67, pp. 73–84.

Streather, H. (1960), 'Army Mountaineering Association Expedition, 1959', *AJ*, 65, pp. 37–47.

Tilman, H. (1947–48), 'Rakaposhi', *AJ*, 56, pp. 329–41.

Tissières, A. (1955), 'Reconnaissance of Rakaposhi 1954', *MW*, pp. 35–6.

Unsoeld, W. (1961), 'Masherbrum–1960', *AAJ*, 12, pp. 209–29.

Vyvyan, M. (1939), 'A journey in the western Karakoram', *AJ*, 51, pp. 231–42.

Walmsley, J. (1958), 'Masherbrum, 1957', *AJ*, 63, pp. 169–84.

Hindu Kush

The Hunza-Nagir Campaign of 1891 brought peace and stability to the area, the immediate result of which was the exploration and rapid reconnaissance of the Hunza valleys. The task was entrusted to Lieutenant George Cockerill (later Brigadier Sir George Cockerill), whose orders were to explore and map the western Karakoram and eastern Hindu Kush, an area which includes some of the most difficult country in the world.

After a lengthy exploration of the Karakoram region Cockerill began his investigation of the still more remote and then unmapped valleys of Chitral in the spring of 1894. His primary mission was the reconnaissance of border passes for military use. He approached the highest peaks from the northeast, passing through Rich, and heading for the Turikho valley. After various excursions he went up the Turikho at the end of June as far as Warkup where he crossed the river by a good bridge, returning northwards on the opposite bank to enter the Tirich valley. After proceeding southwestwards for about fifteen kilometres, his party turned into the Rosh Gol which runs northwestwards into the heart of

the Saraghrar peaks. On 30 June Cockerill left camp at Duru to explore the way to the Kotgaz pass, reaching the glacier after about three kilometres. After crossing moraines the party found themselves in deep snow, while farther on a nearly vertical wall of rock barred the way. Forty years later R. C. F. Schomberg stated that he had never met anyone who had achieved the crossing of this 5,468-metre high pass. Retracing their steps they crossed the Sart pass and descended the Mastuj valley to Mastuj in the southeast.

Cockerill was now determined to complete the exploration of the crest of the Hindu Kush as far as he could, although he was strictly forbidden to enter Afghanistan. Accordingly, at the end of July he went back up the Mastuj and made his way southwestwards to skirt the southern flanks of the Tirich Mir group. This involved a long climb over a seldom used pass of some 5,000 metres into the Dir Gol, a tributary of the Arkari river on the western side of the range. The route led steeply up a moraine, then over huge tottering boulders to a glacier and finally a stiff climb up a narrow gully to the pass. The descent was made down

a very steep couloir, over rotten rocks and across an ice slope to a small circular glacier hemmed in on three sides by steep ridges. During the descent Cockerill's orderly slipped on the ice and hurtled down towards the bergschrund, fortunately finding a snow bridge and so shooting out on the glacier with only the loss of his breeches.

At Arkari, Cockerill turned north and followed the river. Between the villages of Wanakach and Gazikistan they passed the foot of the Lower Gazikistan glacier, descending through a narrow ravine from one of the peaks of the Tirich Mir group. On 8 August he continued towards the Sar Istragh An, a previously unmapped pass. The ascent was steep but he was rewarded with a glorious panorama. Looking eastwards he could see along the great ridge which sweeps upwards towards the magnificent massifs of Istor-o-Nal and Tirich Mir. This marked the furthest Cockerill could go without trespassing across the frontier and, after several side trips, he made his way to Chitral, which was reached on 19 August. Cockerill's reports and maps were printed by the government of India but were not made available to later travellers such as the Vissers and Colonel Schomberg.

(Kurt Diemberger)

Adolf Diemberger (d.1981)
Dr Adolf Diemberger, father of the well-known Austrian mountaineer Kurt Diemberger, never went to the Himalaya, yet through sheer enthusiasm he made himself an authority on the Hindu Kush. He graduated in philosophy and theology and had a great love of his native Alps around Salzburg. In the 1960s, when collaborating on an Alpine yearbook, he developed a passionate interest in the Himalayan regions, particularly the largely unexplored Hindu Kush. At that time climbers were becoming more and more fascinated by these rugged mountains and information was hard to come by. Adolf Diemberger was soon the only person who really knew what had been climbed, and where the most interesting objectives were. The walls of his work-room were covered with photographs and maps and many members of expeditions visited him for information. In return they were expected to report back to him afterwards with details of what they had achieved. His knowledge of the Hindu Kush was outstanding and in painstaking articles he elucidated some of the confusions surrounding ascents of the major peaks. He continued to explore the hills around his home until his death at the age of 78, the result of a small fall while out walking.

Several of the smaller peaks appear to have been down-graded in height. Southwest of Akher Chioh is Koh-i-Tez (7,016, now 6,995 metres), which was climbed by nine Poles from Kraków in 1962 via the west ridge from the north. Polish climbers also made a route up the north ridge. In the Shakhaur group Languta-e-Barfi (7,017, now 6,827 metres), Koh-i-Nadir (7,125, now 6,814 metres) and Keshni Khan (7,177, now 6,745 metres) also appear to have lost their status as 7,000-metre peaks. Languta-e-Barfi was first climbed by the Poles in 1963 by a route up the west ridge and across the southwest flank. The northwest ridge was ascended in 1973 and there have been attempts on the west face. Koh-i-Nadir was climbed twice in 1962 from the Afghan side and again in 1964 via the east ridge. Keshni Khan has been climbed a number of times since the Austrian and Polish ascents in 1963, by the west ridge-north rib and from the east, respectively. Other routes made on this peak include the southwest pillar climbed by the French in 1969 with four bivouacs.

In the 1960s and 1970s there was great activity on the peaks of the Hindu Kush which provide suitable goals for small expeditions. This activity came to an abrupt end with the Soviet invasion of Afghanistan in 1979.

Northern Group

AKHER CHIOH (Akher Chagh)
Wala no. 269
Height: 7,020 metres
Lat./Long.: 36°40′12″ 72°14′
First ascent: 1966 via East Ridge

A small Ö.A.V. group ascended the Uzhnu Gol and the Kotgaz glacier in 1966 and found a point from where they could reach the ridge which wanders east from Akher Chioh. The route led up an ice slope and ridge over Kotgaz Zom, then westward along the ridge to Akher Chioh. From camp (at about 6,200 metres) Hanns Schell and Rainer Göschl climbed the northeast ridge and east face of Kotgaz Zom in deep snow. In two hours they traversed the three kilometres of flat ridge to the foot of the steep summit pyramid of Akher Chioh. They had to turn back, still 300 metres below the top, to avoid a bivouac. A few days later a higher camp was placed near the top of Kotgaz Zom which enabled them to climb the main peak, the last 500 metres being a 45° ice slope.

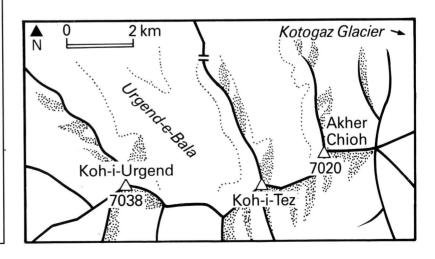

1972. West Ridge and Northwest Face

From camp on the 'Kraków Plateau', between Koh-e-Awal and Koh-e-Tez, Polish climbers got for the first time to the col between Koh-e-Tez and Akher Chioh. Three members completed the very difficult new route over the west ridge. An even more interesting route was a *direttissima* on the northwest face by four other members of the expedition. The 1,800 metre high face was at first snow and ice, then ice and rock above.

KOH-I-URGEND

Wala no. 258
Height: 7,038 metres
Lat./Long.: 36° 39' 48" 72° 09' 30"
First ascent: 1963

On the first reconnaissance in 1962, Polish climbers failed to discover a route from the Urgend-i-Bala valley. However, in 1963, the Swiss found a route up the next valley to the west, the Urgend-i-Payan. During the next ten days they climbed several peaks including Koh-i-Urgend.

1973. East Ridge

Hans Ertl and other German climbers made a number of climbs in this area, including a traverse from Shayoz.

1974. North Ridge

Polish climbers ascended the north ridge of Koh-i-Urgend from the east glacier.

Saraghrar Group

LANGAR ZOM
(Koh-i-Langar)

Wala no. 190
Height: c.7,070 metres (Southeast (or East) Peak (W.192), 7,061 metres)
Lat./Long.: 36° 34' 48" 72° 03' 10"
First ascent: 1964 by traverse from North Peak
(Note: The other peaks of Langar Zom are probably under 7,000 metres.)

A D.A.V. group, led by Dietrich von Dobenek, ascended the Shakawr (Langar) valley to the north of this peak. Of the two route possibilities they preferred the one which led to P.6170, up the northwest spur, down into the col and up a long northeast ridge of the massif. This ends in a high plateau out of which rise various summits. All members climbed one of about 6,750 metres (north peak). Two days later Otto Huber soloed the highest summit with a bivouac below the top; he also reached the south summit (at about 6,850 metres).

1967. Southeast Peak

Climbed by Japanese party.

1968. East Side

The 1968 Waseda University group climbed at the head of the Hushko glacier, to the east. After bad weather they dug a snow cave at 6,200 metres east of the main peak, which was climbed on 18 August.

1976. Traverse

A Polish expedition from Kraków traversed the eight kilometres long ridge of the Langar massif from north to south, including all the highest peaks.

SARAGHRAR

Wala no. 195
Height: 7,349 metres
Lat./Long.: 36° 32' 30" 72° 06' 15"
First ascent: 1959 via Northeast Ridge

The mountain consists of a long and irregular plateau lying at 7,000–7,300 metres, from which jut a number of pyramids, domes and ridges, the whole being surrounded by very steep faces of rotten rock and hanging glaciers.

The 1958 Oxford expedition ascended the Rosh Gol and followed the glacier up into the Northern Cwm which leads to the west wall of Saraghrar. The intended route was up a steep snow couloir at the head of the glacier to the summit ridge, and thence about a kilometre along the easily inclined ridge to the summit. Halfway through the climb, however, P. S. Nelson dropped his axe while crossing the couloir, overbalanced and fell to his death, whereupon the climb was abandoned.

Fosco Maraini's 1959 Italian expedition decided to approach the northeastern side of the peak up the Ziwar Gol to the Niroghi glacier. Eventually, after two weeks' exploration, they launched themselves on the buttress leading to a point (6,790 metres) on the northeast ridge. From the head of the glacier, a great ice shelf led easily to a minor top. Then the buttress became a horizontal ridge of ice and snow more reminiscent of the Andes in its formations; this was the crux of the climb and took a week to overcome. Out of reach of the monsoon the expedition continued to enjoy excellent weather and pushed on to P.6790 where the fifth camp was placed. From there, easy snow led across the plateau to the peak; nevertheless another small two-man tent was placed nearer the summit. Next day, 24 August, G. Castelli and C. A. Pinelli left Camp V very early and caught up with the advance party, F. Alletto and P. Consiglio. All four reached the top shortly before 3 p.m. Curiously, although the whole climb had been over ice and snow, the actual summit turned out to be a narrow ridge of broken slabs.

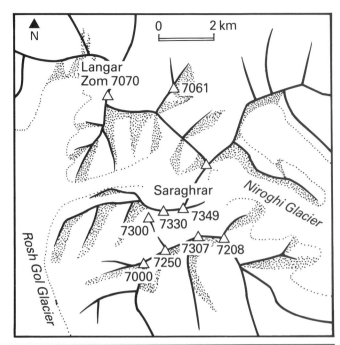

▲
North face and summit of Saraghrar (Fosco Maraini)

◀ *On the southwest ridge of Saraghrar at about 6,000 metres (Fosco Maraini)*

SARAGHRAR SOUTHEAST I
Wala no. 197
Height 7,208 metres (Southeast peak II, 7,184 metres)

The lower peak was possibly climbed in 1971.

SARAGHRAR WEST ('South-South')
Height: c.7,000 metres

1975–77. Southwest Buttress Attempts
A Spanish expedition were held up by the weather and ran out of food and time after thirty-nine days, having reached 6,020 metres on

this steep rock wall. In 1977 another Spanish party passed the 1975 high point and continued along a very severe section to where the buttress merges into the face. At this point it became obvious that more food, ropes and equipment were required, so the attempt was broken off.

SARAGHRAR CENTRAL
Height: c.7,330 metres.

SARAGHRAR SOUTH
Wala no. 196
Height: 7,307 metres
First ascent: 1967 via South Ridge

Japanese climbers discovered a hidden valley leading from Dru in the Rosh Gol, from which a steep ridge at the centre of the south face of Saraghrar gives a direct and short route to the summit of the south peak. The ridge required one camp and a bivouac.

SARAGHRAR II AND III
(Northwest I and II)
Location: third and fourth peaks west of main one
Height: c.7,300 metres (Northwest II – lower western or fourth – peak, c.7200 metres)

1982. Northwest II
Spanish climbers spent a week on the difficult southwest buttress, finally reaching the summit of Northwest II.

SARAGHRAR SOUTHWEST
Height: 7,250 metres (Southwest II, 7,200 metres)
First ascent: 1971 via West Wall

Four members of the Shizuoka Tohan Club took thirteen days to climb this wall of perpendicular rock faces and ridges. On 29 July they reached the lower of the southwest peaks via a snow plateau. Toshio Nagano went on alone to the higher summit.

SARAGHRAR NORTH
Wala no. 194.
Height: 7,040 metres (possibly 6,900 metres)
First ascent: 1959 via Northeast Ridge

Traversed by Fosco Maraini's party during first ascent of main peak.

SHAKHAUR
Wala no. 168
Height: 7,084 metres
Lat./Long.: 36°33′12″ 71°58′30″
First ascent: 1964 via Northwest Ridge from the South

The Polish reconnaissance in 1962 discovered no satisfactory route. A second expedition in October 1963 attempted the north buttress, reaching about 6,000 metres beneath a 800-metre high barrier of séracs. The next year an Austrian group ascended the North Atrak glacier and gained the head basin above the ice-fall. From there it was a fairly short climb to the summit which was reached over steep snow slopes to the northwest ridge, and thence by way of a col, to the top.

1969. North Pillar
Climbed by members of a French expedition. The buttress rises 3,000 metres and was climbed entirely on crampons. The surface was ice, with powder snow higher up and occasionally easy rock; the angle varied between 40°–70°.

1975. East Ridge and Traverse
Polish climbers traversed from the Kotgaz Pass, over Shakhaur to Koh-e-Nadir.

1977–79. Northeast Face and Northwest Face
Polish climbers made a route on the 2,600-metre high central buttress of the northeast face, and another route on the northwest

buttress of the northwest face. Czechoslovakian climbers made a new route on each of these faces in 1979.

UDREN ZOM
Wala no. 169
Height: 7,108 metres
Lat./Long.: 36°32′18″ 71°58′40″
First ascent: 1964 via North Face

Austrians Gerald Gruber and Rudolf Pischinger made the first ascent of this peak which is separated from Shakaur by a 700-metre deep notch. The climbers got on the summit ridge across the icy northern face and a steep snow slope below the summit.

1979. Traverse from Shakaur
By Czech climbers.

UDREN ZOM CENTRAL
Height 7,080 metres
First ascent: 1977

Members of a Japanese expedition climbed to the top from camp at 6,700 metres.

UDREN ZOM SOUTH
Wala no. 170
Height: 7,050 metres
First ascent: 1967 via South Ridge

Japanese climbers made this ascent in two days.

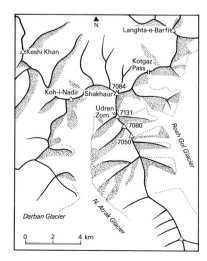

Noshaq Group

DARBAN ZOM

Wala no. 116
Height: 7,219 metres
Lat./Long.: 36°26'42" 71°50'15"
First ascent: 1965 via South Face

Austrian climbers established camp on the Darban glacier. Despite the precarious snow on Noshaq's northern slopes, which they had to traverse to reach Darban Zom, they managed to make camp at 6,400 metres. Ice slopes to a ramp gave access to the basin between the two peaks from which Uli Kössler and Markus Schmuck climbed an ice slope up the southern side to the summit.

1978. Attempt from North

A small international party got to within 150 metres of the summit by a route on the north side before an accident forced a retreat.

NOBAISUM ZOM

Wala no. 101
Height: 7,070 metres
Lat./Long.: 36°24'18" 71°51'15"
First ascent: 1967 via East Ridge

Austrians Kurt Diemberger and Kurt Lapuch made this ascent with one camp.

NOSHAQ

Wala no. 98
Height 7,492 metres
Lat./Long.: 36°26'6" 71°54'
First ascent: 1960 via South Ridge
  from Southeast Ridge of Noshaq
  West

Japanese climbers ascended the upper basin of the Qadzi Deh glacier, crossing a col which leads to the Upper Tirich glacier, and made their way to the foot of the south ridge. This is a narrow but not too difficult snow ridge and steep arête about 700 metres high,

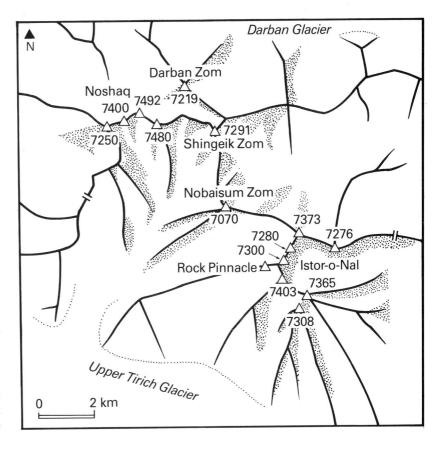

which leads to a broad, gentle snow slope. It took a very long time to ascend this diagonally and the summit pair of Toshiaki Sakai and Goro Iwatsubo suffered from altitude and soft snow. The top, a rocky pile, was not reached until 6 p.m. but the ensuing bivouac caused no problems. Polish climbers repeated the ascent ten days later, possibly by a slightly different route.

1963. West Ridge and Traverse

Austrians G. Gruber and R. Pischinger traversed all the Noshaq peaks on 21 August.

1971. Northwest Spur

Ascended by Austrian climbers. The same year two members of a Bulgarian expedition signalled their successful ascent by rocket but were never seen again. Two more disappeared during the descent from Camp III (7,020

metres), leaving a sick climber behind who was found dead by porters a few days later.

1972. Southwest Face

Polish climbers made an alpine-style ascent with two bivouacs.

1973. Winter Ascent

Near the summit Polish climbers were horrified to see a hand sticking out of the ice, a relic of the 1971 Bulgarian tragedy.

1977. Southwest Face

Yugoslavians made a new route to the left of the 1972 Polish one.

1978. North Face

German climbers traversed three kilometres under the northern slopes to the north face. This was mostly 45°–50°, with quite a lot of bare ice and some objective danger.

▲ *Noshaq (centre left) from Ghul-Lasht Zom, i.e. from the southwest. The crest ridge leads to Shingeik (centre right) and Nobaisum Zom (far right)* *(Kurt Diemberger)*

NOSHAQ CENTRAL
Wala no. 97
Height: c.7,400 metres
First ascent: 1963 by Traverse

Traversed by Austrians who went from Noshaq West to the main summit.

NOSHAQ EAST
Wala no. 99
Height: c.7,480 metres
First ascent: 1963 by Traverse

The Austrians R. Pischinger and G. Gruber continued their traverse of the Noshaq peaks from the main summit to Noshaq East.

NOSHAQ WEST
Wala no. 96
Height: c.7,250 metres
First ascent: 1963

Austrian climbers ascended the rib which rises straight up from the rubble covered Qadzi Deh glacier

to the west summit and traversed all the Noshaq peaks on 21 August.

1971. South Ridge
Ascended by Austrian climbers.

SHINGEIK ZOM
Wala no. 100
Height: 7,291 metres (Shingeik Zom II, 7,170 metres; III, 7,150 metres)
Lat./Long.: 36°25'48" 71°51'
First ascent: 1966

The Bavarian Chitral Expedition of 1966 ascended the Darban glacier to a point below the north face of Noshaq. From there, two members reached the summit of Shingeik Zom without difficulty.

1969. Shingeik Zom II and III
Toni and Ambros Aichhorn, members of an Ö.A.V.expedition, climbed these peaks via the east ridge on 20 August from a camp to the north.

Istor-O-Nal Group

ISTOR-O-NAL
Wala no. 110
Height: 7,403 metres
Lat./Long.: 36°26'38" 71°55'52"
First ascent: 1969 via Southwest Ridge

In 1929 a Survey of India party reached about 6,100 metres on the southwest ridge, from the Upper Tirich glacier. This was the route all subsequent attempts were to follow. In 1935 R. J. Lawder and D. N. B. Hunt chose a slightly different line. They climbed a sizeable couloir covered in hard ice which gave access to the main west ridge of the massif. The exit from the couloir consisted of a rock face 100 metres high. The first part of the ridge was corniced and the climbers were obliged to cut steps on the ice slope below the crest. After several days of slow progress

Istor-o-Nal; at about 7,000 metres on the
Southwest Ridge in 1935 (R. J. Lawder)

Barcelona to unravel the topography of Istor-o-Nal and to make
the first ascent. From the Rock
Pinnacle they traversed the steep
southern slopes to the col leading
to the main peak. From there they
traversed the southeast and south
tops and back to the col.

1971. Southwest Buttress and Ridge

Climbed by members of a Yugoslav expedition. The lower part of
the route gave Grade IV–V rock
climbing. Some of the slopes were
of 60° or more.

Istor-o-Nal seen from Camp I on Ghul-Lasht
Zom (6,611m), i.e. from the west across the
Upper Tirich Glacier (Kurt Diemberger)

they reached a height of about
6,800 metres where the ridge
broadened and was covered in
deep soft snow. The next day
Hunt and two of the porters
almost reached a point which
appeared to be the summit, but
which was subsequently shown to
be about 7,100 metres, in the
vicinity of the 'Rock Pinnacle'.

The next climbers to try the
peak, a two-man American party
in 1955, made the same error in
poor visibility. They saw a snow
plateau which appeared to drop
beyond the highest point, not
realizing that the slope dropped to
a col before rising again to the
separate summit pyramid which is
on a different ridge. In 1968 and
1969 three more expeditions
reached approximately the same
point on the mountain, retiring for
various reasons. It was left to the
1969 Spanish expedition from

ISTOR-O-NAL NORTH
Wala no. 102
Height: 7,373 metres (North II, 7,350 metres; North III, 7,300 metres)
First ascent: 1967 via North Ridge

From a base camp on the head basin of the Upper Tirich glacier, under the northern flanks of the massif, an Austrian group gained a northern spur and made the ascent of this peak. After an hour's traverse of a corniced ridge they arrived on the slightly lower North II peak.

ISTOR-O-NAL NORTHEAST
Wala no. 103
Height: 7,276 metres

A six-man Japanese group failed in an attempt in 1977. From camp on the South Atrak glacier they established camps up to 6,400 metres. Ice formations and difficult rock obliged them to retire from a point only 100 metres higher than that.

ISTOR-O-NAL EAST
Height: 7,100 metres

ISTOR-O-NAL SOUTH
Height: 7,308 metres
Subsidiary peak: Southeast, 7,365 metres
First ascent: 1969 by Traverse from Main Peak

Both peaks were ascended by the Spanish expedition after climbing the main Istor-O-Nal peak.

ISTOR-O-NAL WEST
Height: 7,300 metres (West II, 7,280 metres; Rock Pinnacle on west ridge, 7,200 metres)
First ascent: 1955 or later

The main West top was almost certainly first climbed by the Americans Tom Mutch and Joseph Murphy in 1955. The Rock Pinnacle is mentioned by the Japanese Womens' Expedition in 1968 but may not have been ascended until 1969, when it seems to have been definitely climbed by members of a Czechoslovakian party.

The north faces of the Tirich massif seen from Ghul-Lasht Zom South (6,400m). From left to right–Tirich Mir East, Tirich Mir, Tirich West I–IV.

(Kurt Diemberger)

▼

Tirich Mir Group

TIRICH MIR

Wala no. 30
Height: 7,706 metres (South summit –
*   peak on south ridge – c.7,100*
*   metres)*
Lat./Long.: 36° 15′ 21″ 71° 50′ 32″
First ascent: 1950 via South Ridge

The Tirich Mir massif consists of the main peak; an eastern peak reached by a ridge; and the north-west ramparts which constitute a wall not unlike the Grandes Jorasses. More than thirty years after Cockerill's exploration, Survey of India officials who were in the Tirich Mir region in 1928 and 1929 made unsuccessful attempts to reach high peaks suitable for triangulation. In 1935

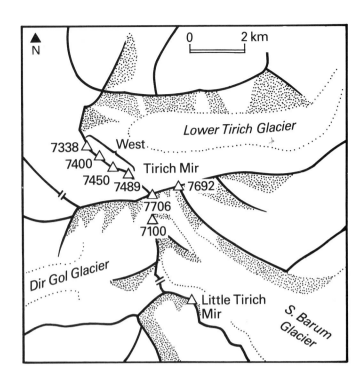

members of a mainly scientific German expedition tried to reach the peak from the south. Three years later a British reconnaissance reached about 6,100 metres from the Owir Glacier and decided that the south ridge looked possible.

Just before the outbreak of the Second World War, Miles Smeeton's party tried an ascent from the south up the Owir glacier. They reached the southern ridge of the massif, dividing the Dir Goland and South Barum glaciers, between Little Tirich Mir and South Glacier Peak. From here they had an impressive view across the col to the south shoulder which looked to be very steep and uncompromising. They decided to turn back for lack of fixed ropes. After the war climbers from several countries had designs on Tirich Mir, but the Norwegians were the first in the field. In 1949 Arne Naess and Arne Randers Heen, one of Norway's most famous mountaineers, carried out a reconnaissance of the South Barum glacier. They reached the

ridges on both sides of the glacier, but were worried about avalanches and the possible dangers should climbers get caught high on the mountain. The easiest but most dangerous route lay up the south face.

▲

Southern side of the Tirich Mir massif looking up the head of the Owir valley (R. C. F. Schomberg)

The following year a full expedition arrived at base camp at the snout of the glacier on 11 June. Most of June was spent establishing advanced base (Camp IV) near the top of the glacier at about 5,400 metres. The first choice of route, the southeast ridge, was inspected and it was found that snow conditions were bad compared with the year before. Meanwhile the predictions about avalanches were coming true. Advanced base was hit several times, but as there seemed nowhere safe they stayed put. The focus now turned to the South Glacier Peak approach to the south ridge, but again conditions were totally different, with several avalanches a day down the steepest

parts. The only course remaining was the short cut running directly to the south ridge high on the mountain. This seemed easy to reach but would be followed by a difficult traverse across a steep, smooth glacier on the main face.

Lastly there was a very steep, partly rocky section before the final slopes. They decided to try it and gamble on the weather holding long enough.

The first snag was an ice edge covered in waist-deep snow which was surmounted by 'swimming' up on snow shoes. Higher camps were set up as far as 6,550 metres. Just as the final assault started, illness struck. One of the climbers developed pneumonia while a porter became crazed over Tirich Mir's legends of evil fairies and had to be restrained. The expedition also suffered the effects of a violent earthquake. Nevertheless an exhausted advance party managed to put a camp at 7,000 metres. With

snow conditions deteriorating, the second assault was launched on 21 July, Per Kvernberg climbing ahead of his support team in an effort to reach the summit quickly. Late that evening when he got back to the top camp on the ridge he announced that he had made the top at about 6 p.m. in beautiful weather. The snow had been very deep and treacherous but the route was not difficult. The leader Naess and two others repeated the climb next day.

1967. Northwest Ridge
Czechoslovak climbers ascended to the col on the ridge between Tirich Mir and Tirich Mir West I from the Upper Tirich glacier, that is, southern, side. This route has been repeated several times.

1971. South Ridge
Members of a Japanese expedition trying to repeat the 1950 Norwegian route switched to an ascent over the South Glacier Peak. From camp in the col north of this peak Shinji Sawamura and Akio Okamoto climbed the main peak with one bivouac. Near the top on the west side they found bleached bones which proved to be of mammals.

TIRICH MIR EAST
Wala no. 31
Height: 7,692 metres
Lat./Long.: 36°15′30″ 71°50′20″
First ascent: 1964 via South Face

In 1962 the Austrian F. Stammberger made a solo attempt on the south ridge, reaching about 6,700 metres or possibly higher. After being slightly injured in an avalanche he returned to base. Two years later Arne Naess and four other Norwegians started from the South Barum glacier and climbed the difficult south face of Tirich Mir East, which is separated from the main peak by a ridge which dips to a col at about 7,550 metres. The route started up sharply and ascended very steep snow, ice and rock. After a prolonged snow-storm they decided on a quick two-man assault. After more difficult rock and snow leading to another steep ice-field, Camp VI was established on a fairly flat snow rib at about 6,500 metres. R. Höibakk and A. Opdal then climbed the third ice-field and bivouaced. Next day a steep ice gully led to a shoulder and the southeast ridge: they arrived on top at 4 p.m. in doubtful weather.

Southeast Spur Attempts

The southeast spur was attempted by Germans in 1970. In 1975 Austrian Stammberger disappeared during his second solo attempt.

TIRICH MIR WEST I

Wala no. 46
Height: 7,487 metres
Lat./Long.: 36°15′48″ 71°49′
First ascent: 1967 from Tirich Mir

Four Czechoslovakians climbed this peak easily from the northwest col of Tirich Mir, from the Upper Tirich glacier.

1975. West Spur

The Italians Guido Machetto and Gianni Calgagno climbed a mixed route of Grade IV-V to the summit before traversing to Tirich Mir itself.

TIRICH MIR WEST II

Wala no. 47
Height: c.7,450 metres
Lat./Long.: 36°16′ 71°48′40″
First ascent: 1974 via Tirich Mir West III

Having climbed the French route on Tirich Mir West III, the Italians Guido Machetto and Beppe Re descended to the linking col and followed the sharp ridge to the top of Tirich Mir West II.

TIRICH MIR WEST III

Wala no. 48
Location: Separated from Tirich Mir West IV by a deep col
Height: c.7,400 metres
Lat./Long.: 36°16′20″ 71°48′15″
First ascent: 1974 via West Face

A French expedition climbed the west face from the Upper Tirich glacier. From camp at 6,100 metres they ascended a rock buttress, cut by steep snow slopes, which ended in a ridge leading to the summit. In the upper part of the route the climbers had to make a difficult traverse to avoid a steep step. The route was likened to the Innomin-ata ridge on Mont Blanc, with steep ice and rock to Grade V. Bad weather and lack of time prevented them from traversing to Tirich Mir II; this was done a month later by the Italians Guide Machetto and Beppe Re.

TIRICH MIR WEST IV

Wala no. 49
Height: 7,338 metres
Lat./Long.: 36°16′18″ 71°48′
First ascent: 1967 via North Face

This is the most impressive of the four Tirich Mir West peaks. Kurt Diemberger and Dietmar ('Didi') Proske started the climb on 31 July. The route went up a broad ice couloir to a long narrow ice ledge in the middle of the face at about 6,300 metres, where they made camp. Further on the ledge petered out above the Lower Tirich glacier and they could see the dauntingly

steep north face with its vertical granite ribs separated by patches of ice and black slabs. Crossing these next day was slow work but they reached 6,650 metres before dumping their loads and descending. On 4 August they collected everything from the dump and started for the summit. The route traversed across steep ridges and deep ice gullies for nearly half a kilometre, ending with a very strenuous Grade IV pitch which brought them to the rim of a hanging glacier where camp had to be made in a crevasse. They could see that the upper part of the face consisted mainly of ice slopes and granite buttresses. Next day they were lucky enough to find another, much better, crevasse camp-site at about 7,000 metres; it was imperative to remain roped at all times in these camps. On the last day, 6 August, they traversed below a wall of polished granite before ascending a steep slope of hard ice which, to their delight, turned out to be the key to the summit. The climb was made possible by the prolonged spell of fine weather, although they suffered from the wind and intense cold.

1976 and 1977. Southwest Face

A Spanish expedition climbed the face to the col between Tirich Mir III and IV, and from there to the top. The route followed a couloir and glacier to a rocky buttress. They spent ten days fixing ropes on the face. Finally, on 22 August Ernesto Fonquernie and Francisco Chavarri left Camp V and climbed to a bivouac at 7,050 metres, reaching the top next day. During the descent Fonquernie had an accident and was later found dead at the foot of the face, probably having untied himself while awaiting rescue. The following year, Italian climbers made a completely

▲

Climbing the North Face of Tirich West IV: Lower Tirich Glacier below (Kurt Diemberger)

new route up the 1,200-metre high rocky face, the first part of which offered sustained and technically difficult rock climbing with no objective dangers. The final obstacle was a 200-metre snow couloir which was in bad condition.

Bibliography

Agresti, H. (1971), 'Shakhaur (716 m), 1969: first ascent of north buttress', *HJ*, 30, pp. 275–7.

Agresti, H. (1971), 'Alpine exploration of the Wakhan', *HJ*, 31, pp. 275–7.

Axt, W. (1971), 'Austrian Hindu Kush Expedition, 1969', *HJ*, 30, pp. 264–9.

Bala, M. (1976), 'Shakhaur, 1975', *HJ*, 34, pp. 115–17.

Burn, D. (1930), 'Istor-o-Nal and some Chitrali superstitions', *HJ*, 2, pp. 68–72.

Chwascinski, B. (1961), 'Polish expedition to the Hindu Kush, 1960', *AJ*, 66, pp. 235–49.

Chwascinski, B. (1966), 'Exploration of the Hindu Kush', *AJ*, 71, pp. 199–214.

Cobb, E. (1951–2), 'Prelude to the conquest of Tirich Mir', *AJ*, 58, pp. 4–5.

Cockerill, G. (1939), 'Pioneer exploration in Hunza and Chitral', *HJ*, 11, pp. 15–41.

Day, H. (1970), 'Tirich Mir, 1969', *AJ*, 75, pp. 79–86.

Day, H. (1970), 'Fourth ascent of Tirich Mir West, 1969', *HJ*, 29, pp. 139–60.

Diemberger, A. (1970), 'The problem of Istor-o-Nal', *HJ*, 29, pp. 168–74.

Diemberger, A. (1970), 'The Saraghrar peaks', *HJ*, 29, pp. 175–6.

Diemberger, K. (1966), 'Some climbs from the Upper Tirich Glacier', *AJ*, 71, pp. 61–7.

Eiselin, M. (1964), 'Auf dem Siebentausender', *Bergsteiger* 31, Jahrgang, Heft 8, pp. 538–41.

Engele, H. (1980), 'Noshaq – a route off the beaten track', *HJ*, 36, pp. 145–9.

Gruber, G. (1964–65), 'The Hindu-Kush, 1963–1964', *MW*, pp. 32–40.

Gruber, G. (1967), 'Panorama of the Hindu Kush', *AJ*, 72, pp. 1–14.

Hechtel, R. (1970), 'Noshaq', *AAJ*, 17, pp. 27–31).

Lawder, R. 'A climb on Istor-o-Nal, 1935', *HJ*, 8, pp. 53–62 (see also, *AJ*, 48, 1936, pp. 118–23).

Maraini, F. (1960), 'A Roman flag on Saraghrar Peak', *AJ*, 65, pp. 151–7.

Miyamori, T. (1972), 'Saraghrar and Langar group: some problems of topography and identification', *HJ*, 31, pp. 322–33.

Montfort, J. (1974), 'Spanish Expedition Hindu Kush, 1973', *AJ*, 79, pp. 199–201 (see also, *HJ*, 33, 1975, pp. 169–72).

Murphy, J. (1956), 'Ascent of Istor-o-Nal', *AAJ*, 10, pp. 66–74.

Naar, R. (1979), 'Istor-o-Nal North I, 1976', *HJ*, 35, pp. 251–3.

Naess, A. (1951–52), 'Norwegian expedition to Tirich Mir, 1950', *AJ*, 58, pp. 6–15.

Schell, H. (1967), 'Akher Chioh (7,020 metres)', *AJ*, 72, pp. 225–31.

Schmuck, M. (1964–65), 'Climbing in the high Hindu Kush', *MW*, pp. 41–6.

Schmuck, M. 'First ascent of Darban Zom, Q6 and M9', *MW*, pp. 33–43.

Schwabe, U. (1972), 'Noshaq on skis', *AJ*, 77, pp. 110–15.

Smida, V. (1968–69), 'Second Czech expedition to the Hindu Kush', *MW*, pp. 59–62.

Trübswetter, I. (1967), 'Shingeik Zom – the smoking mountain', *AJ*, 72, pp. 85–6.

Valic, I. (1972), 'Istor-o-Nal', *HJ*, 31, pp. 290–1.

Zawada, A. (1974), 'Noshaq in winter', *AJ*, 79, pp. 11–14.

Zbinden, O. (1975), 'Solothurner Hindu Kush Expedition, 1973', *HJ*, 33, pp. 173–82.

Pamirs

Situated at the meeting point of Russia, Afghanistan, Pakistan and China the Pamirs are the hub from which spring all the great ranges of central Asia. Historically, they were part of the link between the empires of the eastern and western worlds, part of the 'Silk Road', carrying travellers and trade caravans.

The exploration of the Pamir peaks began in the latter part of the nineteenth century, two Russian geographers, Alexis Fedchenko and N.L. Korzhenevsky, being particularly active in the area. In 1871 Fedchenko, who was always accompanied by his wife, Olga, fixed the position of the highest peak in the northeastern Trans-Alai section, now called Pik Lenin; and no doubt he would have contributed much more had he not been killed in a climbing accident on Mont Blanc two years later. Nevertheless his preliminary mapping enabled others to begin a topographical survey in 1883. In 1878 V. F.Oshanin explored the immense Fedchenko glacier at the head of the Muksu river, but it was another thirty years before Korzhenevsky began to explore the fine peaks which surround it. In 1910 he discovered a high peak which he named after his wife and fellow worker, Evgenia, and in 1926 he found another peak which proved to be the highest in the USSR, now known as Pik Kommunizma. Of the three 7,000-metre peaks in the Pamirs, Pik Lenin is the most accessible and favourable to successful ascents.

Nowadays the Pamirs are notable for the annual Soviet International Mountaineering Camps which have become more and more popular, with climbers from numerous countries participating. Visitors are expected to conform to the Soviet way of doing things but this does not preclude opportunities to tackle high quality routes. Although the summer weather is generally favourable, sudden and violent storms lasting several days are not uncommon.

PIK LENIN (Mt Kaufmann)
Height: 7,134 metres
Lat./Long.: 39° 20' 43" 72° 53' 02"
First ascent: 1928 via Northeast
  Ridge from the South

Pik Lenin is the most accessible, and favourable for successful ascents, of the three 7,000-metre peaks in the Pamirs. It was originally named after C. P. Kaufmann, Governor-General of Russian Turkestan, 1867–82. Although generally an unimpressive peak it possesses a magnificent north face. The two normal routes are the Rasdelnaja Ridge (west side) and Lipkin Spur (northeast). In 1928 a joint Soviet-German expedition, led by W. Rickmer Rickmers, explored and climbed a number of the peaks at the head of the Fedchenko glacier. Then, retracing their steps to the Muksu, they moved eastwards to the Saukhdara glacier south of Pik Lenin. From there they reached the Krylenko Pass (5,820 metres) on the east ridge and followed a long undulating crest to the top.

1934. East Ridge from the North and First Soviet Ascent
The Lenin glacier north of the mountain was followed to a snow dome and terrace at 6,100 metres beneath the upper part of the north face. By climbing a rock ridge (Lipkin Spur) V. Abalakov, N. Chernukha and I. Lukin reached the northeast ridge and the summit.

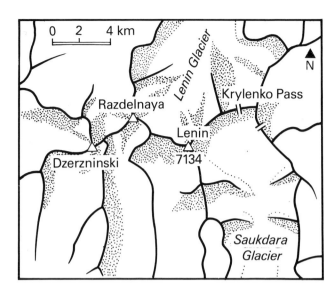

Erwin Schneider on his return from the first ascent of Pik Lenin

Erwin Schneider (1906–87)

The Austrian climber Erwin Schneider had a distinguished career as a mountaineer and mountain cartographer. In 1928 he participated in an expedition to the Pamirs and was in the party which made the first ascent of Pik Lenin. Two years later he accompanied G. O. Dyrenfurth to the Sikkim Himalaya. He was a leading member of the expedition which opened up the Cordillera Blanca in Peru in 1932, making the first ascent of Huascarán and six other major peaks. In 1934 he climbed high on Nanga Parbat before the expedition was overwhelmed. In 1936 he began his mapping work with a survey of the Cordillera Huayhuash in Peru. After the Second World War Schneider devoted much of his time to surveying and mapping the mountain regions of eastern Nepal, and produced a famous map of Mount Everest and its environs. His other maps included sections of the eastern Alps and Mount Kenya. He collaborated with G. O. Dyrenfurth in the production of the book *To the Third Pole*, and with Hans Kinzl on *Cordillera Blanca*, a fine record of the three D.Ö.A.V. expeditions of the 1930s. He was still working shortly before he died in August 1987 in his native Austria.

Pik Lenin from the north (Paul Nunn)
▼

1937. Third Ascent Using Aircraft Supply Drops

1954. First Traverse of Peak

This was made from west to east by two teams comprising five climbers led by V. A. Kovalev.

1955. South Ridge

K. Kuzmin's ascent included a traverse of Pik Oktober (6,780 metres).

1958. First Ascent by a Woman

E. Mamleyeva was one of ten members of a team operating from the Dugoba mountaineering camp.

1958. Soviet-Chinese Ascent

Thirty-seven members of a Soviet-Chinese expedition climbed from the Bolshoi (i.e. big) Sauksai glacier via Pik Profsojuzov and continued up the 1928 first ascent route.

1960. North Face and Traverses

A party led by V. P. Cheredova tried to climb the northeast ridge from the Krylenko Pass but did not reach the summit, being forced to retreat by the illness of one member. V. Kiesel's group made a direct route on the steep north face. In the same year two groups made traverses from east and west to meet on the summit; the traverse included Pik Dzerzhinsky (6,713 metres).

1967. East Face, Austrian Spur

On 12–14 August Austrians R. Hoyer, K. Kosa and E. Weilguny climbed the face by way of a prominent ice rib, 1,800 metres high, on the left of the face.

1967. North Rib via Komplex

A party of six led by Yuri Skurlatov climbed the north rib via the 'Komplex' gendarme and continued up the 1928 route.

1969. East Face (2)

At the end of July, the Russians Jury Ustinov and Oleg Borisenok with Germans Toni Hiebeler and Michael Schneider made a new route by a steep snow and ice ridge on the right of the face, spending four days on the actual face.

1969. Southwest Ridge

A party led by N. Yushin climbed the ridge from the Malaja (i.e. small) Saukhdara glacier.

1974. International Climbing Meet

This gathering of 160 climbers from twelve nations was marred by one of the worst tragedies in mountaineering history. In all thirteen climbers died, including the entire Soviet women's team of eight. This was their first time together as an all-women team on a major peak. They were attempting a traverse. They were seen going for the summit on 6 August. That night, some American climbers on the lee side of the summit ridge barely survived the extreme winds and cold. The storm continued all next day, during which the women made several radio contacts with base camp, reporting first one then two more deaths in the party; finally at 8.30 p.m. that they were unable to move and all resigned to death. On 8 August Japanese and American climbers discovered a string of bodies on the final eastern snow slope. (Three, not five, Estonians died, thus reducing the total from fifteen as reported elsewhere.)

1982. Ski Descent

Czechoslovakian Pavol Rajtar soloed the mountain in four hours, then skied down the northwest ridge and north face. The 3,000-metre vertical descent took two-and-a-half hours on slopes up to 48°. A ski descent was also made by a Soviet girl, O. Agranovskaja, among others.

PIK KOMMUNIZMA (Mt Stalin, also, erroneously, Garmo)

Height: 7,482 metres (or, 7,495 metres)
Lat./Long.: 38°56'26" 72°00'47"
First ascent: 1933 via East (Pioneer) Ridge

The first party to reconnoitre the peak started out from Altynmazar and ascended the Fedchenko, Bivachnyy and Ordzhonikidze glaciers to the eastern flanks of the mountain. The battle for the peak lasted over a month. The climbers started up a gentle rib which soon became severe when a series of gendarmes barred the way between 5,600–6,400 metres. The surfaces were treacherous and Nikolayev fell nearly 500 metres from the second pinnacle when a handhold broke away. The fifth

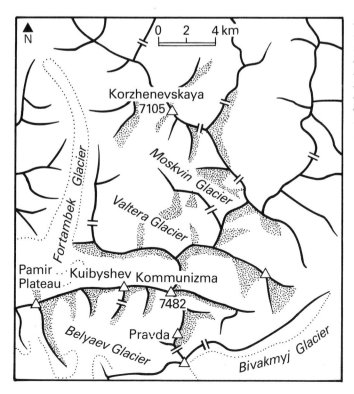

Opposite: Gathering of the international climbing meet for the memorial service to the climbers who died on Pik Lenin in 1974 (John Roskelley)

▶

and sixth towers were the most difficult, and while Evgeny Abalakov was traversing a narrow ledge between the two a falling rock laid open his second's hand. Finally, the section was forced and the last camp pitched on a snow patch at 6,900 metres. The climbers now suffered several days of severe weather and their food stocks ran down almost to nothing. Abalakov remained the driving force in the group. On 3 September he and N. P. Gorbunov donned their frozen outer garments and set out for the top. In loose, deep snow their progress was painfully slow and as Gorbunov began to succumb to altitude sickness, Abalakov unroped and continued alone. On the knife-edge summit crest he had to combat the strong gusts of a side wind, eventually reaching the summit on all fours. The descent became even more desperate with Abalakov snow-blind and Gorbunov frostbitten, while the third member of the party was suffering from the effects of a heart attack.

1937. Second Ascent

During this ascent led by Evgeny Beletsky, Oleg Aristov, one of the leading Russian climbers of the day, fell to his death only a few metres below the summit when he lost his hold on a sharp ice covered ledge.

1955. South Ridge from Belyaev Glacier

A Georgian party under O. Gigineishvily and A. Ivanishvily started from the upper reaches of the Garmo glacier and followed the Belyaev glacier. They then ascended a steep wall to a high col on the crest of the Academy of Sciences Ridge to the south of Pik Pravda (6,400 metres) which was turned to the east. With one more camp the summit was reached by four men in bad weather via the south ridge.

1957. West Ridge from Belyaev Glacier

Kiril Kuzmin's party of ten from the Moscow Burevestnik Sports Society climbed from the Garmo basin, and made the first crossing of the Pamir snow plateau (*Pamirskoje Firnovoje Plato*). Their route to the plateau lay across the top of Pik Kuibyshev.

1959. Southwest Wall, West Ridge

Another Moscow Burevestnik Sports Society group led by K. Kuzmin made a difficult route from the upper Belyaev glacier, skirting the left edge of the south face to gain the west ridge, reaching the summit on 29 August.

1961. East Face from Bivačnyj Glacier

A group from the Moscow Burevestnik Sports Society, led by E. Tamm, went from the Bivačnyj glacier across the icefalls of the Rossiji glacier and plateau near Pik Pravdy, in August.

1965. Nekrassov Route

A party led by Viktor Nekrassov made a route from the Belyaev glacier up the rib between Pik Pravdy and Pik Rossija, then via the south ridge (Georgian route of 1955) to the summit.

▲ *On the way to the final camp; Pik Kommunizma, first ascent*

The South Face of Pik Kommunizma (Zdislav Drlik)

1967. Southeast Ridge

Climbed by a Ukranian Spartak Sports Society party, leader A. A. Kustovsky, in five days during August.

1968. Southeast Ridge via Central (Budanov) Buttress

Leningrad Spartak Sports Society, led by P. Budanov, in August.

1968. South Face (Southwest Wall)

The first attempt at a route in 1962 by a Spartak party led by Vitaly Abalakov failed on account of bad weather. Careful reconnaissance in 1965, and a comparable route on Pik E. Korzenevskoi in 1966, laid the foundation for the successful 1968 ascent, which was made from the Belyaev glacier during 8–18 August. The first part was prepared beforehand. The leader of the Burevestnik group was Anatoly Ovchinnikov. The climbers soon found the climbing difficult on rotten rock and after a few days it was clear that the route could not be made from the plateau; an advanced camp was needed on the face. Work on the route continued intermittently until 2 August when they had to break off to assist in a rescue.

When the four climbers returned to the foot of the face on 8 August to begin the final assault, conditions on the face had changed considerably. The snow had melted, stonefalls were frequent, and the fixed ropes were broken in many places. Dodging the falling stones they accomplished the first 800 metres safely in one day. The route then went up a 50° ice slope to a tent bivouac where two nights were spent. Fresh snow made the next section very difficult, on a rock wall with sloping tile-like ledges; they made only fifteen rope lengths in one day. Between 13–14 August they surmounted this barrier and ascended a snow shoulder in dense mist to another rock barrier. All night, powder snow poured down the face, burying the tent. On the last day they had to overcome several rope lengths of difficult climbing, partly on overhanging rock. At 5.30 p.m. the summit was reached, where they were able to get some food from other climbers, having been on starvation rations. The climbers were V. Gluckhov, V. Ivanov, E. Myslovsky and A. Ovchinnikov.

1968. From Valtera Glacier

The Moscow Burevestnik Sports Society, led by Yuri Borodkin, crossed the Pamir Plateau to P.6950 on the west ridge in August.

1968. Northwest (Burevestnik) Buttress from Fortambek Glacier

Three groups from the Moscow Burevestnik Sports Society, led by V. Bozukov, V. Galkin and W. Maksimov, ascended the north-west buttress, and crossed Pamir Plateau to P.6950 on the west ridge, in August.

1970. Northeast Rib to East Ridge

The Uzbek route, in August.

1970. Southwest Wall via Lefthand Buttress

The Trud Sports Society route; leader W. Onishtchenko, in fiifteen days, summit on 15 August.

1970. Southeast Buttress

Led by V. Voronin.

1971. North Face Routes

From 12–20 August V. Bessubkin and four other Russians ascended the 2,000-metre high north face by way of the Tadzhik (Dusanbe) Route from the Fortambek glacier along the left edge of the north wall to the Pamir Plateau, then to P.6950 on the west ridge. Three kilometres to the west on this vast face the Krasnodarsk Route was climbed by J. Hetmann's group. The route went from the Valtera glacier along the right rib of the north wall of P.6708 and the north ridge of Pik Kommunizma.

1972. Northeast Face

The lefthand edge of the face was climbed from the Ordzhonikidze glacier by a party led by O. Borisenok.

1973. South Face

Climbed by a party led by A. Kustovsky.

1977. American Ascent of Nekrassov Route

Dick Dietz and Chris Pizzo

▲ *North Face of Pik Kommunizma (Courtesy Eugene Gippenreiter)*

climbed this 1,200-metre high route from the Belyaev glacier, safer and more interesting than the Georgian Couloir immediately to its left. After a short ice-fall and 60° ice, the second half was a corniced knife-edge followed by steep rock.

1977. Southwest Face

A party led by A. Nepomnjaschiy climbed the centre of the face.

1978. Northeast Face

Climbed by two parties led by A. Putinsev and G. Chunovkin.

1978. American Ascents on East Side

In mixed Soviet-American parties, Chuck Kroger and Rick Sylvester climbed Pioneer Ridge; while Ben Read climbed the adjacent and slightly more direct Varunia Arête. The routes join at about 6,700 metres. These were the first American ascents on the east side of the peak.

1979. Southwest Face of West Shoulder

Five Moscow climbers, led by V. Nevorotin, made the ascent from the Belyaev glacier using 164 rock and 23 ice pitons; the climb had been attempted many times before.

1980. South Face via Right-hand Buttress on Southwest Flank.

Nine Soviet Army climbers led by K. Valiev climbed this 2,800-metre high face between 29 July and 11 August, using 300 rock and ice pitons, often with sitting bivouacs.

1981. West Face

A party led by V. Solonnikov started from the 'Triangle' face and climbed the centre of the main buttress.

1982. Ski Ascent

Czechoslovakian P. Rajtar and a companion climbed the Burevestnik Buttress and skied twelve kilometres across Pamir Plateau. Rajtar then soloed the summit and skied down.

1986. Winter Ascent of Borodkin Buttress

A combined team of Russian and Uzbek climbers made probably the first winter ascent of a major Pamir peak. The Borodkin Buttress was covered in hard ice and took much preparation. Camps were placed at 5,100, 5,800 and 6,200 metres. On the snow plateau a snow cave camp was made on Pik Dushanbe at 6,900 metres. In all 24 climbers reached the summit in two waves, some suffering from frostbite.

1987. Southeast Buttress

A party led by G. Lunjakov climbed a route on the left-hand side.

1988. Northwest Face of North Ridge

A party led by P. Chotchia climbed a route on the left-hand side of the face.

PIK E. KORZENEVSKOI

Height: 7,105 metres
Lat./Long.: 39°03′20″ 72°01′26″
First ascent: 1953 via North Ridge

This peak is so difficult to reach that it did not become generally accessible until the organization of helicopter transport around 1960. Thus, in 1971 fifty Soviet climbers made the ascent, while in 1972 the total was sixty-five men and ten women. It is named after Evgenia Korzenevskaya, wife of the Russian geographer N. L. Korzhenevsky.

In 1937 a party led by D. Gushchin attempted the peak but only reached the lower summit (6,910 metres). In 1953 a group led by A. Ugarov approached from the Muksu valley, along the Fortambek glacier and through a gorge leading to the Korzhenevsky glacier. From a col on the north ridge the climbers forced their way past three rock towers to the summit of the lower peak. After descending into the gap between the two summits a further climb of 300 metres led them to the main top.

1961. South Ridge from Moskvin Glacier, Southeast Central Spur

This mainly rock route was put up by a group led by B. Romanov.

1966. South Ridge Buttress and Other Routes

A large Burevestnik expedition and a Spartak party made four new routes on the mountain; the south ridge, south ridge buttress, southeast face, and east ridge during August. One group from the Burevestnik expedition went to attempt the south ridge buttress which starts at 5,600 metres. They found the rock easy but friable and had to advance slowly. On the second day they climbed a 40-metre high rock wall, with an overhang, which was followed by relatively easy snow-covered rocks. By mid-afternoon they reached a steep pitch leading to the exit to the south ridge; the height was about 6,500 metres. Next day Anatoly Ovtchinnikov and another leader started to prepare the route which proved so difficult that by noon they had progressed only four rope-lengths. They were then obliged to evacuate a member of the party who was suffering from altitude sickness. On return to base they learned that the south ridge had been climbed but that, like them, the east ridge party had been forced to turn back with a medical casualty.

A few days later the climbers set off again. Attacking the exit from the buttress to the south ridge – the most difficult 300 metres of the whole climb – took a whole day, even though part of it had been prepared during the first attempt. Vertical walls and overhangs alternated with ledges covered in deep snow. Having arrived on top they camped on the broad snowy ridge. Now the summit was quite near but the snow was deep and more fell during the night, while next day visibility was very poor and there was a strong wind. They struggled to the top in two exhausting hours and with great difficulty found the cairn. A message from the east ridge party stated that they had another casualty. On account of the weather they did not stay long and began the descent of the south ridge where they caught up with the others and a rescue party who

had come up to help transport the sick climber; the evacuation took two days. During the same period a Soviet Army expedition repeated the 1961 Romanov route.

1968. Northeast Ridge
Climbed by a party led by B. Sivtsov.

1968. From Mushtekov Glacier
A party led by A. Zaidler climbed the peak from the Mushketov glacier via Pik 6,200 metres.

1973. Southeast Face
Climbed by a party led by D. Dangadze.

1974. West Face
A party led by I. Hatskevich climbed up the left-hand side of the face.

1975. West Face
A route led by A. Putinzev.

1976. South-Southwest Ridge
A route led by Yuri Popenko.

1976. East Ridge
A route led by V. Sviridenko.

1980. West Buttress and West Face
A. Putinzev led six climbers from Tashkent on the 1,900-metre high west buttress, 450 metres of which were Grade VI. It took a Leningrad team led by A.

Bashmakov a week to make a route up the centre of the west face.

1982. Tzetlin Ridge
The Czechoslovak Pavol Rajtar, and three others ascended the Tzetlin (southwest) Ridge. Rajtar and Robert Galfy made the first ski descent of the same ridge, reaching the end of the glacier in three hours.

1984. Southwest Ridge
A route led by V. Markelov.

1986. Winter Ascent
A team from Leningrad ascended the difficult south face, chosen because it was more sheltered from wind; eighteen climbers reached the top.

1986. American Ascent of Tzetlin Ridge
Fully acclimatized after an ascent of Pik Kommunizma, Gary Bocarde, Susan Havens and Andrew Evans made a rapid ascent of the peak, reaching a height of 6,320 metres in two days. The next day was a white-out, despite which six Russians àttempted the summit unroped, one sustaining fatal injuries. On the fourth day the Americans climbed the remaining 700 metres to the summit by way of the airy Tzetlin ridge. (This climb was reported as the Zatelan Ridge.)

1988. West Face
A group led by N. Petrov climbed the right-hand side of the west face 'Triangle'.

Bibliography

Borchers, P. (and others) (1929) 'Bergfahrten im Pamir', *Zeitschrift (Deutscher und Österreichischer Alpenverein)*, 60, pp. 64–160.

Clark, G. (1978) 'Pik Kommuniza', *AAJ*, 21, pp. 451–8.

Craig, R. (1977) *Storm and Sorrow*. Seattle: Mountaineers, (revised edition, London: Gollancz, 1981).

Hunt, J. and McNaught-Davis, I. (1963) 'British-Soviet Pamirs Expedition, 1962', *AJ*, 68, pp. 90–9; 243–50.

Ovchinnikov, A. (1967), 'Expédition Soviétique 1966 au Pamir', *La Montagne*, December, pp. 173–6.

Ovchinnikov, A. (1969) 'The first ascent of the south face of Peak Communism, 1968', *AJ*, 74, pp. 25–34.

Polyakov, A. (1958) 'Conquest of the first 7000-metre peak', *AJ*, 63, pp. 203–6.

Romm, M. (1936) *Ascent of Mt Stalin*. (London: Lawrence & Wishart).

Roskelley, J. (and others), (1975) 'U.S.A.–U.S.S.R. Pamirs expedition', *AAJ*, 20, pp. 68–80.

Slesser, M. (1964) *Red Peak*. (London: Hodder & Stoughton).

Sylvester, R. (1979) 'From Russia with luck', *AAJ*, 22, pp. 62–9.

Vanis, E. (1968) 'Austrian expedition to the Pamirs', *AJ*, 73, pp. 25–34. (See also *MW* (1968–69), pp. 86–93).

Wala, J. (1973) 'Routes leading to Pik Kommunizma', *AJ*, 78, pp. 173–7.

Tien Shan

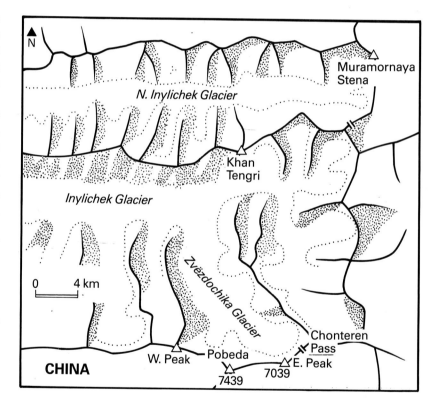

The existence of this great range, otherwise known as the Celestial Mountains, has been known for many centuries. It runs for over 1,600 kilometres from Tashkent to Urumchi, beyond which it rises again as the Bogdo Ola Range. Its southern fringes were first described by the Buddhist monk Hsuan Tsang in the seventh century BC, and they would have been visible from the Tien Shan Nan Lu, the great Silk Road, along which Marco Polo travelled in 1273 with his father and uncle. Later, the mountains would have guided the caravans transporting costly merchandise to Kashgar and the west. However, it is only the central portion, southeast of Lake Issyk-kul which contains the very high mountains. Here the peaks are closely grouped together, mostly in east-west ranges, near or on the Sino-Soviet frontier. Hsuan Tsang wrote of 'encountering nothing but ice and snow. The snow falls both in summer and spring-time. Night and day the wind rages violently'.

Despite the records and acute observations of the early travellers the Tien Shan remained more legend than reality until the mid-nineteenth century when they were visited for the first time by a man of science, the Russian geographer Peter Semyonov. In 1856 he travelled around Lake Issyk-kul and returned to winter in Alma-Ata. The following spring he set off to explore the highest ranges of the Tien Shan, for which he had prepared himself thoroughly, not only by his studies but by climbing in the Alps. His sizeable expedition first crossed the Santash Pass east of Alma-Ata and a further pass before retracing their steps and heading for the Chinese frontier. On 26 June the high peaks came suddenly into view – a cluster of some thirty snowy summits well over 6,000 metres, headed by the mighty Khan Tengri, 'Lord of the Sky – Prince of the Spirits'. Semyonov got no nearer and in the autumn he left the Tien Shan for ever, although subsequently he had a long and distinguished career as head of the Russian Geographical Society.

The first person to attempt to reach Khan Tengri was the Austrian explorer Dr Gottfried Merzbacher in 1902. Approaching from the north he found himself separated from it by the Sarydzhas Range and the deep trench of the North Inylichek glacier. This led him to discover that Khan Tengri does not lie on the main watershed of the Tien Shan which in fact is the north–south spur named the Meridional Range. Merzbacher and his party attempted a fine peak, Mramornaya Stena ('Marble Wall') on this frontier range before returning to Kashgar for the winter. The following year he discovered the snout of the 60-kilometre long Inylichek glacier which leads to the heart of the region. In so doing Merzbacher established the relationship of the various ranges which unite to form a reversed letter 'E'. He studied Khan Tengri itself, noting the overlapping slabs and absence of chimneys, ledges and terraces, and considered that its ascent would require a large well organized expedition.

The height of Khan Tengri was originally determined at 7,193 metres but later surveys reduced this to 6,995 metres which remains its accepted altitude. In form it is a striking white pyramid of near perfect shape. To the west a corniced ridge falls steeply for nearly 1,000 metres to a col while the east ridge plunges to around 5,900 metres; the finest route lies up the southwest buttress, the

Marble Rib. In the 1930s Russian climbers began to suspect that it was not the highest in the range but it was not until 1943 that the height of Pik Pobeda (7,439 metres) was established beyond doubt. Not only are the weather conditions bad, with protracted snow falls, but for many days of the year the peaks are obscured by clouds of loess dust.

KHAN TENGRI

Height: 6,995 metres (formerly 7,193 metres)
Lat./Long.: 42°40'10" 80°16'43"
First ascent: 1931 via West Ridge

Between 1929–31 M. T. Pogrebezky led three Ukranian expeditions to Khan Tengri, reconnoitring the approach routes and climbing possibilities. In September 1931 Pogrebezky and two companions started from below the north face and climbed a steep rib to easier ground, whence they succeeded in ascending the fairly easy west ridge. Later parties started from the South Inylichek glacier to reach the col between Pik Tchapajev and Khan Tengri. Between 1931 and 1962 twenty climbers from five expeditions reached the summit.

1964. Southwest Rib
Climbed by a 33–man expedition from the Moscow Trud Sports Society, led by B. Romanov. The actual Marble Rib rises some 900 metres above a 1,500-metre high bastion of extremely difficult rock and ice. Once on the rib there is little chance of retreat. The route was prepared to 5,100 metres before the six-man assault team set off on 4 August. They made slow progress up brittle ice-glazed rock and had to surmount gendarmes, vertical rock steps and walls of ice. Three days' hard

work were needed before they reached a moderate snow slope leading to the foot of the rib. Now they had to contend with the bitingly cold wind, which appeared to blow incessantly, but in compensation found that the reddish-white limestone of the buttress was only moderately difficult. On the afternoon of 8 August heavy snow began to fall but they were obliged to continue climbing until dark and bivouaced not too comfortably at 6,700 metres. Next morning visibility was down to 20–30 metres. After a few rope-lengths they were at the base of the summit wall which consisted of icy, snow plastered slates. They fought their way up the wall for ten hours in the fury of the storm and had barely enough strength left to erect their bivouac tent just below the summit. Next day they descended the west ridge in pleasant conditions.

1964. West Ridge by a Woman
Lidia Komanova was a member of a party from the same Moscow Trud Sports Society expedition, with V. Vozozhischev as leader.

1964. North Ridge
Five climbers from the Burevestnik Sports Society, led by K. Kuzmin, climbed this route a few days after the ascent of the Marble Rib.

1968. East Ridge
Khan Tengri's east ridge was climbed by a long traverse from Pik Saladin over Pik Shachter (6,700 metres).

1970. Eastern Buttress of North Face
Climbed by a party led by O. Hudiakov.

▲ *On the southwest ridge of Pik Pobeda: in the distance (centre) is the pyramid of Khan Tengri (David Breashears)*

1973. East Face (1) and South-Southwest Ridge
A buttress of the east face and the south-southwest ridge were climbed by a group led by V. Voronin.

1974. North Face (1) and (2)
Two Soviet teams, led by E. Myslovsky and B. Studenin, climbed routes in the centre of the face.

1975. North Ridge
The eastern buttress of the north ridge was climbed by a party led by V. Benkin.

1982. South Face
Led by G. Isachenko.

1982. Southwest Buttress of South-Southwest Rib
Led by V. Sviridenko.

1986. North Face (3)
A new route was made on this very difficult face during 8–21 August by V.Koroteev and seven other Moscow climbers. They bivouaced six times during the ascent. The route on somewhat rotten rock included three nearly vertical rock barriers; at 6,500 metres a 70°, 180-metre chimney led to the summit cone.

1987. North Face (4)
The lefthand buttress of the centre north face was climbed by a group led by M. Gorbenko.

1987. East Face (2)
The centre of the east face was climbed by a party led by N. Shustov.

1988. North Face (5)
Led by N. Zakharov.

1988. East Face (3)
The right-hand side of the face was climbed by a party led by A. Savin and Yuri Moiseev.

1988. Via Pik Chapaev
The peak was climbed by a party led by V. Khrischatyi via the northwest rib of the shoulder of Pik Chapaev.

PIK POBEDA (Russian name)/MOUNT TOMUR (Chinese name)
Height: 7,439 metres
Lat./Long.: 42°02′ 80°08′
First ascent: 1956 via Northeast Spur

During 1936–37 two parties on Khan Tengri were convinced that they had seen another peak to the south which appeared to be

The North Face of Pik Pobeda from base camp: the route climbed by the American-Soviet party rises from the far right (David Breashears)

higher. Professor A. Letavet was so sure that in 1938 he organized an expedition to find and attempt it. From camp on the Zvëzdochka ('Little Star') glacier the view was of a mighty snowy wall, somewhere on which must be the peak they were looking for. Eventually only three members of the party – L. Gutman, E. Ivanov and A. Sidorenko – were fit to make an assault. Worn out and frostbitten they reached the mist-enshrouded crest at about 6,930 metres and climbed a summit (probably Pik Komosomol). In 1943 the geodesist P. Rapasov worked out the results of a new topographical survey and established the height of Pik Pobeda ('Victory Peak') at 7,439 metres but it was not until 1946, when Letavet climbed Mramornaya Stena ('Marble Wall') and photographed Pobeda, that its exact position was confirmed. A number of parties subsequently reconnoitred the peak and made abortive attempts from the east along the Kokshaal-Tau crest and from the north on the immense face at the head of the Zvëzdochka glacier. The death-toll on Pik Pobeda, which now stands at over sixty, began with the deaths of eleven Russians in 1955.

In 1956 the first ascent was made by a 32-man expedition led by the veteran Vitaly Abalakov. From 24 July to 14 August four intermediate camps were set up, the route being the most westerly yet attempted. One camp was on a snow plateau at 5,300 metres, the next on a steep snow and ice slope at 5,800 metres, and the fourth at 6,200 metres. Large snow caves were built and stocked with food and equipment. On 18 August Abalakov and three other senior Soviet mountaineers started the assault on the summit, followed next day by seven more climbers. At Camp IV two days

of bad weather were followed by two more when the cold winds made it impossible to proceed. They then moved on and above 6,500 metres made a long tiring ascent over snow which was alternately hard and soft. Camp was made at 7,000 metres. On 30 August the final climb went up steep, firm snow slopes, crossing two vertical rock ridges. At 4 p.m. they reached the corniced summit, Abalakov having led the climb all the way from base.

1958. East Ridge and Traverse

A large party from Moscow, led by I. Yerokhin, ascended the Zvëzdochka glacier to the Chonteren Pass. On the fifth day of the assault, Pobeda's east peak was reached by forty-four mountaineers including three women; thirteen of them climbed on. They advanced along the crest at a height of more than 7,000 metres, over difficult terrain. Camps were made in snow caves and the traverse took seven days. The party descended the Abalakov route.

1967/1970. Traverses

In 1967 the peak was traversed from west to east by a party led by V. Rjasanov. Three years later V. Rjabukhin led a traverse from east to west.

1971. West Ridge

By twelve climbers from Leningrad, led by O. Hudjakov.

1977. Chinese Ascent from South

Twenty-eight climbers, including six women, ascended the peak on 25 and 30 July via the south face, using four camps.

1982. North Face

Led by V. Smirnov.

1984. North Face of East Ridge

Led by V. Khrischatyi.

(Jósef Nyka)

Vitaly Mikhailovich Abalakov (1906–86)
Vitaly Abalakov was the Soviet Union's most distinguished mountaineer. During the early 1930s he climbed in the Caucasus, often with his brother Evgeny and his fiancée. (Evgeny made the first ascent of Pik Kommunizma in 1933.) In 1934 he made the first traverse of Beluhka, the highest mountain in the Soviet Altai and the following year took part in the first Russian ascent of Pik Lenin. In 1936 he made the third ascent of Khan Tengri in the Tien Shan, as a result of which he lost thirteen fingers and toes through frostbite and was unable to climb for nine years. However, in 1946 he became the leader of the Spartak climbing group and made a series of fine new routes in the Caucasus, on nearly all of the main peaks. In 1956 he led the first ascent of Pik Pobeda, the highest mountain in the Tien Shan. He continued to make severe climbs in the Pamirs and Tien Shan for another ten years, and was the leader of the Russian group on the joint British-Soviet Pamirs expedition in 1962 when Wilfrid Noyce and Robin Smith were killed. Apart from climbing, he designed sports equipment and wrote many articles – in addition to his well-known mountaineering handbook, also translated into other languages but not English. He was awarded many titles and distinctions, including the Order of Lenin.

1985. American Ascent of West Ridge

David Breashears, Randall Starrett and William Garner became the first foreigners to ascend Pik Pobeda which they did in the company of a dozen Soviet climbers. The route climbed was the ten-kilometre long west ridge from the Zvëzdochka glacier on which the Russians had already spent more than a month without reaching the frontier crest. On 17 August the party set off and next day reached the previous high point at 5,800 metres. In the next twenty-four hours over a metre of snow fell but a wind consolidated conditions on the 1,200 metres of steep mixed rock and ice leading to the 7,000-metre high ridge. In the afternoon of 21 August the climbers reached the crest and traversed on the Chinese side for nearly two kilometres to avoid cornices. In deteriorating weather they ascended the summit arête, straddling the narrowest places, and arriving on top at 4 p.m., the deadline set by the Soviet team captain. The six-hour return to camp was made in $-40°C$

temperature and winds exceeding 130 kilometres per hour.

1988. Greater Traverse

Twenty-six climbers in two groups completed a west to east traverse from Pik Vazha Pshavela (6,973 metres) over Pik Pobeda, Vostochnaya and Military Surveyors Summit (6,973 metres). The 20-kilometre long route was completed in seven days.

VOSTOCHNAYA POBEDA/TOMUR EAST PEAK

Height: 7,039 metres (or 7,060 metres)
Lat./Long.: 42°02' 80°11'
First ascent: 1958 via Northeast Ridge

This peak lies on the Kokshaal-Tau crest some five or six kilometres east of the main Pobeda peak from which it is separated by a number of lesser summits. It was traversed from the Chonteren Pass during the second ascent of the main peak.

1984. West Ridge via North Face

This route was climbed by a party headed by V. Solonnikov.

Bibliography

Abalakov, V. (1960–61) 'Pobeda Peak', *MW*, pp. 23–31.

(China) (1979) *Planting the Five-Star Flag on Mount Tomur.* (Peking: Foreign Languages Press).

(China) (1980) *The Tian-Shan Mountains.* (Peking: China International Bookstore.)

Merzbacher, G. (1906) 'Der Tian-Schan oder das Himmelsge-birge', *Zeit. DÖAV*, 37, pp. 121–51.

Merzbacher, G. (1905) *The central Tian-Shan mountains, 1902–1903* (London: John Murray).

Onishtchenko, W. (1966/67) 'Khan Tengri, Lord of the Sky', *MW*, pp. 44–52.

Polyakov, A. (1959) 'The first ascent and first traverse of Victory Peak', *AJ*, 64, pp. 74–7.

Starrett, R. (1986) 'Snow leopards on Pik Pobedy', *AAJ*, 28, pp. 21–6.

China and Tibet

The more remote mountains of China and Tibet have been yielding up some of their secrets in recent years. Sadly they have been shown to be not as high as legend and imagination would have them. The heights of a number of historically recorded 7,000-metre peaks have been reduced substantially as a result of United States aerial photography and the latest Chinese surveys. Apart from the determination of location and probable height, our knowledge of some of these peaks remains much as it was seventy-five years ago, that is, at best scanty and in some cases virtually nil. Even though most of them are currently not ranked as 7,000-metre peaks, they retain their fascination along with that of the travellers' tales which gave birth to their reputations. And there still may be compensations. The latest map has thrown up some previously unrecorded peaks exceeding 7,000 metres in height. Who shall say there are no more?

The modern exploration of Tibet began in the 1860s with the despatch by the Survey of India of the Pundit surveyors, the first and greatest of whom was Nain Singh. At this time the trans-frontier maps north of the Himalaya were almost complete blanks, the 2,400-kilometre long frontier being closed by order of the Emperor of China – 'no Moghul, Hindustani, Pathan or Feringhi shall be admitted into Tibet on pain of death'. In the 1870s European explorers entered Tibet either by way of the Bokalik Tagh (northeast) or Ladakh (northwest) in an effort to avoid coming into contact with the Tibetans, who lived mainly in the south and east. These expeditions, by mostly Russian, French, Swedish and British explorers, continued until the outbreak of the First World War which, coupled with the Russian Revolution, stopped all entry from the north. Amongst these travellers the best known is Sven Hedin, but many others contributed as much, if not more, to our knowledge of the high peaks of these formidable and forbidden regions.

Transhimalaya

The Transhimalaya stretches for approximately 1,000 kilometres, but has neither a marked crest nor a definable drainage system. The highest points are isolated peaks and massifs. The southern boundary of the range follows the curvature of the Himalaya, while the northern boundary is approximately a straight line between the lakes Pangkong Tsho (Bangong Co) in the west and Tengri Nor (Nam Co) in the east. Modern geographers prefer to refer to the main part as the Kailas range (Gangdisê Shan) and the eastern end (northwest of Lhasa) as the Nyenchen Tangla range (Nyain-qêntanglha Feng).

The first recorded information about the Transhimalaya comes from the journeys made by the pundit Nain Singh in 1866–67 and 1874–75. On his first journey he crossed into Tibet from Nepal over the Gya La (north of Manaslu) and made his way to Lhasa, returning along the caravan route to Lake Manasarowar near Kailas. On his outward journey in 1874 from Leh to Lhasa he travelled more to the north and noted 'a vast snowy range lying parallel to and north of the Brahmaputra river'. On this occasion he returned to India by following the Tsangpo eastwards. The next travellers were the British officers Captains Rawling and Ryder, accompanied by Lt. F. M. Bailey, returning from Younghusband's 1904 mission to Lhasa. They followed Nain Singh's 1867 route to Lake Manasarowar and confirmed much of his work.

The last explorer, who claimed most of the credit for the discovery of the Transhimalaya, was Sven Hedin. In August 1906 he slipped into Tibet from Leh, having evaded the British officials, and eventually was allowed to travel as far as Shigatse (Xigazê) where he stayed as the guest of the Panchen Lama. On his return journey he was supposed to follow the route of his predecessors, but he zigzagged his way westwards through the tangle of peaks until, in mid–1907, he once again got on the highway as he neared Lake Manasarowar. As soon as Hedin arrived back in Ladakh he set off again and headed back whence he had come. This final journey achieved only a further demarcation of the mountain barrier designated as the Transhimalaya.

As a result of all these explorations the heights and positions of some thirty peaks were observed, some much more acurately than others.

ALING GANGRI (Nganglong Kangri)
Height: 6,450 metres (historically 7,315 metres)
Lat./Long.: 32°48' 81°00'

This peak was first seen, named and given this location by Nain Singh in 1867. The height of the peak was entered in the official record as 'exceeding 23,000 ft and possibly 24,000 ft' and was based on the amount of snow at the time – September – as seen from the south. It was reported again three times between 1874–1901.

KUHANBOKANG
Location: no high peak in area indicated
Height: historically 7,216 metres

This non-existent peak was supposed to be located at about 31° 57' 83°15'. Nain Singh was the first to record snow peaks at about 32°25' north during his 1873–75 journey. Subsequently it acquired first a name, then a height. The nearest peaks recorded on the US air chart rise only to about 6,500 metres.

LOINBO KANGRI (Lungpo Gangri, Lombo Kangra)
Height: 7,093 metres
Lat./Long.: 29°50' 84°36'

This peak corresponds to Peak W134 of the Ryder and Wood survey of 1904. The US air chart records a peak of 7,324 metres slightly farther west, but the original location and height (slightly increased) have prevailed in the latest Royal Geographical Society [R. G. S.] map.

▲ Illustrations from Sven Hedin's book Trans-Himalaya (Alpine Club Collection)

LUNGMARI
Height: 6,572 metres (historically, 7,100 metres)
Lat./Long.: 30°36' 86°24'

The background for this peak is uncertain. It may correspond to Nain Singh's Targo Gangri peaks (1873–75 journey) which he estimated at about 7,400 metres. Sven Hedin seems to have been the only other western traveller to note it, recording a peak of 6,933 metres slightly to the west. Its more recent height of 7,100 metres has now been reduced to 6,572 metres.

SHAHKANGSHAN
Location: no peak at this specific location
Height: historically, 7,660 metres
Lat./Long.: 31°40' 85°20'

Nain Singh is credited with the discovery of this mountain and its height of 7,660 metres in the course of his 1873–75 journey from Leh to Lhasa. However, his account and map refer only to 'high snow peaks' at about 31°40' 84°45'–57'. Sven Hedin noted it several times, always referring to it as Nain Singh's 'Shahkangsham', and recording the same elevation. Thus the name and height must have come out of the Indian Survey Office. There appears to be no peak at the location recorded and the surrounding peaks shown by the US air chart are all in the region of 6,000 metres. However, the highest point in this locality shown on the RGS map is 6,815 metres.

QUNGMOGANGZE (Chomo Gangar, Kan Lan Shan)

Location: c.100 km WNW of Lhasa
Height: 6,139 metres (historically, 7,000 metres)
Lat./Long.: 29° 48′ 90° 03′

The historical details of this peak derive from the survey by E. A. Ryder and H. Wood – their peak R210, also called Chomo Gangar by the pundit A. K. The US air chart shows several 6,000-metre peaks in this area; the RGS map shows the location but no height.

NINGCHIN KANGSHA (Nodzin Kangsan, Ning-dzing-zonka)

Location: southwest of Lhasa, 2 km from the Lalo La (Karo La) on the road from Gyangze to Lhasa
Height: 7,223 metres (Also given as two summits, 7,252 and 7,158 metres)
Lat./Long.: approx.28° 57′ 90° 12′
First ascent: 1986

This peak was noted and photographed in 1936 by F. Spencer Chapman, who was of the opinion that both the exquisitely fluted north ridge and more gently sloping south one were climbable. The first recorded attempt on the peak was in 1985 by a Japanese party who were stopped at 6,600 metres on the southwest ridge. The following year, twelve members of a Tibet Mountaineering Association expedition reached the summit in twenty days from the highway. They measured the height as 7,191 metres.

NANCHEN TANGLA (Nyainqêntanglha Feng, Nianqintanggula, Nien Ch'ing T'ang Ku La Shan)

Location: c.90 km NNW of Lhasa
Height: 7,162 metres (summit in centre of range)
Lat./Long.: 30° 22′ 90° 36′
First ascent: 1986 via West Ridge

The East Face of Ningchin Kangsha from the Karo La showing the fluted north ridge and gentler south ridge (F. S. Chapman)

▼

This mountain was surveyed by E. A. Ryder and H. Wood, who gave its height as 7,088 metres. It was originally recorded by Nain Singh, then by Gabriel Bonvalot, Dutreuil De Rhins and St George Littledale, all from the shores of Lake Tengri Nor (Nam Co). They roughly estimated its height at 7,300–7,600 metres.

Twelve climbers from Tohuku University in Japan established base camp near a small frozen lake on 5 April at 5,300 metres. After crossing the lake they ascended the south glacier and eventually reached a col (6,270 metres) on the west ridge. Rope was fixed on the upper part of the ridge to the base of the summit rock wall at 7,000 metres. On 8 May three members overcame the Grade IV+ rock to reach the top.

Kun Lun

In its wider sense the Kun Lun encompasses the mountain ranges which run for some 4,000 kilometres from the Pamirs eastwards along the northern edge of the

▲   Nanchen Tangla seen from the east on the Lhasa road (Michael Ward)

KONGUR TOBE FENG
(Qungur I, Qungur Tjube Tagh)

Height: 7,595 metres
Lat./Long.: 38°36' 75°06'
First ascent: 1956 from South Side

In 1873 a very strong British mission to Kashgar, led by Douglas Forsyth, carried out a considerable amount of geographical work, among its many enquiries. Captain Trotter, one of the surveyors, calculated the height of the peak at 7,620 metres. Later nineteenth century travellers to the area included Ney Elias, Francis Younghusband and Sven Hedin, but none of them managed to spot that there were two Kongur peaks. The first to do this was Sir Aurel Stein in 1900 when he photographed the massif from the Karakol lakes. Even so, the relative postions of the two

Tibetan plateau to approximately 113°E. The highest peaks are in the western Kun Lun where the system is narrowest (about 250–350 km); as it broadens eastwards the peaks become correspondingly lower.

The whole mountain system comprises several parallel chains of mountains. In the central Kun Lun the Arka Tagh is the true backbone and is the actual border range of the Tibetan plateau, for none of the ranges which cross Tibet to the south appears to belong to the Kun Lun.

Kongur Tiube from the vicinity of the Karakol lakes (Michael Ward)

peaks were not pinpointed until the 1920s. The then Consul-General in Kashgar, Sir Clarmont Skrine, viewed the massif from the Shiwakte and Tigarman peaks (at about 6,000–6,400 metres) to the east and thus was able to link up previous reports made from the north and south. Coupled with his further explorations, the position and height of Kongur Tobe Feng were fixed, along with conclusive proof of the higher adjacent peak.

After the successful ascent of Muztagata in 1956, a member of the expedition, Kiril Kuzmin, led a party to investigate the southern approach to Kongur Shan itself, possibly reaching Koksel Col. As it was obvious that the peak would require a major expedition including reconnaissances of the north and east sides, Kuzmin turned his attention to a possible ascent of Kongur Tobe Feng from the

south. The climb was accomplished in a single five-day push, the eight climbers being supported by nine others and pack animals. Six Russians and two Chinese reached the summit, the climb being described as 'technically complicated'. The second ascent of the peak was made in 1961 by an all-women expedition from China. The weather was generally bad and the ice-fall of the 1956 route proved to be impassable, necessitating a new route along a ridge. The ice and snow slopes, which varied from 40°–70°, were piled with deep, loose snow. Included in the summit party were two Tibetans. During the descent a climber died in an avalanche.

Summit pyramid of Kongur from the west (Michael Ward)

KONGUR SHAN (Qungur II, Qungur Tagh)

Height: 7,719 metres
Lat./Long.: 38° 36′ 75° 18′
First ascent: 1981 via South Ridge of Kongur Tobe Feng and traverse of Main Ridge via 'Junction Peak'

The existence of this hidden peak was not discovered until 1900 when Sir Aurel Stein examined the massif from the Karakol lakes to the southwest. Its precise location and height were not known until the 1920s when Sir Clarmont Skrine explored the area while resident in Kashgar. The first attempt on the peak was made in 1956, immediately following the Sino-Russian ascent of Muztagata. Coming from the south, the climbers may have reached Koksel Col on the ridge leading to Junction Peak between the two Kongurs. These summits lie on the

▲ *Summit of Kongur from east summit, looking west to Kongur Tiube and the USSR Pamirs (Michael Ward)*

main east-west ridge which has numerous points above 7,000 metres. In 1980 the region was opened to foreigners and the British and Japanese made reconnaissances. Michael Ward's three-man party investigated all sides of the mountain except the east, where they were prevented by bad weather from linking up Ney Elias' 1885 route with Skrine's 1921 explorations.

In 1981 the ten-man British Kongur expedition conducted a programme of altitude research under Dr Michael Ward, as well as making the first ascent of the peak. The climb was made alpine-style and the route was from the south-west, via the Koksel glacier. Higher up the climbers chose the south ridge which rises from Koksel Col to Junction Peak. The south ridge was climbed in one long, very hard day which involved two steep ice pitches and steep,

deep snow. In worsening weather they traversed Junction Peak only to find the summit pyramid of Kongur much bigger and steeper than expected. Although hoping to reach the summit in a day, the knife-edge ridge leading to the foot of the final pyramid took six hours to traverse and they had to return to their snow cave on the plateau. Conditions forced a retreat to base, made by traversing to Kongur Tobe Feng and descending its southern rib. The second assault was made up this route and the climbers re-established themselves in their snow cave. On the far side of the knife-edge ridge they were pinned down for four nights by storm with only unsatisfactory snow holes. The last day's climbing was initially hard and the top was not reached until 8 p.m. where another night was spent. Next morning they decided to climb the northeast peak, just to be sure, and

their descent of the mountain did not commence until late-afternoon. During this an accident occurred to Peter Boardman, caused by a falling stone, and they did not get back to their snow cave until after midnight.

At the same time a Japanese expedition was making slow progress up the east ridge from the Qurghan valley. Meanwhile, three other members of the expedition set off on an alpine-style attempt on the north ridge, carrying nine days' food. They were last seen at 6,300 metres the day before the weather turned bad for a week, and no trace of them was found afterwards. A local man reported having seen a tent on a ridge between the northeast and main summits and it is possible that they reached the top only to be killed in an avalanche during descent. The east ridge climb was abandoned. In 1983 a small American party spent some days investigating the lower part of the Japanese route before choosing a smaller ridge further west that promised easier access to the upper parts of the mountain. Passing two stiff ice faces they gained an enormous snow basin which led directly to the col at the base of the summit ridge followed by the British 1981 party. The summit pair got on the ridge but were too weak to continue.

MUZTAGATA

Height: 7,546 metres
Lat./Long.: 38°12' 75°06'
First ascent: 1956 via West Face

Muztagata lies some twenty-five kilometres east of the Sino-Russian frontier. Between the two runs Marco Polo's Silk Road, now part of the Karakoram Highway. The most straightforward routes of ascent are from the northwest and south; the north side appears to be more difficult, while the east face, which is closed to foreigners, is said to be very impressive. The first western traveller to try to ascend the peak was Sven Hedin in 1894 when he made four attempts, riding up on a yak. The first two attempts were made via the northerly of the two western ridges that leads to the lower northern peak. He claimed to have reached 6,300 metres, but 5,700 metres seems more likely. His third try was up the ridge of the main summit but this failed at about 5,600 metres. For his final attempt he returned to the other ridge, camping at his previous high point, but next day strong winds prevented any advance. Another famous explorer, Sir Aurel Stein, attempted Hedin's northern route six years later. He turned back at 6,100 metres but his two Hunza guides reached about 6,550 metres before finding their way barred by a notch ('Stein's Gap'). An attempt in 1904 by the

(Alpine Club Collection)

Sven Anders Hedin (1865–1952)
Sven Hedin was born in Stockholm, the eldest son of the city architect Ludwig von Hedin. He was inspired to become an explorer after witnessing the triumphal return to Stockholm of Baron Nordenskiöld. In 1886 he made a tour through the Middle East; later he followed the Silk Road east to Kashgar where he met up with Francis Younghusband. On his first major expedition in 1894 he started by exploring and mapping part of the Kun Lun, and made four attempts to climb Muztagata. A year later he just survived a crossing of the great Takla Makan desert in Sinkiang, later exploring the Tarim basin along its northern boundary where he discovered two ancient lost cities. In 1898 he began a series of journeys in the no-man's land between the Gobi Desert and the Tibetan plateau as a prelude to a swoop on Lhasa which took place in July 1901. He was intercepted twice, finally being allowed to leave Tibet by way of Ladakh. In 1906–7 he undertook what were to be his most controversial expeditions when he claimed for himself alone the discovery and exploration of the indeterminate ranges north of the Brahmaputra which he named the Transhimalaya. Throughout his life Sven Hedin displayed a ruthlessness and disregard for others, while at the same time he was a sentimental man who craved recognition and approbation. This he never received from his homeland but for some years he was honoured by the Royal Geographical Society. His extravagant claims regarding the Transhimalaya, coupled with his support for the German regimes in both World Wars, led to his virtual eclipse by the time he died.

Russian geologist Bogdanowitsch also failed.

There are no more recorded climbs until the almost successful ascent in 1947 by Eric Shipton and Bill Tilman. In a fast, lightweight attempt they reached a point some seventy metres below the summit in deep snow. Shipton was badly acclimatized and had frostbitten feet; both agreed it was the coldest climb they had ever made. In 1955 mountaineering was adopted as an official sport in China and the following year, after training in Russia, a large Sino-Russian expedition, led by E. A. Beleckij, attacked the mountain. Following Shipton and Tilman's route they established a line of camps in three weeks and succeeded in putting nineteen Russians and twelve Chinese on top.

1959. Second Ascent
By a party of thirty-three Chinese, including eight women.

1980–81. Ski Ascents
In 1980 a party led by Ned Gillette made the first ski ascent-descent of a mountain of this height. The next year a group led by John Amatt chose a route further south which lay between the Chal Tumak and Tergen Bulak glaciers. Japanese skiers also reached the top, including the lower north peak.

1982. Northwest Ridge and Southwest Face
Members of an American expedition climbed the northwest ridge. Five members of a Sino – Japanese organization climbed the southwest face.

The peak may now be reached from Pakistan, over the 4,960-metre high Kunjerab Pass on the Sino-Pakistani border, a distance of some 100 kilometres.

▲ *Base camp, with the Koksel Glacier immediately beyond and Muztagata rising from the clouds (Charles Clarke)*

MUZTAGATA NORTH

Location: Separated from Muztagata by the Yambulak glacier
Height: 7,427 metres
First ascent: 1981 via North Ridge

The independent nature of this peak was not recognized until recently. It is separated from the main peak by cliffs 900 metres high which border the gorge cut by the Yambulak glacier. Its windy north ridge was climbed on 7 August by the Japanese Tadakio Sakahasa and Koji Matsui, followed a week later by their two companions. The Japanese approached from the northeast but the easiest approach is from the southwest via the Chodomak (Qiaodumake) glacier which descends from an amphi-theatre between the north and northwest ridges.

MUZTAG (E61, K5)

Height: 6,710 metres (historically, 7,281 metres)
Lat./Long.: 36°02' 80°12'

This peak was originally known as E61 and was measured by the Survey of India in 1862 at 7,281 metres, with a location of 35°57' 80° 14'. Sir Aurel Stein variously referred to it as 'Muztagh' or K5 in his 1901 survey. The peak was the subject of some controversy and acrimony for many years on account of the surveyor W. H. Johnson's illicit visit to the region in 1865 and his claimed ascent. It was not until the 1920s that Kenneth Mason demonstrated quite conclusively that Johnson had not even been on the peak. One of the three known points of latitude had been wrongly plotted on his plane-

table when he set off and he was in fact farther south, separated from E61 by the 4,000-metre deep gorge cut by the Yurungkax He river. It has been suggested that he climbed a peak called Zogputaran, but now that E61 is calculated to be under 7,000 metres the possibility of a nineteenth century ascent of such a peak has finally been laid to rest.

P.7120

Location: c.110 km southeast of Mustag: the highest point in 'Aksai Chin' massif
Lat./Long.: 35°22' 81°10'

Approximately 120 kilometres east of Lake Aksai Chin is an area of glaciated peaks, the highest point of which is given as 7,120 metres on the RGS map. During his 1906–8 expedition Sir Aurel Stein noted that the glaciers were the most extensive he had seen in the Kun Lun. This peak may be the same as P.7167 ascended by Japanese climbers in 1986

P.7167

Location: not ascertained
First ascent: 1986 via East Ridge/
   South Ridge

This peak may be the one given in some references as 'Aksai Chin, 7,160 metres' and so may be the same as P.7120. The Japanese expedition from the Tokyo University of Agriculture Alpine Club travelled from Urumchi via Kashgar to the western Kun Lun and sited their base camp some sixty kilometres east of Tansuihai at 5,720 metres on the Litang River, still some twenty-five kilometres from P.7167. The most difficult part consisted of carrying loads across the Doctor and Zhongfeng glaciers. A glacier was followed on its south side to meet the east ridge where Camp III was placed. The climbers followed the east ridge to its junction with the south ridge. Four members reached the summit on 16 August and six others the next day.

ULUGH MUZTAGH (Muztag Feng)

Height: 6,987 metres (historically,
   7,723 metres)
Lat./Long.: 36°25'09" 87°29'47"
First ascent: 1985 from the East

The first Europeans to see this very remote mountain were members of the Dutreuil de Rhins expedition who passed by in 1893. One member, Fernand Grenard, found it dominating and thought it likely to be the highest peak between Turkestan and the Himalaya; he assigned it a height of 7,340 metres. In January 1895 St George Littledale described it as a double peak and measured it at 7,723 metres,

which remained its undisputed height until recently. Nothing more was done about it until a chance conversation between Eric Shipton and American Robert Bates in 1966. The latter raised the problem with one of his fellow climbers, Nick Clinch, in 1973 and they decided to get there and, if possible climb the peak, and determine its height. Negotiations for this were protraced but an agreement was finally signed with the Chinese.

The 1,750 kilometre drive to the mountains took ten days from Urumchi (Ürümqi), passing places visited by Marco Polo, and crossing the Altyn Tagh range before heading out across roadless desert. After stopping at Lake Acchikul the expedition eventually set up base camp on the east side of the mountain at about 5,300 metres.

Camp I was established at the snout of a glacier and the next some eight or nine kilometres farther on. American climbers Pete Schoening and Tom Hornbein spearheaded the route above Camp II, putting in fixed ropes. High winds produced big drifts of snow and the development of windslab danger, and the expedition began to worry about the time factor. This was not helped by original assault plans having to be changed.

Meanwhile the Chinese established Camp IV within easy striking distance of the summit. In view of the weather/time situation the Chinese leader was urged to send his climbers on ahead and the summit was reached by five of them on 21 October. The American assault team awoke next day to find that an accident had happened on the mountain below them. After assisting with the evacuation of the two climbers there was no chance of a second ascent and everyone began withdrawing to base.

CHOLPANGLIK
Height: historically, 7,102 metres
Lat./Long.: c.35°47′ 79°55′

It is difficult to decide who was responsible for some of these western Kun Lun figures, although this

This mountain was probably first seen and named by the Russian explorer Nicholas Przhevalski during his 1885–87 expedition. The report makes no mention of its elevation but the mountain appears to have been one of a group of peaks estimated at around 6,000 metres. Several later travellers contributed nothing to our knowledge of it and it seems probable that the Russians were responsible for the published elevation and location

▲
Ulugh Muztagh (Nicholas B. Clinch)

one probably arose out of a survey by Sir Aurel Stein. The US air chart records two peaks of 6,574 metres in this locality.

SHAPKA MONOMAKHA (Mo-No-Ma-La Shan)
Location: Bokalik Tagh range
Height: historically, 7,720 metres
Lat./Long.: 36°22′ 90°55′

The US air chart has no peak recorded at the specific location (neighbouring peaks being quite low) but it appears to correspond with Buka Daban Feng (6,860-metre) shown on the RGS map at approximately 36°00′ 90°54′.

AMNE MACHEN (Maqên Gangri)
Location: Amne Machen (Anyemaqên) range
Height: 6,282 metres
Lat./Long.: 34°48′ 99°28′
First ascent: 1981 via Northeast Ridge

Possibly the earliest reference to this mountain occurred in the great Chinese atlas of 1707 compiled by the Jesuits for the Emperor of China. It is also noted in the despatches of early Tibetan explorers but the first European to see the mountain was probably Fernand Grenard, of the De Rhins expedition, late in 1894. He noted it as 'dazzling and dominating' but accorded it a height of only 6,500 metres. In 1895 the Russian Roborosky was the first to reach the foot of the mountain, but the hostility of the local Golok tribesmen was for a long time a hindrance to approaching the peak. Stories of its legendary height seem to have started in the early 1920s when the British soldier-explorer George Pereira put it at at least 7,600 metres. An account in the *National Geographic Magazine* widely circulated American Joseph Rock's 1928 estimate of 8,500 metres, later revised to only 6,400 metres. Apart from a hoax report by American pilots flying the 'Hump' route during the Second World War, the last person to add to this myth was the American Leonard Clark who claimed to have surveyed the peak at 9,040 metres in 1949 just before the Chinese took over.

In May 1960 a group of teachers and students of the Peking (Beijing) Geological Institute went to the range and started by carrying out a survey to determine the height and position of the main peak. A reconnaissance party traversed the Gongma glacier from the east, but found themselves unequipped to tackle the steep summit ridge. Two days later another route from the southwest was started, but the terrain became more and more complicated. After reaching a height of 5,200 metres it was late afternoon before they started up two short but difficult ice walls, only to find a bottomless crevasse in front of them. The third attempt was made up the northeast slope and they planned to make the climb in two days. At one stage a dangerous crossing of a large crevasse had to be made. Loss of visibility then made it impossible to advance through the crevasses and they took to a 300-metre high 70°ice slope. Next day they set off before dawn, soon finding themselves in waist-deep snow while crossing a névé basin. Two steep ice slopes brought them at last to the summit.

The results of their very thorough survey showed the height of the peak to be 7,160 metres, but this was not the end of the story, for by 1972 further surveys had shown that not only was the peak climbed only 6,256 metres high, but that it was not the highest in the range. The relevant maps were kept secret and it was not until 1980 that the Chinese Mountaineering Association announced that the real Maqên Gangri was still unclimbed. This situation was rectified by one of the first foreign climbing expeditions allowed into China. On 9 June 1981 the Americans Galen Rowell, Harold Knutsen and Kim Scmitz made the ascent alpine-style in two days from an advanced base at 4,575 metres. The route went up a ridge which ended in steep, deep snow. Next morning they traversed a sharp ridge to the main buttress of the peak. Steep cramponing took them to the summit plateau where they encountered a wide basin of thigh-deep powder snow under wind crust. On top they found no evidence of a previous ascent, although two other expeditions were attempting the peak.

CHUNG MUZTAGH (Qong Muztag)

Height: 6,978 metres (possibly more)
Lat./Long.: 35°42' 82°18'

The record of Chung Muztagh (6,920 metres, location c.35°35' 82°15') may have originated with the British explorer H.H.P.Deasy who crossed the western Kun Lun down to about 34° north in 1896. He was the first real surveyor of these Tibetan mountains, fixing the locations and measuring the elevations of numerous peaks in the western Kun Lun and on the Tibetan plateau. The US air chart of 1974 listed a peak of 7,070 metres at 35°39' 82°20' with a maximum vertical error of ± 336 metres; it is given as 6,978 metres on the RGS map.

Peaks in Central Tibet

MAYÊR KANGRI (Peng-Wa-Lo-Te Shan)

Location: isolated peak c.250 km WSW of the Dupleix Mountains
Height: 7,011 metres
Lat./Long.: 33°24' 86°48'

This peak may have been one of the peaks seen by the French explorer Bonvalot who, in 1889–90, crossed the central Arka Tagh and travelled as far south as Lake Nam Co (Tengri Nor) near Lhasa.

ZANGSÊR KANGRI

Location: c.120 km northwest of Mayêr Kangri
Height: 6,950 metres on RGS map
Lat./Long.: 34°18' 85°48'

The highest point of a small isolated massif lying to the east of two small lakes. Despite its obvious height, which may well have led to its being stated as over 7,000 metres, this peak does not appear to have been recorded previously.

PUROG KANGRI (Mount Dupleix)

Location: 'Dupleix Mountains' c.500 km NNW of Lhasa
Height: 6,929 metres
Lat./Long.: 33°55' 89°14'

This mountain was first seen and named by the Bonvalot expedition. Bonvalot's estimate of its height (8,000 metres) was made in mist and the onset of darkness, and was regarded by Hedin as an exaggeration. Until recently this mysterious range was still thought to be around 7,500 metres high.

P.7353

Location: c.300 km northeast of Lhasa
Height: 7,353 metres
Lat./Long.: approx. 30°55' 93°49'

This appears to be a newly recorded high peak.

Minya Konka Region, Szechuan (Sichuan) Province

MINYA KONKA (Gongga Shan)

Height: 7,590 metres (7,556 metres per latest Chinese surveys)
Lat./Long.: 29°36' 102°06'
First ascent: 1932 via Northwest Ridge

This isolated granite and ice peak on the edge of the Tibetan plateau was first observed by a Hungarian, Count Bela Szechenyi; more importantly he measured its altitude to within a dozen metres of the true figure. In 1929 the American botanist Joseph Rock visited the monastery at the foot of the mountain and brought back the first close photographs. With his simple instruments he grossly

▲ *Minya Konka (Alpine Club Collection)*

overestimated its height, a mistake he repeated in the same year in respect of Amne Machen (Maqên Gangri). The following year Arnold Heim, the well-known Swiss geologist, and Edward Imhof took part in a geological survey, Imhof later publishing a remarkably accurate book about the region, including superb maps.

The first mountaineering expedition took place in 1932, the work of four Americans – Richard Burdsall, Arthur Emmons, Terris Moore and Jack Young. Their lengthy stay in China had familiarized them with Chinese ways and the language and they had been given almost complete freedom to travel across China, surveying, taking pictures and climbing. Burdsall and Emmons left Shanghai in June to reconnoitre the mountain and a month later the others started their own six-week journey to base camp. The party

met up on 19 September with a feeling of winter already in the air. Severe storms could be expected at any time. Emmons wrote: 'Our total climbing personnel consisted of only four men, two of whom had little previous mountain experience, a woefully small number to tackle an unknown 25,000-foot giant.' Porters could only be used as far as the snowline. The small caravan set out on 2 October.

Five days later, Moore and Emmons had reached the crest of the northwest ridge at just over 6,000 metres and the route looked reasonable as far as the base of the summit pyramid at 7,000 metres, but it was threatened by the possibility of loose snow avalanches that could be triggered by the sun's heat or the climbers' weight on the unstable slopes. This happened a few days later as Moore and Emmons were trying to traverse a feature called the 'Hump'. They

finally reached a height of 7,000 metres after a week's exhausting work. It was time for a rest; after another week's climbing the team was in position for a summit bid. The night before the assault Emmons suffered an unfortunate accident to his fingers. This left only the thirty-six-year-old Burdsall and the experienced Moore to make the climb. After a restless night they left at 5 a.m. and made good progress on the crooked ridge, thanks to careful prior study of the route. At 2.40 p.m. they reached the top, an oval platform about six metres across.

Minya Konka remained the highest summit reached by Americans until 1958. There have been several ascents now of the original route, and attempts on others, some of which ended in tragedy; all of which underlines the very considerable achievement of the pioneers nearly sixty years ago.

JIAZI (Rudshe Konka, Da Xue Shan)

Location: Szechuan province
Height: 6,540 metres (previously 7,100 metres)

This peak in the Da Xue Shan was calculated to be 7,100 metres high by Arnold Heim and Edward Imhof during their 1930–31 expedition. The official Chinese figure is now 6,540 metres.

ZHONG SHAN (Sunyatsen)

Location: Szechuan province
Height: 6,886 metres (previously 7,010 metres)
First ascent: 1981 via East Ridge

A Swiss expedition climbed a steep 700-metre snow and ice gully to gain the Ma-tsöko glacier which gives access to several high peaks. Four members approached the col between the south and main summits of Zhong Shan and followed the east ridge to the main peak.

Bibliography

Bates, R.H. (1986), 'The Ulugh Muztagh', *AAJ*, 28, pp. 27–38.

Bonington, C. J. S. (1982), *Kongur: China's Elusive Summit* (London: Hodder & Stoughton.)

Bonington, C. J. S. (1982), 'British Kongur expedition to China', *HJ*, 38, pp. 1–6.

Boothman, F. (1982), 'The mountains of Tibet and the Tibet–China border', *AJ*, 87, pp. 83–99.

Burdsall, R. and Emmons, A. (1935), *Men Against the Clouds* (New York: Harper & Row); (revised edition, Seattle: Mountaineers, 1980).

Cleare, J. (1983), 'Ski mountaineering in China: the ascent of Mustagh Ata', *AJ*, 88, pp. 29–36.

Day, H. (1982), 'Da Xue Shan, Sichuan, China', *AJ*, 87, pp. 117–120.

Gillette, N. (1981), 'American skiers in China's wild west', *AAJ*, 23, pp. 71–82.

Hedin, S. (1895), 'Attempts to ascend Mustagh Ata', *Geographical Journal*, 6, pp. 350–67.

Jardine, M. (1987), 'An electrifying experience', *AJ*, 92, pp. 117–21. (Muztagata)

Jardine, M. (1988–89), 'North Muztagh: Xinjiang's forgotten peak', *AJ*, 93, pp. 84–7.

Kelley, D. and Murphy, J. (1983), 'Gongga Shan – Minya Konka revisited', *AAJ*, 25, pp. 40–7.

Mason, K. (1921–22), 'Johnson's "suppressed ascent" of E61', *AJ*, 34, pp. 54–68.

Molnar, P. (1987), 'Ulugh Muztagh: the highest peak on the northern Tibetan plateau', *AJ*, 92, pp. 104–16.

Morgan, G. (1983), 'China's highest mountain', *AJ*, 88, pp. 65–9.

Murphy, J. E. (1986), *Adventure beyond the clouds* (Minneapolis: Dillon Press).

Nolting, R. (1983), 'Jiazi', *AAJ*, 25, pp. 48–53.

Pai Chin-Hsiao (1962), 'Ascent of Amne Machin', *AJ*, 66, pp. 274–83.

Rock, J. (1930), 'Seeking the mountains of mystery', *National Geographic Magazine*, 57, 2, pp. 131–85.

Rowell, G. (1982), 'On and around Anyemaqen' *AAJ*, 24, pp. 88–100.

Rowell, G. (1985), *Mountains of the Middle Kingdom*. (London: Century).

Shih Chan-Chun (1958), 'The second ascent of Minya Konka', *AJ*, 63, pp. 194–202.

Shih Chan-Chun (1959), 'Ascent of Muztagh Ata', *AJ*, 64, pp. 78–82.

Shipton, E. E. (1947–48), 'Muztagh Ata', *AJ*, 56, pp. 317–29.

Skrine, C. P. (1926), *Chinese Central Asia*. (London: Methuen).

Tilman, H. (1949), 'Muztagh Ata', *HJ*, 15, pp. 75–84.

Tilman, H. (1949), *Two mountains and a River* (Cambridge: Cambridge University Press).

Town, J. (1988–89), 'Amne Machin: a closer look', *AJ*, 93, pp. 77–83.

Vaill, E. (1985), 'Mountaineering in China: one hundred years of first ascents remain', *AJ*, 90, pp. 23–33.

Ward, M. (1981), 'The Kongur massif in southern Xinjiang (Sinkiang)', *AJ*, 86, pp. 7–17. (See also *Geographical Journal*, 140, 1983, pp. 137–52.)

Ward, M. (1982), 'Science on Mount Kongur', *AJ*, 87, pp. 65–7.

Yang Ke-Hsien (1959), *Ascent of Muztagh Ata* (Peking: Foreign Languages Press).

General Bibliography

(Note: The Japanese publications quoted have English summary and/or photo captions.)

Abrego, M. (1983), *Jannu: una primavera del Himalaya* (Pamplona: Aramburu).

Academic Alpine Club of Kyoto (1961), *Ascent of Noshaq* (Tokyo: Asahi-Newspaper).

Academic Alpine Club of Kyoto (1959), *Chogolisa* (Tokyo: Asahi-Newspaper)

Academic Alpine Club of Kyoto (1964), *Saltoro Kangri* (Toyko: Asahi-Newspaper)

(Anon) (1976), *Expedición Navarra Hindu-Kush 1976. Shakaur 7,116 metres, Espolón N.E.* (Spain: Pamplona – Report).

Anderson, W. (1983), *To the Untouched Mountain* (Wellington: Reed), New Zealand ascent of Molamenqing.

Andlovic, J. (and others) (1976), *Kangbachen* (Ljubljana: Mladinska Knjiga), second ascent in 1974 by Yugoslavs.

(Asahi-Newspaper) (1978), *The magnificence of the Himalaya* (Tokyo: Asahi-Newspaper), photo-album of 136 high peaks.

Bahi Alburquerque, A. (and others) (1983), *Arreu de les muntanyes: de Monserrat al Makalu* (Manresa: Centre Excursionista De La Comarca De Bages), includes Tirich Mir and Noshaq.

Band, G. (1955), *Road to Rakaposhi* (London: Hodder & Stoughton) 1955; Cambridge expedition in 1954.

Banks, M. E. B. (1959), *Rakaposhi* (London: Secker & Warburg); attempt in 1956 and first ascent in 1958.

Barenghi, B. (and others) (1955), *Alla conquista del Monte Api. Documentario della spedizione italiana al Garhwal-Nepal-Himalayano* (Milan: Ceschina), Piero Ghiglione's expedition in 1954. Photo-album.

Barker, R. (1959), *The Last Blue Mountain* (London: Chatto & Windus), ill-fated Oxford expedition to Haramosh in 1957.

Barnola, P. and Zuanon, J. (1978), *Sur le toit du monde: l'ascension du pic du Communisme* (Paris: Club Alpin Français,); report.

Bassi, R. (and others) (1974), *Un 7000 Friulano* (Udine: Arti Grafiche Friulane) 1974, ascent of Saraghrar.

Bergamaschi, A. (1977), *Biafo '77. Spedizione 'Citta di Bologna' all 'Himalaya Pakistano* (Bologna: C.A.I., Pinzolo); report. Ascent of Latok.

Bergamachi, A. (1980), *Il Nepal e la HN '79. Spedizione Italiana all'Annapurna Fang-m. 7650, Himalaya de Nepal* (Ancona: Flli. Aniballi); report.

Bergström, P-O. (and others) (1976), *Nun Kun 7000. Svenska Himalaya-expeditionen 1975: Reserapport* (Sweden: Stockholm), report.

Berry, S. (1988), *Thunder Dragon Kingdom* (Marlborough: Crowood Press/Seattle: Cloudcap); Gangkar Puensum, Bhutan.

Boardman, P. (1982), *Sacred Summits, A Climber's Year* (London: Hodder & Stoughton), Gaurishankar.

Bonatti, W. (1964), *On the Heights* (London: Rupert Hart-Davis), from the Italian: *Le mie montagne* (Bologna: Zanichelli, 1962). Autobiography; includes Gasherbrum IV in 1958.

Bonington, C. J. S. (1966), *I Chose to Climb* (London: Gollancz). includes Annapurna II and Nuptse.

Boninton, C. J. S. (1982), *Kongur: China's Elusive Summit* (London: Hodder & Stoughton).

Bonington, C. J. S. (1986), *Everest Years: A Climber's life* (London: Hodder & Stoughton), includes Ogre.

Bonvalot, G. (1891), *Across Tibet*

(London: Cassell) 2 vols.

Braham, T. (1974), *Himalayan odyssey* (London: Allen & Unwin).

Brown, J. (1967), *The hard years* (London: Gollancz); autobiography. Includes Pik Communism and Muztagh Tower.

Bruce, C. G. (1934), *Himalayan Wanderer* (London: Maclehose).

Burdsall, R. L. (1935), *Men against the Clouds* (London: Bodley Head), revised edition, Seattle: Mountaineers, 1980.

Calciati, C. (1930), *Spedizione Mario Piacenza nell'Himalaia Cashmiriano* (Milan: Rizzoli), first ascent of Kun.

Cameron, I. (1984), *Mountains of the Gods* (New York/Oxford: Facts On File Publications).

Chapman, F. S. (1940), *Helvellyn to Himalaya: Including an Account of the First Ascent of Chomolhari* (London: Chatto & Windus).

(China) (1957), *Conquering the Father of the Icy Mountains* (Peking: Foreign Languages Press), photographic record of the Sino-Soviet expedition to Muztagh Ata in 1956.

(China) (1965), *Mountaineering in China* (Peking: Foreign Languages Press), photo-album of Chinese climbing expeditions to Minya Konka, Amnemaqen, etc.

(China) (1979), *Planting the Five-Star Flag on Mt. Tomur* (Peking: Foreign Languages Press), Mt. Tomur is the Chinese name for Pik Pobeda.

China (1980), *Glaciers in China*, edited by the Institute of Glaciology & Cryopedology, Academia Sinica (Shanghai: Shanghai Scientific and Technical Publisher).

China (1981), *High Mountain Peaks in China* (Tokyo: Newspaper Publishing Bureau of Japan/People's Sports Publishing House of China).

Clark, L. (1954), *The Marching Wind* (New York: Funk & Wagnalls – London: Hutchinson, 1955); journey to the Amnemaqen Range in 1949.

Cockerill, G. K. (1896), *Report on Various Reconnaissances in Chitral Territory, 1893–5* (Simla: printed at the Government Central Printing Office).

Colombel, C. de (1981), *Voyage au bout du vide: une cordée alpine au Masherbrum* (Paris: Fernand Nathan); French expedition in 1980.

Conway, W. M. (1894), *Climbing and Exploration in the Karakoram-Himalayas* (London: T. Fisher Unwin); exploration of the Hispar, Biafo and Baltoro glaciers in 1892.

Cooke, C. R. (1988), *Dust and snow* (the author). Includes climbs in Sikkim, particularly Kabru.

Craig, R. W. (1977), *Storm and Sorrow in the High Pamirs* (Seattle: The Mountaineers with AAC); Revised edition, London, Gollancz, 1981.

Czechoslovakia Expedition (1981), *Krokonošská Horolezeckea Expedice Himálaj '79. Manaslu North (7,157 metres)* (Prague: Vydal Merkur); illustrated, maps.

Dainelli, G. (1933), *Buddhists and Glaciers of Western Tibet* (London: Routledge & Kegan Paul), from the Italian, *Il mio viaggio nel Tibet Occidentale* (Milan: Mondadori, 1932). Travels in the Karakoram; Siachen, Teram Sher and Rimo glaciers.

Dainelli, G. (1959), *Esplorati e alpinisti nel Caracorum* (Turin: Unione Tipografico-Editorice Torino); history of exploration and climbing in the Karakoram, with expedition route-maps and illustrations.

Deasy, H. H. P. (1901) *In Tibet and Chinese Turkestan* (London: T. Fisher Unwin); exploration and survey work in the western Kun Lun and on the Tibetan plateau in the years 1896–9.

Deutsche Himalaya Expedition 1973 (ed.). (1974), *Besteigung des Dhaulagiri III 7,715 metres. August 1973 bis Februar 1974* (Munich: The Editors); report.

Diaz Ibañez, J. J. (1983), *Expedición Aragonesa al Himalaya. Baruntse (7,220m)* (Zaragoza: Montañeros De Aragon/Peña Guarra); Baruntse East Buttress.

Diemberger, K. (1971), *Summits and Secrets* (London: Allen & Unwin); from the German: *Zwischen Null und Achttausend.* (Stuttgart: Orac Pietsch, 1970); Includes Chogolisa, Tirich Mir.

Diemberger, K. (1980), *Gipfel und Geheimnisse* (Orac Pietsch); includes Tirich Mir and Shartse.

Dingle, G. (1976), *Wall of Shadows: The New Zealand Jannu Adventure* (London: Hodder & Stoughton).

Dyrenfurth, G. O. (ed.) (1931), *Himalaya: unsere Expedition 1930* (Berlin: Scherl); Jongsong Peak.

Dyrenfurth, G. O. (ed.) (1935), *Dämon Himalaya. Bericht der Internationalen Karakorum-Expedition, 1934* (Basle: Benno Schwabe); Baltoro Kangri, Sia Kangri.

LÉcole Nationale de Ski et d'Alpinisme de Chamonix (1976), *Nanda Devi: l'ascension impossible* (Paris: Laffont). traverse in 1975.

Eiselin, M. (1963), *Wilder Hindukusch: Erlebnisse in Afghanistan und dem zweithöchsten Gebirge der Erde* (Zurich: Orell Füssli); first ascent of Urgend.

Emin, R. (and others) (1979), *Himalaya: Tilicho 7132 mètres* (Chamonix); photo-album.

Fiala, I. (1982), *Priatel'stvo v Srdci Pamira* (Bratislava: Pressfoto); photo-album; Pik Kommunizma.

Filippi, F.de (ed.) (1912), *Karakoram and Western Himalaya 1909* (London: Constable).

Fleming, J. (1976), *Joint British*

Army Mountaineering Association/ Royal Nepalese Army Nuptse Expedition 1975 (Warminster: The Expedition), report.

Forman, H. (1936), *Through Forbidden Tibet: An Adventure into the Unknown* (New York: Longmans Green); (London: Jarrolds, 1936); search for Anyemaqen mountains.

Franceschetti, B. (and others) (1966), *Il paese delle montagne: spedizione organizzata dalla Sezione CAI-UGET nell'Himalaya del Nepal* (Turin: La Nuova Grafica-Zincotipo); includes attempt on Langtang Lirung in 1963.

Franco, J. and Terray, L. (1967), *At Grips with Jannu* (London: Gollancz); from the French: *Bataille pour le Jannu*. (Paris: Gallimard, 1965); Franco's 1959 expedition and Terray's ascent in 1962.

Ghiglione, P. (1954), *Eroismo e tragedia sul Monte Api* (Milan: Garzanti).

Grant, R. (1967), *Annapurna II* (London: W. Kimber).

Gray, D. (1970), *Rope boy*. (London: Gollancz); includes Gaurishankar.

Greig, A. (1985), *Summit fever* (London: Hutchinson); Muztagh Tower.

Greene, R. (1974), *Moments of being* (London: Heinemann); includes Kamet first ascent.

Grob, E.(and others) (1940), *Zwischen Kantsch und Tibet. Erstbesteigung des Tent Peak* (Munich; Bruckmann).

Gunma-ken Himalayan Expedition Committee (1974), *Dhaulagiri IV* (Maebashi: Gunma-ken Mountaineering Union).

Halás, A. and František, K. (1978), *Hindúkuš '74* (Bratislava: Nakladatelstvo ČSTK-Pressfoto); Noshaq. Mostly colour illustrations; English captions and summary.

Hashimoto, S. (ed.) (1973), *Annapurna South, 7,150 metres* (Tokyo: Dôryu Mountaineering Club); central peak.

Hauser, G. (1966), *Eisgipfel und Goldpagoden: Expedition ins Königeich Nepal* (Munich: Bruckmann); Gangapurna.

Heckel, V. (1970), *Schody pod Vesmir* (Prague: Olympia); Tirich Mir. Photo-album.

Hedin, S. (1909–13), *Trans-Himalaya* (London: Macmillan), 3 vols.

Helmle, B. (1979), *Noshaq* (Konstanz: Alpine Hochschulegruppe); north face.

Hillary, E. P. and Lowe, G. (1956), *East of Everest* (London: Hodder & Stoughton); Baruntse.

Hillary, P. (1988), *Rimo: Mountain on the Silk Road* (London: Hodder & Stoughton).

Himalayan Association of Japan (1978), *Nun Expedition 1975* (Fukushima: The Association).

Himalayan Association of Japan (1979), *Trisul, 7,120 metres* (Fukushima: The Association).

Hokkaidô University Alpine Club (1981), *Account of Karakorum expedition* (Sapporo: The Club); Kunyang Chhish North.

(Japanese Alpine Club) (1976), *Indo-Japanese Women's 2nd Joint Himalayan Expedition* (Tokyo: Japanese Alpine Club); Abi Gamin.

Jonas, R. (1954), *Ho, Pasang! Oesterreichische Bergsteiger in Westnepal* (Vienna: Europa–Verlag); Saipal.

Keay, J. (1977), *When Men and Mountains Meet: The Explorers of the Western Himalayas, 1820–75* (London: John Murray).

Keay, J. (1979), *The Gilgit Game: The Explorers of the Western Himalayas, 1886–95* (London: John Murray).

Khanna, Y. C. (1980), *Saser Kangri: Yellow Goddess of the Karakoram, First Ascent* (New Delhi: R. K. Puram).

Kielkowski, J. (1987–88), *Kangchenjunga Himal & Kumbhakarna Himal.* (Düsseldorf) three-part guidebook. In Polish.

Kielkowski, J. (1988), *Makalu Himal.* (Düsseldorf) two part guidebook. In German.

Kielkowski, J. (1986–88), *Mount Everest Massiv* (Frankfurt/ Düsseldorf), three-part guidebook. Part I in German; Parts II and III in German and English.

Klarner, J. (1956), *Nanda Devi* (Warsaw: Cztelnik); Nanda Devi East in 1939.

Kobe University Karakorum Expedition (1976), *Sherpa Kangri 1976.* (Kobe: The Expedition.)

Kohli, M. S. (1962), *Last of the Annapurnas* (New Delhi: Ministry of Information & Broadcasting), Annapurna III.

Kowalewski, Z. and Kurczab, J. (1983), *Na szczytach Himalajów* (Warsaw: Wydawnictwo Sport i Turystyka); well-illustrated history of major Himalayan mountaineering.

Kowalewski, Z. and Paczkowski, A. (1986), *Polskie Wyprawy Karakorum Alpinistyczne* (Warsaw: Wydawnictwo 'Sport i Turystyka'); many illustrations.

Kumar, N. and Ahluwalia, H. *Trisul Ski Expedition* (New Delhi: Vikas Publications).

Kunaver, A. (and others) (1979), *Na Vrh Svijeta. Jugoslavenske ekspedicije od Trisula do Everesta* (Llubljana: Mladinska Knjiga/ Globus); Yugoslavian Himalayan climbing, 1960–1979.

Kurz, M. (1959 and 1963), *Chronique Himalayenne: l'Age d'or 1940–1955*, and *Supplement* (Zurich: Fondation Suisse pour Explorations Alpines).

Lambert, R. and Kogan, C. (1956), *White fury: Gaurisankar and Cho Oyu* (London: Hurst & Blackett); from the French: *Record à l'Himalaya* (Paris: France-Empire, 1955).

Languepin, J-J. (1956), *To Kiss*

High Heaven (Kimber), from the French: *Himalaya, passion cruelle. Expédition Francaise à la Nanda Devi* (Paris: Flammarion, 1955).

Languepin, J-J. (1952), *Nanda Devi* (Paris: Arthaud); photo-album.

Lenser, G. (1963), *Pumo Ri: der schönste Berg der Erde* (Zurich: Orell Füssli).

Longstaff, T. G. (1950), *This my voyage* (London: John Murray).

Machetto, G. (and others) *Sette anni contro il Tirich* (Milan: dall'Oglio).

Malatynski, M. (1978), *W Cieniu Kangczendzengi* (Warsaw: Iskry); Polish first ascent of Kangbachen.

Maraini, F. (1961), *Karakoram: The Ascent of Gasherbrum IV* (London: Hutchinson); from the Italian: *Gasherbrum IV* (Bari: Leonardo da Vinci, 1959).

Maraini, F. (1964), *Where four worlds meet* (London: Hamish Hamilton); from the Italian: *Paropàmiso* (Bari: Leonardo da Vinci, 1963); Saraghrar.

Mason, K. (1955), *Abode of Snow: A History of Himalayan Exploration and Mountaineering* (London: Rupert Hart-Davis) (new edition, London, Diadem Books, 1987).

Meade, C. F. (1940), *Approach to The Hills* (London: John Murray); Kamet.

Mélèze, C. J. (1973), *Directissime Pumori* (Paris: La Cité).

Merzbacher, G. (1905), *The central Tian-Shan Mountains, 1902–1903* (London: John Murray).

Młotieckiego, P. (1977), (ed.) (1977), *Kangbachen zdobyty* (Warsaw: Wydawnictwo 'Sport i Turystyka'); first ascent of Kangbachen. Many illustrations.

Montero Aparicio, S. (1979), *La aventura Nun Kun: diario de un reportero* (Leon: Celarayn).

Monzino, G. (1961), *Kanjut Sar.* (Milan: Martello); many illustrations.

Mumm, A. L. (1909), *Five months in the Himalaya* (London: Arnold; Trisul.

Murphy, J. E. (1986), *Adventure Beyond the Clouds* (Minneapolis: Dillon Press); Minya Konka.

Naess, A. (1952), *Tirich Mir* (London: Hodder & Stoughton); from the Norwegian: *Tirich Mir til topps* (Oslo: Gyldendal Norsk Forlag, 1950).

Naess, A. (1964), *Opp stupet til Østtoppen av Tirich Mir* (Oslo: Gyldendal Norsk Forlag); Tirich Mir East in 1964.

Nagoya YMCA Alpine Club (1974), *Putha Hiunchuli, 7,246 metres* (Nagoya: The Club).

National Railway Climbers' Club (1978), *Karakorum: Prupoo Burhaka* (Tokyo: The Club).

Neve, A. (1913), *Thirty years in Kashmir* (London: Arnold); Nun Kun.

Nottaris, R. (1980), *Pumori: Ticinesi in Himalaya del Nepal* (Agno: Arti Grafiche Bernasconi).

Noyce, C. W. F. (1962), *To the unknown Mountain* (London: Heinemann); Trivor.

Nyka, J. (and others) (1977), *Gipfelsturm im Karakorum* (Leipzig: Brockhaus); Khinyang Chhish, first ascent.

Okayama University Alpine Club (1976), *Dhaulagiri V, 1975* (Okayama: The Club).

Oki, M. (1968), *Dhaula Himal* (Nagoya: The Author); Dhaulagiri II.

Osaka City University Alpine Club (1980), *Expedition to Langtang Lirung, 1978* (Osaka: The Club).

Patey, T. (1971), *One Man's Mountains* (London: Gollancz); includes Muztagh Tower and Rakaposhi.

Pierre, B. (1955), *A Mountain Called Nun Kun* (London: Hodder & Stoughton); from the French: *Une montagne nommée Nun Kun* (Paris: Amiot-Dumont, 1954).

Procházka, V. (1972), *Na Annapúrnu* (Prague: Naše Vojsko), Annapurna IV.

Renner, G. (1975), *Biwak auf dem Dach der Welt: auf Bergpfaden durch Tadschikistan*, (Leipzig: Brockhaus); Pik Korshenevskaya.

Rickmers, W. R. (1930), *Alai! Alai! Arbeiten und Erlebnisse der Deutsch-Russischen Alai-Pamir Expedition* (Leipzig: Brockhaus); includes the first ascent of Pik Lenin.

Roberts, A. (and others) (1954), *Himalayan holiday* (Christchurch: Whitcombe & Tombs); report of New Zealand ascent of Chamar.

Roch, A. (1947), *Karakoram-Himalaya: sommets de 7,000 metres* (Paris: Victor Attinger); ascents of Sia Kangri and Baltoro Kangri.

Roch, A. (1947), *Garhwal-Himalaya: Expédition Suisse 1939* (Paris: Victor Attinger); includes ascent of Dunagiri.

Rock, J. F. (1956), *The Amnye Ma-Chhen Range and adjacent regions* (Rome: Istituto Italiano per il Medio ed Estremo Oriente).

Romm, M. (1936), *Ascent of Mount Stalin* (London: Lawrence & Wishart); Pik Kommunizma.

Roskelley, J. (1987), *Nanda Devi: The Tragic Expedition* (Harrisburg, PA: Stackpole Books).

Rowell, G. (1983), *Mountains of the Middle Kingdom* (San Francisco: Sierra Club Books); (London: Century, 1985); mountains of China.

Rowell, G. (1980), *Many People Come, Looking, Looking* (Seattle: Mountaineers); includes Nun Kun.

Royal Geographical Society and Mount Everest Foundation (1987), *The Mountains of Central Asia* (London: Macmillan); gazetteer and 1:3,000,000 relief map.

Rubenson, C. (and others) (1923), *Med Telt og Husbaat i Kashmir*

(Kristiania: Steenske Vorlag); includes Kabru.

Rudolph, F. (1986), *Chomolungma und ihre Kinder* (East Berlin); on the 100 highest mountains of the Himalaya.

Russell, S. (1946), *Mountain prospect* (London: Chatto & Windus); includes Shipton's 1939 Karakoram exploring expedition.

Rutkiewicz, W. (ed) (1979), *Zdobycie Gasherbrumów* (Warsaw: 'Sport i Turystyka'); includes Gasherbrum III.

Rybár, P. (1980), *Čelenka matky země* (Kruh: Hradci Králové); Czechoslovak expedition to Nun northwest ridge.

San Sebastian, J. (1987), *Cuando la luna cambie. . .* (Bilbao: Printed by Elkar); includes Chogolisa.

Sanrei Ascent Club (1981), *Hachindar Chish Expedition* (Tokyo: The Club).

Satulowski, D. (1964), *In Firn und Fels der Siebentausender* (Leipzig: Brockhaus); Pamirs and Tien Shan.

Schlömmer, L. (1973), *Meine Welt, die Berge* (Graz); includes Momhil Sar. Many illustrations.

Scott, D. and MacIntyre, A. (1984), *The Shisha Pangma Expedition* (London: Granada).

Shateyev, V. (1987), *Degrees of Difficulty* (Seattle: Mountaineers); includes Pamirs.

Shih Chan-Chun (1959), *Conquest of Minya Konka* (Peking: Foreign Languages Press).

Shinshû University Alpine Club (1972), *Annapurna II–1971* (Nagano: The Club).

Shipton, E. E. (1936), *Nanda Devi* (London: Hodder & Stoughton).

Shipton, E.E. (1938), *Blank on The Map* (London: Hodder & Stoughton); Shaksgam, Karakoram.

Shipton, E. E. (1951), *Mountains of Tartary* (London: Hodder & Stoughton); Muztagh Ata.

Shipton, E. E. (1969), *That Un-travelled World* (London: Hodder & Stoughton); autobiography.

Shizuoka University Alpine Club (1973), *Churen Himal, 1970* (Shizuoka: The Club).

Shizuoka University Alpine Club (1978), *Teram Kangri* (Shizuoka: The Club).

Simonov, E. (1958), *Conquering the Celestial Mountains* (Moscow: Foreign Language Publishing House); first ascent of Muztagh Ata.

Sircar, J. (1979), *Himalayan Handbook* (Calcutta: R. Sircar).

Skrine, C. P. (1926), *Chinese Central Asia* (London: Methuen); includes Kongur.

Slesser, C. M. (1964), *Red Peak* (London: Hodder & Stoughton); Pamirs.

Smeeton, M. (1961), *Taste of the Hills* (London: Rupert Hart-Davis); includes Tirich Mir.

Smythe, F. S. (1932), *Kamet Conquered* (London: Gollancz).

Smythe, F. S. (1938), *Valley of Flowers* (London: Hodder & Stoughton); includes Mana Peak.

Steinmetz, H. (1957), *Vier im Himalaya: Erlebnisbericht der deutschen Nepal-Expedition 1955* (Stuttgart: Belser); Annapurna IV.

Steinmetz, H. and Wellenkamp, J. (1956), *Nepal: ein Sommer am Rande der Welt* (Stuttgart: Belser); photo-album; Annapurna IV.

Sterba, O. (1975), *Kde příroda vládne/Pět výprav do Asie* (Prague: Orbis); includes Haramosh.

Svenska Himalaya Expeditionen 1981 (1982) *Annapurna-den Långa Vägen* (Västra Frölunda: The Expedition); Annapurna via Glacier Dome and Roc Noire. Illustrated.

Tasker, J. (1982), *Savage Arena* (London: Methuen); includes Dunagiri.

Temple, P. (1969), *World at Their Feet: Story of New Zealand Mountaineers in the Great Ranges of the world* (Christchurch: Whitcombe & Tombs).

Tilman, H. W. (1937), *Ascent of Nanda Devi* (Cambridge: Cambridge University Press).

Tilman, A. W. (1949), *Two mountains and a River* (Cambridge: Cambridge University Press); Rakaposhi and Muztagh Ata.

Tilman, A. W. (1952), *Nepal Himalaya* (Cambridge: Cambridge University Press); Langtang and Ganesh Himal, Annapurna IV.

Tokyo University Karakorum Expedition (1965), *Khinyang Chhish* (Tokyo: Meikei-dô).

Tokyo University Karakorum Expedition (1973), *Churen Himal, 1971* (Tokyo: The Expedition).

Tokyo University of Agriculture & Technology Alpine Club (1976), *Dhaulagiri II, 1975* Tokyo: The Expedition.

Ungerholm, S. (1978), *Vi nådde Nun Kun* (Stockholm: Wahlström & Widstrand).

Valla, F. and Zuanon, J–P. (1976), *Pamir: escalade d'un 7000 au pays des Kirghizes* (Domène: Imprimerie Sogirep); Pik Lenin and Pamir climbing history, geography, etc.

Venables, S. (1986), *Painted Mountains* (London: Hodder & Stoughton); Rimo.

Verghese, B. G. (ed.) (1962), *Himalayan Endeavour* (Bombay: Times of India); Kamet, Nun, Annapurna III.

Visser-Hooft, J. (1926), *Among the Kara-Korum Glaciers in 1925.* (London: Arnold).

Waller, J. (1939), *The Everlasting Hills.* (Edinburgh: Blackwood & Sons); Masherbrum, Nun and Saltoro Kangri (Peak 36).

Ward, M. P. (1972), *In This Short Span* (London: Gollancz); includes Bhutan.

Whillans, D. and Ormerod, A.

(1971), *Don Whillans: Portrait of a Mountaineer* (London: Heinemann); includes Gaurishankar, Masherbrum, Trivor.

Wilczkowski, A. (1971), *Sniegi pokutujace [Nieves penitentes]* (Lodz: Wydawnictwo Lódskie); Polish ascent of Languta-e-Barfi.

Workman, F. B. and Workman, W. H. (1908), *Ice-bound heights of the Muztagh* (London: Constable).

Workman, F. B. and Workman, W. H. (1910), *Call of the snowy Hispar* (London: Constable).

Workman, F. B. and Workman, W. H. (1909), *Peaks and glaciers of Nun Kun* (London: Constable).

Workman, F. B. and Workman, W. H. (1917), *Two summers in the Ice-Wilds of Eastern Karakoram* (London: T. Fisher Unwin).

Yakushi, Y. (ed.) (1970), *Gurja Himal* (Toyama: The Expedition).

Yamato, M.(ed.) (1967), *Dhaula Himal Expedition*, 1965 (Nagoya: Aichi-ken Mountaineering Union) Dhaulagiri II.

Yang Ke-Hsien (1959), *Ascent of the Muztagh Ata.* (Peking: Foreign Languages Press).

Yoshizawa, I. (ed.) (1977–78), *Mountaineering Maps of the World* (Tokyo: Gakushûkenyû-sha); Vol. 1 – Himalaya; Vol. 2 – Karakoram & Hindu Kush.

Peak Index

Page numbers in italics refer to
captions

Abi Gamin 83, 84, *84*, 85
Akher Chioh (Akher Chagh) 12,
    155–6
Aling Gangri (Nganglong Kangri)
    185
Amne Machen (Maqên Gangri)
    193–4
Annapurna 2
Annapurna II 2, *64*, 65
Annapurna III 4, 65–6
Annapurna IV 5, *64*, 66–8
Annapurna Dakshin (Annapurna
    South, Moditse) 9, *67*, 68
Annapurna Himal 65–71
Api 10, 78–80, *80*
Api-Nampa Range 79
Apsarasas I–VI 8, 9, 127
Assam Himalaya viii, 14–15

Badrinath *see* Chaukamba
Baintha Brakk (Ogre) 8, 114–15,
    114, *116*
Baltistan Peak (K6) 8, 11, 142–3
Baltoro Kangri I (Golden Throne)
    ix, 8, 145, *146*
Baltoro Kangri II–V 8, 9, 146
Baltoro Muztagh 116–24
Baruntse 10, 38, *38*
Batura I–VI 3–6, *104*, 105–7
Batura Muztagh 103–8
Bhutan Himalaya viii, 16–23
Big White Peak *see* Lönpo Gang

Bogdo Ola Range 178
Bojohagur Duanasir (Ultar I) 7,
    107
Bojohagur Duanasir II (Ultar II)
    6, 107–8
Bride Peak *see* Chogolisa
Broad Peak 2, 117, 120–1, *120*,
    114
Bularung Sar 9, 110
Bumthang group 20–3

Celestial Mountains *see* Tien Shan
Chamar 9, 60, *60*, 62
Chamlang 7, 9, 39–40
Changtok I (Chiring) 11, 115
Changtok II 12, 115
Changtse (Zhangzi) 4, 47
Chaukhamba I (Badrinath Peak)
    10, 82, 86, *87*
Chaukhamba II (Badrinath II) 12,
    86
Chiring *see* Changtok I
China 184–96
Cho Aui (Nangpai Gosum II) 7,
    46
Chogolisa (Bride Peak) ix, 4, 143,
    143
Chogori *see* K2
Choksiam *see* Labuche Kang
Cholpanglik 193
Chomo Gangar *see*
    Qungmogangze
Chomolhari (Jomolhari) ix, 7, 16,
    17–18, *17*
Chomolhari Gang (Jomolhari

Gang) 13, 20
Chomolhari Kangri *20*
Chomolhari-Laya group 17–19
Chomolönzo 3, 41–2, *42–3*
Chong Kumdan I–II 12, 13, 129
Chongtar 6, 7, 118
Chongtar South (Mount Spender)
    118
Chumhari Gang 13, 23
Chung Muztagh (Qong Muztag)
    194
Chura Gang 13, 23
Churen Himal 6, 71–2
Cloud Peak *see* Saser Kangri IV
Crown (Huang Guan Shan) 8,
    152, *152*

Dakum *see* Ngadi Chuli
Darban Zom 9, 159
Da Xue Shan *see* Jiazi
Depak 10, 148
Dhaulagiri viii, 2, 34
Dhaulagiri II 3, 72–3, *72*
Dhaulagiri III 3, 73
Dhaulagiri IV 4, 73–4, 75
Dhaulagiri V 4, 74
Dhaulagiri VI 8, 74–5
Dhaulagiri VII *see* Putha
    Hiunchuli
Dhaulagiri Himal 71–6
Diran (Minapin) 8, 136–7
Disteghil Sar 2, 4, 103, 108,
    110–11, *111*
Dome Kang 5, 32
Dongkya Range 32–3

Dunagiri 12, 83, 87–8, *88*, 93
Dunapurna *see* Ngadi Chuli
Dupleix, Mount *see* Purog Kangri
Dyrenfurth's NE-Zacken 101
Dyrenfurth's Silberzacken 101

E61 *see* Muztag
E. Korzenevskoi, Pik 11, 175–6
Everest viii, ix, 1, 15, 25, 34, 91, 169

Fang *see* Varah Shikar
Forepeak (Nanga Parbat) 100

Gama Peak *see* P.7150
Ganchen Ledrub *see* Langtang Lirung
Ganesh I (Yangra) 5, 56–8
Ganesh II 11, 58–9, *59*
Ganesh III (Salasungo) 11, 59
Ganesh IV (Pabil) 12, 60
Ganesh Himal 56–60, *57*
Gangapurna 5, 68–9, *69*
Gang Benchen (Kangpenqing) 9, 53
Gangchen Tag (Kangcheta) 13, 18
Gang Chhen (Kang Chen) 9, 20
Gangkar Püensum (Kangkar Pünzum) 4, 20–1, *20–1*
Gangotri group 86–7
Garhwal Himalaya 82–95
Garmo *see* Kommunizma, Pik
Gasherbrum I (Hidden Peak) 2, 123–4
Gasherbrum II East 2, 121
Gasherbrum III 2, 121–2
Gasherbrum IV 2, 122–3, *123*
Gasherbrum V 7, 123, *124*
Gasherbrum VI 13, 123, *125*
Gaurishankar 10, 48–50, *49*
Ghaint I–III 6, 7, 149
Ghenish Chhish *see* Spantik
Ghent, Mount *see* Ghaint
Ghenta Peak *see* P.7090
Gieu Gang (Gyu Kang) 9, 19
Gimmigela I (Twins I) 7, 27
Gimmigela II (Twins II) 13, 27, *27*
Glacier Dome *see* Tarke Kang
Golden Parri *see* Spantik
Golden Throne *see* Baltoro Kangri I
Gongga Shan *see* Minya Konka
Gulha Kangri *see* Kula Kangri
Gurans Himal 78–80

Gurja Himal (Sauwala) 9, 75–6, *75*
Gurla Mandhata (Naimona'nyi, Namunani) 3, 76–7, 77, 93
Gyachung Kang 2, *41*, 46
Gyala Peri (Jialabiali Feng) 10, 14, 15
Gyu Kang *see* Gieu Gang

Hachinder Chhish (Teigni) 10, 106
Haramosh 6, 140–2, *141*
Haramosh Range 140–2
Hardeol (Tirsuli South) 10, 88–9, *89*
Hardinge, Mount *see* P.7024
Hidden Peak *see* Gasherbrum I
Himalchuli 2, 4, 6, 60–2, *61–2*
Himlung 10, 63
Hindu Kush viii, 154–67
Hispar Muztagh 108–13
Huang Guan Shan *see* Crown
Hungchi 12, 46

Istor-o-Nal 6, 7, 8, 11, 160–2, *161*
Istor-o-Nal group 154, 160–2

Janak (Outlier) 12, 32
Janak Himal 32
Jannu (Kumbhakarna) 3, 35–8, *35–6*
Jasamba (Nangpai Gosum I) 7, 46
Jeje Kangphu 8, 19, *19*
Jialabiali Feng *see* Gyala Peri
Jiazi (Rudshe Konka, Da Xue Shan) 196
Jitchu Drake 19
Jobo Garu *see* Menlungtse
Jomolhari *see* Chomolhari
Jomolhari Gang *see* Chomolhari Gang
Jongsong Peak 5, 24, 32
Jugal Himal 54–5
Junction Peak *see* P.7108; Shartse

K2 viii, ix, 1, 103, 116–18
K5 *see* Muztag
K6 *see* Baltistan Peak
K7 142
K12 5, 150–1
K24 *see* Saser Kangri II
Kabru I (South) ix, 7, 29, *29*
Kabru II (North) 7, 29–31
Kabru III–IV 6, 31
Kabru massif 28, *28*

Kailas 77, 184
Kamet ix, 3, 82, 83, 84–5, *84*, 91
Kamet group 83–6
Kampire Dior (Karambar Sar) 10, 105
Kangbachen 2, 34
Kang Chen *see* Gang Chhen
Kangchenjunga Himal viii, ix, 24, 25–31, *27–8*, *31*, 34–8
Kangcheta *see* Gangchen Tag
Kangchungtse (Makalu II) 4, 40–1
Kang Guru (Naurgaon Peak) 64
Kangkar Pünzum *see* Gangkar Püensum
Kangpenqing *see* Gang Benchen
Kangphu Gang 9, 19
Kangri 23
Kangtö 11, 14
Kanjut Sar 3, 113
Kan Lan Shan *see* Qungmogangze
Karakoram viii, ix
    Greater 102–33
    Lesser 134–53
Karambar Sar *see* Kampire Dior
Karjiang 9, 23
Karun Kuh 7, 151
Kaufmann, Mt *see* Lenin, Pik
Kellas Rock Peak *see* P.7071
Keshni Khan 155
Khangsar Kang (Roc Noire) 5, 69, *69*
Khan Tengri 179–81, *180*
Kharta Changri 12, 47
Khartaphu 9, 47, *47*
Khunyang Chhish 3, 108, 111–12
Kirat Chuli (Tent Peak) 6, 26, *26*, 27
Koh-i-Langar *see* Langar Zom
Koh-i-Nadir 155
Koh-i-Tez 155
Koh-i-Urgend 12, 156
Kommunizma, Pik (Mt Stalin) ix, 5, 168, 170–5, *172–4*
Kongur Shan (Qungur II, Qungur Tagh) 3, 188, *188–9*
Kongur Tobe (Qungur I, Qungur Tjube Tagh) 4, 187–8, *187*
Kuhanbokang 185
Kula Kangri (Künla Kangri, Gulha Kangri) 4, 16, 17, 22, *22*
Kumaun Himalaya viii, ix, 82–95
Kumbhakarna *see* Jannu
Kun 11, 96, 97–8, *97*
Kun Lun viii, 186–94

Labuche Kang (Choksiam) 6, 53
Langar Zom (Koh-i-Langar) 11,
  156
Langtang Himal 53–4
Langtang Lirung (Ganchen
  Ledrub) 9, 53–4, *54*
Langtang Ri 9, 54
Languta-e-Barfi 155
Lapchi Kang *see* Pamari Himal
Latok I–II 10, 115
Lenin, Pik (Mt Kaufmann) ix, 10,
  168–70, *169–70*
Link Sar 12, 143
Loinbo Kangri (Lungpo Gangri,
  Lombo Kangra) 11, 185
Lönpo Gang (Big White Peak)
  54–5
Lunana Group 17, 19–20
Lungmari 185
Lungpo Gangri *see* Loinbo Kangri
Luphar Sar 9, 108–9

Mahalangur Himal 38–48
Makalu II *see* Kangchungtse
Makorum 140
Malangutti Sar 12, 110
Malubiting 5, 8, 137–8
Mamostong Kangri I–II 5, 12,
  129–30
Mana 8, 11, 85
Manaslu East Pinnacle 2, 62
Manaslu Himal *see* Mansiri Himal
Manaslu North 10, 62–3
Mani Peak 140
Mansiri (Manaslu) Himal 60–3
Maqên Gangri *see* Amne Machen
Masa Gang *see* Matsa Gang
Masang Gang *see* Matsa Gang
Masherbrum ix, 3, 146–8, *148*
Masherbrum Range 142–8
Matsa Gang (Masa Gang, Masang
  Gang) 9, 18
Mayêr Kangri (Peng-Wa-Lo-Te
  Shan) 13, 194
Mazeno Peak 11, 101
Melunghi Kang 13, 17, 23
Menlungtse (Jobo Garu, Qiao Ge
  Ru) 10, 50–2, *51*
Minapin *see* Diran
Minya Konka (Gongga Shan) ix,
  4, 194, *195*
Minya Konka region 194–6
Moditse *see* Annapurna Dakshin
Molamenqing *see* Phola Gangchen

Momhil Sar 7, 109
Mo-No-Ma-La Shan *see* Shapka
  Monomakha
Muchu Chhish 5, 107
Mukut Parbat 8, 85–6
Muztag (E61, K5) viii, 191
Muztagata 4, 6, 13, 190–1, *191*
Muztag Feng *see* Ulugh Muztagh
Muztagh Tower 8, 117–18, *117*
Myagdi Matha 74

Naimona'nyi *see* Gurla Mandhata
Nai Peng 12, 14, 15
Nalakankar Himal 76–7
Namcha Barwa (Namjag Barwa
  Feng) 3, 14
Namunani *see* Gurla Mandhata
Nanchen Tangla
  (Nyainqêntanglha) Feng,
  Nianqintanggula, Nien Ch'ing
  T'ang Ku La Shan) 186, *187*
Nanda Devi ix, 3, 5, 76, 82–3,
  89–93, *90*, *92*
Nanda Devi group 87–90
Nanga Parbat ix, 2, 100–1
Nangpai Gosum I *see* Jasamba
Nangpai Gosum II *see* Cho Aui
Nangpai Gosum III 11, 46
Naurgaon Peak *see* Kang Guru
Nepal Himalaya, Central &
  Western 56–81
  Eastern 34–55
Nepal Peak 26–7, *26*
Ngadi Chuli (Peak 29, Dakum,
  Dunapurna) 2, 63
Nganglong Kangri *see* Aling
  Gangri
Ngojumba Kang 3, 4, 47
Nianqintanggula *see* Nanchen
  Tangla
Nien Ch'ing T'ang Ku La Shan
  see Nanchen Tangla
Nilgiri North 12, 70, *70*
Ningchin Kangsha (Nodzin
  Kangsan, Ning-dzing-zonka) 9,
  186, *186*
Nobaisum Zom 12, 159, *160*
Noshaq 5, 6, 8, 159–60, *160*
Noshaq group 159–60
Nun 10, 96, *98–9*, 98–100
Nun Kun Massif ix, 96–100
Nuptse 3, 42–4, *45*
Nyainqêntanglha Feng *see*
  Nanchen Tangla

Nyanang Ri II, 52
Nyegyi Kagsang 12, 14
Nyenchen Tangla 10, 184

Ogre *see* Baintha Brakk
Outlier *see* Janak

P.6705 40
P.6845 103
P.6900 143
P.7000 3, 13, 148
P.7010 (Annapurna) 13, 70
P.7010 (Lupghar Sar West II) 108
P.7010 (Rakaposhi East Peak) 136
P.7011 13, 47
P.7013 12, 48, 55
P.7016 (Schneider's P.6931) 12,
  105
P.7018 12, 48
P.7023 12, 48
P.7024 (Mount Hardinge) 12, 126
P.7032 12, 33
P.7036 12, 63
P.7038 12, 63
P.7040 142–3
P.7044 12, 32
P.7050 12, 55
P.7060 (Savoia-Kangri III,
  Summa-ri North) 12, 118
P.7069 12, 70
P.7071 (Kellas Rock Peak) 11, 48,
  48
P.7090 (Ghenta Peak) 107
P.7098 11, 63
P.7100 (Gasherbrum) 11, 123
P.7100 (K12) 6, 151
P.7100 (Yukshin Gardan Sar
  South) 113
P.7108 (Junction Peak) 11, 74
P.7120 11, 191
P.7139 10, 63
P.7150 (Gama Peak) 10, 74, 144
P.7150 (Ice Dome, Ridge Peak) 3,
  10, 145
P.7167 10, 192
P.7180 (Chongtar South II) 118
P.7183 (Chamar South) 60
P.7186 9, 46
P.7199 9, 42
P.7200 (K12) 6, 151
P.7200 (Masherbrum) 148
P.7239 9, 22, 73
P.7249 8, 74

P.7290 (Chamlang) 7, 40
P.7290 (Rakaposhi) 3, 136
P.7291 8, 107
P.7300 8, 122
P.7308 7, 48
P.7316 (Chamlang South) 40
P.7316 (Dhaulgiri) 7, 74
P.7353 7, 194
P.7385 35
P.7451 5, 32
P.7468 (Jannu East Peak) 38
P.7514 (Ngadi Chuli South
    Shoulder) 63
P.7532 (Kangbachen Southwest)
    4, 35
P.7600 4, 122
P.7640 4, 106
P.7700 4, 71
P.7739 3, 70
P.7772 121
P.7785 100
P.7817 100
Pabil see Ganesh IV
Palung Ri 12, 48
Pamari Himal 53
Pamirs ix, 168–77
Panmah Muztagh 113–15
Pasu Diar 8, 107
Pasu Sar 5, 107
Pathibhara (Pyramid Peak) 10,
    25–6, 25
Pauhunri 10, 12, 24, 32–3, 33
Pauhunri South see P.7032
Peak 11 see Pumari Chhish
Peak 29 see Ngadi Chuli
Peak 33 see Shispare
Peak 38 see Shartse
Peaks 48–51 see Rimo
Peng-Wa-Lo-Te Shan see Mayêr
    Kangri
Peri Himal 63–4
Phola Gangchen (Molamenqing)
    4, 52
Pik E. Korzenevskoi see E.
    Korzenevskoi
Pik Kommunizma see
    Kommunizma
Pik Lenin see Lenin
Pik Pobeda see Pobeda
Pinnacle Peak 96
Pobeda, Pik (Mount Tomur) 5,
    179, 180–1, 181–3
Porong Ri 8, 52
Prupoo Burahka 13, 143

Pumari Chhish (Peak 11) 5, 108,
    112
Pumarikish Southeast 7, 112
Pumori 10, 44–6
Pungpa Ri 5, 52
Punjab Himalaya 96
Purog Kangri (Mount Dupleix)
    194
Putha Hiunchuli 8, 76
Pyramid Peak see Pathibhara;
    Spantik

Qiao Ge Ru see Menlungtse
Qong Muztagh see Chung
    Muztagh
Queen Mary Peak see Sia Kangri I
Qungmogangze (Chomo Gangar,
    Kan Lan Shan) 186
Qungur see Kongur

Rakaposhi 3, 134–6, 135
Rakaposhi Range 134–40
Rakhiot Peak 101
Ratna Chuli 12, 63
Rimo I 6, 128, 129
Rimo II 6, 128
Rimo III 9, 128, 128
Rimo IV 10, 128–9
Rimo Muztagh 127–30
Risum 12, 55
Roc Noire see Khangsar Kang
Rolwaling Himal 48–53
Rose, Mount see Singhi Kangri
Rudshe Konke see Jiazi

Saipal 12, 80
Salasungo see Ganesh III
Saltoro Kangri I–II ix, 3, 4,
    149–51, 150
Saltoro Range 148–51
Sangemar Mar 107
Saraghrar 7–9, 12, 13, 156–8, 157
Saraghrar group 156–8
Saser Kangri 4, 130–2, 130, 132
Saser Kangri II (K24, Shukpa
    Kunchang) 5, 131
Saser Kangri III 5, 131
Saser Kangri IV (Cloud Peak) 6,
    130, 132
Saser Muztagh 130–2
Satopanth 11, 82, 86–7
Sauwala see Gurja Himal
Savoia I–III 10, 11, 118
Savoia Kangri I see Summa-Ri

Savoia Kangri II see P.7180
Savoia Kangri III see P.7060
Serang (Sringi) Himal 60, 62
Shakhaur 11, 158
Shankangshan 185
Shapka Monomakha
    (Mo-No-Ma-La Shan) 193
Shartse (Junction Peak, Peak 38)
    5, 42
Shartse II 42
Sherpi Kangri 6, 8, 149
Shingeik Zom 8, 160, 160
Shisha Pangma 2, 52
Shispare (Peak 33) 4, 107
Shudu Tsenpa see P.7032
Shukpa Kunchang see Saser
    Kangri II
Siachen Muztagh 124–7
Sia Chhish 106
Sia Kangri I (Queen Mary Peak)
    6, 125, 126
Sia Kangri II–III 7, 126
Sichuan 194
Sikkim Himalaya viii, ix, 24–33
Silver Crag 101
Singhi Kangri (Mt Rose, Singhi
    Ri) 9, 126
Skil Brum 6, 118
Skyang Kangri (Staircase Peak) 4,
    118
Sod's Law Peak 112
Spantik (Ghenish Chhish, Golden
    Parri, Pyramid Peak, Yengutz
    Har) 12, 138–40, 139
Spender, Mount see Chongtar
    South
Sringi Himal see Serang Himal
Staircase Peak see Skyang Kangri
Stalin, Mt see Kommunizma, Pik
Summa-Ri (Savoia Kangri I) 8,
    118
Summa-Ri North see P.7060
Sunyatsen see Zhong Shan
Szechuan 194–6

Table Mountain (Zongophu
    Gang) 13, 19
Takaphu see Tserim Gang
Takka Khon 23
Talung 7, 31
Tarke Kang (Glacier Dome) 9,
    70–1
Teigni see Hachinder Chhish
Tent Peak see Kirat Chuli

Teram Kangri I 5, 76, 97, 124, 126
Teram Kangri II–III 6, 124, 127
Teri Kang 13, 19
Tibet 184–96
Tien Shan (Celestial Mountains) 178–83
Tilitso (Tilicho) 10, 71
Tirich Mir 4–7, *162*, 163–6, *166*
Tirich Mir group 154, *162*, 163–6, *164*
Tirsuli 11, 12, 89, *89*
Tirsuli South *see* Hardeol
Tomur, Mount *see* Pobeda, Pik
Transhimalaya 184–6
Trisul ix, 11, 76, 83, 93–4, *94*
Trivor, 3, 109–10
Tsenda 11, 19

Tsenda Gang 23
Tserim Gang (Takaphu) 19
Tsogaka 9, 54
Tsulim Khon 23
Tsunga Ri 23
Twins *see* Gimmigela

Udren Zom 11, 12, 158
Ultar *see* Bojohagur Duanasir
Ulugh Muztagh (Muztag Feng) 192, *193*
Urdok I–II 8, 11, 124

Varah Shikar (Fang) 4, 71
Vostochnaya Pobeda 12, 183

Western Himalaya 96–101

Yalung Peak *see* P.7532
Yangra *see* Ganesh I
Yazghil Dome 4, 7, 111
Yengutz Har *see* Spantik
Yermanendi Kangri 6, 148
Yukshin Gardan Sar 5, 112–13
Yutmaru Sar 7, 113

Zangser Kangri 194
Zaskar Range 82
Zemu Peak 1, *31*
Zhangzi *see* Changtse
Zhong Shan (Sunyatsen) 196
Zongophu Gang *see* Table Mountain

People Index

Page numbers in italics refer to captions

Aas, Monrad 29–30
Abalakov, Evgeny 172, 182
Abalokov, Vitaly M. 168, 173,
    182–3, *182*
Abruzzi, Duke of ix, 116, 118,
    119, 143–4
Agranovskaja, O, 170
Aichhorn, Ambros & Toni 160
Allan, Iain *60*
Allan, Sandy 46, 55, 81
Allen, Rick 46, 59, 81
Alletto, F. 156
Amatt, John 190
Ammerer, G. 144
Ang-Nima, Sherpa 70, 110
Angtharkay 87
Angyal, Rinsing 71
Anma, Soh 39
Anullah, Sherpa 45
Aoki, K. 74
Aota, H. 46
Aristov, Oleg 172
Aschenbrenner, P. 101
Aucher, B. 145
Axt, Wolfgang 149, 166

Babaguchi, Ryuichi 123
Bailey, Lt. F.M. 14, 15, 185
Ball, G. 100
Band, George 134
Banks, Mike 134, 153
Barbuscia, Luigi 142

Bardolej, Rudolf 136
Barenghi, B. 78
Barrard, Maurice 123
Barton, Rev. C.E. 96
Bashmakov, A. 176
Bates, Robert 192, 196
Bauer, Paul 26, 27
Baumann, Heinz 67
Baxter-Jones, Roger 52
Beaven, Bill 38
Beghin, Pierre 37
Beleckij, E.A. 190
Beletsky, Evgeny 172
Bell, George 147
Benkin, V. 181
Bergamaschi, Arturo 115, 133
Bernadjikiewicz, S. 89, 93
Berry, Steven 21, 23
Bessubkin, V. 174
Bettembourg, Georges 43
Bianchi, C. 78
Bich, Jean 113
Bielún, A. 79
Biller, Harald 66
Bishop, Maurie 60
Blanchard, B. 136
Bleicher, Hubert 106
Blench, James 68
Boardman, Peter 50, 55, 189
Bocarde, Gary 176
Bonatti, Walter 122
Bonington, Chris 51, 55, 65,
    114–15, 133, 151, 196
Bonvalot 186, 194
Borelli, Lorenzo 97

Borisenok, Oleg 170
Borodkin, Yuri 174
Botta, Erminio 97
Bourdillon, Tom 50
Bozukov, V. 174
Braithwaite, Paul 'Tut' 114
Breashears, David 183
Bridwell, James 46
Brimmer, S. 67
Brocherel, Alexis and Henri 77,
    92–3
Brosig, G. 144
Brotherhood, R. 151
Brown, Joe 117
Brown, T.G. 146
Bruce, C.G. 83, 85, 93, 96
Budanov, P. 173
Buhl, Hermann 144, *144*
Bujak, J. 92, 95
Burdsall, Richard 195, 196

Calciati, Count Cesare 97
Calgagno, Gianni 165
Campbell, D. 87
Carslaw, J.S. 151
Carson, Bruce 94
Carter, H. Adams *91*, 92, 95
Carter, P. 75
Casarotto, Renato 121
Cassassa, Gino 47
Casolari, Cristiano 111
Caspaar, Valentin 119
Cassim, Ricardo 121–2
Castelli, G. 156
Chakravorty, S. 89

Chand, Daya 93
Chapman, F. Spencer ix, 16, 18, 23, 25, 186
Chaturvedi, P.C. 65
Chavarri, Francisco 165
Cheesmond, D. 136, 153
Cheredova, V.P. 170
Chernukha, N. 168
Chiiwa, Fukashi 74
Choi Han-Jo 50
Choi Mi-Ho 47
Choklang, Nawang 64
Chotchia, P. 175
Chunovkin, G. 175
Clark, Leonard 193
Clinch, Nick 147, 153, 192
Clough, Ian 49, 55
Cockerill, Lt. George 103, 108, 154, 167
Connor, Edward 66, 81
Consiglio, P. 156
Conway, Martin ix, 108, 116–17, 122, 134, 145, *145*
Cooke, C. Reggie 25, 27, 30, *30*, 33
Cotter, F.M. 86
Cousteix, Guy 47
Couzy, Jean 41
Crawford, Charles E. 18, 34
Crawford, Lynn 37
Crowley, Aleister 118
Culbert, R. 140–1
Cunningham, John 44

Dangadze, D. 176
Davis, Dennis 43
Dawa, Passang 18
Deasy, H.P. 194
Decamp, Erik 37, 60
De Lint, Jan 62
De Rhins, Dutreuil 186, 192–3
Desio, Ardito 113, 125
Desmaison, René 36
Détry, Jules 54
Deutschmann, Ferdinand 119
Dev, Harbeh 82
Dewison, A. 73
Dieberger, Adolf 155, *155*, 167
Diemberger, Kurt 42, 144, 153, 155, 159, 165, 167
Dietz, Dick 174
Diplock, J. 64
Dittert, René 26
Dobenek, Dietrich von 156

Dorje, Girme 65, 68
Dorje, Nima 85
Dorje, Pema 61
Dorje, Sherpa 50, 70, 72
Dorjee, Phu 93
Downes, Bob 147
Doyle, K. 136
Driessen, Fons 63
Dubois, P. 145
Dubost, R. 92
Dufour, Guy 60
Duplat, R. 91
Dyrenfurth, Günter Oskar 27, 32–3, *32*, 122, 125–6, 146, 169

Eckenstein, Oscar 116, 118
Edge, R.C.A. 85
Egeler, C.G. 70
Elias, Ney 187
Eliassen, Odd 51
Emery, John 140–2, *141*
Emmons, Arthur 195–6
Enda, Keiji 105
Ercalani, Maria Luisa 123
Ertl, Hans 126, 156
Eto, Yukio 52
Evans, Andrew 176
Evans, Charles 40, 66
Everest, Sir George viii, 34

Fabrizio, Manoni 44
Falconer, H. 102
Fanshawe, Andy 51
Fear, Ronald 73, 81
Fedchenko, Alexis 168
Fellner, G. 136
Field, Captain 14
Firmin, Arthur 60
Fischer, A. 144
Fonquernie, Ernesto 165
Forsyth, Douglas 187
Fosse, Torgeir 51
Fotheringham, Jim 50, 128
Fountaine 108
Fowler, Mick 140
Fox, Capt. Crosby 54
Franco, Jean 35–6, 40–1
Freshfield, Douglas 24
Freudig, Anton 94
Frey, Georg 29
Fujihara, M. 144
Fujimoto, K. 146
Fujioji, Yoshioki 119
Furtner, A. 112

Gajewski, R. 63
Gálfy, Robert 176
Galkin, V. 174
Galmiche, J-M. 145
Gansser, August 17, 23, 78
Gardiner, R. 85
Garner, William 183
Garwood, E.J. 24
Gauchat, Eric 58
Georges, Lucien 86
Ghiglione, Piero 78
Gigineishvily, O. 172
Gillette, Ned 46, 190, 196
Girmi, Sonam 66
Glidden, J. 100
Gloggner, H. 108
Gluckhov, V. 173
Godwin-Austen, Henry H. 102–3, *102*, 108, 113, *114*, 116
Gohar, Ali 109
Gombu, Da 55
Gombu, Sherpa 70
Goodfellow, Basil 65, 68, 81
Gorbenko, M. 181
Gorbunov, N.P. 172
Göschl, Rainer 155
Göttner, Adolf 26–7
Graham, William W. viii, 28–9, *28*, 83, 87, 90
Grant, Richard 65
Grasseli, A. 94
Gray, Dennis 49
Gregory, Alfred 110
Greissl, L. 69
Grenard, Fernand 192–3
Griffith, D. 75
Grob, E. 25, 27
Gruber, Gerald 158–60, 167
Gstrein, Walter 72
Gushchin, D. 175
Gutman, L. 182
Gyalgen, Sherpa 54, 78
Gyalzen 58, 70
Gyatso, Sonam 66
Gyr, H. 140, 153

Hall, Brian 43, 153
Hall, L.R. 65
Hamilton, Scott 142
Harada, Masahiro 61
Hardie, Norman 39–40
Harman, Capt. H.J. 24
Harrison, Ginette *21*
Harrison, J.B. 25, 98, 100, 146–7

Harrow, Geoff 38, 40
Hartog, John 117–18, 133
Hatskevich, I. 176
Hauser, Günther 68, 81
Havens, Susan 176
Hearsey, H.Y. 82
Hedin, Sven 184–5, *185*, 187–90
  190, 194, 196
Heen, Arne Randers 163
Heim, Arnold 78, 195–6
Henderson, A. 65
Herrligkoffer, Karl 136, 153
Hetmann, J. 174
Hiebeler, Toni 170
Hillary, Sir Edmund 38–40, 85
Hinks, Alan 51
Hino, Etsuo 70
Hirai, K. 144, 153
Hirakawa, Hiroko 66
Hodgkin, R.A. 146–7
Höibakk, R. 165
Holdsworth, R.L. 85
Holmes, J. 64
Hooker, Sir Joseph viii, 24
Hori, Ryohei 18
Hornbein, Tom 192
Houston, Charles 91, *91*
Hoyer, R. 73, 170
Hoyte, Chris 136
Hsuan Tsang 178
Huber, Adolf 73
Huber, Franz 50, 72, 81
Huber, Otto 156
Hudjakov, O. 179, 182
Hunt, D.N.B. 160–1
Hunt, John 26–7, 33, 151, 153,
  177

Imhof, Edward 195–6
Isachenko, G. 181
Isono, Sumiya 142
Ito, Tsutomu 151
Ivanishvily, A. 172
Ivanov, E. 182
Ivanov, V. 173
Iwatsubo, Goro 159

Jackson, Jeff 21
Jackson, Monica 54
Jackson, R. 61
Jakubowski, Zdzislaw 62
Jangbu, Sherpa 73
Jillott, Bernard 140–1, *141*
Johnson, W.H. viii, 82, 191

Jonas, Rudolf 80
Jones, M.R.F. 111
Jursa, Jan 97

Kabul 136
Kamei, T. 106
Kami, Ang 50
Kappeler, R. 140
Karpinski, A. 89, 92
Kasai, Yoshiro 110
Kaulback, Ronald 14
Kawazu, S. 74
Kekus, Nick 59, 81
Kellas, Dr Alexander M. 15, 24–6,
  25, 32–3, 83, 85, 95
Keller, Paul 36
Kempe, John 31
Kempson, Edwin 47
Kennedy, Michael 120, 133
Khan, Jawed Akhter 147
Khrischatyi, V. 181–2
Kiesel, V. 170
Kim Ho Sup 71
Kim Ki-Heyg 38
Kim Soo-Hyeon 55
Kitar 77
Klarner, J. 93
Kleissl, F. 70
Klincewicz, Jerzy 62
Knutsen, Harold 194
Kobayashi, H. 149
Koblmüller, E. 144, 153
Kogan, Claude 58, *58*
Kogan, Mme Claude 100
Kohli, Mohan 65–6, 89
Koiko, Shoji 73
Komanova, Lidia 179
Kondo, Katsuyuki 65
Kondo, Kunihiko 98
Kono, S. 146
Koroteev, V. 181
Korzenevskaya, Evgenia 168, 175
Korzhenevsky, N.L. 168, 175
Kosa, K. 170
Kössler, Uli 159
Kovačević, Boris 47
Kovalev, V.A. 169
Kramer, K. 138
Kroger, Chuck 175
Kulhavy, Ernst 72
Kumar, Major K.I. 93
Kumar, N. 18, 93, 133, 153
Kunigk, H. 101
Kurczab, Janusz 107, 133

Kurtyka, Wojciech 122, 133
Kushimi, Osamu 40
Kustovsky, A. 173, 174
Kuwabara, T. 144, 153
Kuzmin, Kiril 169, 172, 179, 188
Kvernberg, Per 164

Lal, P. 93
Lama, Pasang Dawa 86
Lambert, Raymond 48, 54–5, 58,
  110
Lampard, D. 123
Landry, Werner 66
Langmade, D. 61
Lapuch, Kurt 159
Larcher, M. 148
Lauchlan, John 68
Lawder, R.J. 160, 167
Lee Heung Sik 72
Lee Jae-Hong 62
Lee Jeong-Hoon 55
Lenser, Gerhard 41, 45, 55
Letavet, Prof. A. 182
Lev, P. 100
Lewis, Gilmour 31
Lindner, Franz 31, 33
Linford, Craig 46
Littledale, Sir George 192
Lloyd, P. 53, 56, *91*
Lobsang, Phurba 45
Longstaff, Thomas G. ix, 76, *76*,
  78, 83, 85, 87, 90, 92–3, 97,
  124, 130, 133
Lorimer, G. 130
Lowe, George 38–40, 55, 85
Lowe, Jeff 44, 46, 120
Lowe, Mark 112
Lucas, Major F.G. 96
Ludlow, F. 16
Lukin, I. 168
Lunjakov, G. 175

Macartney-Snape, T. 65
McFarlane, Jim 39
McGowan, Dick 147
Machetto, Guido 165
MacInnes, Hamish 44, 55
MacIntyre, Alex 52, 55
McIntyre, Donald 46
Mcnaught-Davis, Ian 117, 177
Maggi, M. 78
Magnone, Guido 35–6, 118
Maksimov, W. 174
Mallik, N. 89

Mallory, George 44
Mamleyeva, E. 169
Mandl, F. 142, 153
Maquignaz, Angelo 24
Maraini, Fosco 156, 158, 167
Marchart, Dieter 110
Marenče, S. 94
Markelov, V. 176
Mason, Kenneth 103, *103*, 125, 140, 151, 191, 196
Mason, N. 64
Mathieu, B. 75
Matsui, Koji 191
Matúš, Jan 97
Mauri, Carlo 122
Mayerl, Sepp 21
Mayr, R. 70
Meade, C.F. 83, 85, 95
Mehl, Gert 45
Merkl, Willi 101
Merzbacher, Dr Gottfried 179, 183
Messner, Reinhold 39
Meyer, Dolf 103
Midorokawa, H. 106
Mills, E.J.E. 111
Milne, Kenneth 112
Mitchu, Gyalzen 36
Mitra, C. 89, 95
Miyazaki, Toyohumi 70
Moiseev, Yuri 181
Molinari, Peter 58
Monier, E. 145
Monks, Steven 21
Monzino, Guido 113
Moorcroft, William 82, 102
Moore, Terris 195
Morgan, Capt. Henry 152
Moriaki, Masaaki 74
Morita 55
Morrison, Don 114–15
Morshead, Henry Treise 14–15, *15*
Mortimer, G. 65
Mulasi, S.P. 89
Mumm, A.L. 85, 93
Murphy, Joseph 162, 167, 196
Murray, W.H. 78
Mutch, Tom 162
Myhrer-Lund, Bjorn 51
Myslovsky, E. 173, 181

Naess, Arne 163–4, 167
Nagata, Hideki 119

Nagoshi, Minoru 98
Nakajima, K. 74
Nakamura, Takeo 111
Nakeyama, G. 74
Namgyal 58, 60
Namgyal, Rinzin 16, 24
Nara, Satoshi 41
Narbaud, Georges 123
Nekrassov, Viktor 172
Nelson, P.S. 156
Nepomnjaschiy, A. 175
Neve, Arthur 96–7, *97*, 100, 124, 129–30
Neve, Ernest 96–7
Nevorotin, V. 175
Newell, Daniel 54
Nieuwkerk, Edwin and Ubbink van 38
Nindra, Tenzing 31
Nishigori, Mitsuaki 105
Nishikori, Ryo 142
Nishimura, Mitsuhiro 70
Nogyal, Major C.S. 130
Norbu, Gyaltsen 40
Norbu, Lakpu 41
Norbu, Pa 40, 58
Norbu, Pemba 68
Norgay, Tenzing 92
Norton, Lt. Col. E.F. 85
Noyce, Wilfrid 109, 133, 182
Nyima, Ang 65, 76

Oakes, Captain 14
Oberhofer, Herbert 106
Odell, Noël 91, *91*
Ogawa, Yoshio 73
Ohtani, E. 136
Ohuchi, Michifumi 20
Okamoto, Akio 164
Oliver, D.G. 129
Oliver, P.R. 87, 95
Olschak, Dr Blanche 17, 23
Ölz, O. 70
Omae, Tsumeo 107
Onishtchenko, W. 174, 183
Opdal, A. 165
Orgler, A. 148
Orizumi, T. 50
Otaki, Akio 46
Otaki, K. 113
Ovchinnikov, Anatoly 173, 176, 177

Pablo, K. de 101
Packard, W.P. 66
Paidar, H. 25, 27
Paragot, Robert 36
Pargätzi 26
Patey, Tom 117–18, 134, 153
Pauer, S. 142
Pawlikowski, M. 63
Pélissier, Camillo 113
Pereira, George 193
Pertemba 50
Petrov, N. 176
Phutar, Pasang 39, 46, 80
Piacenza, Mario 97
Pierre, Bernard 58, 99–100
Pinelli, C.A. 156
Piotrowski, T. 79·81
Pischinger, Rudolf 158–60
Pizzo, Chris 174
Pocock, I.S. 83–4
Pogrebezky, M.T. 179
Pooley, Brian 37
Popenko, Yuri 176
Posada, A. 101
Pressl, F. 144
Proske, 'Didi' 165
Przhevalski, Nicholas 193
Putinzev, A. 175–6
Puzak, Branko 47

Rajtar, Pavol 170, 175–6
Ram, Hari 34
Rapasov, P. 182
Ravier, Jean 36
Rawling, Captain 184
Re, Beppe 165
Read, Ben 175
Rebitsch, Mathias 103, 106, 134, 136
Reinhardt, E. 140
Renshaw, Dick 88
Renzler, R. 148
Reynolds, Jan 46
Rickmers, W. Rickmer 168
Richier, Alain 60
Riddiford, H.E. 86, 95
Rieben, Jean-Pierre 66
Ringdal, Helge 51
Rjabukhin, V. 182
Rjasanov, V. 182
Roberts, Athol 56
Roberts, Jimmy O.M. 65, 72, 74–6, 81, 130, 133, 146
Rocca, A. 78

Roch, André 86–7, 95
Rock, Joseph 193–4, 196
Rohn, R. 75
Roiss, H. 142, 153
Romanov, B. 175, 179
Roncaglioni, M. 70
Roots, E.F. 106
Rosenkratz, G. 78
Roskelley, John 50, 95, 177
Rosso, Enrico 44
Rouse, Alan 43, 55, 151
Rowell, Galen 100, 194, 196
Rubenson, C.W. 29–30, 33
Russenberger, Victor 86
Ruttledge, Hugh 82, 90, 95
Ryall, E.C. 130
Ryder, Capt. E.A. 184, 186

Sadler, Jack 109
Saegi, T. 75
Sakahasa, Tadakio 191
Sakai, K. 50
Sakai, Toshiaki 159
Sapp, Greg 66
Sarthou, S. 75
Sasahara, Y. 46
Sato, M. 65
Saunders, Tony 107
Saunders, Victor 128, 133, 140
Savage-Landor, A.H. 76, 78
Savin, A. 181
Sawamura, Shinji 164
Schauer, Robert 122, 151
Schell, Hans 109, 155, 167
Schindlbacher, Horst 137, 153
Schinhofen, T. 68
Schlagintweit Brothers 82–4
Schliessler, Martl 103
Schmaderer, L. 25, 27
Schmuck, Markus 118, 159, 167
Schmutz, Emanuel 71
Schneider, Erwin 27, *32*, 169, *169*
Schneider, Michael 170
Schoberth, Gostav 30, *30*
Schoening, Pete 192
Schomberg, Col. R.C.F. 154
Schranz, C. 70
Schriebel, Hubert 62
Schubert, Pit 67
Schwarzgruber, Rudolf 86, 95
Scmitz, Kim 194
Scott, Doug 19, *38*, 39–40, 43, 52, 55, 114–15, 133

Secord, C. 108, 134
Segi, Y. 64
Sella, Erminio and Vittorio 24
Semyonov, Peter 178–9
Serizawa, T. 72
Sharma, G.K. 129, 133
Sharma, K.P. 89
Sherriff, G. 16
Sherring, C.A. 76, 93
Shibata, T. 146
Shima, S. 69, 146
Shimakata, Kenji 142
Shin Jang Seop 72
Shipton, Eric E. ix, 47–8, 50, 83, 85, 87, 90–2, *91*, 95, 108, 113, 150, 152–3, 190, 192, 196
Shustov, N. 181
Saidorenko, A. 96
Sillem, H. 96
Singh, Hukram 128, 133
Singh, Nain 184–6
Singh, Natha 34
Sivtsov, B. 176
Skrine, Sir Clarmont 188, 196
Skurlatov, Yuri 170
Slingsby, A.M. 83, 85, 97, 124, 130
Smeeton, Miles 163
Smirnov, V. 182
Smith, Robin 182
Smythe, Frank 85, 87, 91, 95
Sole, A. 75
Solonnikov, V. 175, 183
Sonam, Sherpa 130
Spake, Elliot 54
Spoleto, Duke of 113, 125
Stallbohm, Volker 148
Stammberger, F. 164–5
Starrett, Randall 183
Stärker, Günther 110
Stäuble, Werner 45
Steele, Peter 17, 23
Stefan, W. 110, 133
Stein, Sir Aurel 187–8, 190–1, 193
Steinmetz, Heinz 64, 66, 81
Stephenson 151
Stettner, P. 100
Strachey, Richard 82, 84
Streather, Tony 140–2
Studenin, B. 181
Sugita, H. 64
Sviridenko, V. 176, 181
Sylvester, Rick 175, 177
Szechenyi, Count Bela 194

Tabei, Junko 19, 66
Tagaki, Shinichi 151
Tagliferri, G. 70
Takahashi, K. 74
Takahashi, Michiko 73, 81
Tamagni, V. 78
Tamm, E. 172
Tanabe, Hisashi 61
Tarek, Saad 151
Tashi, Sherpa 43
Tasker, Joe 88
Tegischer, Franz 71
Temba, Ang 55, 64, 66
Tenzing, Lhakpa 75
Tenzing, Nawang 42
Tenzing, Pemba 47, 53, 56
Terlikowski, Z. 79
Terray, Lionel 36, 40–1, 70–1
Tezuka, H. 74
Tichy, Herbert 77
Tietze, J. 140
Tilman, H.W. 'Bill' ix, 14–15, 47, 50, 53, 56, 64–6, 81, 83, 90–2, *91*, 95, 134, 153, 190, 196
Tissières, Alfred 134, 153
Tobita, Kazuo 15
Todd, Colin 38, 40
Traill, G.W. 82
Trebeck, George 102
Trotter, Capt. 187
Tsering, Dawa 92–3
Tsering, Lhakpa 63
Tsering, Mingma 68
Tsering, Pemba 53, 74
Tucker, John 31
Tyson, J.B. 78, 81

Uemura, Naomi 47
Ugarov, A. 175
Unsoeld, Willi F. 92, 95, 147, 153
Ustinov, Jury 170
Uyeo, S. 68, 81

Valiev, K. 175
Venables, Stephen 128
Vigne, G.T. 102
Vignes, G. 91
Visser, Philips Christian 103, 108, *108*, 125, 130, 133
Vittoz, Pierre 58, 99–100
Voronin, V. 174, 181
Vozozhischev, V. 179
Vyvyan, Michael 108, 134, 153

Wada, Minoru 52
Wada, Seishi 53
Wallace, P.J. 58
Waller, James 98–9, 146, 151
Walmsley, Joe 147, 153
Wangdi, Sherpa 36
Wangar Sherpa 40
Ward, Frank K. 14
Ward, Michael 17, 23, 50, 189, 196
Warr, Ted 136
Warren, Charles 47
Warth, Hermann 42, 59
Waschak, Erich 149
Watanabe, H. 63
Wayatt, Geoff 37
Webb, Lt. W.S. viii, 34
Weilguny, E. 170
Weir, Tom 48

Weissensteiner, Adolf 73
Wellenkamp, Jürgen 66
Wendlinger, H. 144
Whillans, Don 49, *49*, 109–10, 147
White, J. Claude 16–17
Wien, Karl 26–7
Wigram, Edmund 47
Wilkinson, D. 128
Wintersteller, Fritz 118
Wood, Capt. Henry 34, 186
Workman, Dr William H. & Mrs
   Fanny B. ix, 96, 108, 124, 138, *138*, 146, 149

Yadov, M.P. 129
Yager, M. 61, 81
Yagihara, Kuniaki 19, 81
Yamamoto, D. 64

Yamashita, M. 136
Yanagisawa, T. 74
Yasuda, E. 74
Yasuhisa 55
Yates, Frank 65, 68
Yerokhin, I. 182
Young, Jack 195
Younghusband, Francis 116, 185, 187, 190
Yu Wang-Yul 47
Yushin, N. 170

Zaidler, A. 176
Zakharov, N. 181
Zebrowski, Alice 144
Zehetleitner, Udo 47
Zuloaga, J.L. 101
Zurbriggen, Mathias 145

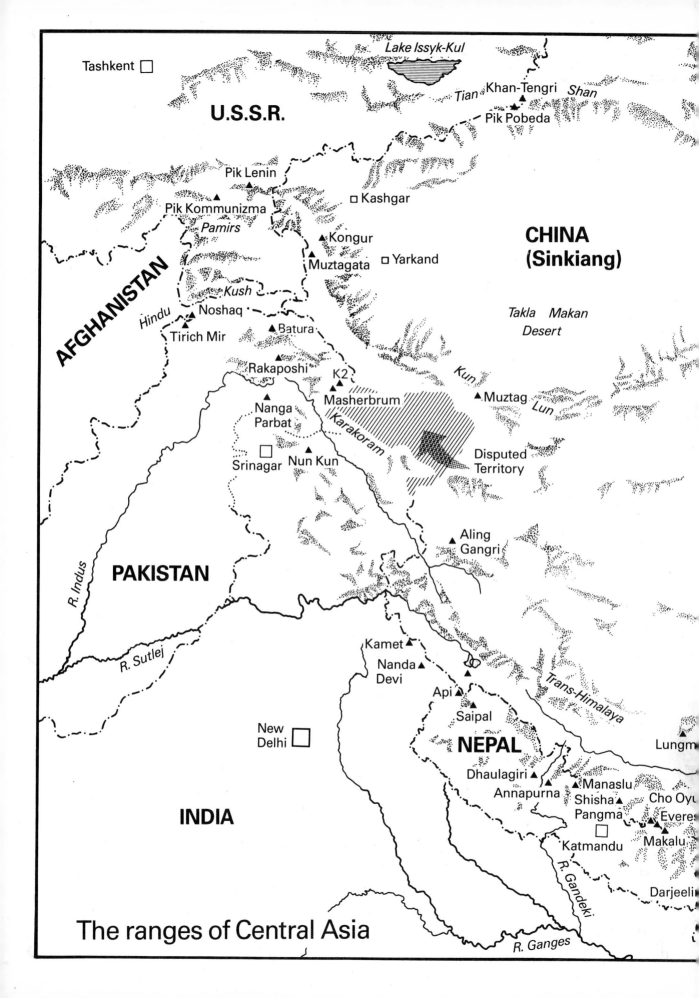

The ranges of Central Asia